SAPPHIC SLASHERS

SAPPHIC SLASHERS

SEX, VIOLENCE, AND AMERICAN MODERNITY

LISA DUGGAN

DUKE UNIVERSITY PRESS

Durham and London

2000

© 2000 Duke University Press
All rights reserved
Printed in the United States of America on acid-free paper ∞
Typeset in Joanna by Tseng Information Systems, Inc.
Library of Congress Cataloging-in-Publication Data appear
on the last printed page of this book.

For Marinelle Green, 1925–1974

CONTENTS

Acknowledgments, ix

Introduction, 1

Part I Murder in Memphis

1   Girl Slays Girl, 9

2   A Feast of Sensation, 32

3   Habeas Corpus, 61

4   Inquisition of Lunacy, 87

Part II Making Meanings

5   Violent Passions, 123

6   Doctors of Desire, 156

7   A Thousand Stories, 180

More Than Love: An Epilogue, 193

Appendix A: Hypothetical Case, 201

Appendix B: Letters, 213

Notes, 233

Bibliography, 281

Index, 299

ACKNOWLEDGMENTS

This book wandered through my life, laced with ambivalence, for years before I was prepared to publish it. I won't say how many years, or give the reasons for my ambivalence. But I will use this proffered space to offer thanks to those who persuaded me that I could publish this southern gothic tale of violence and despair as something other than a repetition, with a politically redemptive as well as elegiac force.

This project began as a Ph.D. dissertation, aided and abetted by the historical imaginations, productive provocations, and support of Carroll Smith-Rosenberg, Judith R. Walkowitz, and Jonathan Ned Katz, whose pioneering research provided the foundation upon which to build. I reinvented it during an endlessly surprising and personally revolutionizing postdoctoral year plus visiting faculty semester at the Unit for Criticism and Interpretive Theory at the University of Illinois at Champaign-Urbana. Drinking at the Fiesta Cafe and driving through the Imported Swine Research Area at midnight, I found reasons to forge ahead. In the company of Paula Treichler, Amanda Anderson, Sonya Michel, Carol Neely, Cary Nelson, Janet Lyon, Alan Hance, Peter Garrett, Michael Bérubé, Robert McRuer, Kirsten Lentz, Linda Baughman, Lee Furey, and other faculty members and students, I packed a decade's worth of intellectual stimulation and transformation into three semesters. I also met two people, also visitors to the cornfields that year, who changed me utterly and made the completion of this particular project imaginable—Kathleen McHugh and Cindy Patton.

After Illinois, I am grateful for a fellowship semester spent at the Virginia Foundation for the Humanities—in my home state, the scene of so many resonant crimes—where I finally submitted the first piece of this research for publication in SIGNS. Then, as Visiting Assistant Professor in the Department of American Civilization at Brown University for two years, I learned more than I wanted to about the challenges of forging an academic career while trying to make research, writing, and teaching matter both within and beyond the classroom. I am deeply grateful to David Savran, Carolyn Dean,

Michael Dyson, Donna Penn, Jessica Shubow, Mark Cooper, Kirsten Lentz (happily transplanted from Illinois), and Sasha Torres for being nice to me, talking to me about my work, or buying me drinks often enough to dissuade me from running away.

Just before the Providence police might have found me on some roof with an Uzi, reenacting rather than writing about a violent history, two miracles saved the day. First, a fellowship to the Humanities Research Centre of the Australian National University beamed me right up to the most unlikely paradise—Canberra! There, during what the North Americans present called Queer Summer Camp (it was winter for the Australians), everything came together—history, politics, long, long conversations, new ideas, road trips, amazing animals, and fabulous food. There is no way to overstate the intellectual and personal debt I owe to Cindy Patton, Henry Abelove, John D'Emilio, Jill Matthews, John Ballard, Carole Vance, Gayle Rubin, Gary Dowsett, and Dianne Chisholm for saving my life that summer. Then second, for divine reasons a very ex-Catholic girl dare not imagine, I was hired to teach in the newly revamped American Studies Program at New York University.

At NYU I have benefited from the extraordinary good fortune of having both dazzling colleagues and astonishing students. Among faculty and visitors in the American Studies Program, History Department, and Faculty Working Group in Queer Studies, I have found fertile environments for the work of finishing this book. Colleagues from these locations and elsewhere have read portions of the manuscript or offered critical support for my work on it, including Andrew Ross, Phillip Brian Harper, Nikhil Singh, Martha Hodes, Cathy Cohen, Ann Cvetkovich, Patty White, Martin Manalansan, Katie Kent, Allan Bérubé, Bert Hansen, Nayan Shah, David Eng, John Howard, Mandy Merck, Jeff Escoffier, Licia Fiol-Matta, Joanne Meyerowitz, Leila Rupp, Jenny Terry, Evelyn Hammonds, Robin Kelley, John D'Emilio, Claire Potter, and Jayati Lal. Walter Johnson made a crucial suggestion, about the possible relationship of the two erotic triangles introduced in chapter 1, that changed everything. Abby Rubenfeld and Debra Alberts opened their Nashville home to me, and spiced some long days of research at the Tennessee State Archives with nights of country singing and dancing. Chris Straayer took me back to the roots of the issues and quests that brought me to this project in the first place. José Muñoz, Carolyn Dever, and Tricia Rose provided that rare combination of daily collegiality and miraculous friendship that preserve life under sometimes inhospitable conditions. My sister, Patrice Samuels, gave me a sense of proportion and made me laugh. Ken Wissoker and Katie Courtland at Duke University Press patiently and calmly led me toward that elusive vanishing point of publication.

There are, in addition, three people whose role in this project has been central, and whose support has sustained me. I bow down in breathless awe before the mighty force of Henry Abelove, whose scholarship, teaching, and writing provide the model I continually aspire toward, and whose generosity and twisted wisdom push me continually to reimagine the possibilities for the politically engaged intellectual life. Our dinner dates have done a lot for my culinary life as well. I extend my hand in profoundest respect for the brilliance and burning determination of the fierce Judith Halberstam, whose work on female masculinity has transformed the scholarship and politics of gender, and whose accessibility, directness of address, zany formulations, and edgy butch style just plain make me smile. Both Henry and Judith read this manuscript, reread it, and came back for more. Their quibbles, questions, and suggestions have vastly improved the quality of the finally final book.

The person who most shaped this project is Nan D. Hunter, who knows everything about ambivalence, southern gothic histories, violence, despair, the importance of elegy, and the sometimes only faintly discernible hope of redemption. In other words, she knew what it would take to get this thing done and out, and she shamelessly supplied me—intellectually, emotionally, politically, and aesthetically. She alone knows what I mean when I say I am grateful.

INTRODUCTION

Opening a U.S. newspaper on a typical day, a contemporary reader confronts the national, international, and local news, arranged on the page according to widely agreed upon hierarchies of significance, and conveyed in familiar genres of "hard" news, news analysis, features, editorials, and special interest or lifestyle reporting on subjects from sports to fashion. Related according to their calendrical coincidence, the differing genres are only rarely substantively linked.[1] The report on the Federal Reserve Board's alteration of interest rates is not explicitly connected to the analysis of new welfare proposals, much less to the latest sex scandal or local crime report. The spatial arrangements and explanatory modes of the newspaper shape readers' commonsense perceptions of the world—provisionally designating matters of public importance, distinguished (always precariously) from questions of lifestyle and private interest.

Newspapers thus operate at the boundaries of public and private, political and cultural, working to define the meanings of such binaries for a national reading public. They perform this work in company with numerous other institutions that together define the parameters of democratic debate and decision making, and of national citizenship itself. College or university classrooms in the United States, for instance, also organize hierarchies of significance and genres of knowledge. Divided into disciplines, knowledge transmitted in these classrooms also shapes widely disseminated conclusions, including: Which topics are central and which marginal? What methods of investigation are appropriate?

The given organization of knowledge in newspapers and classrooms is neither natural nor necessary, however. Each institution's hierarchies and norms have emerged over the past two centuries of political contest and have embedded within them the unequal power and resources of conflicting constituencies. The quotidian practices of the institutions reiterate these inequalities but sometimes also transform them. Especially revealing questions occupy daily decision making and expose the contours of conflict at particular times and places: What counts as "politics" in a newspaper or a classroom? What languages are assumed, taught, forbidden? What parts of the world are privileged as topics and what parts marginalized? Which races, ethnicities, genders, and sexualities are assumed, and which designated?

Sapphic Slashers, a study of the emergence and circulation of the cultural narrative of lesbian love murder at the turn of the twentieth century in the United States, is written in critical relation to the newspaper, the classroom, and other institutions of American modernity that limit the scope of democracy through the containment of knowledge.[2] During the 1890s, the lesbian love murder story developed through the mass circulation press, following upon a sensational crime in Memphis, Tennessee, in 1892—the murder of Freda Ward by her "girl lover," Alice Mitchell. Sapphic Slashers argues that this influential cultural narrative, portraying romance between women as dangerous, insane, and violent, worked to depoliticize, trivialize, and marginalize the aspirations of women for political equality, economic autonomy, and alternative domesticities. The narrative, as it developed from 1892 to the publication of Radclyffe Hall's transformative The Well of Loneliness in 1928, rendered such public goals as private matters of character, morality, and mental health—matters entirely disassociated from central, significant national political concerns.

This cultural narrative did not address itself universally to "women," however, but specifically to the situation, aspirations, and symbolic power of privileged white women. Sapphic Slashers looks at its workings alongside those of the widely analyzed lynching narrative, developed over the same time period in the United States, in order to show their interaction in the emergence of a master discourse of national whiteness at the core of twentieth-century American modernity. The lesbian love murder story and the lynching narrative were not simply analogous or parallel tales of sexual pathology leading to political disfranchisement; they thematized different antagonisms and motivated different forms of social action that cannot be represented as equivalent. The lynching narrative justified campaigns of terror and murder and legitimated the stark inequalities and exclusions of the racial state; the lesbian love murder story interpreted rare homicides and produced normative parameters for domestic order. Despite such disparate operations and effects, these two narratives were nonetheless mutually intertwined in myriad crucial but obscured relations of power. They worked through overlapping institutions, colliding and coinciding in specific times and places to make history. As Phillip Brian Harper has argued, critical investigation of these intertwined histories of race and sexuality can generate a sort of "archaeological engagement" through which we might discover the political logic through which they have been mutually constituted. We might also then uncover a political legacy to inform strategies of resistance to inequalities and exclusions in the present.[3]

Alice Mitchell's murder of Freda Ward occurred in the same year, and in the same place, as the lynchings that drove antilynching crusader Ida B. Wells from the South and onto an international stage. This apparent coincidence, separated in historical accounts as unrelated, reveals the overlapping operations of institutions of publicity and the state in defining the sanctity of the "white home" as the central symbolic site of the nation. The black beast rapist and the homicidal lesbian both appeared, in new cultural narratives at the end of the nineteenth century, as threats to white masculinity and to the stability of the white home as fulcrum of political and economic hierarchies.

Sapphic Slashers centrally analyzes the lesbian love murder story, using the extensive, sophisticated scholarship on the lynching narrative as a secondary focus, to illuminate the shared logics, interrelations, and impact of both within modern American institutions. The goal of the study is *not* to persuasively demonstrate an empirical link between lynching and lesbian love murder, as social practices or cultural narratives—readers will find neither a balanced treatment nor sustained comparison of the two histories. Rather, the project of this book is to offer a juxtaposition of customarily disconnected events and stories in order to show (1) in general terms, how narrative technologies of sex and violence have been deployed to privatize and marginalize populations, political projects, and cultural concerns in the United States, promoting the substitution of moral pedagogy for public debate, and (2) in specific terms, how the lesbian love murder was racialized at the turn of the century in relation to other narratives animating social and political conflict. In pursuing these goals, *Sapphic Slashers* aims to illuminate how institutions of modernity produced the limits and exclusions of twentieth-century American democracy, and to intervene in the continuing disconnections and segmentations of knowledge that perpetuate those same limits and exclusions today. To accomplish this, one version of the cultural narrative of lesbian identity—a pathologizing, mainstreamed version—is shown developing at the heart of national institutions of the state, publicity, medicine, and popular as well as literary culture.

Part 1 of *Sapphic Slashers* focuses on the specific history of Memphis to relate the local story of the Alice Mitchell–Freda Ward murder and the publicity and courtroom proceedings that followed. Chapter 1 elaborates the book's overall argument, introduces key terms, including "modernity" and "whiteness," and explains the method of analyzing cultural narratives as political interventions embedded in concrete, material institutions. Drawing from the work of Judith Walkowitz, Jacquelyn Dowd Hall, Hazel Carby, Judith Halberstam, and Lisa Lowe, this method refuses the separation of social life ("reality") from representation ("myth" or "stereotype") and combines approaches from social history, political analysis, and cultural theory.[4] Chapter 2 analyzes the workings of the mass circulation press, and the strategies of sensationalism that organized reports of the murder and its aftermath. Drawing from recent critical revisions of the theories of Jürgen Habermas, including the work of Mary Ryan, Evelyn Brooks Higginbotham, Elsa Barkley Brown, Nancy Fraser, Miriam Hansen, Lauren Berlant, and Michael Warner, this chapter considers the press as a kind of interactive public sphere in which the production and reception of representations and narratives have been inextricably meshed.[5] Chapters 3 and 4 draw from critical legal studies and critical race theory to show the operations of the state—the law, the police, the courtroom—in conjunction with the press and the medical profession as they together define the issues at a habeas corpus hearing and lunacy inquisition in Memphis during 1892. Throughout part 1, the emerging lesbian love murder story is illuminated through its intersection with the events surrounding the lynching that drove Ida B. Wells from Memphis, and with the developing lynching narrative and its impact through the press, the law, and everyday practices of racial definition. The chapters in part 1 together argue that the multiplicity of racial and ethnic categories, sexual differences, and gendered embodiments are collapsed through cultural narratives that produce stark binaries of race, gender, and sexuality, and erase or privatize the growing inequalities of economic class that marked the 1890s.

Part 2 turns to the role of the Mitchell-Ward murder in the development of nationally circulating narratives of the lesbian love murder in newspapers, medical literature, and literary and popular culture from the 1890s to 1930s. Chapter 5 highlights the appearance of the figure of the "masculine" invert or lesbian, portrayed in competition with white men for the erotic attention of "normal" white women, in a widely proliferating array of newspaper stories through the first quarter of the twentieth century. Several of these stories are reprinted in full in this chapter. They serve to illustrate the argument that such stories contributed four crucial elements that came to characterize the lesbian love murder—a masculine/feminine contrast between the central female couple, a plan to elope, an erotic triangle, and a murder. The stories are also reprinted in order to provide otherwise inaccessible materials for independent analysis by scholars and other readers. Chapter 6 examines the medical and "scientific" literature addressed to race, gender, and desire during this same time period, and through which the lynching narrative and lesbian love murder story were rearticulated. The argument in this chapter elaborates Michel Foucault's account of the production of disciplinary discourses of sexuality in the modern West,[6] to show how sexual knowledge, both homophobic and homophile, has been interarticulated with hierarchies of race, gender, and class to produce a specifically American version of normative national sexuality.[7] Chapter 7 analyzes works of fiction—stories, novels, and plays—that challenge and transform hostile representations of lesbian love during the first half of the twentieth century. The chapter does not offer a critical reading of this fiction, in the manner of a literary theorist, but rather features a more limited historical analysis. The argument focuses specifically on Radclyffe Hall's *The Well of Loneliness*—the widely circulated novel that rescripted the lesbian love murder story, fundamentally and radically contesting it, while also conforming to its central class- and race-marked terms. Chapter 7 and the epilogue that follows argue that the legacy of the lesbian love murder story persists in identity practices and political strategies that claim morality and normality for lesbians and other sexual dissidents, rather than engage in a more thoroughgoing critical examination of the material institutions and cultural inequalities that have fundamentally shaped our sexual modernities.

Sapphic Slashers does not provide a social history of lesbian subcultures or of dissident sexual practices or forms of gendered embodiment at the turn of the century. Rather, this book offers a reconstruction and analysis of dominant narratives of American modernity for the purpose of illustrating the work of sex and violence in making the state and the nation. Narratives of the nation circulated through social worlds, appropriating figures and plots, and generating reappropriations, reworkings, and resistances in an endless cycle of interactions among overlapping social practices, social texts, and economic and political institutions. These interactions were concrete and material, located in specific sites, including the press, the law, the medical profession, and the novel. They were also starkly unequal, constrained by the rules of access to material and cultural resources. Through such interactions, the dominant narratives worked to produce a trivialized, marginalized outside to "real" politics, despite the ambivalences, instabilities, and resistances embedded within them.

Sapphic Slashers centrally and specifically analyzes only one version of the cultural narrative of lesbian identity in the twentieth century—a version that focused on perilous threats to the white home, including the dangerous non-transparency and untrustworthiness of "normal" women (later "femmes"), as well as the displacing competition of gender-inverted lesbians. There were (and are) myriad other such narratives, circulating in relatively broad as well as narrowly constricted public arenas. Further research and interpretation will illuminate these and inevitably complicate and revise the account in Sapphic Slashers. The argument in these pages is thus offered provisionally, with an invitation to debate.

My hope is that Sapphic Slashers can show that the populations and subjects trivialized as "merely" sexual or disruptively violent, as only of private or minority concern, and as properly relegated to the margins of newspapers and disciplined knowledges, have been at the center of politics, imbricated among the defining terms of democratic possibility, all along.[8]

PART **I** MURDER IN MEMPHIS

GIRL SLAYS GIRL

Homicide is, no matter what else it may be, a
social relationship. It might even be called the most
definitive of social relationships. Like all other
human social relationships, it must take place in
terms of culture.

Paul Bohannon, ed., *African Homicide and Suicide* [1]

Monday, January 25, 1892

At 3:00 P.M., nineteen-year-old Alice Mitchell stopped at the home of her friend Lillie Johnson. Alice was driving her family's horse-drawn buggy, as she often did to fill up the afternoons
since completing her course of instruction at the all-white Higbee School for Girls the previous
year. Alice and Lillie usually rode together, but snow and ice — unusual for Memphis, Tennessee,
even in the dead of winter — had prevented their outings for two weeks. So when Alice drove up
to her door, Lillie agreed to join her, and even bundled up her little nephew to take along for the
fresh air.

Alice guided the buggy with its three passengers toward Hernando Street, where her estranged
friend Freda Ward was staying at the home of the widow Mrs. Kimbrough. Freda and her sister
Jo had been visiting there for the past month, and Alice had often driven down Hernando Street
in the weeks before the snowy weather interrupted her, hoping to catch a glimpse of Freda in
the window. On January 25 the Ward sisters planned to take the evening boat back to Golddust,
Tennessee, more than fifty miles up the river where they lived with their married sister, Mrs.
Ada Volkmar. Alice lingered in her buggy in sight of the widow's door until she saw Freda and
Jo leave the house with their friend Christina Purnell, on their way to the boat, the Ora Lee.

Slowly, trailing at a distance, Alice followed the trio toward the river. On Front Street, just
north of the customhouse, the Ward sisters and their friend headed down a slippery walkway
toward the levee to board the boat. Alice stopped the buggy, suggesting to Lillie that they go into

Freda Ward   Alice Mitchell

Fig. 1. Images of Alice Mitchell and Freda Ward from an 1892 Memphis news-
paper (name and date unknown). (Reproduced in Fred Harris, "Lesbian Slaying
Shocked 'Gay Nineties' Memphians," *Gaiety . . . Reflecting Gay Life in the South* 1, no. 5
[Nov. 1975]: 3)

the nearby post office to check for mail. Alice and Lillie climbed out with the little nephew in
tow and walked toward the post office. But when Freda Ward passed them, Alice turned to Lillie
to say she wanted to follow Freda instead, to say good-bye. Lillie declined her friend's invitation
to go along and stepped back into the buggy to keep watch on the horse and her nephew.

Alice inched her way down the icy walk toward Freda. About half of the way down the slope
she caught up to her and reached around her neck. Christina Purnell thought Alice was reaching
to kiss Freda—until she saw blood. Then Jo saw the blood as well and, realizing that Alice
had cut her sister's face, swung her umbrella at Alice and shrieked, "Leave my sister alone. You
dirty dog, you'll hang for this." Alice shouted back, "I don't care, I want to die anyhow," while
slashing at Jo with the razor she still held in her hand. Meanwhile Freda was running down the
walk toward the boat, bleeding. Alice turned and headed down after her, overtaking her at the
railroad tracks and cutting her deeply across the throat.

It was just after 4:00 P.M. Seventeen-year-old Freda lay dying on the railroad tracks as
Alice ran back up the slope to the buggy. Bystanders lifted Freda into a delivery wagon to take
her first to the nearest doctor's office, then on to Stanley & Hinton's undertaking establishment,

where a coroner's inquest was convened within hours. Alice drove her buggy hurriedly toward home, telling first Lillie in the buggy, then her mother in the house at 215 Union Street, that she had cut Freda Ward's throat.[2]

This local tragedy, involving the daughters of several middling to prosperous white Memphis-area families, was obvious grist for the mill of sensational news reporting. The next day's headlines proclaimed, with characteristic hyperbole, that Alice Mitchell had committed "The Most Singular and Shocking Murder Ever Done in Memphis."[3] That a young girl from a respectable family had committed a gruesome murder was enough by itself to provoke such headlines, but this story presented an added twist. Newspaper headlines announced that this was "A Very Unnatural Crime"—the murderess claimed to have loved and wanted to marry her victim. She killed her rather than live estranged from her. Such facts provoked headline writers to herald the murder as "A Tragedy Equal to the Most Morbid Imaginings of Modern French Romances."[4]

Wednesday, March 9, 1892

Early in the morning, Thomas Moss, Calvin McDowell, and Henry Stewart were taken from jail in Memphis, Tennessee, and brutally murdered by a mob of white men. McDowell's body was found with his fingers shot to pieces and his eyes gouged out. Just before death, Moss was alleged to have said, "Tell my people to go West; there is no justice for them here."

The three African American victims of this lynching had been joint operators of the People's Grocery Company, a cooperative store located in a densely populated black neighborhood just outside the city, known as the Curve. When the cooperative opened, it offered competition to another grocery store owned by W. H. Barrett, a white man. A series of disputes between Barrett and his competitors led to a white invasion of the People's Grocery, and the subsequent jailing of over one hundred African American men who were believed to have "conspired" in armed defense of their store.

In the days following the lynching of Moss, McDowell, and Stewart, the arms and ammunition of the African American guard, the Tennessee Rifles, were confiscated, and the criminal court judge ordered the sheriff to take one hundred men out to the Curve and "shoot down any Negro who appears to be making trouble." Rumors circulated that members of Memphis's white business and professional elite were among the lynch mob, including the criminal court judge himself, Julius DuBose. No one was ever arrested for the murders.[5]

Tom Moss had a job on the side while the People's Grocery was struggling to establish itself—he delivered mail. At the offices of the African American newspaper, the *Free Speech*, he made a friend of editor and writer Ida B. Wells. After Moss was murdered, an outraged Wells decided to investigate the causes of the wave of lynchings spreading throughout the region. She was surprised to find that the frequent justification—retaliation for rape (which she had been inclined to believe)—was a deceptive excuse. In the *Free Speech* she began to argue that most lynchings were for other reasons entirely, and to suggest that when sexual relations existed between a black man and white woman, they were often initiated by the woman. In a May 1892 editorial she wrote:

Eight Negroes lynched since last issue of the *Free Speech*. Three were charged with killing white men and five with raping white women. Nobody in this section believes the old thread-bare lie that Negro men assault white women. If Southern white men are not careful they will over-reach themselves and a conclusion will be reached which will be very damaging to the moral reputation of their women.[6]

This editorial provoked heated denunciations in the white newspapers. The *Memphis Evening Scimitar*, assuming the editorial writer to be a man, urged retaliation:

Patience under such circumstances is not a virtue. If the negroes themselves do not apply the remedy without delay it will be the duty of those whom he has attacked to tie the wretch who utters these calumnies to a stake at the intersection of Main and Madison Sts., brand him in the forehead with a hot iron and perform upon him a surgical operation with a pair of tailor's shears.[7]

A white mob later destroyed the *Free Speech* presses while Wells was out of town. She was warned that she would be lynched if she returned, so she traveled to New York to launch an international campaign against lynching.

In taking it upon herself to expose the naked power behind the claims of white men that they were protecting white women when they lynched black men, twenty-nine-year-old Ida B. Wells developed a widely compelling analysis of race, gender, economic control, and sexual power relations.[8] In 1892, she gained international notoriety. She was the second young Memphis woman to do so that year. The first, Alice Mitchell, had not earned her notoriety as had Wells, through outspoken defiance. Mitchell earned hers though desperation and tragedy.

The stories of the 1892 lynching in Memphis, and of Ida B. Wells's reaction and subsequent political activism, are well known and widely circulated in histories of the South, of African American politics, and of race and gender at the turn of the century.[9] The stories of Alice Mitchell's crime, her trials and their publicity, are confined to histories of the nineteenth-century emergence of lesbian identity and are much less well known.[10] The tellings of the stories of these two women don't overlap in our historical texts and memories; they belong to wholly different analytic and historical worlds. And indeed, there is on one level no comparison between Ida B. Wells, one of the most notable and creative political activists in United States history, and Alice Mitchell, a disturbed and destructive young woman responsible for a sensational, ignoble crime. Yet for all their differences, their separation in historical accounts obscures our vision of the history that shapes twentieth-century U.S. modernity. Their lives and stories overlapped, after all, in time and place as well as social and institutional contexts. These overlappings are not coincidental. Understanding them allows us to see crucial parts of the inner workings of change at a formative historical moment.

Alice Mitchell and Ida B. Wells both lived in Memphis in 1892, but they occupied social worlds that were increasingly racially segregated. Though they both belonged to economically prosperous Memphis communities and lived within a few miles of each other, they traveled to different schools, churches, and parties. This spatial separation was a work-in-progress, designed and enforced primarily by the white Memphis commercial elite, concerned to condense a wide range of potentially mixed racial and ethnic identities into a rigid binary, stabilized as a clear hierarchy of white over black. In 1892, this project of condensing and spatializing racial hierarchy was incomplete in Memphis, as it was throughout the South. The scattered experiments in racial democracy that characterized the Reconstruction period had not been wholly extinguished; more racially integrated or egalitarian forms of public life coexisted uneasily with the newly emerging contours of racial apartheid. Force, resistance, and contest formed and re-formed along shifting racial lines.[11]

Yet for all this separation (a separation that in part configures our own historical memories), Alice Mitchell and Ida B. Wells traveled the same streets — the offices of Wells's newspaper, the *Free Speech*, were on Hernando Street, where Mitchell rode hoping to catch a glimpse of Freda Ward. The same mass-circulation newspapers, new to the American urban scene in the 1890s, chronicled the lynching and the murder over an overlapping series of months in 1892, then traced the subsequent fates of Ida B. Wells and Alice Mitchell. The same criminal court judge, Julius DuBose, ordered police actions surrounding the lynching (where he may have been present) and presided over the courtroom where the murder was adjudicated. Not only did the two young women share a very specific time and place, but the same concrete institutions and processes ultimately mobilized forces that banished both from Memphis. All this quotidian sameness, inspected from various angles of vision, reflects large, deeply intertwined historical forces and relations of power at work in Memphis in 1892.

The immediate context in which Alice Mitchell and Ida B. Wells were joined was local, but from this local site their stories produced and circulated national meanings. The 1890s were a crucial decade for such national meanings, as a newly continental United States joined its formerly warring parts to its recently closed frontier. During the 1890s, U.S. modernity, misnamed as "Americanness," was founded upon new narratives of nationhood for the next century. These narratives were the product of local labor, but they were forged of materials of transnational origin; they collectively produced a globally dominant American modernity. Through the institutions, practices, and ideologies of an emerging "corporate liberalism," these narratives scavenged and appropriated multiple alternative modernities, both within the United States and around the world. Thus, though local institutions and processes defined the meaning of "Americanness," they did so in an increasingly interconnected world of shifting global populations, resources, and communications. In other words, the nation was built locally of transnationally gathered materials, to do its work within a global context.[12]

In concrete terms, 1890s U.S. nationality was organized around a master discourse of national race as whiteness—a whiteness that worked to join the regions torn asunder during the Civil War and to unite both to the recently closed continental frontier. The national whiteness of the 1890s, more fragmented and contested than the republican whiteness of a century earlier, was assembled across a landscape of wide variation in ethnic and racial categories. Different regions of the United States produced different variants of the white/nonwhite binary, sometimes in relation to Chinese, Mexican, or Native American rather than, or in addition to, African American populations. And the racial sameness asserted by the legal and social identity "white" was disrupted by the sharp class and ethnic distinctions among waves of European immigrants from the 1840s to the 1920s, when whiteness was again more clearly defined and stabilized.[13]

The American whiteness emerging at the turn of the century was linked through its uneven conglomeration of ethnicities to Anglo-Europe, and to the shared project of imperial domination of "inferior" races, both domestic and foreign. Whiteness united Americans upon an imaginary binary division of race, constitutively thematizing but also predominantly subsuming other racial and ethnic differences, as well as divisions of class, gender, and region. Whiteness joined Americans to Anglo-Europeans and rationalized U.S. imperial domination of racialized peoples. Though neither whiteness nor imperialism was new in the 1890s, the version of whiteness underwriting twentieth-century American modernity was forged then, in the wake of the demise of slavery and Reconstruction, out of the materials of a broad range of social conflicts, economic changes, and cultural wars.

Producing whiteness required substantial labor, discursive and institutional, legal and political, local, regional, national, and global. Such labor required that complex conflicts be condensed into a discourse of binary race—an ideological project of long-term duration and continual instability. After all, the 1890s witnessed multiple upheavals in economics and politics, involving shattering social conflicts of class, gender, economic sector, ethnicity and nativity, and partisan loyalty. The entrenchment of newly nationalizing forms of financial and industrial capitalism met with fierce opposition: agrarian radicalism was at a high tide with the 1892 founding of the People's Party in St. Louis, and class conflict in the manufacturing sector rocked urban centers from Pittsburgh to Chicago. Racial and ethnic differences in excess of the black/white binary energized widespread, often violent struggle—Native American resistance to U.S. terriorial expansion was obliterated with the 1890 slaughter of the Sioux at Wounded Knee, while Chinese immigration to the West Coast inspired employer exploitation, labor competition, and political attack. At the same time, labor disputes in the agricultural Southwest drew on complex, overlapping class and racial conflicts between Mexican, black, and poor white laborers and wealthy white landowners. Such intertwined struggles across race and class hierarchies were also deeply marked by gender. The expansion of women's wage labor and the spread of new practices of consumption undermined domestic ideologies of gender, producing new opportunities for public visibility and political organization.[14]

How and why were these and other major changes and conflicts subordinated, however contingently, to the discourse of American whiteness? One method for illuminating answers to this question is to look closely at the local sites of production for various strands in the tapestry of American race consciousness and examine the narrative components along with the material means of their circulation to a nationalized audience. We can analyze the labor process and relations of production underlying the construction of American modernity upon a foundation of national whiteness during the 1890s.[15]

Memphis was a crucial location for such labor during 1892. A major urban center in the New South, filled with mobile New Women and prosperous New Negroes, Memphis functioned as a local laboratory for new social relations and their institutional and discursive elaboration during the 1890s. In 1892, Memphis became a significant site in the conflicted developmental histories of two significant components of the overarching narrative of national whiteness—the lynching narrative and the narrative of the lesbian love murder. These narratives seem to cover widely disparate territories, but they had a similar active life span—from the 1880s to the 1930s (with extensive cultural afterlives). They thematized the elements of race and gender, subsuming and obscuring the nevertheless organizing category of economic class.[16] They both centrally deployed the narrative technologies of sexuality and violence. And in 1892 they shared a locale as well as centrally powerful players and scenes—the judge, the jail, and the courts; the reporters and the newspapers; a mass mobilization amid the shock and rejection of "the best white people." [17]

In this broad context, the actions of Ida B. Wells and Alice Mitchell acquired meanings, national and transnational as well as local. Both of their lives were shaped by the confluence of historical conditions in Memphis, as their actions in turn intervened dramatically in those very conditions. Their lives and actions became significant elements in the narrative construction of a modern discourse of American whiteness, and in the emerging resistances to it as well.

Ida B. Wells was born a slave in Holly Springs, Mississippi, one of eight children. Her father, Jim Wells, was a skilled carpenter, a leader in the local community, and a trustee of Rust College (called Shaw University before 1890), where Ida was enrolled in the primary school section from age two to fifteen. During her early years, Ida Wells saw enormous racial progress followed by backlash and retrenchment. She saw her father cast his first vote, African Americans being elected to state and local offices, and the passage of a federal civil rights law in 1875. But by the mid-eighties, she had begun to witness the progessive erosion of these gains.[18]

In 1878 both of her parents and her youngest sibling died in a yellow fever epidemic. As the eldest daughter, Ida (aged sixteen) took over responsibility for the surviving siblings, two more of whom died before she moved to Memphis to become a teacher in 1882. In May 1884 on her way to teach school in Woodstock, Tennessee, a conductor on the Chesapeake and Ohio railroad tried to force her to ride in a smoking car with all other black passengers, even though she had paid a first-class fare. The law required equal public accommodations, so Wells got off at the next stop, returned to Memphis, and sued the railroad. In December 1884, the local court decided in her favor and awarded her five hundred dollars in damages, but in April 1887 the Supreme Court of Tennessee (following the increasingly conservative turn in court decisions throughout the United States) overturned the decision.[19]

In 1887 Wells began her writing career with an article on her railroad suit for a church paper. Her career then took off as she wrote for many church papers, then for some of the African American weeklies. She was offered an interest and editorship with the Memphis *Free Speech*, published by Rev. Taylor Nightingale, pastor of the Beale Street Baptist Church. Wells was active in the African Methodist Episcopal (AME) church, but she became responsible for the social message of the *Free Speech*. In 1889 she was elected secretary of the National Afro-American Press convention and began to use her editorship to criticize the inferior conditions in Memphis's segregated African American schools, as well as to argue for equal voting rights. In 1891 she was fired by the Memphis school system for her views and began to devote herself full time to the newspaper business.[20]

A journalist engaged with social issues, Wells joined other dissident African American leaders, including T. Thomas Fortune, to become a member of the Afro-American Council (established in 1889). Wells, Fortune, and their associates argued for social agitation in resisting segregation and disfranchisement and urged African Americans to make use of the economic boycott and emigration in resisting the increasingly hostile racial climate in the South. These leaders diverged from some other black leaders, who by the 1890s were urging accommodation along with "racial uplift" in hopes that increased respectability might improve the situation of African Americans. Though Wells had been deeply immersed in prosperous black Memphis's society rituals, and had briefly subscribed to some very restricted ideas about proper deportment herself, she continued to argue for agitation and resistance throughout her life.[21]

Thus Ida B. Wells encountered and addressed a variety of worsening so-

cial conditions during her years in Memphis. She protested disfranchisement
and opposed segregation, in schools and on the railroad. But it was after her
flight from Memphis in 1892 that Wells made her most spectacularly effective intervention into deteriorating racial relations in the South. She began
to speak about, organize against, and publish her research findings on the
escalating practice of lynching.

The peak year for lynchings of black men by white mobs in the South was
1892. Beginning in 1889, such lynchings had increased dramatically, up to a
high of approximately two hundred per year. Throughout the 1890s, African American men remained the overwhelming majority of lynch victims
(about 75 percent). As the total number of lynchings then declined during
the early 1900s, the racial character of the practice actually intensified (from
1900 to 1909, 90 percent of the victims were black men). Black women were
lynched as well—a total of at least seventy-six during the period from 1882
to 1927. But overall, the practice of lynching was defined at the intersection of gender and race by illegal though unpunished violence against black
men (there were twice as many lynchings as legal executions in the United
States in 1892; lynchers were rarely jailed) deployed to maintain white men's
privileged access to political power, economic independence, and domestic
spaces where their authority was protected from outer intrusion and inner
subversion.[22]

The historical conditions surrounding this campaign of violence were
multiple and complex. Intensified local, state, and national party politics,
economic competition, jockeying for access to public space, new theories
of "natural" racial hierarchy, changing and contested conceptions of domesticity—all shaped the racial and gendered violence of the 1890s. But the
most heated points of conflict centered on three symbolically central sites—
votes and elections, representing the political power bestowed upon black
men during Reconstruction; property and wages, representing the path of
access to middle-class status for black families; and private homes and neighborhoods, representing the bodily integrity, and domestic autonomy and
authority that underwrote claims to citizenship throughout the nineteenth
century. Black men's claims to votes, property, and domestic privacy constituted the attack on white dominance that was thematized as "rape" and that
motivated murders—vengeful murders designed to restore political, economic, and domestic order.[23]

Other campaigns of violence also coexisted with lynching: westward expansion crescendoed in violence against Native Americans in 1890, as U.S.

imperial aspirations beyond the continent consolidated in preparation for the Spanish-Cuban-Filipino–American wars of 1898–1902. This violence was justified with what Sandra Gunning has called a "coalesced rhetoric" of nationalism, eugenics, domestic protection, white racial superiority, and legitimate racial dominance.[24] Justifications for lynching drew on all these themes but rested centrally on the claim to a privileged whiteness—a whiteness constructed partly in and through a culturally powerful narrative. Savage black men, it was claimed, violated white domestic sanctity by raping white women. White men restored order and deterred chaos by lynching the culprits.

The lynching narrative was not the only narrative of racialized sexual danger and depravity circulating in the United States during the 1890s, but it accrued extraordinary cultural authority during that decade and remained influential well into the next century. Like other narratives of sexuality and violence, this one reverberated in newspapers and courtrooms, "scientific" and professional meetings and publications, political and economic institutions, fiction and polemical speaking and writing. It joined political ideology to cultural fantasy, yet worked to reorder the material conditions of everyday life as effectively as any army or piece of legislation.[25]

The lynching narrative of the 1890s was structured through race and gender and operated to reconfigure the boundaries of domestic and public spheres, as well as of political and economic institutions. Thematically, it overlapped with other influential narratives of chivalric rescue, such as those found in popular historical romances and in news accounts of imperial adventure: white manhood intervenes against infantilized or demonized racial others to save the day, rewarded by virtuous and grateful women. Such narratives' deployment of a common superior whiteness countered arguments for equality and justice, whether those of Cuba Libre partisans or of Reconstruction radicals, with melodramatic stories of gendered and racial difference.[26]

During the nineteenth century, most claims to political equality were made in the name of manhood rights, of masculine sameness. All *men*, according to nineteenth-century appropriations of Amercian revolutionary and other natural rights rhetoric, were created equal. This discourse of gender located difference and naturalized inequality at the male/female divide, working in some instances as a form of political resistance to divisions of race and class among men.[27] The chivalric rescue narratives countered this claim by asserting racial difference in gendered terms. In the lynching narrative specifically, African American men were figured completely outside of domestic and kinship relations as hypermasculine marauders of woman-hood. They were represented as bereft of humanizing family lives, as failed and aberrant *men*, so that they might be legitimately deprived of political rights. Having abdicated the proper excercise of manly domestic authority, for the protection of virtuous women, they could not safely exercise civic authority. And having been revealed as corporeal, sexual, and violent, black men could not deploy the disembodied abstract disinterest required for citizenship—or so the logic of the narrative worked.[28]

The lynching narrative operated through multiple reversals, displacements, and exclusions. Interracial desire, sexual coercion, and violence were attributed to black men, a reversal of the common practice of white male sexual attacks against black women. White male fears of disfranchisement, dispossession, and emasculation through the reorganizations of Reconstruction were displaced as these experiences were imposed on black men. And the experience of African American women, both disfranchised and subject to unpunished sexual attacks, was entirely excluded.[29]

The lynching narrative converted political, economic, and social conflict into melodrama through the narrative's mobilizing technologies of sexuality and violence. The story line reflected race and gender relations in a kind of Alice in Wonderland mirror world where everything appeared upside down and backward. The guilty were innocent and the innocent punished for the crimes against them. Race and gender in this mirror world were aligned through the device of the sexual triangle, with the white woman positioned as the passive object of desire. The male rivals were morally polarized, the black villain versus the white hero, with ambivalent desire circulating through all points of the triangle. Set into the melodramatic plot, the triangle connected bodies to identities, through which power and legitimate authority were then established.[30] The sexualized violence of this triangle permeated post-Reconstruction politics in the South and influenced opinion in the North and internationally. The sexual politics of the lynching narrative was always also a politics of citizenship.[31] The sexual rivalry structured by the lynching triangle epitomized a deadly competition over the right to vote, to exercise economic independence, and to protect an autonomous domesticity. The circulation of the narrative through social networks conditioned and justified the outcome of the competition, as U.S. racial apartheid replaced the utopian hopes of radical Reconstruction and settled into place for more than half a century.

Ida B. Wells, in company with many others, rewrote the lynching narrative and circulated a resistant version internationally through speaking, organizing, and publishing.[32] After leaving Memphis in May 1892, she took her research to black women's clubs and northern newspapers. Relying on information drawn from the mainstream white-owned press, she demonstrated that less than one-third of black men lynched were even accused of rape, and that most of those were not guilty. She published the first of a series of exposé pamphlets, *Southern Horrors*, in 1892. In it, and in subsequent essays, she reversed the moral terms of lynching's melodrama, arguing that white men were uncivilized, lawless brutes who murdered innocent black men in order to deprive their race of meaningful equality. She suggested that white female "victims" were often the initiators of consensual relations with black men and that they cried rape (or were forced to make rape charges) to save themselves when caught. She placed black men within a violated domestic world, embedded in an endangered black family. She represented white men as the despoilers of innocents and included accounts of lynchings of African American women and children.

In rewriting the lynching narrative Wells adhered to a gendered structure, but she revised the meanings of gender in constructing what Gail Bederman has called "an alternative discourse of race and manhood."[33] She argued for citizenship rights for black men as "manhood rights," but she reversed the linking of manliness and whiteness to portray white men as unmanly cowards and black men as the manly protectors of African American families. Her most provocative move, however, was her mobilization of a core term of the lynching narrative's erotic triangle—the suppressed agency of the white woman, her passivity and victimization, was refigured in Wells's version as the white woman's *choice* to engage in consensual sex with a black man. The narrative and the practice of lynching itself were produced to deny this possibility of choice, Wells argued. Such choice so destabilized the white domestic scene and white male authority that it had to be obliterated. In this reversal, Wells converted the alleged consent of supposedly promiscuous black women to white male sexual predation (the white racist belief that black women could not be raped) into the consent of white women to alleged black male ravishment (thus countering the belief that white women having sex with black men could *only* be raped). It was this reversal, in particular, that galvanized Memphis's "best white people" to drive Wells out of the state and destroy her newspaper.

Notions of gender constrained Wells's efforts in another way as well. As a particularly vulnerable orphan and single woman, without the protection of father or husband, she confronted attacks against a woman speaking on such sensitive topics in public, and against her personal "virtue" and character. She repeatedly turned to Frederick Douglass and other male supporters in these situations. But she also met these tactics with responses that cleverly turned her gender against her attackers. She delivered the speech that became Southern Horrors in tears and filled it with references to "home" and "friends" to continually reference her place in a protective black domestic world. When the Memphis Commercial countered the success of her speaking tour of England in 1893–94 by circulating accusations of sexual liaisons with male associates at the Free Speech, she shamed them for assailing the character of a lady.[34]

The efforts of Wells and other antilynching activists did not end lynching, but they did put the practice's defenders on the defensive and made it increasingly difficult for northern liberals to accept the lynching narrative and remain silent. Wells's tour of England also shrewdly placed the Anglo-European links established by the discourse of American whiteness at risk by questioning the "civilization" of white men in the U.S. South particularly and enlisting British condemnations of them. Her success consisted, not in simply denouncing the narrative and the gender and racial categories that structured it but in reworking the characterizations and the plot to mobilize a different melodrama, one that called for heroic action against villainous lynchers. She confronted the poisonous politics of race with an ingenious and extraordinarily effective politics of (counter)narrative.[35]

Ida B. Wells's project of converting the privatizing, moralizing lynching story into a public political debate about race and citizenship met with some limited success. By contrast, the alternative narrative of domesticity produced by the Alice Mitchell case—a narrative with profound political implications—was largely subsumed within a newly dominant, moralizing, privatizing public discourse. Alice's narrative, her failures, her crime, and her agony were publicized widely—locally, nationally, and transnationally—and resonated broadly, though ambiguously.

The Memphis newspapers sent the story of the Mitchell-Ward murder out through the press association wire services, which connected news desks nationwide. Some of the largest urban newspapers from as far away as San Francisco and New York covered the story. This widespread interest in the crime, in many ways a very ordinary passion murder, was conditioned by the questions it raised at the moment that it burst into the headlines. The antebellum gender conventions, domestic ideology, and sexual certainties that shaped the lives of the white elite were fading, but no newly "modern" notions had clearly emerged to replace them. Decades of conflict on multiple levels of culture—formal politics, marital and family life, medical discourse, the arts—underlay an apparent new consensus by the 1920s.[36] In the interim, sensational news reports of women's crimes provided a highly focused context for debate and renegotiation of the boundaries of domestic, gender, and sexual deviance.

Women's crimes, especially crimes of violence, raised issues of gender and sexuality more pointedly than did the crimes of men. By definition, violent women criminals had crossed the line of gender to engage in "masculine" activity. Yet most women's crimes, particularly murders, were committed in domestic settings or in response to conflict in personal relations.[37] Thus, news reports drew attention to shifting and contested gender boundaries and to conflict—especially between men and women, often over sexual matters—in the domestic arena. During the 1890s, such conflict centered on the changing dynamics of household power relations as larger numbers of women worked for wages, engaged in social reform, or agitated for political rights.[38]

But not all women who committed violent crimes attracted public attention in the same way. Sensational publicity concentrated on the crimes of white, economically privileged women, and was raised to a fever pitch when the women were young or considered "attractive." In 1892, the trial of Lizzie Borden for the hatchet murder of her father and stepmother in New England drew this kind of highly charged attention. Could one imagine the daughter of a banker to be guilty of such an "unnatural" crime committed in such a "masculine" manner? The public fascination with this case centered around the question of Lizzie's guilt or innocence, and it intensified when it became clear that the basic mystery would not be solved.[39]

The reporting of Alice Mitchell's case in the press presented problems of gender quite explicitly. Had Mitchell's childhood behavior or her courtroom demeanor been "masculine"? Could a normal woman love and plan to marry another woman? Less explicitly, the treatment of her case at all times depended on assumptions about class and race, at the point of intersection with gender. Her crime was treated not simply as the crime of a woman but as the crime of a young white respectable woman. The news coverage of the murder, and the conduct of the legal case, would have been almost wholly different had the defendant been male, black, or less prosperous.

Though the shock of Mitchell's crime was located in her social deviance, the mystery and fascination of the story was generated by the question of her motive. Could the daughter of a prosperous white merchant in a southern city have loved another girl "like a man"? If so, was her love, as well as the murder that resulted from it, a manifestation of insanity? Or was the whole affair attributable to a vicious and depraved character—was Alice Mitchell simply "fast"? Were Alice and Freda innocent of anything "coarse or immoral," or were they guilty of "unnatural practices"? Where was the line between intense but admirable love between girls and perversion? Or could the entire improbable tale of love, loss, and murder have been concocted by clever attorneys to help their client escape the gallows? Was there really a man behind it all?

In 1892 the press was consumed with the battle of interpretations of Alice Mitchell's behavior. The defense and prosecution immediately began to assemble conflicting arguments that were aired in the newspapers. Interviews with the female principals revealed understandings of the issues at sharp variance with those espoused by the male professionals, lawyers, and doctors who controlled the legal proceedings.

The press framed its reporting of this interpretive battle in a familiar way —as the opposing views of defense and prosecution in the trial following a love murder. Such violent attacks on spouses or sweethearts, and the subsequent legal wrangling, were the frequent fare of sensational news. But within this familiar frame, the Mitchell-Ward murder was treated as nonetheless incomprehensible, and unique on American soil. The *New York World*, for instance, repeatedly inserted the adjectives "strange" and "puzzling" into its articles and announced:

A sober American community and an unimaginative American court must deal in matter-of-fact fashion with matters which have been discussed hitherto by French writers of fiction only. Gen. Luke E. Wright and Col. George Gantt, of Tennessee, find themselves compelled to do in open court the work that Balzac did in tracing to physical sources mental perversion. In the Criminal Court of Memphis, Shelby County, Adolphe Belot's Mlle. *Ma Femme* will be the only textbook at hand. Judge DuBose, of Tennessee, will have cited to him, as bearing on the case of an American girl, the creations of French writers whom he and all his associates have looked upon as perverted creatures, dealing with matters outside of real life, or at least outside of American life.

In all the long history of crime and insanity there is no such case recorded.[40]

In fact there *were* other such cases recorded,[41] but in 1892 the same-sex love murder was not recognized as a familiar type of crime by newspaper readers and reporters. Intense, loving friendships between girls were accepted as commonplace—in Memphis such girls were said to be "chumming." But passion of the sort that could lead to romantic obsession and murder was considered startling and newsworthy. In drawing attention to the appearance of such passion in Memphis, the newspapers at first pointed to European sources, particularly notorious French novels just appearing in English translation in Memphis bookstores during the 1890s.[42] This suspicious French origin initially marked the love affairs of girls and women as un-American, but as such relationships were "Americanized," the European references helped serve to mark them as white.

In many respects, the national frame is not a useful one for the study of sexuality. In 1892, New York City's sexual cultures probably had more in common with those in Paris and Berlin than with those in Memphis. Transnational and local framings are in many instances more appropriate for generalization or comparison than the national. Nonetheless, U.S. sources insistently repeated the descriptor "American," understood as racially white and economically prosperous but not European, when textualizing sexual differences. During the 1890s, newspapers, legal proceedings, and other institutions and cultural centers were thus engaged in the production of an "American" national sexuality. This "American" sexuality was produced through a process of radical condensation of differences along multiple axes, represented in texts whose distribution marked the boundaries of the "national."[43]

In Memphis, the murder of Freda Ward by Alice Mitchell almost immediately exceeded the local context. Reports in the local newspapers were rerouted through the interconnected mass circulation press, forming one basis for a new discourse of sexual difference. This discourse reached beyond French fiction for images and narratives, into the extensive new medical literature on same-sex love and sexual passion spreading throughout Anglo-Europe. By 1892, many European-trained American doctors had read Richard von Krafft-Ebing's 1886 opus, *Psychopathia Sexualis*, in the original German (the first U.S. edition of his work, in English translation, appeared later that year). His theories concerning the origin and consequences of the sexual perversions were just being picked up and reworked by a handful of medical writers in the United States. Though the concept of "homosexuality" had not yet been clearly developed by these writers (the term itself was first used in an American publication in 1892),[44] a pathological condition (variously named) involving same-sex love and cross-sex behavior was being described in the medical journals for the first time.

Such borrowings from Anglo-European novels and medical publications shaped understandings of Alice Mitchell's crime in Memphis, even as it began to be labeled "American." The referenced nineteenth-century literary and medical texts emerged from a historical landscape of widely varied and dispersed forms of gendered embodiment and sexual practice. From the seventeenth to the nineteenth centuries, various printed sources refer to passing women and female husbands, tribades and hermaphrodites, romantic friends and female fiends. Forms of gender disguise or presentations of mixed or intermediate gender, deviant sexual practices, and excessive or "unnatural" emotional attachments were variously ascribed to biology (hermaphroditism or an enlarged clitoris), socialization (especially the environment of the girls' boarding school), economic necessity, or political defiance. These multiple forms of difference varied across class, ethnic, religious, and other cultural boundaries, though the forms cited in 1892 Memphis news reports were drawn from elite texts and professional, scientific, or literary languages. By the late nineteenth century, these textualizations of gender and sexuality increasingly worked to figure all such differences as simple and obvious deviance from conventional elite norms. Multiple variations and meanings were condensed into rigidly binary forms of either excess sexuality or inverted gender, "primitive" or overcivilized masculinity and femininity. The production of binaries, and the collapse of sexuality into gender, of difference into deviance, was especially marked in the texts of the new late-nineteenth-century "scientific" sexology.[45]

In the United States in 1892, gender and sexual differences were also multiple and dispersed. In addition to European immigrant cultures, African, Native American, Latin/indigenous mestizo, and Asian cultures contributed to the general diversity, which ranged across regions and classes and along urban/rural and industrial/agricultural spectrums. But in the United States, cultural and political agencies also worked to radically condense such particularities into a mutually constituting network of binary categories of identity. The increasingly rigid racial binary of the 1890s encountered a shifting gender binary and interacted to produce a new sexual binary implicitly marked by race and class. The U.S. version of the Anglo-European homosexual/heterosexual polarity began its century-long discursive career during the 1890s as a phenomenon centered among the white commercial, industrial, and financial elites. The U.S. version was in turn appropriated in Anglo-European texts, which picked up the Mitchell-Ward case as "typical" of their new category of female sexual inversion, but typical in a particularly "American" way. An account of the case was added to later editions of *Psychopathia Sexualis*; by 1901 the first U.S. edition of popular British sexologist Havelock Ellis's *Sexual Inversion* stated simply that she was "a typical invert of a very pronounced kind. . . . There have been numerous cases in America more recently."[46]

The new interacting binaries of race, gender, and sexuality developed unevenly, alongside older categories and other new ones developing in less mainstream locations. In Memphis in 1892, newspapers and other sources referred to "fast" girls and vulgar, painted women (almost always poor and/or "colored") who sold themselves, to "chumming" schoolgirls whose excess emotionality might be cause for concern, to doctors with vague notions of anatomical hermaphroditism as well as with Victorian medical vocabularies peppered with "nymphomaniacs" and "erotomaniacs." Beyond the newspapers and court records, or the literary productions and preserved papers of the well known and prosperous, there were undoubtedly other vocabularies of gender and sexual variation. As the Mitchell-Ward "case" accrued coherence, these other vocabularies remained obscure while the various frameworks of white elites came into focused collision. What emerged from the trials surrounding the case and the reporting of them was a clash of stories and categories; out of this conflict a highly influential though contested narrative appeared. This narrative condensed multiple forms of difference and conflicting vocabularies of deviance into a tale about sexually deviant "types," shaped into a tragic plot and circulated as a national morality tale.

As in the lynching narrative, the characters and plot of the Mitchell-Ward story were produced through an erotic triangle. The elements of this triangle story were not new; they were reworkings of earlier fragments and familiar tropes. The Mitchell-Ward story itself, as it was retold in court and in the press, only slowly assembled these fragments, acquired coherence and stability, and became a widely repeated, powerful cultural narrative. The figures in the triangle included a "normal" white couple, resonant in many ways with the threatened white couple of the lynching narrative, whose potential happy future is torn asunder by a violent third party. But in the narrative assembled through the Mitchell-Ward story, that third party is not a black man but a white woman—a masculine homicidal lesbian.

The word "lesbian" was only rarely used in reference to the Mitchell-Ward case itself and was not widely established as a social identity in the United States until the 1930s or later.[47] But a genealogy of the "lesbian" as she appears clearly on the cultural and social landscape by the 1930s leads back to the mannish "invert," the masculine woman of the late nineteenth century. This figure is a social fiction, a generic construction covering over and standing in for a much broader array of historical gendered embodiments and sexual desires.[48] She appears as a figure in stories and texts but is not a "myth" or simply a distortion. She arises from the fragmented narratives and practices of social life, collapsing and condensing the resistances to gender and sexual convention of innumerable historical women. In the newly dominant narratives of the 1890s, the figure of the lesbian is horrific and negative, used to police the boundaries of gender and sexuality by warning of the unspeakable consequences of transgression. But the traces of resistance, the suggestion of the possibilities for gender transitivity drawn from social life, remain. The lesbian also returns to haunt domestic order as a lived social identity.

As assembled from French novels and Anglo-European sexology through the figure of Alice Mitchell in 1892, the lesbian embodied a series of links from gender inversion, through sexual deviance, to violence. These links were forged through an extended process of cultural labor, performed in courtrooms, in the columns of newspapers, in oral and street corner contexts, and in a vast range of cultural productions. The energy of this labor arose from a sense of danger at the heart of white elite domestic life, understood as the very foundation of legitimate public and social authority.[49] The struggle for feminist political reforms and women's suffrage, the possibility of female economic independence through wage work and the professions, and the specter of manless households of spinsters converged into the figure of the masculine "girl lover" in rivalrous relation to a "normal" man for the erotic loyalty of a "normal" feminine partner.

The mannish woman sought various male prerogatives. Through "masculine" clothing she increased her public mobility; through professional or artistic aspirations she sought economic independence; through her romantic escapades she placed herself in courtship or domesticity in the masculine position. She was a presumptively white and prosperous woman who set out to claim an elite masculine life plan for herself.[50] In the lesbian love murder narrative's erotic triangle, she was figured in competition with the "normal" man, who would deny her her heart's desire by blocking her access to the "normal" woman and thus access to the associated prerogatives of white masculinity. In this he paralleled the white man of the lynching narrative in blocking "illegitimate" access to the economic, political, and domestic privileges of white manhood, thematized as his sexual rights to the white/"normal" woman. In the lesbian love murder story, the lesbian erupted in violence as she pursued her sexual prey. The white man, through his institutions and agencies, responded with the necessary institutional or personal force required to restore order.

But the most troubling figure in this triangle was the "normal" woman. Ostensibly the passive object of desire, she nonetheless acted in persistently confounding ways. She appeared conventionally feminine in identification and embodiment, yet could not be fully known or controlled. She might go either way. She might be seduced by or even choose the lesbian and reveal abnormal desires. Or she might choose or return to the "normal" man. In either instance she could not be distinguished from among the general throng of ordinary "normal" women. She became a figure of potential instability and betrayal located in the position of *any* (white) woman, located alongside the foregrounded image of the fixed, identifiable, deviant lesbian. This nontransparency and instability of the "normal" woman triggered the violent struggle of the lesbian love murder story, as the struggle over the agency of the white woman, another representative of *any* (white) woman, motivated the lynching narrative's murders.

In the lynching narrative the white woman's agency was obliterated, as was the black man's body. But in the antilynching narrative, her departure from proper domestic order consisted in a taste for miscegenation or adultery often judged as base or immoral and involving treachery and deceit, sometimes represented as sadly doomed love or, more rarely, regarded as bohemian or "advanced." In the lesbian love murder and its resistant reversals, the normal woman often embodied a nondomestic or even antidomestic form of femininity—expressed through an affinity for the theater or the arts, an association with the demimonde, a determination to travel as a religious missionary or spiritualist medium, or a lifelong dedication to the education of young girls. She frequently emerged from homosocial public or semipublic worlds that provided some economic independence and social visibility for otherwise "feminine" white women. Her position, though ultimately largely effaced in both dominant and resistant versions of the lesbian love/murder story, functioned as a crucially revealing linchpin nonetheless.

Like the masculine woman in the love/murder narrative's triangle, the normal/feminine woman never simply reflected social life. As the invert or lesbian came increasingly to represent a fixed, pathologized alternative to femininity (standing in for many such alternatives), the "normal" woman in this triangle (a precursor of the deceptive "femme" of the 1950s) was a residual character who carried the possibilities of choice and change over time that were denied in the inverted figure. As she emerged in twentieth-century cultural narratives, she had much in common with the nineteenth-century prostitute or "fast" girl in representing uncontrollable femininity. At the turn of the century, she often all but disappeared from the story, as Freda Ward did from the Mitchell-Ward story in 1892. The focus of attention remained riveted on the more obvious deviant, the inverted lesbian.

The lynching narrative and the lesbian love murder story were not analogous or parallel tales; they organized different forms of violence and exclusion and ordered different arenas of political and social action. The lynching narrative motivated campaigns of terror and murder and legitimated social segregation and political apartheid. The lesbian love murder story did not motivate widespread murders but interpreted rare ones. It did not produce dispersed geographies of difference and inequality but ordered white households for the reproduction of genders and generations. But despite such dramatic differences, examining the lynching narrative and the lesbian love murder story together enables an expanded, more integrated vision of the birth of American modernity in the 1890s. The overlapping of these two cultural narratives reveals a threatened white masculinity concerned to reconfigure political, economic, and domestic order in the face of change and challenge in race and gender relations. The terrifying figures of the black beast rapist and the homicidal lesbian leapt from fearful imaginings of the effects of votes, property, and autonomous homes for black families and independent white women. The white home, built upon control of the white woman's body and underwriting structures of political authority and ideologies of economic freedom, appeared in peril. But these narratives do more than symbolize or manage fear of change: they actively work to produce new strategies for building stable hierarchies. They produce racial categories, reorder gender relations, and cover over deep divisions of class. They perform this work, not in some abstract space of textuality or consciousness but through the concrete, material operations of specific historical, social, cultural, and political institutions.[51]

In Memphis in 1892, Alice Mitchell and Ida B. Wells experienced love and loss and transformed mourning into social action. Their actions interacted with a range of local, national, and transnational institutions, including the press, the law, and the medical profession. Out of such interactions emerged pieces of an emerging American modernity.

A FEAST OF SENSATION

The sensationalism of the average daily paper has, no doubt, created an appetite for things abnormal.

"Indecent Journalism," *The Journalist*, August 5, 1893 [1]

The mass circulation press, newly connecting towns and cities throughout the United States during the 1890s, publicized the lynching narrative and the lesbian love murder story as national morality tales. The specific operations of newspapers—their economic underpinnings, their managed readerships, their generic conventions and taboos—shaped the meanings and material contexts that gave such narratives cultural and political force. It was first and foremost as newspaper accounts that the events that defined lynching and lesbian love murder became recognizable *stories* with repetitive plots and characterizations. And it was in the pages of the mass circulation press particularly that such stories were meaningfully attached to national themes and widely disseminated to an imagined national public.

The 1890s were a directly formative period for the basic institutions of American modernity. Waves of change and crisis in economic relations accompanied the alteration of political practices, as markets expanded and populations moved across local, regional, and national boundaries. The resulting social and cultural ferment created new opportunities for democratic transformations, but the emergence of political alignments and economic forces organized on an unprecedented scale also produced vast inequalities.

This contradictory environment of possibility and containment was crucially mediated by new institutions of mass culture that posited the nation as the fantasied subject of political, economic, and cultural aspiration.[2]

The mass circulation press that emerged during the 1880s and 1890s built upon earlier institutions and genres of commercial culture to create a web of political, economic, and cultural links across the space of the nation. The spread of communication and transportation technologies since the midnineteenth century allowed publishers and editors to gather news, images, and advertising on a national (and international) as well as local and regional scale. Thus, even though few newspapers circulated nationally, as new popular magazines and some mass-produced fiction did, syndicated news and feature services and traveling advertising agents carried news stories and commercial brands to nationwide networks of expanding, mass circulation daily and weekly papers.[3]

These networked newspapers did not simply reflect an emerging coast-to-coast sense of nationality but functioned as crucial linchpin institutions to create that sense. Newspaper advertising helped create the expanded markets necessary for a mass consumer form of capitalism; newspaper reporting through the wire services linked localities and regions to produce an imagined national readership/constituency for federal politics, both domestic and foreign. And as networked publishers selected local stories to circulate as bearers of national significance, cultural narratives of the nation emerged to define the boundaries, preoccupations, and exclusions of Americanness at the turn of the century.[4]

Mass circulation newspapers thus constituted American modernity in the 1890s in at least three ways. First, they provided a vehicle for the mass sale of commodities and the production of an ideology of consumption that linked myriad layers of economic relations and helped stabilize the repetitive crises of production of the late nineteenth century. The literal material circulation of the physical newspaper linked the sites and imperatives of production with sites of consumption—shops, cafés, post offices, streets, porches, and homes. Daily and weekly newspapers forged such links immediately and locally, but they also followed and facilitated the movements of populations and goods regionally, and by the 1890s, nationally.

Second, newspapers organized national meanings through their spatial arrangements of time and place, identity and genre. Page layouts organized reports of temporally simultaneous occurrences across dispersed geographies according to principles of relevance and hierarchies of significance.

These layouts produced modes of relatedness and connection by addressing an imagined "general public" or positing an American identity, then defining the subjects of such general or American interest. Layouts and terms of address also generated modes of disconnection, marginalization, or exclusion through disarticulated identities and interests defined as "special" or marginal, either excluded or confined to separate sections or to the borders and edges of stories and pages.[5]

Such arrangements of time and space, identities and interests, presented newspapers as virtual public spheres, constructed in interactive relation to other spaces and arenas constituted as public. The sequential chronology of newspaper publication, and the interaction of its reporting procedures with the events and populations of multiple public places, brought publishers, editors, and reporters into continual confrontation and implicit dialogue with the interests, identities, and priorities of others. The pages of newspapers thus constituted an interactive, virtual public sphere engaged in mediating the shifting terrain of American modernity. Commercial, elite interests controlled the material means of this mediation through newspaper ownership, organization, and page layout. But the events, populations, forms of identification, and meaning making that constituted the "news" shaped multiple, overlapping, conflicting publics that were never reducible to or controllable by the institution of the newspaper.[6]

Third, newspapers assembled and circulated narratives that accumulated coherence through repetition and power through shaping the material contexts, the rules and policies, the beliefs and behaviors governing the boundaries of private and public life. Newspaper stories drew from a wide variety of other genres of publication, also addressed to public/private boundaries, throughout the nineteenth century. The fictional narratives of story papers, dime novels, and cheap libraries overlapped with the "true stories" of crime pamphlets and police gazettes in tales of romance, adventure, horror, mystery, and mayhem. The popular plot formulas of scandal and sensationalism carried over from one genre to another across the line of news/fiction, drawing a mixed-class readership of both genders for daily newspapers—especially after the dramatic growth of the "penny press" during the 1830s and 1840s.[7]

These strategies for narrating news and marketing newspapers were expanded during the 1890s by mass circulation urban papers. The most aggressive and successful purveyors of "sensationalism," such as Joseph Pulitzer's *New York World* and William Randolph Hearst's *New York Journal*, were attacked by competitors and critics for exploiting crime, sex, and violence, and pandering to the low standards of a mass readership in a crass bid for advertising revenue and profits. But scandal and sensationalism were more complex and significant cultural strategies than such criticisms allowed. More than merely diversionary, pandering, or profiteering and prurient, the strategies of scandal and sensationalism addressed the interests of publishers and readers through politically productive narratives that intervened in prevailing definitions of equality and freedom—through the rhetorical and material organization of public and private life.

News stories in the mass circulation press during the 1890s employed the conventions of scandal or the language of sensationalism to produce plots, characterizations, and emotional contexts organized into a range of historically specific narratives. These narratives worked primarily to naturalize inequalities as reflections of character and moral order, or to privatize political contests through spectacles of normative versus deviant intimacy. But their production of meanings was never monolithic or monologic; sensational news stories carried contradictory meanings and produced diverging interpretations and responses. For instance, dramatic accounts of industrial "accidents" and strikes deployed sensational descriptions to shape public, class conflict through characterizations of individually careless owners or violent, crazed strikers. But such stories also contained narratives of class antagonism stressing the indifference or brutality of the rich and might operate to spread news of a strike to sympathetic workers, as well as to mobilize support for owners. Other commonly told tales featured lawless intimacies (prostitution, seduction, adultery) and revealed, through purple prose and stark moral polarities, that deviant emotions and desires created alarming moral disorder. But the same stories also advertised opportunities for adventure and sometimes included implicit critiques of male sexual privilege.[8]

During the 1890s the lynching narrative and the lesbian love murder story emerged, as local events interacted with nationally circulated sensational newspaper reports. The narratives were assembled over time as structured, politically interested interpretations of events; they circulated in newspapers in critical relation to interpretations located in other public arenas. They specifically registered as well as countered the political impact of expanded postbellum black and interracial public spheres and white women's growing public presence. The dominant versions of the narratives, though never finally fixed, circulated interpretations of events that attacked the democratic possibilities of multiply accessed public spaces—by highlighting their dangers. They reframed political conflicts over votes, property and domestic autonomy—conflicts expressed in and through new, alternative, and oppositional public spheres—as the sensational clash of dangerous sexual deviants with the forces of morality and domestic order.

Such narratives helped rationalize and reconcile the troubling gap between formal political democracy, joined to an ideology of equitable economic opportunity, and the existence of vast, growing inequalities. Political and economic hierarchies appeared in them as the natural result of differences—differences of character attached to collective identities. Social arrangements out of sync with these morally differentiated identities produced danger, crime, and violence. Efforts to democratically reorganize public and domestic life appeared as assaults on nature and decency. Read together in the pages of newspapers, these re-presentations of social conflict as moralized difference ultimately privatized politics, substituting a constraining moral pedagogy for democratic dispute.[9]

Events in Memphis during 1892 contributed substantially to the development of the lynching and antilynching narratives and inaugurated the half-century life of the nationally circulated lesbian love murder story. These events were reported and interpreted in the Memphis newspapers—there were more than a dozen publishing in 1892. Of these, four major dailies adapted the strategies of mass circulation, display advertising, and sensational news reporting pioneered in New York—though none circulated at the level of the *New York World*, the most profitable newspaper internationally, with over 500,000 readers by the mid-1890s. The most successful of the four was the *Memphis Appeal Avalanche*, a morning paper that claimed to have the largest circulation in the South; at 23,000 for the daily, 28,000 for the Sunday, and 96,000 for the weekly edition (distributed regionally), it certainly had the largest in Memphis (population circa 85,000, or more than 110,000 for Shelby County as a whole). Established in 1890, the *Appeal Avalanche* had the advantage of the exclusive Associated Press franchise and the first Linotype machines in town. It competed for morning readers with the *Memphis Commercial*, established in 1889. Meanwhile the first successful evening paper in Memphis, the *Public Ledger*, publishing since 1865, met new competition from the *Evening Scimitar* beginning in 1890.[10]

The different Memphis newspapers were owned and operated by competing factions of the white business elite, an interconnected network of commercial, political, civic, and professional leaders positioned at the nexus of regional commerce. In 1892, Memphis was in the midst of an economic boom, only minimally affected by the coming nationwide depression and panic of 1893. The expansion of regional trade and the strengthening of the elite-controlled municipal government combined to manage a huge influx of freedpeople and Irish immigrants, who helped triple the population from 1880 to 1900. Despite this growing population diversity, the city escaped much of the intense class conflict sweeping agricultural and industrial centers during the 1890s. Populism was at its height in much of the surrounding region—Tennessee had a Farm-Labor governor in 1892—and industrial conflict shook cities farther north. Memphis experienced only some ripple effects. The Memphis Trades Council, formed in 1889, set out to organize skilled workers in the city's small but rapidly growing manufacturing sector. There were occasional strikes, lockouts, and use of scabs—bitter confrontation sometimes resulted, as it did in the wake of a printers' strike at the *Memphis Commercial* in 1892.

But the passions engendered by class conflict rarely disrupted the confident control of the business and professional elite in Memphis, where individual men commonly combined powerful positions in civic life, control of major local industries, and a share in the operation of the city's regionally important cultural institutions—including its newspapers. Numerous examples include the criminal court judge, Julius DuBose, who edited the *Public Ledger* prior to his career on the bench, and Luke Wright, one of Alice Mitchell's attorneys, who had been a founding owner of the *Memphis Commercial*. Like many other newspaper owners and innovators nationwide, these powerful owners of the Memphis dailies employed newly developed marketing techniques and production technologies to reach the largest readerships ever in the city's history.[11]

The news as reported in the Memphis dailies was thus systematically shaped by the perceptions and assumptions of the prosperous white men who controlled newspaper publishing. But this group was by no means monolithic; publishers and editors supported competing political factions and economic strata, while the reporters who worked for them were recruited from less prosperous groups, with conflicting perspectives on the news. Certain consistencies nonetheless emerged—not only in reports of local events but in the stories collected regionally, nationally, and internationally. The points of view of prosperous white men, coalesced and communicated through the increasingly nationally organized news and advertising business, shaped stories designed for a presumptively white, mixed-class, gender-polarized local readership. Though the meaning of "white" varied during the late nineteenth century, and the particular class mix of different newspapers' readers varied, the "general public" of the national news, as reported locally—and the market for mainstream mass advertising—was imagined as white, "middle class," and gendered in interests and tastes.[12]

The sometimes "southern" but frequently now "American" general public addressed in the news, features, and advertising of the Memphis press thus marked out clear parameters for readers' identification or disidentification. Different genres of stories and types of advertisements addressed separate genders or class segments—during the 1890s, for instance, separate women's sections appeared in Sunday papers with features and ads directed to white women imagined as domestic consumers. Some populations were not directly addressed, however; they appeared in newspapers as "others"—social types or characters portrayed through intersecting characteristics of gender, race, and class. By the 1890s, for example, black men rarely appeared in the news as political and economic actors as they sometimes had during the 1870s and 1880s, but were largely confined to brutal or comic roles. Poor men, economically located below the mixed "middle" of the class hierarchy, were described as members of threatening "mobs" or as pathetic "tramps."[13]

Sensational stories in the Memphis newspapers also emulated the leading urban, mass circulation dailies of the 1890s in organizing plots and the characters of "others" into several standard types.[14] The "fiend" or "brute" appeared in headlines and articles as a kind of gothic monster who committed murder, assault and sexual violence without conscience, as in "Crushed Their Skulls, A Fiend Murders a Family," or "Fiends Assault a Bride, Two Tramps Drive Farmer Delk from His Home, They Repeatedly Outrage His Wife." The "maniac" or "crank," a closely related character, appeared as a more or less dangerous individual who acted without comprehensible motivation, as in "Murdered by a Maniac, Awful Deed of a Lunatic in a Little Scotch Village, Two Persons Hacked to Death and a Third Fatally Injured," or "Work of a Madman, A Prominent Physician Killed for a Fancied Wrong . . . An Epidemic of Cranks in Chicago." Those with more benign manias were featured in articles such as "Now It's Jack the Sculptor, A Fellow with a Mania for Defacing Tombstones." Most of these stories focused on the horrifying yet thrilling actions of the villain. The sufferings of victims were more likely to come to the fore in stories about accidents and natural disasters, such as

"Eight Mangled Forms," the story of a St. Louis train wreck, or "Killed by a Swelling Tongue" in Ohio.[15]

Characters such as the "fiend" or "maniac," though not imagined as newspaper readers, nonetheless referred to populations and situations with existences outside the news columns. They regularly challenged or threatened the order of newspaper stories in ways that were themselves sensational. Of course, the story writers struggled to reassert control of the narrative in the face of challenges. When a black man was charged with raping "a little white girl," a Memphis newspaper reported that "Negroes Rescue the Scoundrel and Are Guarding Him." The article never suggested that the "brute" might have been falsely accused, though the story clearly implied that the rescuers thought so. The resistance to the narrative of the brutal black rapist came through, even as the story reasserted itself through the claim that the rescuers were themselves scoundrels for thwarting the just vengeance of the white mob. In accounts of strikes and "riots" in which working men threatened to "Blow Rich Men to Bits," workers' claims that their bosses were brutal insinuated themselves into the stories, even as the rioters were characterized essentially as "fiends." [16]

Though white women appeared regularly in special fashion, fiction, or society features, and "other" women appeared in the news columns primarily as victims of crimes or accidents, they also broke out of these familiar parameters. News accounts of women's rights activities disrupted the ghettoization, for example, as did a standard variety of sensational story—the domestic scandal.

The scandal story revealed conflicts hidden within "private" life and exposed both the existence of male brutality against the women and children they were assigned to protect and the activities of women whose behavior was shockingly unladylike. One of the most common domestic scandal stories was actually a tale of domestic tragedy—murder within the family or the courting couple made the papers nearly every day. Most of the murderers were men, as in "Her Babes Saw Her Murdered, A Husband Murders His Wife and Then Suicides," or "Shot His Mistress to Death." But some were monstrous mothers or avenging wives and mistresses, as in "Torture for Children, An Unnatural Irish Mother . . . Her Brutality Resulted in the Death of a Daughter," or "Vitriol As Revenge," the story of Kate Cosgrove, who swore she would ruin the male lover who had ruined her. Jealous rivalry often appeared as a motive of both male and female murderers, inspiring articles such as "The Old, Old Story, Attentions Paid to Ladies Have a Most Fatal Result" and "Dashed Vitriol in Her Face, Mrs. Julia Olive of Atlanta Takes Terrible Revenge upon a Pretty Girl" who had begun living with Mr. Olive.[17]

Other domestic scandal stories focused on the gender conflicts exposed by divorce or illegitimacy, or on the generational conflicts revealed when a child, usually a daughter, escaped parental control to elope or undertake a life of "immorality." Even when these conflicts were not fatal, the stories often dwelled upon the reality or possibility of violence, as in "She Stooped to Folly, Miss Sallie Mynott Yields to Handsome Mr. Hall . . . [Who] Stole the Baby and Cast It Adrift, Prominent Families Disgraced," or "An Irate Father's Success, He Recovers His Eloping Daughter with a Winchester."[18]

Such stories reported events among all segments of the population, though reporting conventions varied according to race, class, ethnicity, or region. The sensational element of shocked surprise was enhanced when the families involved were referred to as "prominent" or wealthy. Scandal stories offered readers a public airing of private conflicts and tragedies, combined with morality tales that set the terms of respectable, normative intimacy. Violations of such respectable normalcy provided the occasions for public voyeurism and intervention. But readers might also observe that life was not always what it seemed beneath the patina of bourgeois respectability, and encounter some covert, even subversive pleasures as well as overt moral lessons.[19]

The lynching narrative and the lesbian love murder story combined elements of sensationalism, most centrally murderous violence, with elements of domestic scandal, most prominently desiring bodies, personal intimacies, or sex out of place. Of the two, the lynching narrative developed earlier, appearing initially as a story of southern race relations. By 1892 it circulated nationally, helping to destroy fragile alliances of southern freedmen with some white Republicans at the national, regional, and local levels. Tales of racial rape and lynching began to produce the united whiteness of the modern nation, blurring class lines while entrenching the racial, gendered terms of citizenship so starkly represented in D. W. Griffith's widely distributed 1915 film, *The Birth of a Nation*.[20]

The lynching narrative gathered and assimilated tales of violent racial conflict as the dream of a racially inclusive state receded and interracial public space contracted sharply during the 1880s. Pitched battles over voting requirements, economic opportunities, and access to public spaces and resources from trains to schools produced repetitive scenes of violence and warring interpretations in the pages of both the mainstream white news-papers and the African American weekly press. In the black press the issues were framed as political and economic; white violence against blacks ap-peared as the assertion of raw power in the service of white supremacist practices of political exclusion and economic containment. In the stories of the white mass circulation press, white violence acted to contain black criminality. The defense of the symbolically central white home against black men's lawless sexual violations became the core imperative that structured the lynching narrative during the late 1880s and 1890s.

Newspapers provided the necessary public field for the emergence of the lynching narrative, and for the opposition to it. The mass circulation dailies interacted with events and populations to produce the practices and the *spectacle* of lynching as a repetitive, structured ritual featuring mass white participation in the destruction of the black "fiend" or "brute."[21] The black press meanwhile recorded and circulated the collective experience and views of African Americans, produced and communicated in and through the institutions of the postbellum black public sphere—churches, schools, neighborhoods, and political organizations. The black press collated the emergent political analyses, presented weekly to vie with lynching's moral pedagogy for publicity and impact. These opposing accounts of events and their meanings did not meet head-on in an abstract, egalitarian space of pub-lic discourse; they circulated unevenly, deploying vastly unequal cultural and material resources.[22]

In Memphis, Ida B. Wells launched her career in journalism when she assumed coeditorship of the Beale Street Baptist Church's *Free Speech and Head-light*—after the church pastor, Rev. Taylor Nightingale, fled to Oklahoma to avoid incarceration in the county workhouse. Charges of assault and battery against Nightingale arose in the context of disputes within the congrega-tion, suspiciously in the wake of attacks on the *Free Speech* by the *Memphis Public Ledger* and *Weekly Avalanche* for its editorial support of resistance to lynchers in Kentucky. The white newspapers accused Nightingale of using his church to encourage hate and violence; soon after, city officials brought the criminal charges against him.[23]

Ida Wells assumed her editorship in Memphis following previous battles over access to public space and resources, with a railroad company and the local school board.[24] She used the pages of the *Free Speech* to extend her advocacy of black economic autonomy, political equality, and personal freedom. She joined other black editors, prominently including Frederick

Douglass and John Mitchell of the *Richmond Planet*, in militantly opposing disfranchisement, legal segregation, and violence and criticizing other more accommodationist black leaders. Following the 1892 lynching in Memphis, she pursued this path into direct criticism of the tenets of the developing lynching narrative. The Memphis lynching clearly took aim at black economic and political power; the competition for grocery store trade set off the conflict, which was resolved through extralegal but politically sanctioned force. Wells highlighted this clear context to counter the now widely repeated and accepted terms of national as well as regional support for extralegal white violence against blacks—the lynching narrative's tale of rape and revenge.

For this, Wells was forced to flee the South, and the *Free Speech* was destroyed—as other black papers had been before. (And others would continue to be attacked thoughout the 1890s.) By the end of the century the black press had been virtually eliminated in Tennessee (though there was a strong resurgence after 1900).[25] Meanwhile, Wells launched her antilynching campaign through the black-owned *New York Age*.

The lynching and antilynching narratives structured multilayered contests over political power, economic opportunities, and domestic and personal security. The lynching story worked materially, through the circulation of newspapers nationally, to shape political decisions, economic relations, and the institutions of public life. The story argued that constraints on black populations were necessary to defend moral order—specifically the constraints of legal segregation, which provided a kind of cordon sanitaire around the threat of black deviancy. Black resistance to such constraints was met with escalating violence throughout the 1890s, crucially accompanied by attacks on the critical public arena of the African American press. Justifications for segregation, black disfranchisement, and white violence were provided on grounds of character, decency, and defense of the white home.

The lesbian love murder story also emerged as a defense of the white home from another threat posed by deviant sexuality and violence. The new narrative of lesbian menace drew upon and reformulated earlier sensational stories of female sexual depravity, vulnerability, and death—stories of young women of questionable moral reputation endangered by predatory men or by the risks of their own choices. Sensational news accounts of murdered prostitutes, or "fast" girls found dead, had developed as a familiar genre throughout the nineteenth century. Such stories defined a dangerous "outside" to respectable domesticity and enshrined a vision of the protections provided to virtuous women by the properly maintained white home. Of course, they also advertised the possibility, even the adventure and allure, of undomesticated lives for some women.[26]

By the 1890s, dramatic shifts in the economic and political workings of the household engendered a new elaboration of the imagined threats to the still symbolically central white home. In addition to the prostitute, the "fast" girl, and the morally loose "colored" woman, the "girl lover," invert, or lesbian appeared as a figure of mass culture. This figure threatened to establish an alternative domesticity, founded on female economic independence, sexual autonomy, and political aspiration. Like the enfranchised, wage-earning black man, the lesbian threatened white manhood's privileged access to the bodies of white women and to the political power and economic control such access anchored at the site of the white home.

The figure of the lesbian and the sensational lesbian love murder story emerged in the mass circulation press in response to the expansion of women's public activities and institutions at the end of the century. The growth of homosocial contexts, and expanded heterosocial public spaces, produced new nonfamilial identities as increasing numbers of women attended or taught school, worked for wages in collective settings, attended the theater and other sites of public, commercial leisure, or organized social services at the local, state, and national levels. This expanding publicness supported collective demands for full citizenship, political rights, and economic opportunities.[27]

In Memphis, two generations of women reformers had reshaped and diversified women's public presence by the time Alice Mitchell enrolled in the private Higbee School for young white girls from prosperous local families. The first generation included Mrs. Elizabeth Avery Meriwether, born in 1824 and married to one of the most powerful men in Memphis, who rented the Memphis theater in 1876 to argue for women's suffrage. Mrs. Lide Meriwether, born in 1829 and married into the same family, founded the first suffrage club in Memphis. Both Meriwethers became active in national suffrage organizations and promoted their views to women active in religious organizations, the Women's Christian Temperance Union, and the women's club movement. By the 1890s this kind of women's social activism supported the national convention of the Association for the Advancement of Women, held in Memphis in 1892.[28]

Such elite white women reformers relied on race and class privilege to protect them from serious public censure. Unlike Fanny Wright, whose establishment of the interracial Nashoba community near Memphis in the 1840s had earned her pariah status, the Meriwethers and their generation of elite reformers maintained economic and racial barriers. Though Elizabeth Meriwether had risked opprobrium for advocating the emancipation of her husband's inherited slaves before the war, in 1867 the Tennessee Ku Klux Klan was founded in her living room. According to her son, when asked what she thought of the plan to wear white robes and terrorize Negro voters, she replied:

It may work. Negroes are very superstitious. They may become too scared to vote; then when you are allowed to vote you can elect intelligent men to tax you and make the laws that govern you. But when will women have the right to vote? I have been taught to believe that taxation without representation is tyranny.[29]

The second generation of women reformers in Memphis represented more diverse constituencies and were especially active in the areas of education and employment. The growth of public education and the expansion of private secondary schooling provided a limited independence to ever larger numbers of young women teachers, both black and white, from the 1870s forward. A few of these teachers went on to exercise leadership in the public system or to head private institutions of their own. During the late 1870s, two white girls' schools of particular note were founded to provide a rigorous education of the highest quality—the Conway Institute and Miss Higbee's School for Young Ladies. Both sent graduates to northern colleges, but Clara Conway, a disciple of Margaret Fuller, placed more stress on academic achievement than Jenny Higbee, whose catalogs focused on the development of dutiful Christian women. This contrast was illustrated in the founders' often quoted mottoes: Conway admonished her students to "Hitch your wagon to a star," while Higbee reminded her girls, "He prayeth best who loveth best, all things, both great and small." Alice Mitchell, Freda Ward, and Lillie Johnson were among the approximately three hundred students led by twenty-five teachers at the Higbee School in 1892.[30]

The experience of these private girls' schools was for the daughters of prosperous white families only. But the new independence of young women was shared, in some respects, across class and racial lines. Opportunities for wage earning and education expanded steadily for both black and white women; a privileged few attended colleges or entered the professions. Some attended new southern institutions, including African American coeducational institutions like Fisk University in Nashville or women's colleges such as Spelman in Atlanta; both trained young women to be teachers, nurses, and community organizers, such as Mrs. C. H. Phillips and three of her classmates from Fisk who led the black Memphis WCTU. European American women could attend single-sex colleges in the South, like Mary Baldwin in Virginia or Agnes Scott in Georgia, complete teachers' courses at one of the many normal schools established after the war, or they could leave the region to enroll in first-rate coeducational as well as women's institutions.[31]

Highly educated, economically independent women remained a tiny minority, even among the white elite in Memphis, well into the twentieth century, however. In 1890, of the 8,200 women reported employed in Memphis (2,200 of them white, out of a total labor force of 20,000), the vast majority were employed as servants and laundresses, and another large proportion worked as dressmakers and seamstresses. Many of these working women struggled against impoverishment and dependency to establish a collective public presence as wage earners. Only about 3 percent were found in the professional occupations that paid well enough for a degree of individual economic independence, including teachers (256) and physicians (7).[32] Women like Ida B. Wells — a teacher, writer, and editor, though not a college graduate — remained rare through the end of the nineteenth century. Nonetheless, that such women existed at all signified a profound cultural shift and constituted a dramatic challenge to existing hierarchies of race, class, and gender.

In addition to forging new opportunities for education and work, women in Memphis also expanded their opportunities for public, collective recreation and leisure during the late nineteenth century. Organized by both commercial and noncommercial institutions (Memphis supported two theaters presenting regular programs of drama and opera performed by nationally known companies in 1892, and its citizens were active in a growing proliferation of churches), these opportunities allowed for more unsupervised heterosocial interaction among young people while also generating new homosocial worlds.[33]

By the 1890s, New Women, defined by their independence and mobility, were visible and voluble in Memphis, as in other cities across the nation. The overlapping and diversifying sites of female publicness produced new identities based in homosocial institutions, new market-based aesthetics of consumption and display, and collective social action as well as domestic and religious life.[34] The virtual public sphere of the daily newspapers helped

create, shape, appropriate, and constrain these new identities, in advertising
and news columns as well as feature stories. In 1892, the Memphis dailies
responded to the perceived dangers of such identities in their reporting of
Alice Mitchell's murder of Freda Ward. From the raw material of these reports, the mass circulation press gradually assembled the elements of the
lesbian love murder story—at first, a moral tale of the consequences of the
unchecked aspirations of schoolgirls who dreamed of their own alternatives
to the domestic isolation of the white home.

Alice Mitchell's murder presented an abundance of the elements of a sensational news story: a domestic scandal complete with violence in a prominent family, a bloody murder committed by a fiend—or was she a maniacal
crank? Such elements alone boosted the story to prominence in the national
as well as local news. But this story burst the boundaries of familiar sensational narratives. A love murder involving two girls presented an astonishing and confusing twist that confounded the gendered roles of villain and
victim.

The sensationalism surrounding the Mitchell-Ward murder escalated
quickly and dramatically. Some newspapers around the country were not
content to print only the abundant wire service copy: a few large urban
dailies, including the New York World and the San Francisco Chronicle, commis-
sioned their own correspondents to interview the principals in Memphis.

The stories that were printed in the days following the murder stressed its
sensational aspects. All the papers headlined the class, gender, and age of the
principals, while race was emphasized in descriptions (such as "her white
bosom"—a reference to Freda Ward's corpse).[35] All proceeded to report the
bloody crime in lurid detail. Hyperbole was universal, though out-of-town
newspapers were freer to employ it, as their readers were less likely to spot
it. (Memphis readers would have known that the Mitchells, though prosperous, were not "among the first families of Memphis," as the New York World
claimed, and that Freda Ward was not a familiar figure in "society," as the
New York Times reported.[36]) Imagination bloomed, especially in descriptions
of the violence, with reporters filling in sights and sounds for their readers in
purple prose borrowed from popular fiction. The San Francisco Examiner, which
announced that it was "Investigating the Story of Strange Passion and Death,"
admitted that in reports of this murder, "Fact Merges into Fiction."[37] The
Memphis Public Ledger was especially ambitious on this front, including many
descriptions like this one of the murder scene:

Grasping her by the hair Miss Mitchell pulled her head back, exposing the round, white throat. Again the keen razor was brought into play, and this time it did its work with frightful completeness. The girl was almost beheaded, and fell fainting to the ground, which was soon drenched with her rushing blood.[38]

Proceeding from the foundation laid by such passages, the process of narrativization of the murder unfolded day by day in the news columns. Yet the papers also found themselves mired in narrative confusions. Reporters found it difficult to sketch out a clear plot or strike a consistent moral pose: was Alice a poor, helpless victim of mental disease, or was she a truly monstrous female driven by masculine erotic and aggressive motives? Theories and images proliferated and jockeyed for space in the news columns.

The legal strategies that began to emerge after the initial reports of the murder ultimately shaped the narrative morass into contending accounts provided by defense and prosecution. When Alice was charged with murder, her family hired defense attorneys who decided to rely on medical experts. They consulted physicians, who argued that she was insane and should be committed to the state lunatic asylum rather than be tried for murder. The prosecutor, influenced by Freda Ward's family, rejected the plea of "present insanity" and argued that Alice was not insane but rather rational and vicious. The defense strategy protected the Mitchell family's class- and race-based moral reputation by arguing that their daughter was not bad or "fast" but ill. The prosecution attacked Alice Mitchell's respectability, with the goal of holding her legally responsible for the murder. In the days before the first courtroom proceedings, these opposing sides constructed their own competing narratives and struggled to influence the public through the press.

From the beginning, the defense had a clear advantage in constructing and presenting its case. Alice's father, George Mitchell, the retired senior partner of the furniture merchants Mitchell & Bryson, accompanied his daughter to jail when she was arrested less than one hour after the crime. Prosperous, privileged, and well known locally as lovable "Uncle George," he had the sympathy of police, jailer, and press. He was able to exert control over his daughter and shape a coherent public account of her actions, quickly and effectively. He hired prominent attorneys Gen. Luke Wright and Col. George Gantt, who arrived at the jail to interview Alice by 8:00 P.M. on the evening of the murder.

By the next day, the newspapers were reporting the attorneys' version of events. Since reporters were not permitted access to Alice herself, the attorneys' account of her statements and motives appeared as the only firsthand information available. The day after the murder, headlines proclaimed "Miss Mitchell Was Strangely Enamored of Her Victim, She Says She Loved Her So She Had to Kill Her."[39] Then each subsequent day, the defense released a little more information to the press as "evidence" of Alice's odd beliefs and activities accumulated.

Within a few days, the attorneys provided reporters with the text of an extensive statement, which was printed as if it were a first-person interview with Alice. In it, she said she had been engaged to marry Freda:

The day for our wedding was set, and then not all of the powers in the world could have separated us. It was our intention to leave here and go to St. Louis, and I would have been Freda's slave. I would have devoted my whole life to making her happy. . . . But when Freda returned my engagement ring it broke my heart. It was the most cruel thing I ever suffered. I could not bear the idea of being separated from her: her whom I loved more dearly than my life. I wrote to her and implored her not to break off the engagement, but my letters availed nothing. I could not bear to think of her living in the company of others. Then, indeed, I resolved to kill Freda because I loved her so much that I wanted her to die loving me, and when she did die I know she loved me better than any other human being on earth. I got my father's razor and made up my mind to kill Freda, and now I know she is happy.

Whatever the origin of this statement, Alice Mitchell's lawyers released it for publication as "evidence" of her insanity. To confirm the impression, they supplemented it with tales of her peculiar beliefs and behavior—she claimed that she and Freda had agreed to kill each other if ever separated; she had written letters signed "Alvin Ward" and "Fritz Ward," and one telling of her own death; she showed no emotion when speaking about the murder; she believed Freda was still alive; she wanted to lie down next to her beloved at the funeral home; she took no interest in the coming trial and didn't seem to understand that she might be hanged.[40]

In order to persuade the public (and eventually a jury) that Alice was insane, the defense attorneys worked to shape an image of her that would fit the specific medical definition of a mental disease. They solicited the contributions of physicians, who spoke to the press both before, during, and after the courtroom proceedings in the case. The first diagnosis to appear in the press was "erotomania," defined by an unnamed "prominent physician" quoted in the Memphis Commercial as "an unnatural affection between two persons of the same sex."[41] This was a novel definition for a diagnosis with a long history. For more than two centuries, the term had referred to love-sickness or love-melancholy felt toward someone of the other sex. In the 1892 edition of D. Hack Tuke's authoritative *Dictionary of Psychological Medicine*, "erotomania" was defined as a term "used for those forms of insanity where there is an intensely morbid desire towards a person of the opposite sex, without sensual passion. Others define it as synonymous with Nymphomania and Satyriasis."[42]

Following this first radical reinterpretation, unnamed Memphis physicians continued to try to explain their theories through the press. "Erotomania" was further defined in varying ways—first as "a malady of the mind" caused by the "training, habits and associations" of those affected, and later as a disorder caused by "a diseased brain" which "prompts unnatural practice" that may "lead on to murder" if interrupted.[43] Over time, different medical terms and contradictory definitions were offered. By the time physician-experts testified in court, the "erotomania" diagnosis had been almost entirely displaced by other disease syndromes.[44]

Whatever the diagnosis, however, the defense was at pains to squash any suggestion of "unnatural practices" between the girls that appeared in medical discussions. When a reporter asked one defense attorney whether, in the case of Alice and Freda, there had been any "gratification of the perverted mental passion," the answer was no—the girls' love was "purely . . . mental."[45] None of the mainstream papers did more than hint, through such questions and quotations, that anything "coarse or immoral" could have occurred among respectable white girls.[46] But an "entertainment" paper in Lincoln, Nebraska, took sensationalism one step further than the mass circulation dailies could and reported that medical testimony would show that Alice's insanity was caused "by this unnatural and unholy love, a love which could not be satisfied as nature intended it should be, and unnatural methods had to be resorted to."[47]

Attempts at diagnostic categorization of Alice's emotions and sexuality were accompanied by other efforts to fulfill the definitional requirements of insanity. In 1892, this meant that a "hereditary influence" was necessary. It was found in the mental history of Isabella Mitchell, Alice's mother. Defense attorneys told reporters that Mrs. Mitchell had once been an "inmate" of an asylum in Ohio and had been treated in Memphis for "dementia" at the time of Alice's birth.[48] Ultimately, the ambition of the defense was to construct a comprehensive story of Alice's life as a medical "case history" and to recruit "experts" to support its view in court. Instances of Alice's defiance of gender boundaries were to be centrally featured. As Colonel Gantt explained to the *Appeal Avalanche*:

. . . the history of Alice Mitchell's life, everything she has done, her peculiarities, whether during her infancy she played with dolls or other such toys in which the average female child delights, whether she had fondness for those of her own or the opposite sex, all these will be circumstances going to show the state and quality of her mind.[49]

The defense image of Alice as insane, or as a female "maniac" whose motives were pathological and explicable only with reference to science, was countered by the prosecution. Attorney General George B. Peters, fortified with "evidence" provided by Freda Ward's family and others, set out to show that Alice's motives were perfectly understandable though evil. To the prosecution, Alice was a sane but monstrous female, a vile and vindictive "fiend" with an ungovernable temper, inspired to murder by simple jealousy and plain malice. The *Appeal Avalanche* summarized this division of opinion:

The preponderance of public opinion is in favor of the theory that Alice Mitchell is insane. It is held that even though she were of sound mind and discretion in regard to the ordinary affairs of life, she was the slave of a passion not normal and almost incomprehensible to well-balanced people, but absolutely irresistible; consequently she was not a free agent. There are a few persons, however, who decline to accept the theory of perverted and destructive love, and hold that there are circumstances in the case that justify the belief that the murder was the act of a sane woman with a violent and vindictive temper and morbidly sensitive.[50]

The prosecution was unable to assemble a really coherent case, however. Alice Mitchell was not required to answer Peters's questions, and he was never able to develop a unifying theory of her motives. He and his allies directed their efforts toward questioning defense assertions and offering a range of alternative scenarios. These included the possibility that Alice had attacked Freda for ignoring her or slandering her, or for winning away the affections of some unidentified man. Repeated suggestions that there was "a man at the bottom of it" functioned both to counter the defense picture of Alice as a legally irresponsible "erotomaniac," indifferent to the attentions of men, and to represent her as "fast."[51]

The prosecution's account of Alice's questionable moral character, as well as the evidence they held in their possession, had been passed on by the Ward family. Peters interviewed Freda's sisters Jo Ward and Mrs. Ada Volkmar, who presented him with a bundle of correspondence between the two girls. Though these letters were identified to the press as love letters, their specific content was closely guarded; Peters would only hint that they contained crucial evidence to support the prosecution's view, expressed by Mrs. Volkmar's husband, an "old Memphis boy":

She is a bad girl. She committed the murder at the dictate of a cold, wicked heart. It was done deliberately. She was no more crazy than I am.[52]

The two primary accounts of Alice's character and motives offered by the defense and prosecution were not presented evenhandedly by the press. In a common move that appeared to enhance the newspaper marketing of sensational news, the two major morning papers took opposing sides. The *Appeal Avalanche* generally supported the defense, reporting that its version of events held sway with the public. The *Commercial* presented defense claims with considerable skepticism, however. Summarizing the evidence to be presented in court, its reporter commented that "there has been but little disclosed to show that Alice Mitchell was more than an ungovernable and at times, vicious girl." Examining the specific claim that Alice suffered from erotomania, the reporter argued strenuously:

It is extremely doubtful if such a minor degree of insanity would absolve one from legal responsibility. If Alice Mitchell unnaturally loved her victim, and through jealousy killed her, she would stand much in the legal relation of a jealous man who had killed his rival or his sweetheart. Her fondness for another woman would naturally be supposed to produce a soothing effect, rather than a vicious tendency. She knew she had done wrong when she killed Miss Ward, because she cowardly ran away. Had she been wholly irresponsible and insane, she might have acted differently after drawing the razor across Miss Ward's throat.[53]

In addition to such direct argument, reporters also used the narrative strategy of characterization to construct moral meanings. They created their characters primarily through description, both physical and psychological. Alice, the center of controversy, was featured as the "fair murderess" or the "fair slayer."[54] She attracted especially careful observation and strongly ambivalent evaluation from reporters.

Most often, Alice was described as unnaturally calm or cool, showing no emotion, expressing no remorse. This description of placid self-control was used at different points to fill out two very different visions of her—as a cold and "hardened criminal" or as a simpleminded, uncomprehending lunatic. At other times, she appeared as a "bloodthirsty Amazon" who murdered to "satisfy the craving desire of her mad mind"—an image of out-of-control frenzy, understood as either fiendish or maniacal.[55] The images of frenzy were generally connected to descriptions of the murder itself, while the calm, cool, and controlled Alice appeared primarily in courtroom scenes.

Alice was available for firsthand observation only on the few occasions when she went to court, so at those times her appearance and demeanor were most closely scrutinized. She was frustratingly opaque, wearing a heavy veil and saying little. When she appeared for her arraignment on February 1, the *Commercial* unsympathetically observed:

Miss Mitchell is slight and her blue dress fitted tightly about her figure, while over this she had a short jacket. She raised a veil when the indictments were read and disclosed a face that is far from prepossessing. She has an expressionless face, with low forehead, eyes close together, and blotches that robs [sic] her of any pretence [sic] to a fair complexion.[56]

Following her second court appearance, the *Appeal Avalanche* and the *Public Ledger* offered readers detailed observations, and both described her as "pretty." The *Appeal Avalanche* recorded:

Alice Mitchell was clad in a tan and brown checked ulster with a short cape. The dress was rather abbreviated for a street costume, and displayed a small pair of feet encased in black Oxford tie shoes with high heels that added an inch or more to her height. On her head was a sailor hat decorated with a black feather, while an impenetrable dark blue barege veil, tied closely, concealed her features. . . . The [veil] being removed, a pair of large blue-gray eyes looked out quite complacently toward the judge. Those orbs are unusually large, but not so much as to be out of proportion. The face revealed by Alice Mitchell is quite a pretty one. . . . The complexion is rather pale and sallow, and the cheeks are rather thin, but there is an attractive expression there.[57]

In order to draw a clear connection between such descriptions and Alice's character, reporters repeatedly contrasted Alice with either Freda Ward or Lillie Johnson. In stories of their friendship, Freda figured as Alice's opposite—a gentle, refined girl to whom the more "masculine" Alice had been devoted.[58] Lillie Johnson—Alice's companion at the scene of the murder, who had been arrested and jailed as an accomplice—provided a continuing counterpoint. Her conventionally girlish behavior was highlighted, casting

Alice's deviance in bold relief. When the two appeared in court together, descriptions of them were paired meaningfully:

Lillie Johnson has been in a condition of slight nervous prostration in the nature of hysteria since the indictment was found against her. . . . Alice Mitchell does not seem to be troubling herself a great deal about the situation. . . .

Miss Johnson's color changed when the name of Freda Ward was mentioned but Alice Mitchell's blood was too cold for the dread words to suffuse her face.

[Miss Mitchell] stood as rigid as a statue. . . . Miss Johnson would have sunk to the floor but for the support of her father's arm.[59]

The Mitchell murder story was also populated with numerous other secondary and minor characters. The fathers of Alice Mitchell, Freda Ward, and Lillie Johnson often appeared together as "the three sorrowing fathers" whose sufferings touched observers. George Mitchell was presented as a retired businessman, "fond of rod and gun" and "well suited to leisure." Under the pressure of his daughter's imprisonment he had become a "poor old man" with "the sympathy of all Memphis in his affliction." Thomas Ward, formerly a machinist with the Memphis Fertilizing Company, now a merchant and planter in Golddust, Tennessee, was described as "frantic" and "almost unmanned" by the news of his daughter's fate. No occupation was ever mentioned for J. M. Johnson (though the city directory listed him as a painter), but he was lauded expansively for his devotion to his daughter. He spent several nights at the jail, remaining awake and alert to any signs of danger or distress.[60]

Though the news reports thus showed the fathers as broken down in their grief, they were nonetheless present and to some extent ennobled by their daughters' ordeals. The mothers, however, seemed to collapse and disappear. Isabella Mitchell, labeled early on as mentally unbalanced, was never otherwise described in any news report. She seldom appeared in public, was rarely observed or quoted, and no reporter was permitted to interview her at home. Freda Ward's mother was deceased, and her older sister/mother surrogate, Ada Volkmar, was "not well" and unable to appear in court. Mrs. Johnson (along with her daughter) swooned repeatedly and was confined to her room with "nervous prostration." Even the widow Mrs. Kimbrough, the Ward sisters' host in Memphis, was "prostrated" by heart trouble caused by the excitement.[61]

The younger women connected to the case were not incapacitated or silent like the older women, however. Jo Ward and Christina Purnell appeared as witnesses to the murder at the coroner's examination and before the grand jury, and they did not hesitate to speak to the press. Their appearances were described and assessed, positively. They were "beautiful," "modest," or "becomingly attired"—always gender appropriate as the ingenue characters in the press scenarios.[62]

Other minor characters included the judge, Julius DuBose, whose reputation for tyrannical and pompous behavior made him the favored target of reporters' satirical prose.[63] The jury appeared also, even before it was chosen, as representative of southern gentlemanly "chivalry" toward young white respectable women. The Memphis Commercial opined that only a jury of women might find Alice Mitchell guilty of murder—but women didn't sit on juries, and:

> . . . there [are] not twelve men in Shelby County who would render a verdict of murder in the first degree, even though there were cords of undisputable evidence in that line, sworn as they are to render a verdict according to "law and evidence." Their chivalry exceeds their sense of justice.[64]

These characterizations in newspapers, used to establish narrative meanings, were inherently unstable; they were often contested and open to disruption by the "characters" themselves. Individuals involved in the events surrounding the murder of Freda Ward alternately resisted and cooperated with the press in their efforts to control information and shape the story. Attorneys and principals, for instance, sometimes approached reporters and sometimes refused interviews. In addition, readers were often moved to come forward and claim a part in the drama.

Neighbors of the Mitchells and others who had had some contact with Alice volunteered information to reporters in the hope of influencing her characterization or perhaps of appearing as characters themselves. Often, they reinterpreted past events in the light of what they had read about the murder. John Perry told the Public Ledger:

> I live next door to Mr. George Mitchell and have known Alice for nine years or more, and have never considered her strong mentally. Her manner has been always flighty and unsettled and her ways different from that of most girls. She was of an impulsive disposition, and given to doing very much as the present mood inclined her, whether it was to snatch up a rifle and stand about her yard shooting sparrows or to

ride a bare back horse at a break-neck speed about the premises. I have never seen anything about her conduct that was at all immodest, nor was she the least bit fast as regards men. On the contrary, she seemed to care nothing for them and rather preferred the society of her own sex. . . . From a long and close knowledge of Alice Mitchell her act was that of an insane woman.[65]

Even the out-of-town papers found witnesses eager to talk. The *San Francisco Examiner* quoted a young man who claimed to have been a "sweetheart" of Alice's; he hadn't known his "rival" in Golddust was a woman.[66] And out-of-town readers also contributed to the story. A postmaster in Kentucky reported receiving a letter from Memphis asking if two girls could marry there. He had thrown it out, assuming it to be the product of a "crank," until he read about Alice Mitchell in the newspaper.[67] Mr. C. G. Hubbard of Cincinnati recalled to a Memphis detective that three years earlier, Alice had "made love like a man" to his daughter, now deceased.[68]

As the volume of anonymous letters sent to prosecutor Peters's office attested, the imaginations of some newspaper readers were vivid.[69] Some apocryphal tales were reported as fact: the *New York Times* didn't question a claim that Alice and Lillie had appeared in men's clothing while searching for Freda days prior to the murder (testimony at trial verified that they had been attired in dresses and veils).[70] Other stories were openly ridiculed—usually those told by members of suspect social categories. The testimony of two "colored girls," presented by a white woman in order to be accepted at all, was treated less seriously than other patently preposterous scenarios.[71]

Readers responded to newspaper stories collectively as well as individually; crowds appeared as participants and observers at events reported in the press. Though created and fed by the papers, these crowds were often ridiculed by reporters as greedy, pushy hordes who insisted on their "feast of sensation." They showed up at the undertaker's door (where they were "almost ghoulish" in their desire to see the "mutilated face" of Freda Ward),[72] at the funeral (where "hundreds of people of all kinds, colors and conditions gathered" and "tore pickets off of the fence" to get into the church yard),[73] at the jail (where there was a "constant stream of visitors" who tried many gambits to get in to see Alice and failed),[74] and at court (where they were "much disappointed and disgusted at losing their anticipated feast of sensation" when proceedings were delayed).[75]

Though all crowds were ridiculed, gatherings of women and black Memphians were especially sharply satirized. Groups of women were referred to as "displays of millinery" who "hung about the rooms and passages . . . nearly pestering the life out of . . . the sheriff's young deputy with their questions."[76] The "colored folks" who gathered while the grand jury met were said to be interested because "their favorite weapon was used."[77]

Individuals in the crowds sometimes provided comments or asked questions that created a kind of Greek chorus effect in the news stories. Anonymous observers at court commented, "What delicate hands to commit such a horrible deed!" and asked, "Honest, now, is Alice Mitchell crazy or just mean?"[78] A "well known priest" observed that the murderess had a "strong but not masculine" face that indicated a "disordered" brain, while a "prominent minister" warned that public discussion of the case could lead to harm and should be left to "specialists."[79]

The chorus of commentary included explicit comment in the editorial (as opposed to news) columns of the newspapers—both the local publications and those from other cities that were regularly excerpted in the Memphis Commercial. Many editorialists agreed with the prominent minister (quoted above) and the Appeal Avalanche:

It is most devoutly to be wished that the trial of Alice Mitchell and Lillie Johnson may take place at a very early date, and the case removed from public consideration. Its prolongation would be deplorable. It is one of those cases which appeals strongly to morbid sentimentality and which tends unduly to excite diseased or weak minds. It is liable to be provocative of other crimes, for such is the usual baleful consequences of sensational and novel homicides. The exploits of the Whitechapel fiends were followed by others of kindred character in various parts of the world. The court therefore, should act quickly, and the testimony should be as brief as justice will permit.[80]

This was an ironic position for a newspaper that advertised that it would contain "From Day to Day a Complete Report of the Progress of the Unparalleled Mitchell-Ward-Johnson Girl-Murder Trial in all its Details, Fully Illustrated" (see fig. 2).[81] It was an irony that largely defined the moral stance of the newspapers, however.

Most editorial commentary was focused more narrowly on the actions of the principals and endorsed or attacked either the defense or prosecution positions in the case. The Jackson, Tennessee, Tribune-Sun wrote:

The murder of Miss Freda Ward by Miss Alice Mitchell at Memphis has been the subject of more newspaper comment than any other crime that was committed in

Fig. 2. Banner advertisement for Mitchell-Ward trial newspaper coverage. (*Memphis Appeal Avalanche*, Feb. 24, 1892)

the South, and of the many opinions expressed not one of the newspapers . . . seem
to doubt the insanity of the slayer of Miss Ward.

Yet the Hot Springs, Arkansas, *Graphic* argued:

Alice Mitchell, the Memphis girl murderer, hopes to escape by a plea of insanity. Her
insanity was of the mushroom growth. It developed first when she committed the
atrocious murder, and it would likely end with a verdict of acquittal in the murder
trial.[82]

These two contending master narratives, whether presented in the voices
of principals, legal advocates, reporters, or editorialists, were not always internally consistent. As new information and witnesses surfaced, new claims
had to be assimilated into the structure of each argument. Ultimately, coherent assimilation of all the "facts" was impossible. Huge ruptures inevitably
appeared; a cacophony of miscellaneous voices was heard, suggesting other
viewpoints, other stories.

The defense and prosecution did what they could to silence disruptive
voices as they struggled to construct coherent narratives. But the only one
they could control completely was Alice's. No one was permitted into her jail
cell to speak with her other than her family and her attorneys; she was permitted to make no unmediated statement until she appeared on the witness
stand in July (over her attorneys' objections). Other principals and witnesses
were warned by defense attorneys or prosecutors not to speak to the press,
but since they were not jailed they could not be completely restrained. Numerous contacts between reporters and witnesses, crowds, and individual
moral experts (as noted above) could not be monitored at all. A sense of
narrative chaos often resulted, subtly subverting news reports that generally
followed the familiar plots. Occasionally a coherent alternative story suggested itself.

One of the other stories to emerge in newspaper accounts was a tale of
conflict between girls, whose close bonds had developed in the homosocial
world of the school, and their more domestically confined older female relatives, whose nonfamilial attachments had been more limited. Lillie Johnson,
who was interviewed by several reporters before her arrest the day following the murder, said that Alice and Freda had been "chums" for two or three
years, since meeting at the Higbee School. This unremarkable kind of attachment had continued unbroken until Mrs. Volkmar objected to the "unnatural
affection" between the girls and wrote a letter to Mrs. Mitchell the previous

summer, asking that contact between them be forbidden. Since that time, according to Lillie, Allie had been "a changed girl" who seemed to be brooding, in deep despair.[83]

Another story came briefly to light when letters from Alice to a young man in Missouri were produced for publication before the prosecutor could suppress them. The young man had placed an ad in a matrimonial paper for young lady correspondents and received a reply from Memphis signed "Freda Ward." The handwriting of the letters had been identified as Alice Mitchell's, however. As published—first in a St. Louis newspaper, then in the *Appeal Avalanche*—their contents revealed a dense web of fantasy about a life of excitement and adventure. Alice, largely homebound and idle since leaving the Higbee School, described herself in the letters as Freda Myra Ward, an actress who had run away from home with a young man to go on the stage. She told of rising from a poor opera girl to play important roles with small companies and included much detailed stage gossip in her epistles.[84]

These letters were the first of Alice's words to appear in print without the mediating influence of her attorneys. Since the actual Freda Ward had demonstrated dramatic talents, including an exceptional singing voice, the letters suggested that an imaginative identification with Freda played an important role in Alice's psychic life. (This suggestion was corroborated by the existence of a second set of similar letters and the fact that Alice had signed Freda's name to coal receipts when deliveries were made to the Mitchell home.) They hinted that a yearning for escape and adventure had been at the heart of Alice's hopes for a future with Freda.[85] They also revealed a world of nondomestic heterosociality—elaborated in the pages of newspaper ads as well as in the world of the theater—that overlapped with Alice and Freda's homosocial world and helped define their aspirations to live beyond the limits of the white home. But this overlap was disentangled and polarized in the legal wrangling surrounding the Mitchell-Ward murder. The opposing legal strategies tended to separate the homo- and heterosocial landscapes for public life in Memphis—with the defense stressing the experience and dangers of the girls' school and the prosecution focusing on the moral menace of unsupervised heterosocial leisure. These separated emphases supported the emergence in mass culture of the "lesbian" and the morally untrustworthy "normal" woman as distinct threats to domestic stability.

The newspapers in Memphis began to shape the story of the Mitchell-Ward murder in the weeks prior to any extended courtroom proceedings. They slowly assembled a sensational account according to the gendered genres of the domestic scandal and the love murder and circulated it within the material networks and structural logics of newspaper publication. The story, as it emerged at the beginning of 1892, appeared on pages laid out to separate and rank news accounts according to subject and significance. As an attention-grabbing sensational domestic scandal, the Mitchell-Ward story received prime placement, but it was located, presented, and narrated as "about" private morality and character or perhaps bodily or mental health. It was not placed or narrated as "about" politics, public policy, or questions of freedom and equality. It was unconnected to stories thematizing such subjects. Though they appeared on the same physical pages of black and white type, the categories of stories were interpretive worlds apart.

As the lesbian love murder story was assembled through the Mitchell-Ward case, it appeared alongside the lynching story in the columns of the mass circulation press. These narratives, also presented as having nothing whatsoever to do with one another, helped define the parameters of the American "general public"—the readers of the newspapers whose moral fitness for citizenship, or for the domestic morality underwriting it, was assumed. They accomplished this through their construction of unfit "others," social types who negatively defined the normative characteristics of Americans. Along with the advertisements that defined the mainstream consumer as presumptively white and domestic, the news stories worked to produce a new form of mass culture and an emerging American modernity at the turn of the century.

HABEAS CORPUS

Scarcely any political question arises in the
United States that is not resolved sooner or
later into a judicial question.

Alexis de Tocqueville, *Democracy in America* [1]

By the late nineteenth century, a new form of American nationalism had replaced earlier concepts and practices of republican democracy in the United
States. An augmented national constitution extended the mantle of citizenship to former slaves and for the first time exceeded the importance of state
and local governments in allocating rights and protections among the popu-
lace. A nationalizing governing structure began intervening more aggressively in world affairs, as well as asserting authority internally. This expanded
structure of nationhood coexisted with simultaneous contractions of the
scope of political democracy. New restrictions on the franchise combined
with the decline of mass party politics and the rise of state bureaucracies to
narrow the scope of electoral participation. Other forms of access to citizenship and democratic politics were increasingly restricted by myriad means,
including segregation and immigration laws or more extensive policing of
public space.[2]

The resulting contradiction between the expansion and rising significance
of national citizenship and the multiplying constraints and restrictions on
democratic public life dissolved into the form of American nationalism formulated through the mass circulation press. The newspapers provided a

sense of national membership through their imagined general public of readers, a collectivity more expansive and inclusive than formal citizenship or
access to political participation. Readers with limited access to democratic
politics were nonetheless invited to join the affective unity of the nation
through their consumption of news and advertising that addressed them as
Americans. But this more inclusive nationalism also segmented its constituencies, most centrally through the gender binary, and marginalized or excluded large populations of "others," primarily through the deployment of
racial categories.[3]

Criminal trials provided newspapers with exceptional opportunities for
delineating the boundaries of national membership. Though most trials
were local events that proceeded with little public notice, some attracted
enormous attention and comment. Located at the intersection of the law,
which defined the interests and powers of state institutions, and the press,
which circulated meanings through nationwide networks, trial stories were
especially potent nationalizing narratives. They captured public interest
through dramatizations of major social conflicts — conflicts often born of,
played out through, and provisionally resolved in scenes saturated in violence.

Criminal trials staged the impact and influence of law and its enforcement, a social process involving a wide range of institutions, formal procedures, and informal practices that combined rules of decorum, access, and
fairness with patterns of hierarchy, coercion, and violence. The processes
of *enactment* of this law represented Americanness, as personified by politicians and dramatized through electoral campaigns. Formally democratic
elections and legislative votes at multiple levels of government legitimated
American law, and the U.S. state, as products of popular consent. But these
processes were shaped at every level by bloody conflict, violent coercion,
and terrorism. During the 1890s, social policies of official and unofficial violence produced racially exclusive state structures, class-inflected legislation,
and gendered forms of citizenship.[4]

Formal structures of law systematically obscured their undemocratic and
violent sources — processes of *enforcement* were somewhat less opaque. The
semivisible process of selection in practices of policing and arrest, only half-
heartedly and unconvincingly denied by politicians and police authorities,
enabled patterns of extralegal violence to operate as shadow extensions of
public policy. This effect was spectacularly obvious during the 1890s in the

systematic failure to arrest members of lynch mobs, who were well known to their local communities. A similar (and related) impact resulted from the enforcement of rape laws, which so markedly depended on the social identity of the accused and the perceived respectability, coded as "virtue," of the aggrieved. The overall policies of deference to privilege and surveillance of poverty, and of widely varying standards for different races and genders, were both blatantly apparent and routine.

In Memphis, as elsewhere, the vast majority of arrests were for various violations of public order by the poor. Of 5,177 arrests during 1892, 1,887 were for the specific offenses of disorderly conduct, drunkenness, or vagrancy. Smaller numbers of people were arrested for crimes such as gambling, obstructing the street, fast driving, or using profane language. There were also a smattering of property crimes, from larceny (293 arrests) and embezzlement (4) to arson (3) and counterfeiting (4). But arrests for crimes of violence were still relatively rare in 1892 (though Memphis later became known as the "Murder Capital of the World"). Most of these were for assault and battery (532 arrests); only a few were for murder (15), intent to kill (39), rape (2), or intent to rape (3).

Of the total arrests, 4,360 (84 percent) were of men; of these, 49 percent were European American and 51 percent African American. Only 817 arrests (or about 16 percent) were of women; of these more than 77 percent were African Americans, most often charged with public order offenses.[5]

Of course, these arrest statistics do not represent the actual crime rate: the failure to make arrests in the 1892 lynching of Moss, McDowell, and Stewart was only the most obvious example of the selectivity of police action. Many instances of violence, condoned by the police and the courts, never appeared in arrest statistics. On the other hand, those statistics were swamped by "crimes" created and defined by regulations designed to control the poor— vague statutes penalizing "vagrancy" or "disorderly conduct." The resulting skew in arrests, presented as a socially neutral enforcement of the law, actually constructed "criminals" and the public perception of criminality in class- , race- and gender-specific ways.

The courtroom scenes following such arrests naturalized structures of social domination. Over and over again, poor and black men, along with far smaller numbers of black and white women, were fined or jailed by white prosperous men. These repetitive, routinized enactments of power came to seem part of the natural order of things, so unremarkable and utterly predictable that they possessed no interest for the white "general public" of the press. Reports of courtroom news in the papers were perfunctory lists of the "usual" crimes and sentences, unless unusual violence, comedy, or salaciousness drew a reporter's notice.[6] The most attention went to the rare prosperous defendants—especially those accused of dramatic crimes. The trial of attorney H. Clay King for the murder of another lawyer, in a case involving adultery and intrigue, was the only Memphis criminal case other than the Mitchell-Ward murder to receive sustained attention during 1892.[7]

Once the social drama of law and its enforcement reached the courtroom, the theatrical arena of prosecution, defense, and judgment at once opened up and constrained the possibilites for exposing and contesting the workings of the legal institutions. This moment of *interpretation* of the law was in a sense pre-scripted by the social interests of the most powerful actors, but it nonetheless allowed for unexpected reinscriptions of legal and cultural meanings.[8] Like the newspaper, the trial format operated as an interactive public sphere that allowed multiple publics to participate and shape its content, while also imposing structural limits on the nature of participation as well as on the fundamental, material control of the rules and outcomes. Only white men, predominantly but not exclusively from the prosperous elite, might act as counsel, judges, and jury members. Anyone might appear as a defendant with the opportunity to contest a charge or challenge a law, but defendants were enabled or hobbled as dramatic actors by their ability to secure effective counsel and to attract public attention that might become sympathy—both abilities usually (but not always) tied directly to their social standing. Within these constraints, and those of the rules regulating speech and evidence in this setting, defense and prosecution maneuvered to tell persuasive stories that might reinforce or undermine routine patterns of lawmaking and law enforcement.[9]

Occasionally, startling stories, surprising outcomes, or unpredictable public responses produced effects that were anything but routine. Highly publicized notorious or sensational trials not only reflected the social forces and cultural assumptions arrayed through particular conflicts but actively reformulated, refocused, or reframed ideas and constituencies. Since the founding of the new republic, some trials were widely recognized as significant political events. From the trials of John Peter Zenger for seditious libel in 1735 and of Aaron Burr for treason in 1807, to the trials of John Brown following the raid at Harpers Ferry in 1859 and of the Chicago anarchists following the Haymarket massacre in 1886, the courtroom arena appeared as a constitutive center for political conflict and nation formation.[10]

Other sensational trials were not publicized under the sign of "politics" but thematized issues tagged primarily or solely as "moral," in religious or psychological terms. From the 1836 trial of Richard P. Robinson for the murder of prostitute Helen Jewett in New York to the Beecher-Tilton scandal and civil lawsuit of 1875, conflicts of gender and sexuality received high-profile national press attention. The central issues were promoted in the press as matters of public morality or attacked as dangerous influences or prurient distractions from matters of public importance; they were rarely intepreted as "about" freedom, equality, democracy, citizenship, or politics. As the lynching narrative deployed themes of sexuality and violence to render racial conflict "moral" rather than political, thus legitimating the racial state's refusal to prosecute murders interpreted as moral revenge, so the narratives and processes of the law, the courts, and the mass circulation press generally interpreted conflicts of gender, and sexuality as matters of character and morality, not politics. Though played out for national audiences in public arenas, such conflicts of race, gender, and sexuality appeared as "private" concerns, proper to the realm of moral pedagogy rather than democratic debate.[11]

Alice Mitchell's murder of Freda Ward appeared as a moment of contested interpretation of the law in press reports—the enactment and enforcement of the homicide statute was uncontroversial, as if the state and the community opposed and punished murder in a coherently straightforward way. But legal and extralegal responses to violence were anything but straightforward. The overt concern with character, morality, and responsibility for violence that organized the primary controversy in this case—was Alice Mitchell insane or vicious?—covered over the underlying, fundamentally consequential political question—which acts of violence would be sanctioned, openly or covertly, and which punished, by whom, and through what means? The work of answering such questions, of redefining legitimate and illegitimate violence along with legitimate and illegitimate sexuality, occupied the core institutions of American modernity. Often focused on issues represented as marginal, or consequential but "private," this labor nonetheless set the terms and boundaries of American nationalism and the limits of U.S. democracy at the end of the nineteenth century. The trials surrounding the Mitchell-Ward murder engaged such consequential questions of civic life, represented within the terms of private character, individual psychology, and domestic order.

The public courtroom scenes in the Mitchell-Ward murder case began on February 23, 1892, when the Criminal Court in Shelby County, Tennessee, was called to order for the first day of testimony. The proceeding itself was neither a trial for murder nor the anticipated inquisition into the mental state of Alice Mitchell. Instead, Judge Julius DuBose presided over a brief and relatively minor hearing that nonetheless set the terms for the months of legal debate and extensive press coverage to follow.

Attorneys for Lillie Johnson, who had accompanied Alice Mitchell in her buggy on the day of the murder, filed a writ of habeas corpus with the court and planned to argue that their client should be released on bail, rather than held for trial as was customary in capital cases. To be successful, they needed to persuade the judge that the indictment against Lillie for murder (returned by the grand jury along with the indictment against Alice Mitchell) had been based on evidence insufficient to sustain a conviction.[12] They therefore intended to challenge the state's case in court. Witnesses were to testify, lawyers were to joust, stories and arguments about the murder and its meanings were to receive their first live public airing.[13]

The Memphis press and public prepared for a major event, even though the outcome of the hearing would determine no one's final fate and even though testimony would be focused on the role of a secondary character only. Everyone anticipated the untold secrets sure to come out in court. In preparation for the expected crush of curious onlookers, Judge DuBose arranged to have his courtroom enlarged. As the work of construction repeatedly delayed the opening of the hearing, reporters ridiculed the vanity of the judge but expressed appreciation for the special press stand to be provided in the new courtroom—now said to be the largest room in the city except for the theaters.[14]

The opening of Lillie Johnson's habeas corpus hearing was a popular community event, organized and reported much like an extraordinary public entertainment. The daily newspapers created and sustained this popularity with extensive, heavily promoted reports of each day's courtroom action. Headlines emphasized the theatrical qualities of the occasion: "Women in Gaudy Raiment Strove for the Choice Seats, A Court-Room Scene Seldom Witnessed in the South," or "Another Day of Thrilling Interest in the Criminal Court, The Attendance Was Even Greater Than on the Opening Day,

Opera Glasses Leveled on the Cowering Defendant Witness." [15] The *Public Ledger* made this implicit comparison explicit, beginning its coverage with:

Twenty-nine days ago, a few minutes after 4 o'clock in the afternoon, the curtain rose on one of the most remarkable tragedies of our times. In one respect it was unique; the story was developed after the denouement, and the motive is still in doubt, though the victim has been nearly a month removed forever from the view of mortals.

The scene is laid in Memphis, and the action of the drama begins on the 25th of January, 1892. The leading characters are two young persons just passing the border line that separates the fair domain of girlhood from the gracious and fruitful realm of womanhood. They have been very dear to each other. For years they were knit together in ties which set at naught the laws of sex, and though they had reached the period when school-girl affinities are dissipated by maturer fancies, 'like Juno's swans, still they went coupled and inseparable.'

Then something came between them. What it was shall appear hereafter. So far only the dim outline of the trouble can be discerned. The lights are turned down, the actors mute and no prompter stands between the wings to supply the missing lines.

Thus far the prologue.

The news report went on to describe the entire crime in acts and scenes, then slotted in the courtroom proceedings as the continuation of the drama. [16]

The use of such theatrical metaphors sometimes functioned to frame the courtroom action as an entertainment that the public could consume, whether through actual attendance or by reading the news accounts in serial format in the papers. Many observers, including the judge, evinced no embarrassment in regarding courtroom events in this case as an entertaining public diversion. [17] But the metaphors also evoked something deeper. At the hearing, and later at the lunacy inquisition, the events of the crime and the conflicts of interpretation surrounding it were literally "staged" and performed by witnesses and attorneys. The turn-of-the-century trial (or public hearing or inquisition) was understood as a specifically theatrical form of legal decision making.

The spectators at a trial attended a ritualized performance in which the story of a crime was told by witnesses, a conflict was organized and enacted by counsel, then all was resolved by judge and/or jury. The drama existed on several levels. [18] On the most immediate level, narratives of the crime itself, told by defendants, victims, and witnesses, formed a drama of social relationships gone awry: stories of love, pain, and betrayal, of envy, greed, exploitation, and hatred were often the most gripping feature of a trial. The direct address to the courtroom, and the appeal to imaginative understanding, worked to persuade audiences to accept a particular version of the story of the crime.

On a more abstract level, the conflict of prosecution and defense organized varying interpretations of the crime into two competing master narratives, each designed to sway judge or jury toward specific evaluative actions. These narratives competed according to standards of classic realism: the winning story would be the one best able to represent a "reality" recognizable to the white men who customarily rendered legal decisions.[19]

The clashing master narratives of defense and prosecution in courtrooms allowed for a public, ritual performance of disturbing social conflicts and mandated public enactments of resolution. The resolution provided by judge or jury was, as Ann-Louise Shapiro has argued with reference to nineteenth-century French trials, a "moment in the inscription of social and semantic boundaries," a ritual that fixed for a brief and unstable moment a judgment deeply embedded in current social hierarchies, cultural assumptions, and political equilibrium.[20]

Of course, this resolution was not arrived at by social or legal consensus but through the exercise of culturally legitimated authority vested in the law, the judge, and the jury. Though trials thus ultimately dramatized and legitimized the social authority of prosperous white men, they allowed for rare public contests in which other social groups actively participated. At the Johnson habeas corpus hearing, the social drama was also a drama of race and class. The gender relations enacted were those of the elite white population, though spectatorship was more broadly democratic. These social relations, of groups and individuals, were structured by—not merely reflected in—courtroom proceedings. In company with the newspapers, the legal rituals engaged the population of Memphis in a process productive of new, contested meanings and re-formed sexual and social order.

The social drama and legal ritual in the courtroom involved dynamics of spectatorship and performance that were endlessly examined in the press reports. At the Johnson hearing, as at other sensational trials, the race, class, and gender of the players and audience triggered anxieties about lines of authority and the possibly destabilizing impact of problematic "mixing" (see fig. 3). The first newspaper stories noted that more people arrived on Febru-

SAMPLE SPECTATORS.

Fig. 3. Courtroom "mixing" generated anxious representations in the newspapers. (*Memphis Appeal Avalanche*, July 26, 1892)

ary 23, and on the following two days, than had ever been in the criminal court before. Observers and participants expressed astonishment, not just at the size of this crowd but at its nature. The *Appeal Avalanche* reported that when the judge entered the courtroom and saw how "confused" was "the congregation of both sexes and all colors, nationalities and previous conditions of servitude," he issued a "ballroom order": "Ladies to the right, and gents to the left."[21] This effort at classification couldn't solve the whole problem of inappropriate mixing, however. The presence of a broad spectrum of the female population, who seemed to make up half the estimated attendance of one thousand, drew special attention. The *Public Ledger* noted:

Staid matrons and their young daughters sat cheek by jowl with women of doubtful character and women whose lack of all character was blazoned on their faces as plain as pikestaff. There were white women and black, mulattoes, quadroons, octoroons and a sprinkling of the genus whose class has never been distinctly defined— all eager to see two of their own sex in peril of their lives, and hoping, perhaps, to hear something excitingly naughty.[22]

Such large, diverse crowds were not business-as-usual at the criminal court, which generally accommodated only those charged with crimes, courtroom professionals, and a small group of spectators from less privileged backgrounds. Women were only occasionally present in court; rarely were any "staid matrons" or "ladies" among them — except in high-profile cases such as this one.[23] At the Johnson hearing, women's enthusiastic pursuit of places in the courtroom audience was treated with ridicule and condemnation in the press. Some women were so determined to watch the courtroom spectacle from an advantageous position that they claimed to be reporters and were seated in the press section. In addition to these pretenders, two of the professional reporters present were women — a fact that led the *Public Ledger* to paraphrase a nursery rhyme: "When a lady reporter is good she is very, very good, and when she is not she is horrid." The *Appeal Avalanche* commented simply, with less ambivalence: "The best place for the ladies to sit during the trial is about four feet back from their own hearthstones." These attacks, though constant, were manifestly ineffective as a "tidal wave of craning necks with bonnet plumes and artificial flowers flashing up in a confusion" filled the courtroom daily.[24]

Judge DuBose responded to the presence and "mixing" of so many women, not only by separating the genders but also by setting boundaries of "respectability" for female spectatorship. On the final day of the Johnson habeas corpus hearing, he evicted Sarah Davis, "an octoroon" who looked "like a Mexican," was dressed in "pronounced colors," and was seated between two white ladies. The newspapers reported her resentment:

During the progress of the trial she hung around the corridors of the courthouse, fuming and working up her resentment, and after the adjournment of court she approached Judge DuBose and began to abuse him. She lit into him in pretty good style.

"Go away, woman; I don't want to talk to you," said the judge.

"I won't go away. I know my rights. I won't be ordered out."

"Mr. Officer, take this woman to jail."

She showed up in the following day's court news, tagged with the alias "Buckskin Lou" and charged with vagrancy.[25]

Performance as well as spectatorship — the dynamics of being looked at as well as looking — were treated as problematic for women. Ambivalence circulated in descriptions of the female defendants and witnesses, who were the focus of intense visual inspection but also believed to be endangered by it. Respectable white women particularly risked an inappropriate and sullying "publicness" when they appeared on display in the courtroom. Alice Mitchell and Lillie Johnson were "on exhibition" in court; Lillie Johnson was "devoured" by eyes that "almost started from their sockets" while she was on the witness stand. The defendants were described repeatedly as resisting this visual centrality by wearing veils and avoiding crowds.[26] To be looked at was both to compromise expected female modesty and to lose control over the interpretation of one's character.

These multiple levels of gendered interaction at trial—between defendants, witnesses, attorneys, judge, and spectators—were reflected in the newspaper illustrations. Before the opening of the hearing, all the illustrations had been portraits of the female principals—Alice Mitchell, Freda Ward, Lillie Johnson, and Jo Ward—along with a few symbolic props, including a razor and a bloody coroner's slab.[27] Beginning with reports of the hearing, men began to appear in the woodcuts as well. The judge, the attorneys, the sheriff, the chief of police, the clerk of the court, and male relatives of the defendants appeared, along with female participants, in portraits or in poses connoting their roles—speaking, reading, or watching warily. Relationships were represented in courtroom scenes, in which gendered performance and spectatorship shifted with the levels of courtroom drama depicted. For instance, when the Memphis Commercial printed a drawing captioned "Scene in the Court Room during Miss Ward's Examination," Jo Ward was shown centrally, in black, head bowed, testifying before the judge, the attorneys, and an audience represented as entirely male. The drawing emphasized the female story of grief as told to male authority (fig. 4). On the following day, another drawing, captioned "Scene in Court Yesterday," presented the judge as a central figure facing spectators rendered as entirely female. Here, male authority was shown in legitimate control of a world of women (fig. 5).[28]

All the figures in the illustrations were represented as white, thus constituting the relevant "public" of the hearing for the newspapers. The raced and gendered roles set in motion at trial intersected with the mode of address of the press, to render an anxiety-provoking, shifting, mixing array of publics as containable within identifiable hierarchies.[29]

The assembled publics awaited the start of the action of the hearing, which centered on the question of twenty-year-old Lillie Johnson's responsibility in the murder of Freda Ward. Always secondary in the pre-hearing publicity, she now moved to the center of public concern. The specific question at issue as the habeas corpus hearing began was Lillie's knowledge of Alice's intentions on January 25; knowledge, if proved, would imply complicity. But crucially linked to that manifest legal issue was the heavily weighted question of Lillie's character. Was she a good girl led astray by a domineering, insane companion? Or was she a bad girl who shared her friend's secrets and wayward impulses?

Counting in her favor was her exaggeratedly feminine behavior—her meekness in public and her tendency to "nervous prostration" and "hysteria" in private. Such a girl was considered an unlikely accomplice to murder; newspapers reported that most Memphians thought her innocent. But counting against her were three categories of suspect activity: (1) Before the

Fig. 4. Scene in the courtroom during Jo Ward's testimony. (*Memphis Commercial*, Feb. 24, 1892)

Fig. 5. Judge DuBose in control of his courtroom. (*Memphis Commercial*, Feb. 25, 1892)

murder she was rumored to have flirted with conductors on the electric streetcar. She was also known to have exchanged letters with unknown men using a pseudonym. This information was treated as a sign of possible immodesty and deception. (2) On the day of the murder Lillie accompanied Alice in following the Ward sisters, then waited in the buggy while the murder was committed. On the Friday before, she had boarded the *Ora Lee* with Alice, searching for Freda. (3) After the murder she went to the Mitchell home and later was placed in Alice's cell at the jail, without any expression of outrage or fear.[30]

Such questions of character revolved around the appropriateness of Lillie's intimacies and emotions—with Alice and with her unknown male correspondents—and around the propriety of her movements through public space—on the streetcars, in the streets, on the riverboat. But unlike Alice Mitchell, Lillie Johnson was never represented as "masculine." The investigation at the hearing focused on whether her body and emotions were centered on home and controlled by family, as fitted her social status, or whether her movements and attachments were suspiciously extradomestic and unsupervised—thus morally suspect. If insufficiently domesticated, Lillie Johnson might just be the kind of girl to bond with another, more "masculine" girl like Alice Mitchell—for immoral purposes from flirtation to murder.

This debate over the meaning of Lillie's story was to be the central drama at the hearing. But the defendant shared the stage of the courtroom with several other star players—the attorneys as the sparring interpreters of her case and the judge. At the defense table were attorneys Malcolm Rice Patterson, Col. George Gantt, Gen. Luke Wright, and Squire Pat Winters. In the context of a Memphis trial, this was the heaviest legal artillery a defendant could muster.

Patterson was the first attorney retained by Lillie's family. The Johnsons were of only modest means, and he was their neighbor—young and relatively unknown at the time of the murder. He was the son of a well-known former Confederate commander, Col. Josiah Patterson, who had been a representative to the Tennessee state legislature, a candidate for governor, and a force in launching the state drive for black disfranchisement during the 1880s. In 1890, Josiah Patterson was elected to Congress after waging a vigorous white supremacy campaign.[31] Young Malcolm, born in 1861 and called Ham, had been attorney general of the criminal court in Memphis from 1884 to 1890 and was a member of his father's law firm, Gantt and Patterson. During the hearing the local press called him "one of the most promising young men at the bar" who, though younger than the other attorneys, was "never outclassed." His promise was eventually fulfilled—an active Democrat, he went on to be elected to Congress in 1900 and became governor of Tennessee from 1907 to 1911.[32]

The importance of the case mandated that Patterson be joined at the defense table by his senior partner Col. George Gantt. Both Gantt and Wright were among the most influential men in Memphis and had been community leaders since the days of desolation and struggle following the yellow fever epidemics of the 1870s. Gantt had a reputation as the most effective trial lawyer in Memphis. During the hearing the *Public Ledger* noted that as a "tear starter" he was in a class all by himself, while the *Commercial* asserted that he and Wright were two of the strongest lawyers in the South. This assessment may have been influenced by the fact that Wright was one of the original investors in the *Commercial* Publishing Company. The son of a Tennessee Supreme Court justice, he had been an attorney general of the criminal court of Shelby County (this was the source of the honorific "General" that he bore), and he went on to become governor-general of the Philippines, the first U.S. ambassador to Japan, and secretary of war under President Theodore Roosevelt.[33]

These legal advocates for the defense clearly represented the Memphis elite. Even their research assistance was provided by "one of the shrewdest attorneys in Memphis," constitutional lawyer Pat Winters.[34] Their opposition was only slightly less prominent. Attorney General George B. Peters Jr. had been a member of the state legislature and had earned a reputation as a highly successful prosecutor. In addition, he was no stranger to the issues of sexual transgression, insanity, and murder raised by the Mitchell-Ward-Johnson case. His father, Dr. George B. Peters Sr., had murdered Confederate Major General Earl Van Dorn in 1863, allegedly out of revenge for Van Dorn's adultery with Mrs. Peters. The later insanity and suicide of George Jr.'s brother Thomas was tied to this scandal.[35]

Peters was assisted in the prosecution by a gaggle of very young assistants—altogether, a group that was not an even match for the assembled defense team. But counsel in the case were collectively strong enough for the *Commercial* to predict with confidence that "the flight of oratory will be memorable."[36]

This legal talent was to be displayed before Judge Julius DuBose, an eccentric and tempestuous man who was alternately feared, despised, and ridiculed. The son of a wealthy planter, DuBose had been a Confederate soldier, an early leader in the Tennessee Ku Klux Klan, and an editor of the *Memphis Public Ledger*. He was elected criminal court judge in 1886, but his arrogance on the bench, and the many personal animosities he incited, led to an extended impeachment drive against him beginning in 1893.[37] His 1912 obituary was headlined diplomatically, "Career Was Picturesque, Of South Carolina Family and of Unique Personality."[38]

The newspapers reported the rituals of the hearing's opening and described the players in detail for those readers sadly unable to attend the proceedings. Lillie Johnson and Alice Mitchell arrived in the courtroom escorted by their fathers and brothers; none of their female relatives attended. Their attire and demeanor were observed by reporters—Alice was said to be thinner and Lillie to be pale and downcast. Other participants and observers were characterized by the *Commercial* in order of their arrival:

> Presently the attorneys in the case began to stroll in—Col. Gantt, with his nervous mouth poised for some telling witticism; Gen. Luke Wright, with his fine legal brow, and Gen. Peters, with his handsome face. The younger members of the bar took advantage of the privilege which their profession gave them, and came within the railing. The older members were hardly as prominent as the young ones. By this time the aisles were jammed with men and women.
>
> Deputy Sheriff Bob Harrell, chief gatekeeper, was attempting to keep down conversation while the soft, lulling tones of Deputy Sheriff Cole rolled over the sea of heads. Magistrates, merchants, doctors, and all sorts of professional and business men began to file in.[39]

Once the crowd was settled in and the pounding of the judge's gavel rang out, the first order of business was a decision on Alice Mitchell's motion for access to letters (between Freda and herself) in the possession of the attorney general. The judge denied the motion, and Alice and her entourage left the courtroom. Lillie moved to front and center, creating a tableau of contrasts described in the press:

> . . . and with her veil off her fresh, young face, loomed up between the gray heads of Col. Gantt and Justice Winters—a striking picture. Her distressed father was just behind her.[40]

On the first day of the hearing, courtroom action didn't focus further on Lillie Johnson, however. The testimony of the day's first and primary witness, Jo Ward, provided the central drama. Her ascent to the witness stand to testify evoked the kind of close physical observation, subtly sexualized description, and gender-specific evaluation accorded solely to respectable young white women of undisputed virtue. The *Appeal Avalanche* reporter wrote:

> A figure that might attract the admiration of an artist, but heavily draped in black from head to foot, so that not a speck of brightness relieved the pall of mourning, was announced as Miss Jo Ward. Before she removed the long, somber veil that hid her features there was ample time to survey her figure, and its exquisite outlines and classical proportions repaid more than a cursory observation. She mounted the

witness stand slowly, and after taking the chair, slowly lifted up her veil, being admonished thereto by Judge DuBose. . . . The face revealed is one of rare charm. It lacks color, but the white oval contour, set off by the densely dark background, is perfect. The features are prominent enough not to obtrude, but to present each a separate charm. The eyes are large and limpid. The nose is large and regular, the lips full, round and rosy, were it not for the pallor occasioned by the fright that no doubt possessed her at that time. Seated on the stand throughout the course of the examination, Miss Jo Ward was the picture of modesty in distress.[41]

Jo Ward's ordeal on the stand was a protracted one; she was examined twice each by Ham Patterson and George Peters, as both the defense and prosecution struggled to shape and reshape her story. During her first interrogation, by Patterson, she was asked to tell the history of her relations, and those of her sister Freda with Alice Mitchell and Lillie Johnson. Jo reported several years of visits and friendly correspondence, marked by special attachments between Alice and Freda, and between herself and Lillie. One short spell of trouble—between Freda and Lillie—had been quickly patched up. Patterson's questioning was aimed at demonstrating a lack of hostility among the girls, and thus the lack of a rational motive for Lillie to have participated in a murder. Under his questioning, Jo affirmed Lillie's "gentle disposition." [42]

Patterson also led Jo into a description of the events of January 25—from her walk with her sister and Christina Purnell toward the riverboat landing, followed by Alice and Lillie, to the actual scene of the crime on the railroad tracks. This section of her testimony was filled with the horrifying details of murder:

What first drew my attention to the cutting was Miss Purnell's screaming, and as she screamed I turned around. . . . Miss Mitchell was right at my sister then, and was nearly cutting her. She was cutting at her, and I struck her with the umbrella. She turned to me, said: "I'm doing just exactly what I wanted to do, and I don't care if I do get hung."

After she said that, she jumped up and flew up the levee, running very fast. . . . She had blood on her face and on her hands, with a great deal on one side.[43]

In eliciting such an emotion-laden tale, Patterson emphasized through repeated questioning that Lillie was not present at this scene but rather waiting more than three hundred feet away, over a hill and out of sight and earshot.

When the attorney general then approached the witness, he set out to counter the story of friendship and goodwill among the four girls. Jo admitted to Peters that at the time of the murder, she and her sister were not on speaking terms with Alice and Lillie: during August 1891, their elder sister had forbidden them to have any further contact with their two friends. The witness then identified a note to her from Lillie, asking the reason for the estrangement (which was reprinted in the papers complete with grammatical errors):

Memphis, Tenn., Jan. 5, 1892

Dear Joe—I know you are angry with me and I won't asked you to be a friend of mine, but please tell me why you are angry. I want to know, so that when people asked me I know what to tell them. Tell me what you are angry with me for and I will tell them what you tell me to say.

Lillie.[44]

If Peters hoped to establish a possible motive with this story of broken friendship, Patterson countered forcefully by bringing out, over the resistance of the witness and the objection of the prosecution, the reasons for the elder sister's actions. The story he painstakingly elicited was considered "the sensation of the morning" and was featured in headlines trumpeting the days' events: "Plot to Elope and Marry . . . Unnatural Love between the Murdered and Murderess."[45]

The outlines of this tale had already been reported in the newspapers—the newly sensational quality was imparted by the context of the telling. Patterson extracted reluctant admissions from the murdered girl's sister with long leading questions:

Patterson: Is it not a fact that your sister forbade your having anything to do with, or writing to Miss Johnson and Miss Mitchell, because Alice Mitchell and your sister were engaged to be married, and your sister was about to elope with her, and had gotten on the boat for that purpose?

Witness: . . . That was one reason.

Patterson: Was not that the controlling reason?

Witness: Yes, sir.

Patterson: [Freda] intended to take the boat, did she not, and to come to Memphis, and then they intended to go to St. Louis?

Witness: Yes, sir.

Patterson: And there marry? Well, now, in that arrangement to marry, Miss Ward, who was to be the man? Miss Mitchell?

Witness: Yes, sir.

Patterson: And your sister was to be the wife, was she, and they were to arrange it in that way?

Witness: Yes, sir.

Patterson: And was not Miss Mitchell to be called Alvin J. Ward after they married?

Witness: Yes, sir.

Patterson: Your sister was to be called Mrs. Alvin J. Ward?

Witness: Yes, sir.

Patterson: That was all made up and understood, and planned, and your sister discovered it all, and after making that discovery she forbade your further correspondence with them?

Witness: Yes, sir.[46]

As he constructed this story, Patterson repeatedly emphasized that the relations between the girls had not been disrupted by anything Lillie Johnson had done, that Jo Ward would not have suspended relations with her had not Mrs. Volkmar demanded it, and that no love letters or elopement plans had passed between the witness and the defendant. Patterson thus aimed to show that his client had no motive for murder and that her character was unsullied.

Attorney General Peters responded to this move by redirecting the witness's attention to a secondary reason for Mrs. Volkmar's interdiction of relations with Lillie Johnson. Earlier in her testimony Jo had briefly mentioned that Mrs. Volkmar thought Lillie was "wild." Peters asked for elaboration:

Peters: Tell us, Miss Ward, exactly what you mean, and what your sister said, and what you found out, and all the reasons why your sister prohibited you and your sister Freda from associating with Miss Lillie Johnson, and the reason why you did do it?

Witness: It was because she visited the union depot quite often, and she flirted a great deal. She flirted with men. . . . When she was visiting us last summer, my sister also forbade her waving at the boats and the men. That is all. She was just considered quite a flirt.[47]

By joining such testimony with an emphasis on the closeness of Lillie and Alice, Peters hoped to raise the specter of a conspiracy to commit murder by two girls already prone to behavior outside the respectable bounds of domestic virtue.

Jo Ward was followed on the stand by four minor witnesses whose testimony concluded the day's proceedings at 1:00 P.M. The *Commercial* summarized the major legal issues:

It is difficult to form a just opinion of Miss Johnson's complicity in the affair at this stage of the trial, although but few of the hearers in the court room have any doubt as to Miss Mitchell's insanity. Miss Mitchell's insanity, however, does not necessarily excuse Miss Johnson from legal responsibility, unless it be shown that she was wholly unacquainted with Miss Mitchell's purpose as they followed the Ward girls to the levee.[48]

The *Appeal Avalanche* commented on the day's quotient of sensation:

There was nothing in the evidence or other portions of the proceedings yesterday to offend the modesty of any lady whose constitution is attuned to tales of bloodshed of the ordinary kind.[49]

Nonetheless, Lillie Johnson was said to have nearly fainted, later requiring medical attention at the jail.

The second day of the hearing was an even greater trial for Lillie, however. After the testimony of three eyewitnesses to the murder, including Christina Purnell, she was called to the stand. Her appearance, which "showed signs of physical weakness as well as of weariness of spirit," elicited compassion from observers. When, midway through her cross-examination, she wept, the *Appeal Avalanche* reported that "many another handkerchief was raised to sympathetic eyes among the spectators outside the railing."[50]

Before another crushing crowd in the courtroom, Patterson led Lillie through the history of her relations with Alice, whom she'd known for five years, and with the Ward sisters. He also elicited the details of the day of the murder. She had gone to the blacksmith's with Alice, returned home for dinner, gone into town shoppping with her sister, walked homeward, passed Alice on the street, and agreed to go riding—taking her young nephew along. Patterson was careful to emphasize that the afternoon ride that day had been unplanned.

Lillie continued with her story, providing details and dialogue. She and Alice had driven past Mrs. Kimbrough's house, where they spotted Freda in the window, then proceeded to the office of Lillie's brother on Madison Street. When they climbed back into the buggy and passed the Ward sisters and Christina Purnell, Lillie said she asked Alice repeatedly not to follow them. Alice pulled the buggy up in front of the post office and got out, with the professed intention of retrieving her mail, when she exclaimed, "Oh,

Lil! Fred winked at me. I am going down to the corner to take one more look at Fred and say good-bye!" Lillie returned with her nephew to the buggy to wait, and the next thing she said she saw was Alice running up the hill, jumping into the buggy:

Patterson: What did you say as she ran up the hill?

Witness: Oh! What have you done to her?

Patterson: What made you say that?

Witness: I saw blood on her face.

Patterson: What did she say?

Witness: . . . When she got to Court Street she told me, "I have cut Freda's throat." I said: "No you haven't, have you?" She said: "Yes, I have."

Patterson: What did she do then?

Witness: She asked me the quickest way she could kill herself. I said: "Don't do it while you are here with me. Go home and tell your mother what you have done." . . . She asked me: "Is there much blood on my face?" I said "Yes." "Take my handker-chief out of my pocket and wipe it off," she said. I started to do it, when she said: "Oh, no; it's Freda's blood. Leave it there. I love her so."[51]

During Patterson's examination, Lillie insisted that she had known noth-ing of Alice's intentions. She explained that though Alice had been hurt when Freda stopped speaking to her, she had never threatened Freda but continued to love her. The witness then concluded her initial testimony by relating her history of sick headaches—a recurring illness that had necessitated her with-drawal from a convent school in Indiana as well as from the Higbee School in Memphis. This evidence of physical weakness crucially bolstered the image of Lillie Johnson as appropriately feminine, dependent, and domestic rather than bold and publicly gregarious.

The prospect of cross-examination brought out yet more reticence in the witness and compassion in observers. The *Commercial* noted:

The slender figure of the witness seemed to shrink, and the small head drooped even more pathetically than before, as her eyes piteously turned from her counsel to the Attorney-General, in evident dread of what was to follow, and even his sympathy was aroused for the poor girl, whom he had to cross-examine.[52]

Peters carefully prodded Lillie to affirm that her relations with Alice were extremely intimate, that they had been inseparable, that they rode together nearly every day and conversed freely on all subjects. He then asked whether Lillie hadn't therefore known Alice's feelings and intentions toward Freda.

The witness faltered somewhat in reponse to these questions, saying she had known of the estrangement between Alice and Freda but that Alice hadn't talked about it much. She added that she had only gone aboard the *Ora Lee* looking for Freda because Alice begged her to, and had gone to the Mitchell home after the murder because Alice "asked me to stay, and I would do anything for her."[53]

Peters returned to the issue of Lillie's character by interrogating her about letters she had exchanged with unknown men using the pseudonym Jessie Rita James and giving her brother's office address to hide the correspondence from her mother. She said that Alice had given her the name (and that she had never heard of the robber Jesse James). This testimony, not directly relevant to her knowledge of or participation in the murder, raised the specter of unsupervised heterosociality. It invoked an image of Lillie as possibly "wild," independent of domestic ties, and therefore untrustworthy and *bad* enough to be guilty. Her response to this exchange was to recoil. The *Public Ledger* reported that as she left the stand, she nearly fell.[54]

The defense then countered whatever negative impression Peters had been able to convey with five character witnesses: a neighbor and a business associate of Lillie's brother who attested to her good reputation, her father and brother who verified her history of "delicate health," and her sister (the mother of the nephew in the buggy on January 25) who corroborated Lillie's account of her activities on the day of the murder. By the end of the day's testimony, though the prosecution might have hoped that Lillie's claim to complete ignorance of Alice's murderous intentions would be received with skepticism, it couldn't have fully anticipated the overwhelming effect of her drooping, fearful, weeping presence. The *Commercial* simply concluded:

Her testimony has undoubtedly aided her case. In fact, few of those who heard the words of this unfortunate girl and the testimony of others yesterday morning, believe that she is guilty of murder as an accessory.[55]

And the *Appeal Avalanche* similarly opined:

So far as the direct evidence adduced yesterday goes, there was nothing to show that Lillie Johnson knew of the crime in advance of the occurrence; in fact, nothing derogatory to her character was brought out, unless it be considered that maintaining a correspondence with various young men whom she had never seen might be considered in that light. She had not been a party to Alice Mitchell's love affair, . . . but was overcome by the more powerful will of the amorous Alice. . . .[56]

The third and final day of the hearing was less well attended than the first two. The *Appeal Avalanche* reporter expressed puzzlement at that fact:

> The attendance in court was not so large yesterday as on preceding days of the inquiry or trial. The reason therefor is not apparent. While there was no evidence of importance to be taken . . . the argument was on the tapis, and that was certainly not an uninteresting feature of the proceedings.[57]

The *Public Ledger* suggested that the reason was gendered:

> As usual both races were fully represented, but the women were not present in force as before. The impression had got abroad that there would be nothing very bad brought out in the testimony today and the petticoat brigade does not take much stock in the eloquence of counsel.[58]

Whether distinguished by gender or not, some proportion of the Memphis public was apparently more interested in the emotional drama of personal testimony than in the rhetorical conflict of counsel.

After the remaining spectators settled into their seats under the judge's gaze, testimony continued with another character witness for Lillie Johnson—her family priest, Father Veale. The priest was followed by the Johnson family physician, Dr. Z. B. Henning, who testified that Lillie suffered from "nervous headache." He insisted that her confinement in jail would affect her very seriously.

Though Peters had not bothered to cross-examine any of the character witnesses, he interrogated the doctor closely. Led by Peters, Dr. Henning admitted that nervous headache was a very common complaint, that Lillie's complaint had not seriously affected her before her confinement to jail, that he had not been called upon to treat her during the twelve months prior to her imprisonment, and that she had not been confined to her bed for the ailment. The doctor also acknowledged that Lillie and Alice's jail room was large, light, and well ventilated, though he did insist that jail was not a healthy place for any previously active person.

Dr. Henning was the last witness. Arguments by counsel then began with Ham Patterson's plea for Lillie's release on bail. Patterson reviewed the relevant constitutional law and outlined the facts of the case. Of course, he embellished his version of the story with rhetorical flourishes designed to win sympathy for his client. He described Alice Mitchell as the "active and assertive spirit" in the crime and presented Lillie Johnson as her "passive companion" in his arguments:

When Alice Mitchell turns the corner in that insane and most unnatural walk, and takes her lover by the waist, and cuts her throat, this girl takes the little baby in her arms and goes back to the buggy. Conspiracy indeed! Reverse human nature—reverse the whole order of things—but do not say that a girl is guilty of conspiracy upon such a state of facts as this.[59]

He concluded with his opinion that the judge and attorney general should go beyond granting his client bail:

. . . the State should withdraw from the prosecution, should add not another gray hair to the devoted father's head or wring another tear from the mother's heart.[60]

Following Patterson's conclusion, Attorney General Peters declined to argue the state's case, choosing to simply assert the guilt of both Miss Johnson and Miss Mitchell, as charged in the indictment. The *Appeal Avalanche* commented:

Whether his refraining from [arguing the state's case] was due to a confidence of the strength of his position, [or] to a feeling of indifference whether the prisoner was held in the jail or out on bond, the Attorney-General alone knows.[61]

Colonel Gantt next stood to make an argument on the defendant's behalf, and his emphasis soon clarified the reason for the extensive testimony about the state of Lillie Johnson's health. Gantt argued that the judge could release Lillie on bail, regardless of the evidence in the case, if confinement in jail could be shown to threaten her life or health. To encourage Judge DuBose to pursue this option, Gantt "devoted much of his time to pathetic pictures of the girl's wretched health."[62]

Gantt didn't confine himself to the issue of his client's health, however. He also reinforced his colleague's portraits of Alice Mitchell as insane and Lillie Johnson as good, respectable, and innocent:

[*On Alice Mitchell*] A girl that thinks to assume the mask of a man, can shuffle off the baptismal name given her and take on the name of Alvin J. Ward, take the place of a man and marry a woman—Your Honor knows there was madness at the bottom of that.

[*On Lillie Johnson*] If we had a strong man here, a man accustomed to crime and oaths, and who bore on his front the evidence of broils, against whom many indictments had been found, these circumstances against the defendant might appear consistent. But when we select the prisoner from the fireside of one of the homes of the city of Memphis, one of the best homes—a home not too rich, and not too poor to be good—. . . . Why, there is not a skeleton in the closet of that home. . . . This girl from that fireside is supposed to go forth to kill, and instead of bringing an Arkansas toothpick by way of weapon brings a baby. . . . These are circumstances that we can't reconcile with the others that may look incriminating.[63]

Both Gantt and Patterson's arguments received high praise in the newspapers, described as "earnest and powerful," "eloquent" and "very touching." Spectators were said to have been moved to tears, as were Lillie and her father. As the final court day drew to a close, everyone had only to wait for the judge's decision.

Judge DuBose kept everyone waiting for two days, then read a decision that upheld his reputation for toughness, yet avoided outraging public opinion. On the issue of the evidence, he decided:

The proof is evident that the defendant aided and abetted in the commission of the crime, a crime the most atrocious and malignant ever perpetrated by woman.[64]

But DuBose nonetheless released Lillie Johnson on $10,000 bail, owing to the condition of her health. Though newspaper reports indicated that relief at Lillie's release was practically universal, there were glimmers of skepticism about the rationale. The *Public Ledger* commented on the defendant's departure from the courtroom:

As she stepped across the sidewalk to the carriage, she moved with a sprightly step for one so ill.[65]

Such comments revealed that reporters, and their reading public, remained aware of the contrived, performative nature of courtroom testimony and legal arguments, even as they were also persuaded by the performances. Reports of events at the trial sometimes took on the quality of a theatrical review, as the effectiveness of the "weeping witness" and the skills of the attorney as a "tear starter" were evaluated.[66]

The defense at the Lillie Johnson hearing generally got high marks for its presentation. This success was in part a function of the familiarity of the scenes constructed by defense witnesses and attorneys. The story conformed largely to the conventional form of melodrama. Lillie Johnson appeared as the innocent, fragile maiden falsely accused of a crime, suffering in the bosom of her devoted family—a family modest of means but rich in love. Though the prosecution contested, and the judge ultimately resisted, various elements of this story, it proved largely irresistible to the press.[67]

This first hearing set the terms for the inquisition of lunacy focused on Alice Mitchell to follow. "Character" and "health" became and remained the key questions, as addressed specifically to the cases of "respectable" white women. Character was to determine guilt, though responsibility might be mitigated through health. But at the Johnson hearing and later, the figure of the white woman began to split—not only according to the binary of good/domestic versus bad/public that commonly marked differences of class coded as respectability but also along lines of masculine/abnormal and feminine/normal. Lillie Johnson's involvement in the events surrounding Alice Mitchell's murder of Freda Ward raised questions about the latter binary: Might the apparently normal feminine woman actually be the deceptive, secretly "wild" partner of that other kind? Such questions spilled over into related questions about the other partnership at the center of the case—the relations of the "girl lovers" Alice Mitchell and Freda Ward. The lunacy inquisition to follow extended questions raised by the habeas corpus hearing to ask: Might a female pair, dominated by the abnormal partner, seek to displace the fundamental gendered terms of white domesticity itself? The threat of such a question ultimately produced the figure of the homicidal lesbian. In this case, in the figure of Alice Mitchell, she not only embodied the social violence and cultural impossibility of her goals, but her actions also reassuringly obliterated the specter of the apparently normal but dangerously untrustworthy collaborator who might sit at any prosperous white fireside in the city, undetected.

INQUISITION OF LUNACY

The evidence given by psychiatric experts in criminal courts has three qualities: (a) It has, or may have, the power of life and death; (b) It functions as a discourse of truth, being scientific—it is given by people qualified within scientific institutions; (c) When one reads the transcripts, they make one laugh.

Such testimonies are an integral part of the daily juridical discourse.

Michel Foucault, from a 1975 lecture [1]

Between the first courtroom proceedings of the Mitchell-Ward murder case in February 1892 and the second round of proceedings that began in July of the same year, the racial conflicts surrounding the lynching of Thomas Moss, Calvin McDowell, and Henry Stewart gripped Memphis. From the grocery store competition leading to an armed standoff in the Curve neighborhood, through the March murders, to the destruction of the *Free Speech* and the final departure of Ida B. Wells from the city in May, the daily newspapers were filled with news of ominous conflict and violence. The dailies sided with white citizens who felt threatened by the specter of armed black neighbors ready to defend their store and themselves, and printed accounts of the lynching so detailed as to suggest that the reporter had been present or had interviewed a participant. The editorial columns did not actually endorse the practice of lynching, but neither did they promote prosecution of any member of the white mob. The police, the politicians, and the courts did nothing to punish the murderers. No arrests were made and no charges filed against any white citizen of Memphis for the lynchings, the destruction of the *Free Speech*, or the terrorist threats against Wells. The state and the law, the police and the courts, collaborated with the mainstream press to racialize "justice" in Memphis more firmly and emphatically than had been obvious since the end of the Civil War.

Meanwhile, the nationwide network of black newspapers covered events in Memphis extensively, some black Memphians organized a streetcar boycott, and Wells and others called for mass black emigration. The city's white elite took some notice of the impact of such protest. Efforts were made to assure blacks of their safety and access to basic (though inferior) services and protections in the city. There were no more open racial conflagrations, but the outlines of the racial state and the limited boundaries of the fully enfranchised "public" had been made clear. Along with new voting restrictions and segregation laws, the publicizing of the lynching and the subsequent inaction of the state worked to dramatize the parameters of the new post-Reconstruction world of racial apartheid in Memphis.[2]

In July 1892, intense press attention returned to ponder questions of gender, romance, and conflict among white women. In the case of Alice Mitchell's murder of Freda Ward, the state intervened to process the meanings of murder, which seemed opaque, puzzling, and debatable. Here, rather than the swift actions and clear inactions of their responses to racial conflict during the 1890s, the local institutions of the state mobilized an extended dispute over desire and domesticity among the white elite. Alice Mitchell's defense team brought in regionally prominent medical men to elaborate their side to the press and in the courtroom—an option available only to prosperous or notorious defendants. The legal dispute then took shape around the controversial theories, explanations, and diagnoses of the experts on mental life. In court, under examination by defense and prosecution, they pronounced their learned opinions on the role of deficient health, character, willpower, intellectual functioning, and moral reasoning in revealing insanity and generating violence.

Alice Mitchell appeared before the Criminal Court of Shelby County, Tennessee, on July 18, 1892, to face an inquisition of lunacy rather than a trial for murder. She did not plead "not guilty" of murder by reason of insanity as many other defendants in her position might have done. Her attorneys presented a plea of "present insanity" instead—a move roughly comparable to the plea of "incompetent to stand trial" in contemporary U.S. courts. A jury's finding of "presently insane" would delay a trial, sending Mitchell to the state lunatic asylum until physicians pronounced her recovered. At that time, county officials would decide whether or not to prosecute. A finding of "presently sane" would lead to an immediate trial on the indictment for murder.

On one level the choice of plea made very little difference in the handling of Mitchell's case. The lunacy inquisition proceeded very much as a murder trial would have. The presentation of evidence covered the circumstances of the murder as well as Alice's life history and mental status.[3] A finding of "presently insane" would also involve substantially the same consequences as a finding of "not guilty" by reason of insanity—commitment to the asylum with very little chance of eventual discharge.[4]

On another level the choice of plea revealed, and was designed to resolve, a contradiction at the heart of the definition of Alice Mitchell's "insanity." She was not a furious "maniac," an obvious "lunatic," or a hopeless "idiot." In the framework of turn-of-the-century psychiatry, she seemed to suffer from "partial insanity." Consulting physicians conceded that her ability to reason and control herself remained substantially intact; they argued that her mental disorder revealed itself only in discrete thoughts, feelings, and behaviors that were not always apparent to an untrained observer. Such partial insanities were regarded by many (but not all) alienists as mental diseases resulting in irresponsibility for criminal behavior. But they sometimes failed, as diagnoses of defendants, to persuade juries to acquit by reason of insanity.[5]

In choosing a lunacy inquisition over a murder trial, Mitchell's attorneys avoided having to demonstrate their client's insanity under the M'Naghten rule, which prevailed in Tennessee criminal courts (as well as in most other states) during the 1890s. This rule required that in order to be found irresponsible for a crime, defendants must be unable to distinguish between right and wrong and unable to appreciate the consequences of their actions. The strict application of this rule, which emphasized pervasive intellectual impairment as the sole basis for an insanity acquittal, could (and often did) lead to the conviction of defendants diagnosed with partial insanities.[6] At a lunacy inquisition, the legal standard was broader and more vague. In Tennessee, the legal code stated:

> When the plea of present insanity is urged on behalf of any person charged with a criminal offense, punishable by imprisonment or death, the court shall charge the jury, that if from the evidence they believe the defendant to be insane, and that it would endanger the peace of the community to set him at liberty, they shall so find.

As Judge DuBose further elaborated on this point for the jury in the Mitchell case, "The question is, whether the defendant has mental capacity sufficient to make a rational defense to the charge in the indictment."[7]

Mitchell's attorneys undoubtedly calculated that their chances of demonstrating "present insanity" were greater than their chances of winning an acquittal under the M'Naghten rule in a murder trial.[8] Yet their strategy also revealed their overwhelming pessimism about their client's situation. There is no indication that they ever considered a "mania transitoria," or temporary insanity, defense of the kind sometimes used to win acquittal for defendants accused of crimes of passion.[9] There is no record of any attempt to get the charge reduced. Nor was any hope expressed for Alice's speedy recovery. The most anyone aimed for (apparently) was escape from the gallows and commitment to the asylum—a fate likely to amount to lifetime incarceration.

The position of the defense was thus fundamentally paradoxical: Alice Mitchell was not "insane" enough for a straightforward acquittal under the M'Naghten rule, yet she was too "insane" to risk legal strategies that might have resulted in her immediate or eventual freedom. This paradox, rooted in an assessment of Alice Mitchell's sanity and her legal prospects, ultimately reflected the puzzling quality of her crime—at once so familiar, yet so alien. In so many respects it was an ordinary crime of passion—the murder of a loved one following upon abandonment, with its attendant grief and rage. Such crimes, when committed by respectable white citizens in defense of socially legitimated relationships, often garnered public sympathy and sometimes led to legal acquittals. The stories of seduction, abandonment, or betrayal by a man, often deployed in such circumstances to render women's crimes "justifiable" or at least comprehensible, were not available in this case. The stories of sexual competition or jealousy often used to explain women's attacks on other women seemed both less sympathetic and less coherent (given the existing evidence), though they were picked up by the embattled prosecution.[10] In this instance, the motive for Mitchell's crime proved ultimately incomprehensible to her contemporaries. For Alice Mitchell to have loved and acted "like a man," even like a sane or only temporarily insane one, she must have been completely, unpredictably, dangerously mad.

The attorneys hired by George Mitchell confronted this paradox and decided that the only sympathetic story his daughter had to tell was a story of illness. This decision was based on their assessment of the narrative possibilities of their client's situation — a situation shaped by gender, race, and class as well as by the commission of a violent crime. The defense needed a persuasive, sympathetic story that could explain a murder committed by a prosperous young white woman to a jury of white men. A man from a background similar to Alice's might have been more likely to receive the kind of defense that would ultimately set him free; a black or poor defendant of either gender would have been unlikely to receive any plausible defense (and almost certainly not a psychiatric one). Alice Mitchell's predicament required a "respectable" woman's defense — one that would protect her family's reputation, while also containing any danger she might represent to the stability of the white home. From the point of view of Alice's family and defense team, the plea of "present insanity" offered a workable strategy. It framed Alice's ideas and actions as the result of an illness for which she could not be held morally or legally responsible, though those ideas and actions might be wholly condemned and Alice herself socially quarantined in an asylum.[11] Ultimately, the story of illness was used by the defense to "explain" the unexpected and seemingly inexplicable — the otherwise unnarratable — motives and actions of Alice Mitchell in a way that preserved, as far as possible, her respectability and her family's reputation.

The defense attorneys actually constructed a written version of the story underlying their legal strategy — a "hypothetical case" that brought together the testimony they planned to present in court and fashioned it into a coherent tale of illness, a medicalized life story.

The hypothetical case was a variation of the legal practice of presenting "hypothetical questions" in court to expert witnesses. The experts rendered their opinion based on the "facts" presented in different questions formulated by defense and prosecution. The determination of which set of facts had been most persuasively established through testimony or other evidence was left up to the jury. Nineteenth-century alienists generally opposed this legal practice, because it limited their ability to deliver uncontested and fully authoritative opinions in the courtroom. Nonetheless, it persisted in American courtrooms into the twentieth century.[12]

The hypothetical case was modeled on the medical case report as developed in professional journals since early in the century. It was presented to medical experts, who offered diagnoses of the defendant based on its content, whether in courtroom testimony or through written deposition. In theory, both defense and prosecution might offer different hypothetical cases to the same experts for diagnostic evaluation. At Alice Mitchell's trial only the defense constructed one, which they then circulated widely through the press.

The hypothetical case (reprinted in appendix A) was carefully crafted according to the conventions of the genre of medical case reports. It provided a clinical portrait of the defendant that linked an account of the crime to a history of peculiar behavior and deviant social relations, and explained it all by reference to evidence of bodily pathology. The conceptual grid of the hypothetical case was drawn from the somatic theories of late-nineteenth-century psychiatry. Though a chain of pathology leading to insanity might be set in motion by emotional or environmental factors, the circle of cause and effect always ran through a material, physical foundation. The condition of the body and brain, revealed through mental symptoms as well as physical signs, was the ultimate ground of "true" insanity, as distinguished from immorality or malevolence.

The hypothetical case was not simply a psychiatric portrait, however; it was also (at least) a double narrative, with legal as well as medical aims. Its rhetorical structure positioned it as a call to action: it was constructed to lead inexorably both to a specific medical diagnosis and to a desired legal outcome. As Kathryn Montgomery Hunter has argued with respect to oral case reports in medical settings, it operated like a Sherlock Holmes mystery as recounted by Watson. It was presented as a puzzle by someone who knew its solution.[13]

At the Mitchell lunacy inquisition, the hypothetical case had yet a third function. The high public profile of the proceedings provided (or burdened) the defense with another arena of influence beyond the medical experts and the legal actors in the case—the press and the public. The case's narrative was therefore directed toward eliciting a diagnosis of medical pathology, meeting the legal standard for "present insanity," and persuading the jury and the public that, in commonsense terms, Alice Mitchell was crazy. It was designed to accomplish this by presenting a personal history of hereditary pathology, physical illness, odd behavior, and inappropriate emotions and relationships.

All of the elements of the hypothetical case were supported through court-room testimony. Family members, neighbors, acquaintances, experts, and witnesses to the murder provided the evidence intended to corroborate the case's implicit findings. As integrated by the hypothetical case narrative, this testimony was aimed at linking Alice's violations of law and custom—her inappropriate gender deportment, her "misunderstanding" of the nature of romantic love and marriage, and her use of unsanctioned violence—to an explanation rooted in her body's sickness. If it was persuasive, such testimony would strip her crime of its social meanings, its possible explanation in social relations gone awry, and substitute somatic meanings. Instead of a young woman who, in a desperate, angry, or confused state, took hostile, aggressive, and tragic action, she would become a passive victim of biological events and thus worthy of some sympathy. She would then merit commitment for "treatment" rather than imprisonment or execution.[14]

The hypothetical case thus constituted a crucial point of intersection for the different institutional processes and professional discourses that intersected as the lunacy inquisition began. The newspaper reporters, writing sensationalist accounts of the proceedings, labored to "translate" the legal strategies and relatively alien psychiatric notions, organized through the hypothetical case, for their readers. The medical experts were selected and examined by the attorneys, who worked to shape both the psychiatric diagnoses and the press reports for legal use. Principals and witnesses, supporting or disputing elements of the hypothetical case at trial, entered into this complex dialogic intersection—sometimes in a confused way but often with some strategic savvy of their own. Each day's events were marked by this multifaceted jockeying for position.[15]

On Monday morning July 18, 1892, the first witness called by the defense was George Mitchell, Alice's father. He tearfully responded to Gen. Luke Wright's questions about his family tragedy, beginning (as the hypothetical case did) with the issue of Alice's heredity. Since heredity was considered so important a factor in the etiological schemas of nineteenth-century psychiatry,[16] some family history of mental disturbance was required to bolster the defense plea. George Mitchell chose to tell a story of illness about his wife, Alice's mother, who did not herself appear in court.

Isabella Scott had become the second Mrs. Mitchell in 1856 and had borne seven children from then to the birth of Alice, her youngest, in 1872. According to George, she suffered from "puerperal insanity" following her first child's birth and was committed to a lunatic asylum for several months by her physician. The child soon died while in the custody of Isabella's sister. George testified that she was "never the same" after that, becoming gloomy and indifferent rather than her formerly sociable self.[17]

"Puerperal insanity" was commonly diagnosed among nineteenth-century women who bore many children under traumatic conditions. The symptoms described by physicians often included behaviors that broke the taboos constraining respectable women. Patients were furious or lewd and cursed, threatened, or insulted those around them.[18] According to the hypothetical case, Isabella Mitchell became "wild and ungovernable" and developed a "groundless and absurd" antipathy toward relatives and friends. Her physician, Dr. Thomas Griswold Comstock, stated in his deposition (read in court) that Mrs. Mitchell had been "ferocious in her delirium," passing from melancholia to hallucinatory insanity to acute mania before her recovery and release from the asylum.[19]

Isabella Mitchell was reported to have suffered from similar mental disturbances at the births of each of her seven children, four of whom lived to adulthood.[20] Her life history was thus repeatedly marked by the trauma and pain of difficult childbirths and death; according to the hypothetical case, while she was an infant her parents also had died. Death was thus unsurprisingly featured in many of her delusions. Reportedly, she had once believed herself to be dead and later threatened to kill a stepdaughter believing that the twelve-year-old girl wished to murder the infant Alice, then commit suicide.[21]

Isabella Mitchell's rage, frustration, disappointment, and despair were expressed in the symptoms of "puerperal insanity," which was then explained medically. Her intense emotions were understood primarily as the products of a diseased body rather than as distressed or distorted expressions of personal loss, vexed social relations, or compulsory pregnancy.[22] This medical explanation relied in part on heredity, so depositions were also presented in court to verify the insanity of Isabella's brother Vance Scott, her cousin, and several other relatives.[23] Alice Mitchell's crime was then placed in this frame as the latest rotten fruit borne of the diseased family tree.

Though alienists argued that most insanity was acquired through heredity, they didn't believe that it necessarily appeared in every child of an insane parent. In order to establish that Alice's crime was the result of insanity inherited from her mother, evidence of specific physical pathology was added to the evidence of diseased heredity. There was very little of it available, however. Alice's two sisters, Mattie and Addie, testified on successive days that when Alice was about twelve years old, or "about the time her womanhood was being established," she suffered from violent headaches and her nose bled frequently—Mattie said that she was "quite nervous at times in consequence." But these were the only indications of physical malady that the Mitchell family could reveal.[24] Other signs of somatic abnormality had to await discovery and interpretation by the medical experts.

Most of the testimony presented by the defense focused on Alice Mitchell's behavior, described by relatives, neighbors, and observers in commonsense terms as peculiar, odd, or strange.[25] Various family members reported that since childhood, Alice had showed marked "peculiarities." At the top of this list was Alice's preference for games, sports, and activities considered "boyish." Her brother Frank (age twenty-four) testified that she "could pump in a swing" in baseball better than he could, while her half-brother Robert (aged forty) brought into the courtroom the toys he had found in her room after the murder—a sack of marbles, several baseballs, tops, and other "boyish" playthings. There were, significantly, no dolls.

Next in importance among Alice's peculiarities was her failure to form appropriate emotional bonds and social associations. She seemed always to be choosing the wrong gender or refusing to be friendly at all. Robert testified that she was fond of playing with boys as a child and preferred her brother to her sisters. She wouldn't associate with other girls of her age and social standing, according to her father, who said she seemed inclined to spend much of her time alone. Her sister Addie added that once grown, Alice cared nothing for the society of young men and wouldn't receive them when they called at the house. She also kept an odd distance toward family members, according to both Frank and Robert, who said she developed inexplicable prejudices and sometimes refused to speak.

This portrait of Alice, carefully constructed by the defense from the raw materials of Alice's social environment, was confirmed by the testimony of friends, neighbors, and acquaintances selected by counsel. Lillie Johnson tried to cooperate but contradicted herself. She claimed that Alice generally conducted herself as other girls did, but was nonetheless "more like a boy than a girl"; she cited as evidence Alice's membership in the girls' baseball club at Miss Higbee's school. Lillie's brother James (age twenty-one) testified that she had refused to dance with him at a picnic, preferring to sit in the hammock with Lillie instead. The neighborhood butcher said he had called her a tomboy, but she hadn't seemed to mind. Even vague testimony from remote acquaintances was solicited. Charles Mundinger complained that when he saw her in church she was peculiar and indifferent, though entirely proper. Mrs. Mundinger said simply, "I felt there was something wrong with her, but I could not say what it was." [26]

The culmination and expression of all this strangeness was the remarkable friendship Alice formed with Freda Ward. Mitchell family members provided the court with accounts of various aspects of that relationship and brought with them "evidence," including correspondence (reprinted in appendix B, section 1) and the engagement ring engraved "From A. to F." George and Robert Mitchell knew very little about Alice's feelings or activities before the murder—most of the information they provided the court was collected after January 25. Frank seemed to know a little more; correspondence from Freda's sister, Mrs. Volkmar, had been forwarded to Isabella Mitchell through him. But much of his testimony was also based on conversations with Alice in jail. His version of Alice's suicide attempt (she once had taken laudanum in despair over Freda's infidelities) was not grounded in firsthand observation and conflicted with the chronology of the hypothetical case.[27]

Alice's sisters also reported little knowledge of her personal affairs; her mother did not testify at all. Among all the witnesses in the case, only Lillie Johnson and Lucy Franklin, the "Negress" employed as a cook in the Mitchell household, had directly observed Alice's distress in the months prior to the murder. Lillie repeated testimony she'd given at her own hearing—about Alice's love for Freda, her jealousy of Freda's men friends, and her anguish at their forced separation. Lucy Franklin described Alice's box of letters, kept in the kitchen and often reread. In the months prior to the murder, Alice told Lucy that she'd rather be dead than alive and that she loved someone dearly to whom she wasn't allowed to speak. Her relatives, she said, had turned against her. At one time she held a rifle to her ear and at another time accidentally fired it. Franklin testified that she tried to reassure Alice, telling her "there was no use to worry as she had plenty of money." [28]

Of course, the ultimate proof of the strangeness of Alice and her relations with Freda was the murder itself. Lillie Johnson repeated her story of the crime, and the defense produced various eyewitnesses (the same ones who testified at the earlier hearing). Family members also reported Alice's odd behavior following the murder: she spoke as though Freda were alive; she saved a thumbstall stained with Freda's blood; she showed no remorse for the crime; she seemed calm and reasonable on every subject except her love for Freda.

This overall picture of insanity constructed by the defense in the days before the arrival of the medical experts was summarized in press commentary. The *New York World* explained:

> The engagement to marry which she proposed to Freda and the non-fulfillment of which was the primary motive of the killing; the fact that she once attempted to commit suicide in Freda's presence through some unaccountable whim; her violent jealousy of a young man who paid Freda some attention; the utter despair to which she was reduced by the separation from her girl lover, all these are given to show the insanity of the accused.[29]

But there was some confusion about the precise grounds upon which such feelings and such conduct were considered insane. Usually, Alice Mitchell was depicted as "like a man" or as "the man in the case" when the elopement plans were mentioned. Yet her behavior *also* appeared as an exaggerated enactment of ordinary feminine "lovesickness,"[30] with her insanity consisting in her aberrant choice of object. The *Memphis Commercial* commented:

> Had she slain a man who had deceived or betrayed her, the idea of insanity might never have been presented, but she slew a girl for whom she entertained a passion such as exists ordinarily between members of the opposite sexes, and the peculiarity of the case at once gave color to a suspicion of insanity.[31]

It seemed clear to observers that a gender inversion was involved in the case, but which gender lines were crossed in what way remained a shifting, ambiguous matter.

The prosecution worked not to contest the assertion that the boundaries of propriety had been crossed but to undermine the suggestion that "insanity" was the determining cause. Invoking the voluntarist assumptions of legal discourse to counter the determinist medical argument of the defense,[32] Attorney General Peters tried to show that Alice Mitchell was responsible for her freely chosen acts. This was no simple matter, however.

No effort was made to dispute testimony about Alice's diseased heredity or physical maladies.[33] The prosecution focused its efforts on the odd-behavior issues, attempting to disrupt the logic of the picture presented in the hypothetical case. Prosecution witnesses disputed the unselfconsciously contradictory defense testimony by insisting alternately that there was nothing very unusual about Alice Mitchell's admitted "tomboyish" behavior *and* that she was actually conventionally "girlish."[34]

Freda Ward's brother-in-law, William Volkmar, opined that Alice liked boys and fun well enough and was certainly not "crazy." But he also confirmed the defense's story of Freda's near elopement (which he interrupted at his wife's behest, Winchester rifle in hand). Jo Ward stated her belief that the marriage proposal had been "very strange" but not "crazy." She also revealed Alice's membership in the "Pleasant Hour" social club: she had attended one of its dances with a male escort. But Luke Wright's questioning further revealed that Alice stayed the night with Freda after club events, while the escort was under sixteen years old. Letters from Alice to several young men (selected from ads in matrimonial newspapers) were read aloud in court (reprinted in appendix B, section 2). But Lillie explained that Alice actually "hated" boys, and didn't mean what she said when she wrote to them, pretending to be Freda.

Thus the prosecution countered the defense narrative—with objections but not with a clear counter-narrative assembled from the evidence. Peters faced his most formidable challenge during the second half of the lunacy inquisition, however. Beginning on the sixth of the ten days of proceedings in the case, the defense brought on its medical experts to tie together the other testimony into an overarching narrative with a clear psychiatric interpretation.[35]

The defense presented five physicians: two elder statesmen of the Tennessee medical community, two young turks whose reputations were still on the rise, and one young physician who had been originally contacted by the prosecution but had decided to support the defense instead.

Only one of the five had anything approximating a national reputation: Dr. John Hill Callender, a sixty-year-old native of Nashville, who had been the medical superintendent of the Central Hospital for the Insane in his home city since 1870. He was Professor of Physiology and Psychology in the combined medical departments of the University of Nashville and Vanderbilt University and was known throughout the state as an authority on nervous diseases who was often called as an expert witness. His national reputation had been established when he was called to testify in the case of Charles Guiteau, charged with the assassination of President Garfield in 1881. (Though he left home convinced that Guiteau was sane, after an examination of the prisoner he testified that he was insane.) In that same year, he became president of the Association of Medical Superintendents of American Institutions for the Insane—the youngest and the first southern man to hold that position.[36]

Callender was treated with great deference during the trial, as was Memphis's own Frank L. Sim, the fifty-eight-year-old founder, Professor of the

Principles and Practice of Medicine, and Dean of the Faculty of the Memphis Hospital Medical College. He was also a founder of the local medical association and for ten years had edited the *Memphis Medical Monthly*. His reputation, though not national, was firmly established in the South, where he was known as an important figure in the growth of the institutions and authority of "regular" medicine. Locally, he was remembered especially for his efforts during the cholera, smallpox, and yellow fever epidemics that scourged the city decades earlier.[37]

Of all the experts, only the relatively younger Eugene Paul Sale had studied abroad—in London, Paris, and Edinburgh. He returned to practice medicine, as a specialist in gynecology in Aberdeen, Mississippi, where he became president of both the state medical association and the state board of health. In 1889 he arrived in Memphis, later becoming Professor of Materia Medica and Therapeutics at the Memphis Medical College. At the lunacy inquisition he explained that he attended lectures on diseases of the mind under the best lecturers while in London and read much on that subject. He believed that the diseases of the female in which he specialized were "more or less of the nervous kind."[38]

Younger still was Dr. B. F. Turner, who had practiced in Memphis for two years after studying diseases of the mind and nervous system in Baltimore and under the eminent physician Allan McLane Hamilton in New York. Turner eventually became the first "neuropsychiatrist" in Memphis; he later taught that specialty at the Memphis Hospital Medical College and the University of Tennessee College of Medicine. In 1892, he was at the very beginning of this career. The prosecution took advantage of that fact to aggressively attack his experience and knowledge, and challenge (unsuccessfully) his credentials to testify as an "expert" in the case.[39]

The testimony of thirty-six-year-old Michael Campbell was especially satisfying for the defense; he had been brought to Memphis to testify by the attorney general but changed his mind. He was the first medical superintendent of the Eastern State Hospital for the Insane, founded in Knoxville in 1886, and Professor of Nervous and Mental Diseases at the Tennessee Medical College since 1889.[40] Like most of the experts in the case, he had been educated close to home and had only a very limited knowledge of the newer European theories of "sexual perversion."

The testimony of all these experts created a general impression of unanimity. All agreed that Alice Mitchell was insane, probably incurably so, and all provided similar accounts of her symptoms and the etiology of her mental disease. This agreement was organized partly by the circulation of the hypothetical case, which though not read to the jury (the prosecution persuaded Judge DuBose that not all of its elements could be "proved" without reliance on inadmissible hearsay evidence), had been given to expert witnesses along with the defense's questions prior to trial.[41] Experts had clearly been "guided" in their interpretations of Alice Mitchell's condition.

Basing their accounts on the information gathered by defense attorneys, all the expert witnesses explained how the "hereditary predisposition" to insanity had been transmitted from mother to daughter; and each noted that mothers were more likely to transmit disease, and daughters more likely to inherit it. They went on to explain that this underlying tendency to insanity was later triggered by an "exciting cause"—in this case, the emotional disturbances of love, jealousy, anger, and grief.

The doctors supplemented the information they gathered from the hypothetical case with interviews with Alice herself: each had seen her at least once, for at least an hour. They all reported that she exhibited low intelligence and seemed much younger than her twenty years. In assessing her general appearance and demeanor, several noticed a vacant expression and a lack of expected emotion and remorse for her crime. E. P. Sale testified specifically that she was left-handed and lacked facial symmetry. Drawing again from the hypothetical case, Dr. Callender noted the significance of her nosebleeds, or "vicarious menstruation," and the probable connection to uterine and circulatory disorders.

Testimony concentrated on the relationship between Alice and Freda, however—and the murder itself. Alice's feelings were variously described as a "perverted affection," "insane love," or a "morbid perverted attachment." Special care was taken to distinguish these "unnatural" feelings from the common, intense friendships of schoolgirls known locally as "chumming," and also from sexual immorality or "depravity." Doctors Sim, Callender, and Turner specified that no evidence existed that the relations between the girls involved "sexual love," which Sim insisted was as different from "platonic love" (or the love that existed between the sexes *before* marriage) as black from white. The experts carefully pinpointed the abnormal romantic *feelings* that distinguished Mitchell's attachment to Freda Ward from disreputable actions or relations, as well as from normal, intense friendship. These distinctions nonetheless remained unstable and contested throughout the trial and afterward.

The medical experts ultimately emphasized the planned marriage, and not the abnormal feelings alone, as the surest sign of insanity, however. Alice's belief that she could marry Freda was specifically diagnosed by the various experts as a "fixed delusion," an "insane idea," a "false judgment," or "impossible idea." Dr. Callender noted, in his statement reprinted in Frank Sim's article on the case in the *Memphis Medical Monthly*:

> She seemed in her simplicity and weakness of mind to have no conception of the preposterous character of the marriage she looked for, and spoke in detail of the preparations as to man's apparel for the occasion, the procurement of a license for the ceremony, of the clipping of her hair after the fashion of men, and the cultivation of a mustache, if Freda wanted her to wear one. The frankness and sincerity of her manner on this topic was evidence either of a gross delusion or the conception of a person imbecile, or of a child without knowledge of the usual results of matrimony or the connubial state, or of the purpose of the organs of generation in the sexes.[42]

Nearly all the experts shared Callender's perception of Alice's honesty and seemed as stunned by the fact that she would tell them of her plan, without apparent shame or deceit, as by the plan itself. But different medical witnesses focused attention on different aspects of the marriage plan. Following Callender's emphasis on the strangeness of Alice's plan to cross-dress and pass as a man, other experts delineated a range of other socially central aspects of the institution of marriage upended by Mitchell's insane proposal. B. F. Turner focused on the need for economic self-sufficiency and the ability to create a reproductive household. He recreated a conversation he had with Alice in jail for the court, to demonstrate obvious defects of mind for judge, jury, and public:

BFT: Alice, do you not know that you could not have married another young lady?
AM: Oh, I could have married Freda.
BFT: But some one usually has to support a family in a case like that.
AM: I know it, but I was going to work and support both.
BFT: But a girl like you could not earn enough for both.
AM: But I was going to dress as a man. . . .
BFT: But Miss Mitchell, do you not know that usually when young people get married they look forward to the time when they shall have children growing up around them?
AM: Oh, yes sir.

BFT: Well, did you and Freda propose to have children?

AM: No, we were not going to have children.

BFT: How do you know you were not?

AM: Oh, I know we were not.

This exchange was published in the *Memphis Appeal Avalanche* and Frank Sim's *Memphis Medical Monthly* article under a heading meant to convey irony: "Alice's System of Logic."[43] It pinpointed the crucial nexus through which turn-of-the-century psychiatry functioned. In distinguishing abnormal from normal desires and relationships, feelings and attachments, psychiatric experts intervened in the state regulation of household formation. As expert testimony at trials such as Alice Mitchell's clearly shows, medical experts on mental life understood the psychic foundations for existing economic and social relations of gender, race, and class. They construed the desire for romance leading to domestic privacy supported through personal economic autonomy as definitional of white masculinity. During the 1890s, the agitation of other aspiring citizen-subjects for these prerogatives met with a wide range of institutional responses. Among these, the regulation of marriage was pivotal. Whatever institutional shifts an emerging modernity might bring, continuing (though altered) constraints on the social symbolism and law of marriage set boundaries for gender, class, and racial formation. Psychiatric experts at Alice Mitchell's lunacy inquisition participated actively in delineating and conserving such constraints.[44]

The act of murder provided the pathologizing framework for judging the plan to marry. That indisputably horrific event retrospectively cast Alice Mitchell's feelings, thoughts, and behavior under medicolegal suspicion and tainted otherwise unremarkable characteristics and behaviors as possible signposts on the road to disaster. The type and kind of roadway, designated by the official diagnoses, provided an explanatory map of causes and consequences—a "scientific" etiology. But diagnoses were the hotly contested core components of widely debated theories. Though there might be agreement about a broad conclusion, as there was with regard to Alice Mitchell's insanity at her lunacy inquisition, there was considerable controversy about the causes, manifestations, effects, and legal implications of specific mental maladies in any particular case.[45]

In diagnosing Alice at trial, three of the five physicians testified that she was under the influence of an "imperative conception" or "imperative impulse" to slay Freda. Echoing the obsessive concern of turn-of-the-century psychiatry with the maintenance and/or loss of "willpower" and self-control by individuals, these experts explained that Alice had been "dominated" by an insane desire to kill. In presenting an example, Turner hypothesized a state of conflict within the mind much like the battle between a runaway horse and driver. If the horse (impulse) is too strong, or the driver (will) too weak, control (of the self) is lost.[46] E. P. Sale offered a different kind of diagnosis — "simple insanity," under the subdivision of "erotomania" — though this was not reported in Sim's article nor in one of the two most important daily newspapers. Michael Campbell did not offer a diagnosis, but he agreed with the others that Alice's form of insanity was often invisible to ordinary observers; he noted that his asylum was full of people who conversed on most subjects with complete rationality.[47] And all the experts concluded finally that Alice Mitchell's malady could not be cured, though it might be temporarily improved through treatment in an asylum. Callender called for special attention to the defendant's uterine functions but ultimately predicted only progressive mental degeneration.

In addition to presenting these expert witnesses at the lunacy inquisition, the defense gathered depositions from other physicians to submit for the court's consideration. These depositions were never produced. The inability of defense witnesses to fully "prove" the assertions of the hypothetical case, upon which the opinions in the depositions were based, rendered them inadmissible. Frank Sim did publish them in his *Memphis Medical Monthly* article, however.

If presented at trial, the depositions might have disrupted the appearance of unanimity that inspired the *Memphis Commercial* headline, "They All Agree, No Diversity of Opinion among the Experts."[48] Frank Ingram, a New York physician who lectured on nervous and mental disease at the New York Polyclinic, diagnosed Alice's disturbance as "paranoia," as did William Baldwin Fletcher, a European-educated alienist and proprietor of a private sanatorium in Indiana called Neuronhurst.[49] The diagnosis of "paranoia," based on the German "primäre verrücktheit," or original insanity, had begun to replace the diagnosis of the partial insanity commonly known as "monomania" earlier in the century. It became one of the most frequent diagnoses applied to "homicidal cranks" as the century drew to a close and was used to designate a thought disorder eventually resulting in delusions of persecution. The "imperative conceptions" or "imperative impulses" described by the trial experts were generally interpreted as symptoms of various mental disorders, and not as diagnoses in themselves, by those with more special-ized or elite psychiatric educations.[50]

The addition of this diagnosis to those offered at trial might have exposed, in a way detrimental to the defense, the lack of agreement among alienists and neurologists about the etiology, diagnosis, and treatment of insanity. In his deposition, the eminent neurologist William A. Hammond arrived at yet another diagnosis—"emotional morbid impulse." He also included an explanation for the differing diagnostic labels in this case and others:

> Different names would be applied to such a form of mental derangement by dif-ferent authors. Just as some people would speak of a "house," others would call it a "mansion," others a "dwelling," others a "domicile," and so on; but all would agree in regard to the essential nature of the structure.[51]

But all did *not* agree on the essential nature of the structure (though the con-flict never came to light in court). Frank Sim and B. F. Turner had pointedly rejected the diagnoses of "paranoia" or "monomania" in their testimony. Turner specified that Alice's disorder did not belong even to a similar clas-sification as "paranoia" (though Sim testified that "imperative conceptions" *might* lead to a "morbid impulse").

On one crucial point all the experts clearly did agree, however: Alice Mitchell was insane. The attorney general was unable to produce a single expert to dispute this claim. Not only did Michael Campbell turn on him, but the superintendent of the Western Hospital for the Insane at Bolivar, Tennessee, refused the prosecution's request to testify as well. The testi-mony he had read in the newspapers convinced him that the defendant was insane.[52]

Without an expert to call their own, the prosecuting attorneys were forced to rely on close questioning of the defense witnesses in order to make their case. During cross-examinations, they carefully picked apart each element of the narrative establishing Alice Mitchell's insanity, hoping thereby to under-mine the structure of the defense's argument. With each witness, the prose-cutor asked whether love between members of the same sex was necessarily indicative of insanity. As the questioner might have wished, he obtained a variety of opinions on this point. Dr. Sale testified that the love between Alice and Freda was an insane or pathological love, while Campbell stated that such passionate fondness was not insane in and of itself—only when carried to an extreme, like murder, was insanity clearly indicated. B. F. Turner tried to explain the difficulty of assessing these situations. As reported in the *Memphis Appeal Avalanche,* he was asked:

"Is there authority in any of the law or medical records for classifying perverted affections as proof of insanity?"

The answer to this was that if the perverted affections were slight they would not be indicative of insanity, but if they were extremely passionate there might be insanity. It is hard to draw the line on a hypothetical case, but the line must be drawn somewhere on these cases of perverted affections as between sanity and insanity.[53]

The distinction was problematic enough that J. H. Callender's comments were reported differently in the press than in Frank Sim's article for the medical press. In the former he was supposed to have said that perverted love, while more ardent than normal love, was not insanity; in the latter he was quoted as arguing that perverted passion might be insane in itself.[54]

When the prosecution proceeded from the question of love to the project of marriage between two women, the attorney general tried to counter defense descriptions of the elopement plan as an "insane idea." He mentioned the case of Annie Hindle, a well-known male impersonator who had once lived in Memphis and later married another woman; no one had ever argued that Hindle was insane rather than merely eccentric.[55] This effort met with the same equivocation as the previous line of questioning. As Dr. Turner explained:

If a girl desires to marry another girl, even knowing that certain incidents of the marriage could not exist, such as physical pleasure and giving birth to children, it would scarcely of itself be sufficient to denote insanity. When one girl showed very great affection for another, and had an uncontrollable desire to be with her, and even to marry her, it might indicate it.[56]

The press had a tendency to simplify the careful answers of the experts, however, invoking clear agreement where none existed. Some reporters also introduced issues and questions that were largely neglected at the inquisition. The *Memphis Appeal Avalanche* reported:

The fact that Alice Mitchell had a passionate love for Freda Ward is admitted by all the experts to be no indication of insanity per se; for there are frequent cases of perversion of the sexual passions where there is no taint of insanity. But the experts point out that Alice's love was based upon an insane delusion, to wit: The delusion that she could marry Freda, and live with her as a husband, the fact being that Alice could not perform the duties of a husband. The only apparent defect in this reasoning is the fact that it has not been proved that Alice could not perform the duties of a husband. None of the experts who have testified before the court have made an examination for the purpose of ascertaining that point, though several of them have expressed the belief that the perversion of which Alice was the victim, was purely of a mental character. This side of the question has not been gone into to any extent whatever by counsel for either side. . . .[57]

The suggestion that Alice's "perversion" might involve some physical abnormality—by implication, hermaphroditism—invoked a centuries-old assumption that gender ambiguity in behavior was rooted in ambiguous genitals. Specifically, sexual relations between women were often understood as a cause and/or effect of an enlarged clitoris in at least one of the partners.[58] In this case, both defense and prosecution avoided any such suggestion, undoubtedly because of the severe moral stigma attached to genital sexual activity on the part of respectable white girls. Yet experts felt compelled to mention the issue, in order to reject its implications. Frank Sim explained:

> No physical examination was made of the prisoner. Had the case been viewed as a purely *sexual* pervert, an examination might have thrown some light on the subject, but as there is no evidence that such is the case, nothing of the kind has been suggested.[59]

Callender reported that he asked Alice's mother about any "physical malformation of the sexual organs." But Peters didn't follow up this statement by asking what Mrs. Mitchell said; he skipped instead to other issues of Alice's general health.

Peters didn't hesitate to focus on other instances of the defendant's alleged physical abnormality, however. He patiently elicited admissions that left-handedness, asymmetrical facial features, or unusual head shape were not indications of insanity, though several experts insisted that, taken together with other abnormalities or "eccentricities," these factors would have their diagnostic weight.[60]

The prosecution continued, with each witness, to raise these and other questions that might expose holes in the defense scenario. Assistant Attorney General William Fitzgerald asked whether, if Alice Mitchell was insane, mustn't Freda Ward be considered insane as well? Campbell answered that "Freda Ward was not the active agent in the business. She was dominated by Alice Mitchell, the stronger-willed of the two girls."[61] Prosecutors asked repeatedly whether a man who killed his sweetheart from jealousy would (like Alice) be considered insane. Sim replied that it would depend on the extent of the jealousy, but E. P. Sale made a sharp distinction:

> Oh, that is done on the spur of the moment and is an ebullition that might occur with every normal man. But here is one girl who supposes she can marry another and arranges to run away, and fancies that she can work and support the family.[62]

Witnesses were also required to explain how Alice's apparently rational behavior, in planning her crime and in the courtroom during the trial, was compatible with their theories of insanity. Callender pointed out that elaborate plans were not incompatible with certain types of insanity; Turner had a more difficult time arguing that people might appear perfectly sane to observers and yet be clinically insane.

Only once during all this prodding and probing did the prosecution suggest a hypothetical scenario of its own, however:

Peters: Now doctor, assuming that Alice Mitchell was not feigning but was really in love with Ashley Roselle, who was paying attention to Freda, and that in addition to her fondness for Freda Ward she had carried on an extensive correspondence with young men, went out driving and met young men and was fond of the attention of young men, and that she was in correspondence with Ashley Roselle, in the course of which she expressed great admiration for him, and that she became jealous of the attentions he was paying Freda Ward, that she wrote to Freda that she should not marry Ashley Roselle, and that she finally killed Freda Ward, might not all those facts exist in entire harmony with a theory of sanity in this defendant?

Callender: Yes, I think that such a theory is tenable.[63]

This proffered narrative of love, jealousy, and murder did not strike medical experts as a story of insanity, but it didn't strike them as compelling either; given the evidence organized by the defense, they didn't take it seriously in forming their opinions.

The expert witnesses most often resisted the efforts of the prosecution by refusing to separate the elements of the case, by denying that insanity could be determined from a single event or characteristic, by insisting on contextualizing their opinions within the *entire* narrative—understood as a whole that was more than the sum of its parts. Nineteenth-century psychiatrists responded to the doubt and controversy surrounding their theories in the courtroom by generally refusing to provide clear definitions of insanity, preferring to examine specific cases in full before rendering an opinion. As Michael Campbell told William Fitzgerald during cross-examination, there was no definition to which there would not be exceptions.[64]

The three days of expert testimony left the prosecution still at a loss for a convincing counter-narrative, but the questions it raised did help transmute widespread popular skepticism about psychiatric experts and their theories into doubt about Alice Mitchell's allegedly insane motives.[65] The *Memphis Appeal Avalanche* expressed such a skeptical view:

> The testimony given by the expert witnesses is peculiar in so far as it shows what alarming symptoms of insanity may be found in a subject who, during a course of twenty years, led the life of a young woman, moving about in society, in school and in the home, without ever giving her most intimate associates reason to suspect the insane temperament which possessed her, until it erupted into activity with an atrocious homicide. From all the evidence it would appear that prior to the homicide Alice Mitchell was considered an ordinary young lady, of ordinary habits and with ordinary mental capacity, and ordinary accomplishments. Now, it is found, to use the words of the experts, that:
>
> She is insane.
>
> She is undeveloped mentally.
>
> Her conversation is that of a person much younger than she is.
>
> There is a lack of symmetry in the facial conformation.
>
> She is of nervous temperament.
>
> Her love was such as the passion a beast feels for its offspring.
>
> She is a victim of erotomania, a subdivision of simple insanity.
>
> She is left-handed.
>
> She is the last child born to an insane mother.
>
> She was eccentric in youth.
>
> At puberty she displayed symptoms of excitability.
>
> She has always found boys more congenial as playmates than girls.
>
> She was the victim of an insane but an imperative delusion.
>
> She was vacillating.
>
> She became maniacal.
>
> She is of a low grade of intelligence.
>
> There is a vacuity in her conversation.
>
> She intended to commit suicide, but forgot.
>
> Her face is larger on one side than the other.

She is too dangerous to be turned loose on the community.

She is very childish.

She is weak minded.

She dominated the mind of Freda Ward.[66]

At the conclusion of the expert testimony, the state's attorney called only four witnesses to support his case: Mrs. Volkmar (Freda's married sister), Ashley Roselle (Freda's erstwhile beau), Christina Purnell (a witness to the murder), and Alice Mitchell herself.[67] Ada Volkmar added nothing new but stated her belief that there was nothing especially peculiar about Alice or her mother; she described Alice's behavior as "wild, bold, willful," but not insane. Christina Purnell concurred, saying there had been nothing in Alice's conduct that was different from other girls.

Ashley Roselle, the twenty-three-year-old postmaster of Featherstone, Arkansas, was a figure of some fun in the news reports for his less than soberly conservative and decidedly nonelite appearance. The *Memphis Appeal Avalanche* designated him "The Man in the Case" and offered a description:

He is making an effort with some degree of success to raise a moustache. He had no vest on, and an ornate pink shirt front, embellished with a blue necktie, furnished the most striking part of his apparel, with a blue pair of pants a close second. He has a round, close cropped head, and his eyes do not open very wide.[68]

Roselle had ceased his correspondence with Freda Ward (at Freda's request), then opened one with Alice Mitchell.[69] His letters to Alice mentioned a possible future marriage, but he testified that he knew she only wrote to him to ask about his relations with Freda—he never thought she was in love with him. He assured the prosecutor that on the two or three times he'd met her, Alice had never impressed him as insane. But he conceded to the defense that the last time he'd seen her, she did mention wanting to kill herself.

These witnesses didn't particularly strengthen the prosecution's position in the case—but none damaged it as surely and irreparably as the testimony of Alice Mitchell.

Alice's presence in the courtroom, and in the Shelby County jail at other times, had been duly noted in the press throughout the trial. She was described in three major modes as "docile," "obedient," and "reasonable" in jail, where she was usually attended by her mother, and as "smiling," "cheerful," "confident," and "composed" in court—or alternatively as "indifferent," "unembarrassed," or "listless" during testimony.[70] She was reported to have openly displayed emotion on only two occasions; when Lillie Johnson took the stand she wept, and when Jo Ward testified she "flushed."

The concern underlying all of these descriptions, explicitly or implicitly, was the question of Alice's sanity. Did her emotional expressions seem ordinary or insanely inappropriate? Different conclusions were reached on different occasions. On July 19 the *San Francisco Examiner* opined:

> But if Alice Mitchell is really insane her insanity is of a type that could never be discovered by any one save an expert. There is not in her face even an indistinct trace of it, and her conduct, barring the killing of Freda Ward, is no more indicative of mental unsoundness than is that of hundreds and thousands of others who walk the streets of this and other cities at their own sweet will. She has at all times taken a rational view of her surroundings, and in conversation has betrayed no evidence of a mind diseased or warped.[71]

On the other side of the question, the *Memphis Commercial* observed:

> Alice, herself, was as unconcerned as ever. An occasional smile lightened, and an occasional frown darkened her countenance, but neither seemed to be occasioned by the evidence. Nothing that was said affected her in the least. If not insane, then she is one of the most marvelous actresses ever known.[72]

Each day of the lunacy inquisition, the courtroom was filled with spectators avidly interested in the case, and the newspapers continued to note the large representation of Memphis's women and girls (except during the expert testimony, when there seemed to be some falling off of female interest). On the day when Alice was called to the stand by the attorney general, there was a general stir of excitement through this crowd, but the anticipated appearance of the star witness was delayed when the defense objected to her testifying.

The judge heard arguments—from the prosecution, wondering why (if they were so certain she was insane) the defense attorneys objected to putting Alice on the stand, and from the defense, declaring that "the family may not care to have her made the object of scrutiny to some sensationalist." He could find no legal precedent on the question and decided to set his own by ordering Miss Mitchell to take the stand.

This decision was a pyrrhic victory for the attorney general. Alice Mitchell's testimony was widely interpreted as the climax of the trial's drama, firmly establishing her insanity in the minds of the jury. The *Memphis Appeal Avalanche* commented:

The last prop was knocked from under the opposition to the insanity plea when Alice Mitchell herself was put on the stand and under examination of counsel told in her own childish, simple way of her relations with Freda and how and why she killed her.

There was no escaping the evidences of insanity marked on her face, shadowed in her conversation and apparent from her system of logic and scheme of reasoning. She appeared to the jury and spectators as described by the experts who had previously examined her in private; and the fact became apparent to the representatives of the State that no amount of testimony that could be brought before the jury could remove the impression already made by the brief appearance of Alice Mitchell on the witness stand.[73]

The same paper reported that Alice herself seemed "tickled" at the prospect of going on the stand, however, and expressed "satisfaction" at her testimony's conclusion. Here was an opportunity to tell her own story, and she told it (according to the newspapers) in a well-modulated voice, without hesitation.

During most of her testimony, Alice told the story of her relationship with Freda, weeping several times as she said she loved her in a special way:

Peters: What person did you love the most in all the world?
Alice: Freda Ward.
Peters: Did you not love your relatives?
Alice: Yes, but nothing to what I loved Freda.

She went on to detail her plans for marriage:

Peters: Did you really expect to marry Freda?
Alice: Yes. . . .
Peters: Did you think it was a proper thing for two girls to marry?
Alice: No, but then I thought if I dressed myself up as a man they would not know the difference.
Peters: Then where were you going to?
Alice: Well, Freda said she wanted to go to St. Louis.
Peters: What business did you expect to engage in there?
Alice: I didn't have any business.
Peters: How did you expect to make a living?
Alice: I don't know. . . .
Peters: Did you never talk to her as to what you would do when you got to St. Louis?
Alice: No, sir. You see we didn't have much chance to discuss it. We were afraid to

say anything about it in our letters, as they were being intercepted. The only time we had to talk about the matter was when we were at Golddust.

Peters: Which of you suggested the elopement?

Alice: I did.[74]

Alice also told the court about Freda's relations with young men: Harry Bilger asked her to run away and go on the stage with him, and Ashley Roselle asked her to marry him. When Freda told Alice she had accepted Ashley's proposal, Alice said she tried to give laudanum to both Freda and herself. Then later, after Alice and Freda were finally separated, she formed the plan to kill Freda, explaining: "I wanted to cut her because I knew I could not have her, and I didn't want anyone else to have her."

Alice provided an account of the murder itself with a combination of "zest" and "indifference," according to the newspapers, and explained that she had also intended to kill herself:

My intention was to cut Freda's throat and then my own, but Jo's interference made me cut Freda again.[75]

When, at the close of her testimony, the jury was permitted to ask questions directly, she told one juryman that she still wanted to die.

During her time on the witness stand, Alice refuted some of the defense assertions about her—she said that she *knew* Freda was dead, for instance. But she confirmed much of what various defense witnesses had said. She also directly countered the favored theories of the prosecution, asserting clearly that she had no interest in young men. In addition, she made several statements that no doubt puzzled jury members, giving them a commonsense impression of insanity: She said it would give her pleasure to be able to look at the thumbstall she saved with Freda's blood on it; she expressed no anger at Freda, saying the separation wasn't her fault.

Reporters seized on two particular aspects of Mitchell's testimony as particularly indicative of insanity—her unrealistic thinking and her strange lack of expected behavior and emotions:

. . . her suppositions and conclusions appeared those of a child who would be capable of forming plans without taking into consideration the responsibilities of life. It seemed she had built an airy fairy castle in which she and Freda were to spend their days, without reference to the matter of victuals nor the necessary associations with the rest of the world.[76]

The spectacle of a girl who has not yet reached her 20th birthday—one born of refined and christian parents, reared with tenderest care, amidst surroundings whose
every influence was good—calmly and nonchalantly admitting the perpetration of
an awful crime, is rare enough and sad enough in all conscience. But that was not
all. Into every horrid detail she entered with apparent relish.[77]

The overall impact was decisive enough that both prosecution and defense
agreed to turn the case over to the jury without argument.[78]

Judge DuBose postponed the conclusion of the case while he prepared
his written charge to the jury. On Saturday, July 30, he read it aloud before
a crowded courtroom. Billed as the "last act in the drama,"[79] the jury began
deliberations. It was out for only twenty minutes, during which time Alice
Mitchell was described as smiling, "her bright and careless face contrasting
strangely with the haggard, anxious looks of her father and brother."[80] The
jury's decision, finding Alice "presently insane" and dangerous, was read by
foreman Col. M. C. Galloway, a state senator and former newspaper editor.
She was taken to the Western Hospital for the Insane at Bolivar, Tennessee,
on Monday, August 1. Before departure, the press reported that she was escorted (at her request) to Freda's grave in Elmwood Cemetery, where she
wept and "seemed to be suffering from remorse."[81]

Reporting that the verdict met with the approbation of the "whole community," local newspaper editors expressed great relief that nothing "revolting" came to light during the trial. The *Memphis Appeal Avalanche* commented
in an editorial titled "The Mitchell Case":

> The *Appeal Avalanche* cannot too highly commend the conduct of the court and its
> officers in this distressing prosecution. There has been a very close observance of
> proprieties and no disposition has been shown to harass the defendant, or to go
> into a line of investigation which, because of its suggestiveness, might have com-
> promised her moral character. It has, however, been made clear that while the State
> did not pursue such a course there were no unsavory revelations to be made; that
> the defendant was a child of feeble will, seized with grotesque ideas, but guiltless
> of offenses against nature. Therefore, so far as the insinuations against her personal
> character are concerned, she stands acquitted, and there remains only pity in the
> heart of every one for the girl, who, in a moment of mental aberration, struck down
> her friend.[82]

The *Memphis Commercial* congratulated the defense for establishing that there
was "nothing depraved, sensuous or degraded in her character" and thanked

the prosecution for refraining from any "unnecessary mortification of the family [or] humiliation of the community."[83]

Approbation and relief: these reactions greeted a decision that seemed to suit the gender and social position of the defendant, and the needs of the "community" represented by newspaper editors, attorneys, physicians, judge, and jurors.[84] The decision allowed for the removal of a troubled and dangerous individual, yet did so on grounds that didn't threaten the "character" of respectable white women. "Immorality" in one young woman (understood primarily in sexual terms) raised the specter of a more widespread potential problem. "Insanity," on the other hand, was an individual, seemingly containable aberration.[85]

The satisfactory resolution of this case depended on a clinical portrait of insanity that was constructed from a wide variety of disparate elements. Characteristics and behaviors rarely viewed as insane were integrated into a narrative plotted as a story of disease. Tomboyishness, romantic friendship or "chumming" between girls, plans to "pass" as a man and marry another woman, even passion murder—all were regarded as either ordinary or only eccentric. Together in the narrative mobilized and circulated in the Mitchell case, these elements were provided with a pathological, physiological "cause" that drained them of ordinariness and normality, making them all links in a chain leading to murder.

This physiological foundation was only hypothetical, however. As Luke Wright explained during the lunacy inquisition:

> The jury can only judge of a person's insanity by his acts and words. The brain cells of the subject may not be dissected and viewed. Acts and words are the only proof. . . .[86]

But acts and words are always open to interpretation. And in fact, each element of the defense's clinical portrait had been disputed at some point: tomboyishness was called unexceptional, Alice was described as sensible, the murder was compared to "ordinary" passion crimes. The crucial effort of experts and other witnesses to distinguish clearly among normal "chumming," unnatural love like Alice's for Freda, and sexual depravity was especially difficult to sustain—in 1892 the Victorian boundaries between spiritual love, romantic love, and sexual desire were disintegrating.

The clinical portrait had succeeded in this case, over the efforts of the prosecution and the widespread skepticism of "experts," in large part because the alternatives to commitment in an asylum—a trial for murder and a jail sentence or execution—were unacceptable, given the facts of the case and the social position of the defendant. The structure of the law, the discourse of psychiatry, and the needs and expectations of the "respectable" white community—as constituted through the newspapers—interacted, shaping and being shaped by their differing parameters, to produce a verdict of insanity.

In constructing the clinical portrait that ultimately sustained the verdict, the attorneys and physicians also drew from the newly emerging European literature on "sexual perversion." Dr. Sim indicated his awareness of the limited clinical literature in this area, and Dr. Callender used language derived directly from European studies: "contrary love" and "morbid" or "perverted sexual attachment."[87] But this newly emerging literature played only a minor role in the case—partly because the medical experts were not specialists in this field, and partly because of their effort to avoid reference to any specifically "sexual" deviance. The boundaries of decorum of the press, along with the social deference accorded a respectable white woman's family at trial, interacted to produce broad social recognition for a new abnormal "type" of woman with aberrant desires for other women—desires conceived as characterological and independent of sexual acts.[88] Though thus disassociated from disreputable sexuality, the new "type" was linked to insane violence—specifically, to murder in pursuit of her heart's desire: domestic life in the marital mode with a "normal" white woman.

Focus on the clinical portrait supported by expert testimony at trial obscured other stories that peeked through the testimony and evidence. The letters produced by various relatives of the principals contained especially well-developed alternative narratives but received little attention or analysis. The letters between Alice Mitchell or Lillie Johnson and various young men were mentioned during the questioning of witnesses, and many of the letters themselves had been printed in the newspaper (see appendix B, section 2). The jury had been asked to consider them either as evidence of Alice's genuine (and morally questionable but completely sane) interest in boys or as a (morally harmless) pastime and expression of her (possibly insane) imagination. The letters revealed a heterosocial world of fantasy and flirtation at the boundaries of respectability in turn-of-the-century Memphis. Prominently featuring the "matrimonial" ads as modes of social connection, and the theater as a site for imagined romance and adventure, this world and its relative freedom challenged the family control of young white women. Generational conflict over the attractions and dangers of these new forms of heterosocial leisure occupied much testimony at the Mitchell trial.

The letters between Alice Mitchell and Freda Ward were also published in the newspapers (see appendix B, section 1); referred to as "Mysterious Letters, Inexplicable Allusions and Endearing Epithets without End," and as "probably the most remarkable epistles to make their way to a court of justice,"[89] they were barely commented upon in testimony at trial. On the surface they were primarily love letters, filled with endearments and expressions of attachment and affection. Alice explained during her testimony that she and Freda had used a cipher that they called the YBIR alphabet—the cipher letters for love. In addition, the letters were filled with the conventional endearments of courtship, such as "Sweetheart," and with special pet names like "Petty Sing." The letters also told the story of the planned elopement and included the "post-marital" names for Alice and Freda—"Alvin J. Ward" and "Mrs. A. J. Ward." But beneath this surface of high hopes and warm feelings, the letters tracked the story of a long-running conflict between the lovers over the nature of their relationship.

The issue at the center of the conflict between Freda and Alice, as recounted in the letters, was Freda's fidelity. Her flirtations and possibly serious relationships with young men threatened Alice profoundly, and she took drastic actions to put a stop to them—threatening to buy a pistol and shoot either Freda or Ashley, and attempting suicide. Freda responded to Alice's bids for control with deceit and manipulation; she promised to try to be "true" to Alice but suggested that she couldn't with such provocative lines as, "Maybe other women are not happy when they love others beside their husbands, but I will be perfectly happy when I become Mrs. Alvin J. Ward."[90]

Freda's letters were laced with ambivalence—attempts to reassure Alice combined with indirect evasions of her lover's attempts to impose limits. Alice's letters were filled with anxiety, anger, and hope that the longed-for marriage would end the difficulty over Freda's fidelity:

Sweet one, you have done me mean, but I love you still with all your faults. I wish we were married. . . . I am afraid some boy will take you from me if we wait too long. You are so changeable. Fred, do you love me one-half as much as you did the first winter? I believe you loved me truer then than you ever did. You didn't fall in love with every boy that talked sweet to you then.[91]

Alice expressed hope that the conventions of gender and marriage could be reconfigured, then mobilized in her favor. If she could transform herself into Alvin J. Ward and marry Freda, then Freda might provide her with the loyalty and obedience expected of proper wives of her class.

Another document, produced at trial by Robert Mitchell, reflected Alice's sentimental, orthodox Victorian view of her future marital happiness with Freda. It was described (but not published) in the *Memphis Commercial*:

> In another document Alice gives her ideas of what a model wife ought to be and do. She must never deceive, must know how to keep house, must know how to cook, she must be able to sew on a button and must be her first love and her last love. She closes the essay by saying if a certain brown-eyed girl keeps her promise she will show a model husband and wife within a year. This reference is, of course, to Freda.
>
> Freda supplemented this by a dissertation upon the model husband, which was not unlike the other in tone.[92]

These documents—involving highly conventional fantasies of a wedding as the happy resolution to the story of Alice and Freda's romance—contrasted sharply with another indicating the bitterness and desperation of the conflict between them. The heading "How to Kill" in Alice's handwriting was followed by a gruesome list: "Cut throat, poison, stab, shoot, hang, smother," and "ten grains of atrophia."[93] Whether this list was intended to facilitate suicide (as she told her brother) or homicide, it clearly expressed lethal desperation. Combined with the strange references to the reported "death" of "Freda Ward" (possibly a reference to an alter ego of Alice's) in the letters, it demonstrated an obsessive interest in death as the best or only alternative to marriage.

These severe difficulties in Alice's relations with Freda preceded the interference of Mrs. Volkmar, whose actions (with Mrs. Mitchell's cooperation) effectively ended Alice's efforts to secure her relationship with Freda. In a state of profound isolation and defeat, Alice lost weight as she contemplated the probable marriage of Freda to someone else. She slowly shed any hope for a satisfying future of any kind.[94]

The power struggle between Alice and Freda, prematurely cut off and painfully resolved through a conflict with female authority, had ended in an act with a double meaning. According to the story told through the letters, the murder was at once Alice's last bid for control over Freda's future, and a pyrrhic victory in its implicit admission of complete and hopeless defeat. From the evidence of the letters, examined together with Alice's testimony at trial, the murder appeared as an act of domination *and* self-destruction following overlapping episodes of conflict and despair. The conflict between the two girls over the nature of their relationship was folded into a generational conflict over proper supervision and control of respectable white daughters. Nurtured in the homosocial life of the school, fed by fantasies of freedom found in the newly emerging world of heterosocial leisure, the girls' conflicted romance and planned elopement hit the wall of familial authority.

At the center of conflict, before and during the inquisition, was the planned marriage of Alice Mitchell and Freda Ward. In Alice's letters, the marriage appeared both as a romantic fantasy of union, and as a means of controlling Freda and their relationship through the imposition of class- and race-based gendered conformity. In Freda's writing, ambivalence and deception circulated around marital plans with a variety of possible partners. To the maternal authorities, Mrs. Volkmar and Mrs. Mitchell, the elopement plan signaled a possible loss of respectability through a definite loss of control over the younger women. The elder female kin retained enough control to stop the plan to marry, however. Once Alice's lethal desperation led her to murder and put her on trial, the marriage proposal became evidence of insanity.

Marriage played a central role in the conflicts in this case, as marital law and symbolism played a crucial role in the core institutions of American modernity at work in Memphis and elsewhere in 1892. The ideology and practice of marriage defined gender, in class- and race-specific ways, by mediating economic opportunities and wage rates, shaping housing options, determining property rights, and legitimating authority relations across genders and generations. Antimiscegenation and segregation laws, combined with naturalization rights and immigration restrictions, differentiated by gender and marital status, produced the racial composition of the nation through the regulation of household formation. Marriage thus appeared as the most significant institution at the boundary of domestic privacy, economic opportunity, and citizenship at the turn of the century. As such, it became the focus for extensive political agitation—both on behalf of greater freedom or equality and in favor of social restrictions and cultural hierarchies. For Alice Mitchell, as for so many other marriage reformers, the quest for marriage to Freda Ward carried both meanings.[95]

As the approved motive for marriage for respectable young white ladies shifted unevenly during the nineteenth century, from explicit economic necessity to romance and happiness, disorders and crimes of desire proliferated. The lynching narrative preemptively defined a socially insubordinate form of interracial desire as rape by definition, never courtship—falling outside the boundaries of social possibility inscribed in antimiscegenation laws as well. The lesbian love murder narrative, as circulated in the Mitchell-Ward case press coverage, defined romantic desire between respectable white women as insane—outside the boundaries of social possibility inscribed *as* the law of marriage.[96]

But as with the clinical portrait in the context of Alice's trial, the pathologizing narrative of the desire of "girl lovers" never held sway completely. It was in a sense "coauthored" by many social interests—always unstable, located in a field of conflict over the authorship, language, and plots of appropriate versus dangerous love and courtship. The tale of this particular conflict in a U.S. context, the narrative of lesbian love murder, extends from the events of Alice Mitchell's trial to its transformative reworking in Radclyffe Hall's *The Well of Loneliness* in 1928.[97]

In 1891, when Alice Mitchell wrote to Freda Ward, "How I love thee, none can know," she occupied a conflicted position between the new possibilities emerging in the lives of her peers and her profoundly isolated position at home and within the regulatory institutions of Memphis. Her desire, her frustration, her dreams for a future of work, love, and adventure with Freda were, at that moment, in that place, paradoxically commonplace and familiar yet culturally unintelligible. The violent end of her romance was interpreted within the terms of the discourses of sin or sickness and reported in the language of sensationalism. In 1892 in Memphis, Tennessee, there were no other coherent, available narratives for the tragedy of Alice Mitchell and Freda Ward.

PART II **MAKING MEANINGS**

VIOLENT PASSIONS

Think back, in the meshes of your musical
memory, of just the opera notices, of the images
these little outline forms have left in the back of
your mind. How many bodies wearing the veil of
darkness, how many criminal and consumptive
women wearing white shifts stained with blood,
how many wrapped in tears and murders?

Catherine Clement, *Opera, or the Undoing of Women* [1]

Only days following Alice Mitchell's journey to the Tennessee state asylum, Lizzie Borden was arrested for the ax murders of her father and stepmother in Fall River, Massachusetts. In another setback for the reputation of the white home and its daughters, the murder, arrest, and subsequent trial were publicized through the nation. The attention focused on the contested place and possibly dangerous desires of unmarried white women through the central question posed at trial: Was Lizzie a dutiful daughter incapable of insubordination, not to mention parricide? Or was she socially ambitious, materially greedy, stifled by parental control, and out for independence by any means necessary? [2]

During the 1890s, the publicity surrounding the Borden trial spotlighted the social anxieties of prosperous elites about the stability of their domestic arrangements and the fascination of the spectacle of violence for an ambivalent voyeuristic public. Though the Borden trial resolved itself in favor of bourgeois domesticity through Lizzie's acquittal, it participated in widespread reconsiderations of the place of single white women in the worlds of work, commercial leisure, and household organization. The period of relative autonomy emerging for some young women during adolescence and early adulthood, generated by wages and new, unsupervised heterosocial pleasures, became the target of anxious publicity and state intervention. The possibility that this period of relative autonomy might be extended into alternative homosocial domesticities produced social opposition through moral judgment, contempt, or ridicule, as well as through visions of apocalyptic violence in parricide or love murder.[3]

The Mitchell-Ward murder case collected energy within this anxious field and became the basis for a cultural narrative circulated nationally beginning in the 1890s. But the materials collected and organized by this narrative, its characters and plot lines, were anything but new. Narrative fragments and characterizations were assembled from a wide range of contexts—from the police and crime papers and the penny press, from mass-marketed as well as literary fiction, and from the social practices and self-representations of Anglo-European women over the previous century. The lesbian love murder story of the 1890s drew on all these sources but especially on two class-marked narratives commonly circulated from the late eighteenth, throughout the nineteenth, and well into the twentieth centuries: the story of marriage, featuring a "female husband" who passed and worked as a man among workingmen, or as a farmer or laborer in an agricultural setting, and who wed an otherwise ordinary woman, and the tale of romantic friendship in which respectable girls and women made passionate commitments to each other within a gender-segregated female world.[4]

These narratives circulated in multiple arenas, but the forms most influential in the 1890s production of the lesbian love murder appeared in the mid-nineteenth-century police and crime papers. These newspapers pioneered some of the reporting strategies of the later mass circulation press —including sensationalist language, a focus on the public/private boundaries of crime and domestic scandal, and the construction of an imagined national audience.[5] The best known and most widely circulated of these, the National Police Gazette, ran two stories of the "female husband" and "romantic friendship" type during 1879, both of which later recirculated along with the Mitchell-Ward story. On October 25, the story of Lucy Ann Lobdell appeared:

A CURIOUS CAREER

Remarkable Adventures of Lucy Ann Lobdell, an Eccentric Female
Character who Figured Successively as Hermit, Hunter, Music Teacher, Author
and "Female Husband"

A correspondent writing from Delhi, N.Y., under the date of the 8th says: News of the death of Lucy Ann Lobdell Slater, known throughout the Delaware valley as the "Female hunter of Long Eddy," has been received here, and it recalls a most singular life-history. In 1851, Lucy Ann Lobdell, daughter of a lumberman living on the Delaware, near the boundary line of this county and Sullivan, was married to a raftsman named George Slater. She was then seventeen years old, and was known far and wide for her wonderful skill with the rifle, not only in target-shooting, but in hunting deer and other game, for which the valley was then noted. After a year of married life Slater deserted his wife and a babe a few weeks old, and has never been heard from since. Mrs. Slater's parents were poor, and she left the child in their charge, laid aside the habit of her sex, donned male attire and

ADOPTED THE LIFE OF A HUNTER.

The mountains of Delaware, Sullivan and Ulster counties of this state, and the Delaware river county in Pennsylvania, were then filled with game. For eight years the unfortunate wife and mother roamed the wilderness, where she erected rude cabins for her shelter. She never appeared at the settlements except to procure ammunition and needed supplies, for which she exchanged skins and game. Her wild life was one of thrilling adventure and privation, and it was not until she was broken down by the exposure and hardships of it that she returned to the haunts of civilization. She wrote a book detailing her adventures in the woods, and giving an account of her sufferings from cold, hunger and sickness. She recorded in this book that she had killed 168 deer, 77 bears, 1 panther, and numberless wildcats and foxes. When she returned to Long Eddy she, for a time, resumed the clothing of her sex, but after recruiting her health she again put on male attire and disappeared. She did not retire to the woods, but, assuming the name of Joseph Lobdell, she went about the country making a living

AS A MUSIC TEACHER.

While engaged in teaching [at] a singing school at Bethany, Penn., where she was known, she won the love of a young lady scholar, a member of one of the leading families of the village. The two were engaged to be married, but the sex of the teacher was accidentally discovered, and she was forced to fly from the place in the night to escape being tarred and feathered. Shortly after this she returned to Long Eddy, put on women's clothing, and, being again in failing health, applied for admittance to the almshouse in this place, where her child had been placed some years before. When the child, a bright little girl, was ten years old, it was adopted into the family of a farmer in Damascus, Penn. The mother remained in the poor house.

In the spring of 1868 a woman about twenty-five years of age applied to the poor authorities of Delaware county for

ADMITTANCE TO THE ALMSHOUSE.

She was in miserable health, but was apparently of more than ordinary intelligence, and to all appearances, respectable. She said her name was Marie Louise Perry Wilson. She was from Massachusetts, where her parents lived. She had eloped from home with a man named Wilson, to whom she was married in Jersey City, but who had deserted her, leaving her destitute. She had too much pride to return home. Having heard that her husband, who was a railroad man[,] was in Susquehanna, she had started out to find him, but was taken sick in the cars, and not having money enough to pay her way, was put off at Lordville. No other alternative presenting, she was forced to enter the poor-house. She was taken into the almshouse with the understanding that as soon as she was able to, she could communicate with her family and

HAVE THEM REMOVE HER.

She recovered her health, but in the meantime had made the acquaintance of Lucy Ann Slater. A strong affection sprang up between the two women, notwithstanding the difference in their habits, character and intellect. They refused to be separated, and in the spring of 1869 they left the poor-house together, and for two years they were not heard from in Delhi. In the summer of the above year a couple calling themselves the Rev. Joseph Israel Lobdell and wife appeared in the mountain villages of Monroe county, Penn. For two years they roamed about that section, living in caves and cabins in the woods, subsisting on game, berries and on the charity of the lumbering foresters scattered about in this region. They generally appeared at the settlements leading a bear which they had tamed. The man delivered meaningless harangues on religious subjects, and

PROCLAIMED HIMSELF A PROPHET.

Finally they became public nuisances, and were arrested as vagrants in Jackson township and lodged in Stroudsburg jail. While they were in jail the discovery that the supposed man was a woman was made, and soon afterwards the prisoners were recognized by a raftsman from the upper Delaware as Lucy Ann Slater and Marie Louise Perry, the paupers of Delhi. They were returned to this place. They remained here for some time when they again left, and until 1876 roamed the woods of northern Pennsylvania, leading their vagrant life and insisting that they were man and wife. In 1876 they were living in a cave in Moosic mountains, near Waymart, Pa. Lucy Ann continued her use of male garments. She was arrested one day while preaching in the above village, and lodged in the Wayne county jail. She was kept there several weeks. Her companion finally prepared a petition to the court for the release of her "husband" from jail on account of "his" failing health. The document was a remarkable one, and is still in the records of Wayne county. It was couched in language which was a model of clear and correct English, and was

POWERFUL IN ITS ARGUMENT.

It was written with a pen made from a split stick, the ink being the juice of poke berries. Lucy Ann Lobdell was released from jail. The two went to Damascus township, and in 1877 purchased a farm, which they worked together until a few days since, when Lucy Ann Slater, or Joseph Israel Lobdell, as she insisted on being known, died after a brief illness. She was nearly fifty years of age.

The child that was born to Lucy Ann Lobdell and George Slater was a girl. She found a good home in the family of the former, into which she was adopted, and grew up to be a handsome and intelligent girl. A young man, named Kent, sought her hand in marriage, but his character was not good, and she rejected him. Shortly afterwards, in August, 1871, Miss Slater went from her home to a neighbor's on an errand. When she started home it was dark, and a thunder-storm was coming up. As she was hurrying along the road, she was seized by three men, dragged, grossly maltreated, and taken to the Delaware river and

THROWN INTO THE STREAM.

She was washed up on an island, where she regained consciousness. She was discovered by a man who lived opposite the island and taken to his house. She left there supposing she could find her way home. She wandered into the woods, and, although parties were out searching for her she was not found until three days afterwards. She was insane and nearly dead from hunger. She was returned home, but it was a long time before she regained her reason. Kent and two others were arrested on suspicion of being the parties guilty of the outrage, but nothing could be proved against them. Most people, however, believed that they were the criminals, and they finally disappeared from the place.[6]

This story repeated a familiar tale of female destitution and vulnerability to male perfidy, resulting in a "passing" strategy to secure physical safety and economic survival. The passing itself was regarded as merely "eccentric" and benign, and the marriage of the "female husband" was not marked with deviant sexual desire or pathological psychology. Such marriages were nonetheless regarded as socially marginal and dangerous, as the near tar and feathering in this story indicates. The mid-nineteenth-century passing and marriage stories focused largely on poor and desperate women or sometimes on adventurous ones in distant or exotic locales. The "romantic friendship" story concerned white respectable women and engaged the routine rather than exceptional experiences and observations of the assumed "general public" of female newspaper readers. Accounts of such ordinary passionate friendships were nonetheless laced with ambivalence and danger; they might become too intensely romantic or substitute for marriage.[7] These stories were less likely to include actual passing or planned elopements, though they might include masculine attire or characteristics in one or both partners or homosocial but respectable living arrangements. They were more likely to focus on the psychological states of love or jealousy and to feature emotional conflict or violence within the couple or the family. On June 7, 1879, the *National Police Gazette* told the cautionary tale of Lily Duer and Ella Hearn:

A FEMALE ROMEO.

*Her Terrible Love for a Chosen Friend of Her Own Alleged Sex Assumes
a Passionate Character, that*

BLAZES INTO JEALOUSY

*Of so Fierce a Quality that it Fires Her to the Sacrifice of the Life of the Object
of Her Unnatural Passion.*

A QUEER PSYCHOLOGICAL STUDY.

Pocomoke City, Md., May 28.—The sad tragedy of last November, in which Miss Ella Hearn, a beautiful young girl just blooming into womanhood, lost her life, accidentally or designedly, at the hands of her bosom friend Miss Lily Duer, has again become the paramount topic of interest in this quaint little Eastern Shore town, on account of the trial of Miss Duer on the charge of murder, now in progress at Snow

Hiss, an indictment having been found against her in the first degree by the grand jury, on the 21st, as she refused to allow a plea of insanity to be put in for her.

The widespread publicity given to the startling tragedy at the time of its occurrence through the press, combined with the remarkable features of the distressing affair, will lend to the trial a remarkable interest that will extend throughout the entire country. Snow Hill is full of strangers and the trial is the sole and absorbing topic of conversation. Public sentiment is divided, with the majority of the opinion that Miss Duer will be acquitted. She is now a prisoner in the National Hotel under the surveillance of the officials. Since her removal at the hotel she has borne her imprisonment with comparative cheerfulness, and is allowed the companionship of her relatives and intimate friends under certain restrictions. Her sister is her constant and devoted attendant. She converses pleasantly on every-day topics and local incidents, but now resolutely refuses to allude even indirectly to the tragedy, which has destroyed the peace and happiness of

TWO WELL-KNOWN FAMILIES.

Miss Duer spends her time principally in reading, preferring books of a romantic or poetic character. Byron is her favorite poet. Her friends do not think that she fully realizes the gravity of the charge for which she stands indicted. Able counsel are employed for the prosecution and defense, and the trial promises to be memorable in the record of criminal trials, the circumstances surrounding it being stranger in many respects than a French romance. Miss Ella Hearn, the victim, rests peacefully in the old Episcopal churchyard, her grave, as yet, unmarked save by the green sod and a bunch of roses and sweet violets. Miss Hearn was originally from Laurel, Del., where she spent most of her youthful days, and where her pretty face and sweet ways are remembered by a large number of friends and acquaintances. That she was the fairest and most lovely girl in all the country about is the testimony of all who knew her, and her photographs, which are now preserved as interesting momentoes, with all the defects a country artist could make, warrants one in believing that

SHE WAS REALLY BEAUTIFUL.

Somewhat below the medium height, she possessed a slight, graceful but well-developed figure, and there is a sweet smile lingering about the mouth in the pictures, which is said to have been habitual to her. At the time of her death she was scarcely seventeen. She was a girl of high spirits, and was gay, cheerful and dashing in her disposition. She was highly esteemed among her friends and those who knew her as a young girl of sweet and pure disposition. Although her education was limited to the acquirements possible at the high school at Newtown, she was fairly accomplished, without any brilliant attainments or pretensions.

For some years during the last of her school days she had permitted rather than encouraged a growing intimacy with Miss Lily Duer. The two girls, while not belonging to the "old families," mingled with the best people in town, and were received to some extent in the best circles. Miss Lily Duer is about twenty or twenty-one years of age, and has lived all her life in Newtown. She is by no means pretty, and somewhat awkward in her movements, as though her female habiliments trammeled her, and she would be better able to get about in male attire. Her eyes are large and unflinching, she meets your gaze with a steady, firm, somewhat defiant stare. The face is rather thin and clearly cut, and her forehead is strikingly high and broad. Her thin lips close tightly, which causes the firmness of her expression to

STRIKE THE OBSERVER AT ONCE.

With short and very dark hair parted at the side, she wears a roll at the top of her head. Altogether the face is one which would not fail to excite interest anywhere. She talks quite intelligently, and with ease, appears to have entire confidence in herself and acts as though she would much prefer to be a man than a woman. During last spring and summer the two girls were constantly together, much like sisters. Miss Duer appears to have obtained a mastery over her more womanly but weaker-minded companion, and it was an affection more mixed with fear than love that controlled Miss Hearn's actions.

It seems strange that she could love such an unsexed being as Miss Duer appears, from what is told of her, to be. She would smoke, with the *sang froid* of a Frenchman, and even was fond of tobacco in its other forms. Her dresses were always worn short, and a little jacket with inside pockets, like a boy's, filled with tobacco or licorice, with a boy's hat, which she always tipped when acknowledging a salute, composed the most striking articles of her usual costume. The young girls with whom she associated tell numerous stories of

HER CURIOUS IDIOSYNCRACIES.

She never cared for the society of the sterner sex and would make hot love like a Romeo to her female friends. Sometimes they would laugh these strange fancies away, at others she would frighten them with her vehemence and they would run away from her. She was always a mystery, and a young lady who knew her well says that it was a favorite theory of hers that two women could be quite as happy and get along quite as well married as a woman and a man. In all outdoor sports she excelled all her lady friends, and could jump, shout, and play base ball as well as any young man in the town. She always carried a pistol and was an expert shot.

There was a reception at one of the country houses near the town at which Miss Duer was present. Miss Duer was during the afternoon exhibiting her skill with the pistol, when a lady present rather curtly said that such sport was in no way becoming a woman. Miss Duer said nothing at the time, but the next day wrote a challenge to the fair critic of her target sport, insisting that the insult should

BE WIPED OUT IN BLOOD.

She further demanded that time, place and weapons should be named. No notice was taken of the message and Miss Duer was about to have the lady "posted" as a coward, strictly according to the *code duello*, but was dissuaded by her friends, and the matter dropped. It is said that all of her dresses were made with a pocket for her pistol, and it is certain that she always carried one and was fond of using it. But with all these peculiarities she was looked upon in Pocomoke as a bright, intelligent woman, with queer notions, which time would correct.

The tragedy occurred on the 5th of November last. The professed friendship of Miss Duer had become very unpleasant to Miss Hearn, and every effort was made to break off the acquaintance. Miss Duer chafed at this, and would frequently upbraid her "dearest friend" for the coldness of her manner and the evident weakness of her affection. The truth was that Miss Hearn had reason to fear that her life was not safe while with her. Upon one occasion while the two girls were in the woods gathering fallen leaves for decorative purposes, Miss Hearn started home some distance ahead of her companion, when she called upon her to wait. Not obtaining instant obedience to her somewhat abrupt command she called again quite sharply. This second summons was not heeded, when, without warning, Miss Duer pulled out her pistol and shot twice directly at the now thoroughly frightened girl. When asked why she shot, the only reply was that if she had not halted then the next shot

WOULD HAVE BEEN MORE EFFECTIVE.

From that time Miss Hearn began to be seriously alarmed when in company with her friend, and on one occasion it is related when she, with strange vehemence, asked Miss Hearn if she did not love her and went so far as to actually propose that they should get married she fled from the parlor, where they had been talking, and locked herself in her room. These little difficulties were gotten over finally, however, and the intimacy was renewed, but not so warmly as before. Miss Duer was constantly complaining that "her passionate love was not returned" and sighing over her "lost hopes of bliss with her dearest friend when they would be always together." There was a young man of the town who about this time began to pay marked attention to Miss Hearn, about which Miss Duer remonstrated with her in the most passionate manner, telling her that she would shoot the man that took her friend from her. A Miss Foster was also a friend whom Miss Hearn was very fond of, and the two began to be very close friends. On the morning of the 4th of November Miss Foster and Miss Hearn had taken a walk together, and upon her return home she found a note from Miss Duer requesting her to call at her house, as she wished to see her urgently. Late in the afternoon she went with her little sister and when the two met Miss Duer asked Miss Hearn to take a walk the next day with her in the woods. With the fear of a possible repetition of the former shooting in her mind, she very decidedly refused. This appeared to arouse all the ire of

JEALOUSY OF MISS DUER'S NATURE.

She passionately and upon her knees begged that her request might be complied with, but in vain.

The next day, at an early hour, Miss Duer called at Miss Hearn's house and was shown into the sitting-room where the latter was sitting with her mother. The conversation that occurred in the room was of a general nature, and nothing was said there of the walk. When Miss Duer was about to go Mrs. Hearn requested her daughter to accompany her to the door, and the two girls passed out into the passage. After a few moments had elapsed a shot was heard and Miss Hearn rushed back into the room with the blood streaming from a pistol shot in the mouth. She was immediately placed under medical treatment, when it was discovered that the ball had entered the mouth and lodged about an inch deep near the right upper jaw. Miss Duer had followed her in with a smoking pistol in her hand, but did not remain long. A young man named Clark was near the house and heard the shot, and when he appeared Miss Hearn was lying upon the sofa in the sitting-room, while Miss Duer, in a frantic manner, was rushing about crying wildly, "I have shot her! Oh, my God, she will die!" Miss Hearn lingered for a long time between life and death, being at times

DELIRIOUS AND RAVING.

She would hold up her right arm before her face in her moments of mental derangement, calling out nervously, "Lily, don't shoot, please don't shoot me; I will go with you and always love you." The arm had been bandaged on account of a severe burn, supposed to have been caused by the flash of powder when she was shot.

Miss Hearn lingered between life and death for a month, and at one time seemed in a fair way for recovery, when suddenly she became rapidly worse, and died peacefully and quietly. The coroner's jury who sat on the case were not unfavorably disposed to the accused and returned a verdict that "the deceased came to her death from nervous depression caused by a shot from a pistol in the hands of Miss Lily Duer." Miss Duer then gave bail in $2,500 for trial.

A full statement of the circumstances of the shooting was detailed to the grand jury by a lady who attended Miss Hearn for some time previous to her death. During a lucid interval Miss Hearn talked to her a good deal about it and

RELATED HOW IT CAME ABOUT.

The substance of that statement is as follows: As soon as the door of the sitting-room had been closed, on the fatal morning when Miss Duer called at Miss Hearn's house for an explanation of the "coldness" of the latter, who had accompanied her alone to the hall, as described above, Miss Duer, turning about, looked at her intensely for a moment and said, "Ella, why will you not walk out with me? Do you not love me?" "Oh, yes, I love you," said Miss Hearn, "but I am afraid of you." "Do you love Mr. ———?" To this question she received no reply, when she became very much excited and spoke again quickly. "Do you love Miss Foster better than you do me?" The answer was "Yes!" This appeared to terribly excite Miss Duer, and she rushed wildly about in a terrible state of excitement. "Don't say that, Ella; don't say that," she kept repeating, while Miss Hearn stood rooted to the spot by the vehemence of her manner. Presently Miss Duer came close to her and said, "If you say that again I will shoot you," and took out her pistol and cocked it. Then she appeared to become more calm and seemed to want to "make up" with her now thoroughly frightened friend. She attempted to kiss her, but was repulsed by Miss Hearn, who put out her arms to warn her off. This caused her to slip and fall upon her knees.

SHE WAS THEN FURIOUS.

"She gave me such a fearful look that I shall never forget in my dying day," said Miss Hearn in relating the circumstances. "She pointed the pistol right at my head. I held up my arm to warn it off, and I cried out, 'Oh! don't shoot me, please, Lily; don't shoot me, I will go with you, I will love you.'" But it was too late, and the next second the pistol was fired and the ball had done its deadly work.

Miss Duer, on her part, has declared that the shooting was purely accidental. She says: "I called to see Ella for the purpose of taking a walk. She did not wish to go. I begged her. She refused. I then wanted to kiss her. I had the pistol in my hand after giving up the attempt to kiss her, and was looking at the cartridges counting them, when the pistol went off. I am not a murderess. I visited her twice during her illness. The first time she heard my voice and called me. I went into the room and she received me by putting her arms around my neck. Then she said, 'Lil, what's the matter with me?' I told her that she was hurt. 'Who hurt me?' she asked. 'I, Ella,' I replied.

'IT WAS I WHO DID IT.'

'Then you did not do it purposely, did you?' " Miss Duer denies the statement which has been circulated that she had left Pokomoke City for Baltimore in male attire.

Miss Hearn's statement will probably be ruled out, although it is not improbable that, if it can be proved that her statement to her father to whom she is said to have reluctantly admitted that she knew the shooting to have been done designedly and not accidently, was made when she knew that she was about to die, it will be admitted, and if, as the defense will find it difficult to save her, for a dying declaration in the knowledge or belief of approaching death is very strong legal evidence, and as there were no other witnesses to the shooting and Miss Duer cannot testify, the former's statement will be hard to disprove, if not impossible. Still it is the general belief that she will not be convicted or that, at the worst, the conviction will not exceed manslaughter.

The line of defense will be not that the accused fired in a frenzy, but that the shooting was accidental and without motive, and that her possession of a pistol, however foreign it was to the strict laws of taste, was an habitual possession.[8]

In the wake of the Mitchell-Ward case, such earlier "similar cases" as well as subsequent ones were circulated. Newspaper editors selected from among the tales told locally or published around the nation and featured stories sharing one or more of four central elements of the emerging lesbian love murder story: (1) a contrast between the masculine woman and her feminine partner; (2) a love triangle organizing competition between the masculine woman and a "normal" man over the loyalty of the feminine woman; (3) a marriage plan, often triggering conflict with female domestic or institutional authorities, and (4) violence (most often involving knives but sometimes pistols), leading to intervention by male-dominated institutions of mental management or the state, as well as to widespread publicity. The assembly of these elements was uneven and protracted and drew initially from diverse temporal, geographic, class, and racial contexts. Earlier narratives and many events and characters were integrated into this emerging story, which combined aspects of the Female Husband and Romantic Friendship narratives. Many lost and found stories, as well as newly discovered ones, were interpreted in light of the Mitchell-Ward case and offered for public contemplation in the newspapers. The Duer-Hearn tale reemerged in the *Memphis Commercial* in the midst of Lillie Johnson's habeas corpus hearing:

SIMILAR CASES RECALLED.

Several Noted Instances Characterized by the Same General Features.

The Buffalo Courier recalls the fact that the case of Miss Mitchell, of Memphis, who killed Miss Ward because the latter refused to marry her, is not wholly unprecedented. In October, 1878, Miss Lily Duer shot and mortally wounded Miss Ella Hearn, at Pocomoke City, Md. They had been warm friends, and strange stories were told of Miss Duer's love for Miss Hearn and desire to marry her. It was asserted that one of Miss Duer's letters to the girl she murdered maintained that two women had a right to marry as though one of them was a man. Much was said at the time of Miss Duer's masculine bearing and her dislike for some feminine occupations. She was convicted of manslaughter and let off with a fine of $500. There is a Scottish story of a Miss Macpherson Grant and a Miss Temple who entered into an agreement never to marry, but to live together until death. But Miss Temple weakened and married, and when a year or so later, 1776, Miss Grant died she let her property, amounting to 300,000 [pounds], go to distant kinfolk, although she had previously made a will bequeathing it to Miss Temple. A still more famous case was that of Lady Eleanor Butler, sister of of the Earl of Viscount Duncannon, and Miss Sarah Parsonby. In 1765 these two young women retired together from society, in fact, "eloped" to the vale of Llangollen in Wales, where they passed the remainder of their lives. They became famous, and their home was a place of pilgrimage for sentimental travelers. One of their visitors was Anna Seward, the eulogist of Maj. Andre. She kept up a correspondence with the "recluses" and wrote queer poetry about them. Lady Eleanor and Miss Grant are described in the two stories as excellent horsewomen and somewhat mannish, their companions as pensive and girlish.[9]

This compendium of stories attached distant tales of benign romantic friendship to the more contemporary American stories of Duer-Hearn and Mitchell-Ward, emphasizing the masculine/feminine contrast in all, the triangle and marriage wish in most, and violence in only two of the four accounts. The inclusion of Anglo-European examples, usually British, marked the conglomerate narrative as white and its class context as generally elite.[10] Some "similar cases" came from other locations, however, often marked by those elements deemed most characteristic of the referenced "others" by prosperous white newspaper editors; elements of passion and violence were, implicitly or explicitly, imported from their more customary sites in exotic elsewheres into the story of bourgeois romance via comparisons with the Mitchell-Ward murder. For example, the *Memphis Public Ledger* published a tale of passion and violence in an exoticized "pirate" enclave in Louisiana just after the Mitchell-Ward murder in January 1892:

UNITED IN DEATH.

A Tragedy Almost Identical With That of Monday.

A GIRL'S LOVE FOR A GIRL.

How It Caused a Murder and a Suicide Twenty Years Ago.
A Story of a Fisher Colony on the Northern
Coast of the Gulf Of Mexico

"That killing on Monday was not the only one of the kind that has happened in the South," said an old citizen to a Ledger reporter last night. "Just 20 years ago today one almost identical occurred in C——— Parish, La. I remember the date because I was living there at the time and chanced to be on the Coroner's Jury. The case made such an impression on me that I never could forget even the details of it.

"At that time there lived on a little arm of the gulf that extends about two miles inland, two families named Desplaines and Peroda, who lived by fishing and hunting. It was a great place for red snapper and oysters, and in the season the marshes were alive with woodcocks. . . . Consequently these two families made a good living—at least as good as their lazy habits would let them. They and their fellow-hunters and fishermen of the vicinity were descended from pirates of Lafitte's band, who scattered and settled here and there along the coast after their leader had been transformed from a cut-throat into a patriot by Gen. Andrew Jackson. But they could never get the wildness out of their blood or their dislike for the usages of their more civilized neighbors. The neighbors returned the compliment with compound interest, and the consequence was that the two classes remained as far apart as if they hadn't belonged to the same species. These descendants of the pirate kings were a law unto themselves. They settled their differences in the simple old way, with bullet and blade, and there was none to molest or make them afraid; for no sheriff would have dared attempt to make an arrest in their territory without half the parish at his back, and if he had caught any law-breaker, the whole colony would have sworn him out of custody, in no time. The women were as expert as the men in the handling of . . . weapons and just as ready with knife or gun on occasion. A carpetbag parish official found this out to his cost a few years before my story begins. He got gay with a girl down there and then quit her. A week later his dead body was found floating in the bay. On his breast was a cross cut in the flesh, and, in his heart the point of a very pretty old-fashioned silver mounted dagger that the girl used to carry.

"The Desplaines and Perodas were neighbors and as thick as thieves, as they had a right to be, considering they were only one generation removed from the worst gang of scoundrels that ever flew the black flag, and that the original Desplaines saved the life of the original Peroda on one occasion when the band tackled a Spanish merchantman that happened to have a company of soldiers aboard. The pirates got licked and drew off. Peroda was shot down on the merchantman's deck, and would have been left there, had not Desplaines borne him back aboard his own ship on his brawny shoulders.

"Annette Desplaines was the belle of the settlement. I saw her once, and a prettier creature never made a man's heart go pitapat. Her bosom friend and constant companion was Clara Peroda, a girl of nearly the same age, and a good second in point of looks. Strange to say, Clara was not at all jealous of Annette, so far as the attentions of the young men went. On the contrary, she seemed to think that all the world ought to adore her chum as she did. But for Annette's returning the passion of any of her admirers — well, that was a horse of another color, as you will see. Annette was fond of Clara, but not wrapped up in her, while Clara loved her with the fierce affection that a tiger cat shows for its young. It was the talk of the settlement, accustomed as the people were to lawlessness in feeling and act.

"One day there came to the place a young Spanish creole, who owned an oystering operation in Barataria Bay. His name was Pedro Gomez. He was as handsome as a picture himself and had an eye for beauty in the opposite sex. Annette captivated him at first sight, and before long it began to be noticed that he hung about the Desplaines place more than there was any need for, unless he had matrimony in view. He gave no sign of such an intention, so far as the gossips knew, but he put desperate court to the girl all the same. Clara was his enemy from the first, because he took up so much of Annette's time and thus infringed on what she considered her vested rights. For a month or two Annette seemed indifferent to her admirer, and would only blush when any one attempted to tease her about him. This comforted Clara, and she made no objection to her idol's little flirtation. But a change was coming. Pedro's devotion began to take effect, and it was not long before Clara realized that Annette was looking on him with more favor than formerly. She taxed her friend with the fact, and was answered rather sharply. Thenceforward Annette grew cool toward her comrade and spent more and more of her time in company with Gomez. Clara took the snubs meted out to her uncomplainingly and continued to hang around Annette whenever the father would let her.

"But at length the storm broke and the neglected girl's forbearance snapped under the strain. One evening Annette called at the Perodas and took Clara out for a walk. She was unusually gracious, for she had a secret to tell. It was . . . [that she]was going to marry Gomez at the end of Lent, then two weeks distant.

"Annette expected that Clara would raise a row, and she did. The girl raved like a madwoman and swore she would never live to see another take her place in the heart and society of the pretty Annette. The other tried to quiet her with assurances of her continued regard, and finally succeeded, to all appearances. The two returned home and separated in their usual affectionate manner.

"From that time forth to the close of Lent Clara busied herself with the humble trousseau of her friend, and scarcely left her during the day, but at night, when Gomez' turn came, she wandered about on the shore until her father would come out and order her to bed. The wedding day arrived and everything was ready. The priest had been summoned from the nearest civilized village and the whole colony invited to witness the ceremony and take part in the feast and dance that were to follow. Clara would permit no one but herself to dress the bride, and with the taste in such matters that seems to be the birthright of the Latin races, she worked wonders. If Annette had been charming before she was positively ravishing now. Gomez, too, was rigged out in all his finery, and a more picturesque figure than he was never seen among that picturesque people.

"The wedding was to take place at [7] o'clock in the evening. It was the month of June, when in that climate the sun does not set until nearly 8 o'clock. At half-past 6, when all was ready, Clara begged Annette to take a walk with her to a live-oak grove on the beach where they had spent many happy hours together. The bride did not wish to go. Clara was not in her mind at that time and she was afraid of mussing her pretty clothes. But at last she consented and the two went out together.

"AT [7] O'CLOCK THE GUESTS

began to assemble at the Desplaines home, and in half an hour the house and little yard in front were crowded. The good priest sat out in front in the only arm chair and received the respectful greetings of the assemblage. Gomez came and was much annoyed to learn that his bride was not there. Eight o'clock arrived and still Annette had not returned. Then Gomez and a dozen volunteers went out to look for her.

"She was found only too soon. The search party went straight to the grove, and there under a great oak that stood sentinel on the shore in advance of its companions, they saw two female figures lying in the moonlight in a close embrace. One sprang up at their approach; the other lay still and white in the moonlight. Gomez rushed forward to raise her in his arms, but he had no sooner touched the prostrate form than he shrank back, screaming with horror. The girl was dead. A red splotch on the lace covering her bosom, in the center of which a poignard was sticking, told the story.

"Clara threw herself down by the still warm corpse and caught it up in her arms. 'She is mine,' she cried, 'and you can't have her.' And before they could seize her she drew the weapon from the heart of her friend and plunged it into her own. They buried them in the same grave. A year or two afterward Gomez was lost in a storm on Barataria Bay.

"The double tragedy caused such a stir that for once the fisher people called in the law. At least the priest did, and they consented to it. A coroner's inquest was held on the bodies of the two girls, and I was a member of the jury. That is how I came to know the story I have told you." [11]

Not all such stories of the passion and violence of exotic racialized others was set in the past, however. In February 1892, the *Memphis Commercial* ran a rare account of a relationship between a "mulatto" and a black woman:

INSTANCES MULTIPLY

Mobile Develops a Case that Has Peculiar Characteristics.

Mobile, Ala. — Eleanora Richardson is now lying at her home in this city, between the borders of life and death from seven stab wounds, the most severe being through the lower rib. She will die. She is a handsome and well-formed mulatto, 17 years of age. Emma Williams, a black but comely woman of 23, is in jail, awaiting the results of the wounds she inflicted upon her friend. . . . The motive was a paroxysm of jealousy resulting from an unnatural passion similar to that case in Memphis, which has caused the world to wonder. The two women have been living in the same house for nearly a year. Eleanora says the past six months Emma Williams has been taking the most unusual interest in her. She has been showering caresses upon her daily and hourly, and though both were seen, the Williams girl went to work, and her wages supported and clothed her and the girl. If the Richardson girl spoke to a male acquaintance, the woman would upbraid her, and beg her not to allow any man to ever separate them. If any males called at the house the Williams woman would see them alone, invent excuses and resort to all artifices to prevent any interview with her companion. Last week Eleanora Richardson left the house where the Williams woman was and took up her residence with a married sister in another part of town. Her companion, wretched almost to the point of madness, yesterday afternoon was told by someone who knew of her unnatural infatuation, that Eleanora had left her because she was going to be married. This the Williams woman answered, "Never mind; I'll get her." She went immediately to the girl's house and . . . asked when . . . [she] was coming home. Her companion replied she would be back when her sister tired of her. Bursting into a fury of rage, the Williams woman said: "You are lying and trying to deceive me; you shall never marry that—," and rushing upon her she drew the murderous knife from her stocking and attacked her, plunging the knife into her body repeatedly, saying with each stab "Oh, you darling." The girl's screams finally brought her sister's husband on the scene, and the furious woman was seized and disarmed, but not until she had inflicted wounds which the physicians declare dangerous and possibly fatal.[12]

This story and the tale from the Louisiana "pirate" enclave included the elements of the love triangle and the violence but omitted the masculine/feminine contrast and the marriage plan. The existence of passion and violence fit the white elite view of "Latin races" and black life, but anxiety over gender and domesticity were focused on the white home.

The threat to the white home was figured in the lesbian love murder narrative as located in institutions offering "public" lives to women as alternatives to domestic privacy. The institutions of the *brothel* and the *theater* offered such alternatives across class lines and appeared most typically in versions of the story set in the past or in relatively disreputable or economically deprived circumstances. In March 1892, the *Memphis Weekly Commercial* reached into the barely respectable white working class to tell the melodramatic story of Addie Phillips and the allure of the brothel:

A STRANGE AFFECTION.

Addie Phillips Shows Traces of Alice Mitchell-Fondness.
Another Case Partially Paralleling the Famous One.
She Runs Away From Her Home on Main Street.

Mrs. Garrett Stack, the Girl's Mother, Speaks of Addie's Conduct
Toward a Companion—No Manifestation of Violence.

Sunday before last Addie Phillips, a fine looking young lady 17 years old, and the daughter of Mrs. Garrett Stack, left her home at 151 Main street in company with

Minnie Hubbard, a girl of about her age, who also lives in the tenement house at 151 Main street with her parents. They did not return at night and their parents were very uneasy and immediately sent in search of them. They heard all kinds of reports and began to make a tour of the disreputable dives of the city.

After a day's absence, Miss Hubbard returned to her parents and gave a satisfactory account of herself, which investigation afterward substantiated. She had been visiting some of her mother's relatives.

When questioned in regard to Addie Phillips, she said she had not seen her after the first day, and knew nothing whatever about her. This information startled Addie's mother, Mrs. Stack, and she became almost frantic with grief. She was determined, however, to prosecute her search until convinced as to the truth or falsity of reports that were in circulation. She found Addie yesterday evening, and though she would not tell where, evidently in a questionable resort on the outskirts of the city.

Mrs. Stack was in tears and suffering untold anguish on account of the waywardness of her daughter and her only child.

She told a pitiful tale last night of her daughter's possible downfall.

At reference to the place in which her daughter was found, Mrs. Stack burst into a flood of tears [and] for sometime she was unable to speak.

"I would rather see her dead than know even what I do," she said, "and God knows that I am [in] ignorance of her actual conduct.

"The girl has not appeared to be herself in several months. Within that time she has developed an unusual and even abnormal fondness for Minnie Hubbard. I could not keep her out of her company and, to tell you the truth, I was afraid it would develop into a Mitchell-Ward affair. Addie told me last week that she would rather be dead than be separated from Minnie; she cared nothing whatever for the society of men; at least she said she never expected to marry a man; that if she was rich she would marry Minnie, if it could be done, and if not, then she would buy a place and live with her the balance of her days.

"I have spoken to Mrs. Hubbard, Minnie's mother, about the unnatural affection existing between the girls and begged her to take some steps towards breaking it up.

"I am worried to death over my poor dear child," and at these words Mrs. Stack sobbed bitterly, and again allowed her feelings to control her.

"Where is your daughter to-night?"

"She is at Mrs. Holman's, a friend. I sent her there to get her away and out of my sight until I had time to reflect as to the best course to pursue.

"I educated my daughter carefully, and she was well advanced for one of her opportunities. She attended school at St. Catherine's Academy and at Holly Springs.["]

Mrs. Stack is a woman of fair intelligence. She is employed as a housekeeper at the Young Ladies' Boarding Home, and has served there in that capacity for two years.

She is prostrated and almost frantic with grief over her daughter's waywardness.[13]

The lesbian love murder story, and other narratives of female sexual danger and deviance, developed in relation to the the brothel and the figure of the prostitute throughout the nineteenth century. In close cultural and social proximity, the theater and the actress also played central roles, positioned at the boundary of female sexual respectability. Both settings, tainted as clearly or possibly immoral, provided extrafamilial living arrangements and economic support for some women and produced fearful images of untrustworthy femininity and suspect female masculinity—both referenced by the epithet "fast."[14] The exploits of such "fast" characters were featured in the Memphis Public Ledger's February 1892 story of a male impersonator and her admirers at the local variety theater twenty years earlier:

> The Case of Male Impersonator Marie Hindle,
> Who Beaued the Girls at Broome's Variety Theater. . . .
> Almost a Parallel Case.

Discussion of the Mitchell-Ward murder has brought to light a number of similar cases of abnormal affection existing between persons of the same sex, differing only in that they did not end in the death of one "lover" at the hands of the other. But there was a case of the kind located in Memphis, which narrowly missed being a prototype of that which is now engaging so much attention all over the country. It dates back nearly 23 years, but is still fresh in the memory of citizens who were familiar with the local life after dark of that period.

In 1869–70 the bright particular star of Broome's Variety Theater, on Jefferson Street, was Marie Hindle, a very attractive woman, who played male parts. Nature had especially fitted her for that line of the business. Her features and voice were masculine, and her tastes in accord with her physical peculiarities. Though by no means chary of accepting the admiration of the other sex, she cared nothing for men as such. Her inclination was altogether toward women, and she inspired in them a like feeling toward herself. It was remarked by the stage hands and those among the habitues who were admitted to the inner circle of the performers that Marie was a reigning beau among the petticoat brigade, from the well-paid high kicker to the humblest "chair warmer."

Two of the former class were special favorites of hers. The girls were named Ione and Lizette, both pretty and clever and both madly in love with Marie. She distributed her favor with so much tact that each considered herself the queen bee in the Hindle hive, and neither had any eyes for the male creatures in their train when she was present. They were jealous of each other in a way, but Marie always managed to prevent active hostilities occurring between them. But the fires of rivalry were kindled and only needed occasion to break forth in flame.

The time came toward the close of the season when Marie had made ready to go on to New York to fill an engagement at the Bowery Theater. Ione and Lizette were wild with grief at the thought of parting from her, and would scarcely let her out of their sight. Naturally, each grudged the other a moment of their common idol's time, and jealousy gave place to hatred. When the day of separation came they were wrought up to a pitch that made them reckless of consequences. Both had laid on their war paint and got ready for action.

The night of Marie's departure found them in a state bordering on frenzy. Each had resolved to act as Marie's special escort from the Overton Hotel, where she was stopping, to the train that was to bear her away; and neither was aware of the other's intention. They chanced to meet at the ladies' entrance to the hotel. It was a match to the magazine. Instantly there came an explosion which attracted the attention of several men standing near, one of whom was Dick English, the river editor of the Appeal. He knew of the enmity existing between the two girls, and fearing lest they should do something desperate he ran toward them. By the time he reached the spot they had clinched and were struggling around in the alley. He kept on after them and reached them just as they pulled out knives and began carving each other. He seized them, and with the assistance of another man, who had followed him, succeeded in separating them and wresting their weapons from their hands, but not until both had received ugly slashes on the face and bosom. But for his timely arrival and prompt action there would have been murder done.

Marie Hindle repeated in New York the professional conquests of her Memphis career. Again she became a successful rival of the gilded youth in the affections of the girls of the company and not a few among her audience. One of the latter she singled out for a favorite and they lived together up to the time of her death, which occurred not long ago. After this it was reported, and published in the papers, that she had actually married the girl.

"Mrs. Hindle" was interviewed by a New York paper soon after her partner passed away. She seemed overcome with grief at her loss and said that Marie had been "a dear, good husband."[15]

This story, ambivalently comic, contemptuous, and admiring, emphasized the narrative element of masculine/feminine contrast, with Hindle
clearly positioned as the locus of difference, and her admirers imagined as
any ordinarily feminine members of the variety theater company or audience. This account was unusual in its depiction of violent competition between feminine admirers. Hindle's role as star of the variety theater placed
her at the apex of the triangle; her competition with male actors was imagined as general rather than specifically personal. The story of Hindle in Memphis contained all four elements of the lesbian love murder story, except that
the location of violence was shifted and the marriage set in another time and
place. The danger was also contained on the margins of respectability, set in
the past, and ultimately averted (by a newspaper man!).

The Memphis story featuring Hindle was based on the Memphis appearances of male impersonator *Annie* Hindle (see fig. 6). *Vanity Fair*, a theatrical
newpaper in Lincoln, Nebraska, published another account of her career just
following its report on the Mitchell-Ward murder in February 1892:

MARRYING A MAIDEN!

Can a Woman Legally Marry a Woman?
The Moon-Struck Memphis Maidens and the Sad Ending of Their Love
Annie Hindle and Annie Ryan's Romantic Marriage
and Happy Wedded Life

. . . .

But all girl loves have not terminated so sadly, as the following bit of true history
of a theatrical couple will attest:

From out of the concert halls comes the strangest story that ever was true. There
was a funeral of the Jersey City Heights the other day, and it brought together as
mourners a dozen men and women who were once famous in an odd way on the
American stage. They gathered in the little parlor of a pretty cottage; they sat for
a little while around a handsome coffin; they talked in low and sad voices about
the masses of flowers which were heaped on the bier; they had a good word to say
for the woman who lay dead among the palms, the roses and the smilax; and they
seemed genuinely sorry for the chief mourner. She was a striking person in every
way, says Durandal. Her face was masculine in all its lines; her eyes were gray, but lit
with a kindly expression; her mouth was firmly cut, and though her lips trembled
with emotion one could detect that this mourner was a woman of great mental force
and capabilities. She was probably between 45 and 50 years of age. Doubtless she

Fig. 6. Annie Hindle as she appeared on stage (*New York Sun*, Dec. 27, 1891; reproduced in Laurence Senelick, "The Evolution of the Male Impersonator on the Nineteenth-Century Popular Stage," *Essays in Theatre* 1, no. 1 [1982]: 35)

had been in her prime an excellent type of what is called the dashingly handsome girl. Once, indeed, audiences in every city had gazed in wonderment and admiration upon her, and perhaps she is not yet entirely forgotten; but here she was a mourner by the side of her dead—that dead a pretty woman, and in life the wife of the woman who now shed tears over the coffin. The wife of a woman. The expression sounds absurd, yet it is absolutely, literally correct. Annie Ryan, the wife, was dead, and Annie Hindle, the female husband was burying her. No stage romance in this, no fable of grotesque imagination, but simply proof anew that truth is stranger than fiction. Listen to the facts, told as plainly as one can tell a story that almost tests human credence.

When Annie Hindle was five years old, the woman who had adopted her, and who gave the protégé her own name, put her on the stage in the pottery district of Hertfordshire in England. The little girl sang well even so early. There was a fearlessness in her manner that tickled her rough audiences, and they made a favorite of her from the very first. At the outset she sang tender songs with love as their theme, but as she grew up and traveled to London, she enlarged her repertory. One day, half in jest, she put on a man's costume and sang a rollicking ditty about wine, women and the races. A shrewd manager who listened to her saw a new field open to her. In a week Annie Hindle was a "male impersonator," and all London was talking about the wonderful and minute accuracy of her mimicry. An American manager bargained with her, and about 1857 she went to New York, to triumph there as completely as she had triumphed in London. She was a blonde, about five feet six with a plump form, well shaped hands, small feet, and closely cropped hair, which on and off the stage, she parted on one side, brushing it away from the temples as men do. Her voice was deeper than alto, yet it was sweet, and she sang true and with great expression. She was the first out and out "male impersonator" New York's stage had ever seen. Ella Wesner had not yet ceased to dance . . . in the ballet with her sister; Maggie Weston was yet to come along in the crowded ranks of Hindle's imitators. But in 1867 all the glory was Hindle's, all the novelty was hers, and she got all the money, too.

It is a fact that this dashing singer was the recipient of as many "mash" notes as ever went to a stage favorite of this country. Once she compared notes with H. J. Montague, that carelessly handsome actor at whose shrine so many silly women had worshipped; but Hindle's admirers outnumbered his, and they were all women, strange as it may seem.

Traveling through America, about this time, was Charles Vivian, the English comique. He was a handsome fellow, a ready wit, a free spender, a great entertainer and an admirable actor of the Lingard type. He was famous before he went there, and on Broadway—our Vanity Fair then had a variety house on every third block—he never worked for less than $150 a week. His path crossed Hindle's one night. She was earning as much as he was; she was as famous in one way as he was in another. Their home was across the sea, and there was much in common between them. Charley Vivian speedily fell in love with Annie Hindle. Nobody was surprised. The couple seemed devoted, and they made the courtship brief. On September 16, 1869, Charles Vivian and Annie Hindle were married in Philadelphia. They started at once for the pacific coast, as happy, apparently, as a couple of young doves, yet they did not travel far together. At Denver Vivian and his wife separated. They never met again. He told his friends that their honey-moon had lasted but one night. Hindle has since said that he did not tell the truth.

"He lived with me," she declared bitterly, "several months—long enough to black both my eyes and otherwise mark me. Yet I was a good and true wife to him."

Vivian did not get a divorce. He had no cause. Hindle did not seek one. He was free enough, yet unhappy, and in March, 1880, Vivian died in Leadville. He had not prospered in his latter days. He should have had thousands of friends, for he it was who founded the great Order of Elks. Yet he was practically penniless when he died, and they buried him in an unmarked grave, which waited seven years before the Elks put a monument over it to the memory of their order's founder.

Hindle's strangest romance came later. In all her travels she had carried a dresser. Ella Wesner was once high factotum to this dashing male impersonator, and half a dozen women since known to the stage had at various times since helped to "make up" Hindle and dress her. In the summer of 1886 Annie Hindle's dresser and faithful companion was a pretty little brunette of 25, a quiet, demure girl who made friends wherever she went. She accompanied Hindle to and from the theatre, and she was a most valuable help to the singer. One night in June, 1886, Annie Hindle and Annie Ryan left the Grand Rapids theatre, where Hindle was then engaged, and drove to the Barnard House. In room 19 a minister of the Gospel, Rev. E. H. Brooks, awaited the couple. There was a best man, jolly Gilbert Saroney, who, oddly enough, was a female impersonator; but there was no bridesmaid. At ten o'clock Rev. Dr. Brooks performed the marriage ceremony, and solemnly pronounced Annie Hindle the husband of Annie Ryan. The female groom wore a dress suit; the bride was in her traveling costume.

The minister put a fat fee in his pocketbook, and Mr. Saroney, the female impersonator, and Miss Hindle, the new husband, opened a bottle of wine and smoked a cigarette or two. There was a sensation in Grand Rapids, of course; but the clergyman defended his action manfully. "I knew all the circumstances," he said. "The groom gave me her—I mean his—name as Charles Hindle, and assured me that he was a man. She was a sensible girl, and she was of age. I believe they love each other, and that they will be happy."

The bride was happy, and the clergyman was right; her happiness ended only with her death, for she it was around whose coffin Annie Hindle and her friends gathered the other day in the little cottage on Jersey Heights. For four and five years Annie Hindle and her wife lived in this cozy nest, which Hindle had built years ago with her savings. The neighbors respected them. The outer world did not disturb them with its gossips. That they could live together openly as husband and wife, the husband in female attire always, and yet cause no scandal, is the best proof of esteem in which those around them held them. No children were born to them, and perhaps that is why Annie Hindle, with tears in her eyes, told your correspondent that the best of her life is gone. A man's widow and a woman's widower, is she not a strange figure on the American stage?

Linked to the Mitchell-Ward murder report in the pages of *Vanity Fair*, this benign and even somewhat heroic version of the career and marriage of Annie Hindle appeared as a kind of rebuttal—to the notions that female masculinity was dangerously deviant or that marriage between women necessarily insane. The unpathologized Female Husband was set beside the girl-lover-as-murderer as a kind of counterpoint. To underscore the effect, the *Vanity Fair* stories included an additional local note:

It may not be improper in this connection to state that Lincoln has a couple of ladies so thoroughly devoted to each other that some two years ago a marriage contract was entered into between them, which has since been religiously observed. They are ladies in the highest sense of the word and enjoy the respect, confidence and esteem of their many acquaintances. Their marriage is known to but a few, and is as happy a one as can be found in this city. There will hardly be an application to the divorce courts.[16]

Such counterpoints issued forth from the public sphere of the late-nineteenth-century theater through the theatrical press. Though the theater and its surrounding institutions in some respects echoed the dominant forms of economic, social, and cultural life, in other respects they offered alternative public arenas, especially to white women. The theater did not constitute an oppositional or counterpublic, as the black press or the women's rights movement, for instance, certainly did. But the theater created a space for diverging or dissenting performances of class, gender, and sexual relations, for complexly ambiguous interpretations of actors' speech and acts, and for forms of shared living and economic support outside the white home.[17]

By the 1890s, the theater had departed from earlier mixed-class spaces like the mid-century variety stage, and it increasingly segmented genres of performance and audiences into "high" and "low" forms. In Memphis, Alice Mitchell and Freda Ward attended the respectable theaters, the Lyceum and the Grand Opera House. In fact, the Memphis newspapers noted that they were "stage struck," with extensive fantasies of running off to join a touring company (see the letters in appendix B). Their noted fascination with the lives of actresses was widely shared by young white women in many U.S. towns and cities, who were attending performances unescorted in increasing numbers during the 1880s and 1890s. A fairly extensive periodical literature at the turn of the century worried over the moral future of a huge mixed-class surge of "matinee girls" or "stage struck girls," too many of whom ran away to join theater companies.[18]

Young women were drawn to the lives and careers of actresses despite widely publicized worries and warnings about possible family rejection, unemployment, or exploitation by theatrical agents. Actresses appealed to their fantasies of desirability and romance, and, on the "legitimate" stage, also appeared to combine economic self-support and social freedom within the boundaries of a precarious respectability.

When Alice and Freda attended the theater in Memphis, they might have seen any of a wide variety of dramas, musical operas, drawing room comedies, or melodramas. They were likely to have seen women performing male parts in dramas or comedies featuring both cross-dressed men and women. If not for the crime and trial, they might have seen Sarah Bernhardt appearing in *La Tosca*, *Fedora*, or *Jeanne d'Arc*. The reviews of Bernhardt's performances, running in the same Memphis newspapers that carried reports of Lillie Johnson's habeas corpus hearing, strangely overlapped with accounts of Alice Mitchell's crime. Whether appearing as the cross-dressed Jeanne d'Arc or as the histrionic tragic heroine of *La Tosca*, Bernhardt elicited responses phrased in language almost identical to that used to describe the murder of Freda Ward. *La Tosca*, an opera in which the heroine shows "maddening jealousy" and commits both murder and suicide, was described in the *Memphis Commercial* as a "sensational tragedy" in which a "love sick" Bernhardt produces scenes that are "thrilling, startling, and almost bloodcurdling."[19]

Sarah Bernhardt must have noticed this overlap. She took an interest in the Mitchell-Ward murder and was rumored to be keeping a scrapbook of clippings to present to *La Tosca* librettist Victorien Sardou as the basis for a new opera. One newspaper speculated about which part Bernhardt would play, concluding that Alice Mitchell's was too villainous, Freda Ward's too brief, and thus Lillie Johnson's the only suitable one for the star. The papers also reported that Bernhardt visited the jail but was denied permission to visit with Mitchell or Johnson.[20]

The Bernhardt-Mitchell/Ward/Johnson connection underscored the central role of theatricality in Alice Mitchell's life and in her crime. The emotionalism, spectacle, and sensational narrative of turn-of-the-century romantic melodrama, with its obsession with passion and death, ran through late Victorian lives as well as theaters. Representations of cross-dressing were also a central preoccupation of many different genres of theatrical production. In a circle of connections, Mitchell moved from fascinated spectator, to social actor, to possible model for a "typical" Bernhardt "pageant of vibrant death."[21]

More important still than the brothel and the theater, the prostitute and the actress, in the developing lesbian love murder story were the *girls' school* and the adolescent student, however.[22] The homosocial school was not mixed by race or class, and so it proved the most suitable ground for a story about possible threats to privileged white ideals of gender and domestic life. Alice and Freda began "chumming" at Miss Higbee's School; similar schools provided the setting for innumerable other stories of adolescent female passion. Not all such stories repeated the pathologizing trajectory of the Mitchell-Ward narrative, however. Girls' secondary schools, especially boarding schools, also produced defensive rewritings of the lesbian love murder story.

A typically rewritten account of romance and conflict between young white bourgeois women appeared in a long article published in the *New York Advertiser* and reprinted in the *Memphis Commercial* in February 1892; it was an importantly altered cautionary tale attributed to Letitia LaGrange, a girls' school principal from the Middle States who wrote in response to "that lamentable school-girl tragedy at Memphis" and the "wrong construction" some in the press had put on it:

LIKE MISS MITCHELL

An Infatuation Which Existed Between Two School Girls
Frustrated in an Elopement, One Attempts Suicide . . .
. . . Warning and Advice to Parents

. . . When Blanche's parents brought her to our school and confided her to my care she had just passed her sixteenth birthday. She was of a vivacious disposition and of a will rather inclined to be imperious . . . Blanche was a very high-minded girl. Her ideals were all lofty. Though strangely ignorant of the real significance of love, courtship, and marriage, she was very free with her criticisms of the attitude of men toward women. Her ideas on this subject were plainly derived from the literature of chivalry. . . .

Blanche lost no time in cultivating the friendship of Mary, the sweetest and most angelic of our flock. In disposition Mary was to Blanche as the soft spring rain is to the electricity which explodes and precipitates it to earth. She was of about the same age as Blanche, and equally innocent and ignorant. She seemed to yield with passive happiness to the new friendship held out to her. In a few weeks the individuality of Blanche seemed to have absorbed her individuality completely. They were constantly together, and both were supremely happy.

. . . Mary, like the ideal lady love, was softly and yieldingly affectionate. She leaned upon Blanche, looked up to her and trusted her as one whose strength and courage were wholly to be relied upon. Blanche on the other hand, exhibited the spirit, dash, and valor with the deferential devotion of the knight, the record of whose glorious career rested beneath her pillow. . . .

. . . And when in a gayer mood I have seen her seize Mary unawares in the darkened hall or behind a door to steal a kiss, as is the fashion of more modern lovers. Neither made any attempt to conceal her infatuation from other pupils of the school, and as there were other cases of a similar kind, their behavior occasioned no particular comment. . . .

[Mary goes home to tend her sick mother and returns after several weeks, a changed girl.] Mary had been playing a medley of gay dance music while Blanche stood regarding her gloomily from a corner of the room. Presently she approached the piano, and seizing Mary's hand to hers, exclaimed passionately:

"Mary, Mary, don't you love me anymore?"

"Yes, my dicky bird—passionately," answered Mary gaily.

"But not as you used to," broke in the poor girl.

"Well, if you were a nice young man now, for instance," said Mary, smilingly, "the case would be—"

"Ah, you are false," broke in Blanche, wringing her hands. "You who promised to be true till death! What is it you have in that locket?" she demanded angrily. And while the rest of us looked on too astonished to move, Blanche snatched the gold ornament hanging at Mary's throat, opened it, and with a cry of rage dashed it on the floor. . . . A miniature photograph and a lock of dark hair were broken loose from their frame and lay on the carpet. Blanche stamped upon them and fled, weeping, to her room.

The photograph was that of a handsome, manly-looking young fellow, such as almost any girl might be pardoned for falling in love with. He was Mary's cousin, and it was their growing attachment for each other that had so long delayed Mary's return to school, after her mother had been pronounced convalescent.

Mary's compassion soon overcame her anger. She went to her friend's room and on the following day I noticed that their reconciliation seemed complete. But I was not at all pleased to see that Mary was again apparently under the influence of her irresistible girl friend. Day after day Blanche's attitude toward her grew more and more loverlike. They were constantly together. It was plain that the handsome dark-haired cousin was forgotten. . . . I noticed the sparkle of a little diamond on the third finger of Blanche's left hand.

"Why, what does this mean?" I asked.

"It means that we are engaged," said Blanche innocently. "I am so happy."

"Engaged! To whom?" I demanded.

"Why, to my darling Mary, of course. To whom else?"

I glanced at Mary's left hand. The third finger bore the duplicate of Blanche's diamond. At first I was very much alarmed but gradually, as nothing further happened out of the ordinary, I concluded that my anxiety was groundless. . . .

In later years, when experience had burdened my knowledge of such matters, I would have acted on the warning which was now given in the actions of Blanche. She could not bear to have Mary out of her sight. . . .

[Blanche and Mary then make two attempted escapes from the school. On the first they are quickly caught, but on the second they make it off the school grounds, leaving a note for the principal:] DEAR MISS LAGRANGE: It is useless for you to follow us. We have gone away, Mary and I, to be married, for we love each other, and have sworn never to be separated. Farewell, BLANCHE.

[But the girls are caught in the town and brought back] . . . As Dr. Greene [from the town] came quite close, I saw beside him in his carriage the muffled-up figures of Blanche and Mary, while at their feet was the bundle which the eloping couple had taken with them. Mary was pale and frightened. Blanche was perfectly calm. Neither said a word.

When Dr. Greene drove back to the village he carried two telegrams. They were addressed to the parents of Blanche and Mary respectively, and urged their immediate presence at the school. Mary's parents arrived the next day, much alarmed. They agreed that it was best that Mary be taken home at once.

"Have you any objection to her cousin," I asked, "the manly-looking fellow with the dark hair?"

They had not the slightest objection to him.

"Then," I said, "invite him to your house and Mary will be herself again in less than a week."

It was arranged that Mary's departure should be unknown to Blanche—at least, I supposed I had so arranged it. But the carriage had hardly passed the great gate when the sound of a pistol shot in the north dormitory created a panic in the house.

It was true. Poor Blanche had proven faithful to her ideal of lover, even to the extent of providing herself with the means of self-destruction. I had forgotten that her window commanded a view of the highway. She lay at full length on the floor. In one hand was the smoking pistol, and in the other a photograph of Mary.

The wound was not serious—the shock was even beneficial, for when Blanche was restored to consciousness after the lapse of several hours, she wept copiously, begged forgiveness for her rash act, and willingly accompanied her parents to her home. I learned afterward that a year of travel abroad not only restored her to a proper condition of mind, but supplied in the place of Mary a young gentleman who was in every way worthy of her, and to whom two years later she was happily married.

If the foregoing shall point a moral that will remain fixed in the memories of parents who read it, I am persuaded that they need never bewail such a misfortune as has plunged two Tennessee families into despair.[23]

In this story, the principal was concerned to argue that schoolgirl friendships, even extremely intense ones, were not morbid or pathological but simply based on ignorance and excessively romantic notions. Regulation of them could safely be left to vigilant female authority. She was therefore at considerable pains to portray the students as innocent of sexuality and to provide a suitably happy ending. Nonetheless, the story contains the narrative elements of the masculine/feminine contrast, the love triangle, and the marriage plan. But the violence is averted, and respectable futures await both girls.

The girls' school thus appears, like the brothel and the theater, as a public arena defined within prevailing norms of class, race, and gender; such schools were officially designed to reproduce the white home. But, also like the brothel and the theater, the school produced alternatives to domesticity for privileged white women and even generated political dissent. Such public sites were an ambiguous, shifting blend of dominant and counterpublics, existing both within and against the institutions of white domesticity. The lesbian love murder story worked in relation to such institutions, ambiguously reinforcing official hierarchies while publicizing alternative possibilities. Of the three institutions referenced by the developing lesbian love murder, the school was the most socially homogeneous and homosocial —it became the central referent for stories of same-sex romance among prosperous white women well into the twentieth century.

The lesbian love murder story, developing in the mass circulation press during 1892 and after, featured neither clearly "lesbian" characters nor explicitly sexual relations between women. The parameters of journalistic decorum, and taboos on openly sexualized descriptions of respectable white women, ruled any such explicitness out of bounds during the 1890s. Rather, it produced intimations of an emerging social identity based on same-sex desire among women through the four core, repetitive elements of the narrative.[24] The masculine/feminine contrast implied the possibility of sexual desire "like" that believed to exist between men and women. The contrast also served to split the perceived danger of "girl love" between relatively fixed and identifiable figures who competed with men and the possibly wayward desires of ordinary women. The elements of the love triangle and the planned elopement worked to signify the danger—that partnerships between women might supplant "normal" marriages. The element of violence worked to abort the trajectory of love and household formation, to signal the pathology and destructiveness of alternative passions and domesticities for women.

These elements were assembled unevenly, within an unstable narrative structure that drew its elements from a wide range of other narratives and social "types."[25] Other versions circulated in subcultural sites, within alternative and oppositional publics including urban demimondes, specialized organs of publicity, and a wide range of genres of cultural production. Developing in blues lyrics, prison populations, scientific literatures, or high as well as low literary cultures, narratives of female passion proliferated during the 1890s and later.[26] The lesbian love murder story, with its four core elements, was a privileged version that circulated nationally and marked the emergence of a new recognizably American type—the mannish lesbian or invert, a prosperous white woman whose desires threatened the comfortable hegemony of the white home. Her imagined partner, the normal white woman, shadowed her throughout the narrative's development. Never cast starkly in the spotlight, like Freda Ward she often disappeared from the story altogether. But her centrality to the narrative signaled the anxieties generated by growing alternative publics and the possibility of independence for white women: Might ordinary women reject the terms of marriage and family life, not by nature but by choice?

Oppositional "lesbian" agents and stories did not emerge into widespread publicity until the 1920s. In the meantime, more limited rewritings of the lesbian love murder appeared from within public sites and institutions and insinuated implicit rebuttals and resistant meanings into mass publicity. This instability of the narrative produced complicated possibilities for identification among readers and rewriters. The most hostile, elite-produced version of the story presumed identification with the normal man and his desired but imperiled home, disidentification with the dangerous masculine woman, and ambivalence toward the passively unreliable normal woman. In this reading, female violence must be contained by vigilant male and female authority in defense of the home. But as José Muñoz and Diana Fuss have argued, the paths of identification and desire never proceed straightforwardly;[27] other paths of possible identification, disidentification, and counteridentification appeared, in which female independence might be valorized (as was Annie Hindle's) or nondomestic female authority vindicated (as in Letitia LaGrange's account). Fragments of the narrative were collected from social lives, like Alice Mitchell's, in which violence might be read not as a sign of deviance or insanity but as a marker of overwhelming social opposition and isolation—forces that might be countered with stories of benign female masculinity or respectable and happy women's partnerships.

The mass culture narratives were available to be read, reworked, or reinvented in quite unpredictable ways for a variety of social purposes. The range of readings, and modes of reinvention, expanded as sexually defined subcultures proliferated at the end of the nineteenth century.[28] But the economic, political, and cultural constraints of the mass circulation press defined the terms of the most widely circulated rewritings; the elite white context and its class and race inequalities were generally unquestioned, and the moralizing terms of normality versus deviance, respectability versus degeneracy, remained central. The success of the mass circulation newspapers, for purposes of preserving white elite ideals, lay not in the lesbian love murder's ability to fix a negative portrait of the violent lesbian's deviant desires—this project was always contested and unstable. The narrative's success lay rather in its capacity to shift the terms of contest from the grounds of politics and citizenship to those of morality and normality. This was also part of the success of the lynching narrative's work—to produce a moralizing, normalizing response to white violence and black terror. The narrative solicited opposition framed as a defense of the black home, "normal" black masculinity and domesticity, and black respectability founded in class distinctions, rather than a more direct attack on racializing institutions and political injustices. Though Ida B. Wells and others produced stories and strategies that consistently exceeded such limited "resistance," much black opposition to the lynching narrative and related demonizing tales was focused on producing moralizing practices and stories of black life.[29]

During the 1890s and later, to resist by normalizing gender or moralizing sexuality was to accept the terms of attack, and could not work effectively—then or now—to directly challenge hierarchies of race, class, and gender.

DOCTORS OF DESIRE

There are many women with perverted sexual instincts and a psychosensory insanity who, at each menstrual epoch, become possessed with a strong homicidal impulse, and those nearest and dearest are often the ones to suffer death at their hands, or perhaps anyone who may at the time displease them.

Edward C. Mann, Medical Superintendent,

Sunnyside Sanitarium, 1893 [1]

The developing newspaper narratives of lesbian love murder interacted extensively with the emerging literature of scientific sexology from the 1890s through the first two decades of the twentieth century. Both forms of publication expanded throughout the nineteenth century in Anglo-Europe and the United States, and shared some central structures and features: a precariously professionalizing authorship (in medicine and journalism), a proliferation of varieties (of specialties and news formats), and local and regional client/reader constituencies increasingly imagined as national. But the two literatures of news and sexology also differed substantially, in ways that shaped the nature of their interactions.

The mass circulation press expanded most rapidly and dramatically in U.S. cities, while the literature of sexology appeared first in continental Europe and Great Britain, especially Germany, in a climate of competitive nationalism at the turn of the century. Uneven borrowings across these geographic

boundaries produced concepts of sexuality and new sexual "types" sometimes perceived as nationally distinctive. The formulations and descriptions
of these concepts and types also diverged in language, depending on venue
of publication, following rules of decorum considered appropriate for particular publics. The newspapers circulated to an imagined "general" public,
while scientific medical texts reached a narrower audience of professionals,
plus some proportion of the educated, elite public. The contrast between
these venues was especially marked in discussions of women's sexuality.

News reports and sexology texts also differed in their relative emphasis
on distinct yet overlapping genres of storytelling—the sensational crime report, and the scientific case history. The lesbian love murder and the lynching
narrative, produced primarily as sensational news reports, did not appear
with all their elements of plot, character, and conflict in the scientific and
medical literatures. But they did draw sustantially from "scientific" notions
of race, gender, and sexuality, and they in turn contributed distinctively
American "types" to Anglo-European sexology's panoply of sexual deviants.

Anglo-European sexology emerged during the mid-nineteenth century from
a complex field of scientific, medical, and popular writing about global and
historical human populations. Following several centuries of global coloni-
zation and economic imperialism, the nineteenth-century human sciences
concentrated resources on the project of classifying and rank-ordering the
"races" of people found around the spacial field of the globe. From eighteenth-century comparative anatomy, through nineteenth-century evolutionary biology, paleontology, and anthropology, biological medicine,
alienism, neurology, and psychiatry, to turn-of-the-century genetics and eugenics, succeeding cohorts of scientific professionals devoted their lives'
work to this project.[2]

These myriad professional specialties proposed multiple and conflicting
definitions of "race" and paradigms for classification and comparison. Yet
they also generally had in common the methods of collapsing space into
time and analogizing individual bodies to populations. Relying on a master
discourse of "evolution" after mid-century, the scientific professionals regarded human races and classes as analogous to animal species. They mapped
populations onto a teleological vector of *development* from primitive to civilized. Populations from differing geographical locations were identified as
having reached specific, measurable points on the vector, as were differing
economic, ethnic, or racialized groups coexisting in a single location. Indi-

viduals from within a given group could also be placed on the vector of development, moving from the most primitive point during fetal life to the point characteristic of the individual's group over the course of a lifetime. Groups and individuals might *progress,* as the overall story of evolution proposed, become *arrested* prematurely and fail to reach potential individual or group maturity, or *degenerate* and slide backward to a more primitive condition. This procedure allowed "lower" class Europeans to be compared and ranked in relation to contemporary Africans or ancient Greeks, as space and time, economic change, and physical differences were merged onto a vector of development.

The key term *development* allowed economic domination achieved across space and over time to be interpreted as the naturalized progress of the species, led by superior classes from more evolved races. The mechanism that moved the story of development forward was *heredity,* another key term in the master discourse of sociobiological evolution that allowed the transmission of economic inequality to appear as a natural process, linked to species progress. Groups and individuals inherited their place in human hierarchies through the intergenerational transmission of resources and capacities. The struggles and achievements of biological ancestors might be passed on, contained in the germ plasm of the organism.

The master discourse of evolution, and the key terms of development and heredity, centrally concerned overlapping hierarchies of race, class, nation, ethnicity, and religion evaluated through measures of mental abilities, body configurations (especially skull shape), political formations, and cultural productions. Gender and sexuality were key markers at all points on the developmental vector and for all measures. Gender differentiation was observed to increase from the primitive state of hermaphroditic organisms to the most highly differentiated gender binary of the civilized classes of nineteenth-century Anglo-Europe. Along with this differentiation, an increasing capacity for the finer feelings of romance marked the more civilized populations—as opposed to the senseless protoplasmic hunger or indifferent if repetitive mating habits of the primitive.[3]

This overarching schema embraced widely varying theories of race and civilization throughout the nineteenth century—theories with flexible, contested and changing political valences. The most politically progressive versions featured a neo-Lamarckian stress on environment and pointed to possibilities for change over time that might ameliorate social inequalities. The more reactionary versions emphasized the relatively fixed biological innateness of inequalities or pointed to the need to prevent degeneration by use of coercive restrictions on the lower orders.[4]

Sexology, embedded in this larger field of social-scientific endeavor, grew slowly from the mid-nineteenth century, primarily, though not exclusively, as a minor subspecialty within forensic psychiatry. It ranged outward from a small group of asylum superintendents and courtroom consultants, called upon to determine insanity or criminal responsibility, to include university-based medical and biological scientists, neurologists, or psychiatrists in private practice, as well as an increasingly motley crew of social commentators and reformers. The institutional basis for this loosely defined field shifted from its mid-nineteenth-century medicolegal moorings, focused on the evaluation of impoverished and dependent populations, to the private practices and exclusive clinics more likely to support sexologists' undertakings by the end of the century. This shift in material underpinnings multiplied the tensions and contradictions marking the practices and texts of the profession during these decades. The hostility or condescension that characterized depictions of asylum-housed or prison-bound populations was increasingly mixed with the sympathetic, if ambivalent, treatment of voluntary patients from the educated elite.

The figure most identified with the growth, tensions, and changes in the field of sexology from the middle to the end of the nineteenth century is Richard von Krafft-Ebing (1840–1902), whose *Psychopathia Sexualis* appeared in twelve German editions from 1886 to 1903. Krafft-Ebing began his career as an assistant physician at an insane asylum and branched out from that post to become one of the first expert witnesses for the Austrian and German courts. He began to collect case histories of asylum inmates and accused criminals from his own experience as well as from newspaper reports. As he continued his career as a neurologist in private practice, a university professor of psychiatry, and a director of an exclusive private clinic, he added patient cases from his own practice as well as those of fellow physicians. His first major publication was a textbook of forensic psychopathology for use in Austria, Germany, and France and published in 1875. He followed this with a textbook on insanity, based on clinical observation, published in 1880.[5]

The immensely successful first edition of *Psychopathia Sexualis* reflected Krafft-Ebing's career trajectory. It was subtitled *A Clinical Forensic Study* and included forty-five case histories from his collection, reported and analyzed in 110 pages addressed primarily to forensic psychiatrists, lawyers, and other interested medical professionals. The tremendous success of this first edition, and its wide circulation beyond its intended audience, generated substantial response and correspondence from which Krafft-Ebing selected material for subsequent editions. The text ballooned, including 203 cases by the last edition in 1903—cases more extensively detailed than the brief notes of 1886. The book's classification system also shifted and expanded, as the authorities cited ranged more widely.

This expanded last edition of *Psychopathia Sexualis* repeated the evolutionary framework of the first and reiterated the hierarchies of racial progress, stories of development, and mechanisms of heredity characteristic of nineteenth-century Anglo-European science. But within this framework, the text encompassed pervasive analytical tension and contradiction, to the point of incoherence.

In setting out an overall classificatory system for the major perversions—sadism, masochism, fetishism, and antipathetic sexuality, also called contrary sexual instinct—Krafft-Ebing drew on the work of preeminent theorist of degeneration Benedict Augustin Morel (1809–1873), leading criminal anthropologist Cesare Lombroso (1835–1909), and pioneering neurologist Karl Westphal (1833–1890) in defining them as neuropathic conditions or psychic atavisms, tainted through a hereditary process of degeneration. In his global survey of the perversions, Krafft-Ebing demonstrated how these diagnostic evaluations were to be differentially applied. In primitive races and lower orders of the European population, perverted behavior might be characteristic of the arrested evolutionary development of the entire group and not an indication of individual pathology. Among the advanced classes of the civilized, however, perversion indicated either pathological degeneration or individually arrested development. The result was a hazy, unstable distinction in the text's analytical framework between vice or immoral perversity, most characteristic of those lowest on the vector of development, and the condition of perversion, which might be found without hint of vice at the higher end of the vector. Krafft-Ebing's text then equivocated as to whether the conditions of perversion might be regarded as diseases to be treated or as unfortunate but natural anomalies to be understood and tolerated.

Krafft-Ebing's ambivalence toward the condition of civilized sexual perverts drew, for its positive valence, on the pioneering theories of Karl Ulrichs (1825–1895) and the extensive research and polemics of Magnus Hirschfeld (1868–1935).[6] Ulrichs's writings, published between 1865 and 1879, influenced all twelve editions of *Psychopathia Sexualis* and contributed concepts and arguments to the field of sexology well into the twentieth century. Ulrichs described a variety of man-manly love and defined its practitioners as Urnings, or members of a third, intermediate sex characterized by male bodies with female psyches. Urnings, including Ulrichs himself, represented nonpathological anomalies of nature whose sexual feelings were not immoral but instead often spiritual and noble. Ulrichs argued that such feelings should not be considered evidence of disease or criminality.

Ulrichs, and later John Addington Symonds (1840–1893) and Edward Carpenter (1844–1928) as well as Hirschfeld,[7] resisted the pathologizing evolutionary narratives of sexual deviance as arrested or degenerate by countering the vertical vector of development with a horizontal scale of benign variation. And where pathologizing accounts featured metaphors of reversal of the natural gender binary for some perversions, such as antipathic sexuality, contrary sexual instinct, or sexual inversion, Ulrichs and his legatees invoked a kind of gender pluralism through metaphors of intermediacy.

This strategy of resistance did not work equally for all perverts or perversions, however. Embedded in the overall evolutionary schema, the horizontal scale and intermediate types were located across the top. The defense, which rested on claims of virtue, fine romantic feeling, intellectual achievement, and moral worth, was mounted on behalf of Anglo-European men of the civilized classes. Those races, ethnicities, or classes lower on the vector of development were rarely credited with any of the qualities invoked in Ulrichs's defense of the Urning. Even Edward Carpenter, whose romantic utopian theories of natural variation substantially upended the vector of development, reiterated many aspects of the evolutionary model. Though he found nobility and virtue among "primitive" folk, and considered sexual variation among them innocently natural rather than perverse, he nonetheless retained the primitive/civilized scale and framed his defenses primarily around the fine qualities, high achievements, and sensitive natures of civilized intermediate types. In addition to these limits, all of the defenses of perversion, from Ulrichs to Carpenter, applied only to those termed antipathic, contrary, inverted, intermediate, third sexed, or homosexual—conditions that together might include the contemporary identity categories of transgender, transsexual, transvestite, homosexual, bisexual, or intersexual. Other perversions cataloged by sexologists, from nymphomania and satyriasis to sadism, masochism, or fetishism, were seldom defended.

The place of women in both the pathologizing and naturalizing frameworks for the perversions was profoundly vexed. The development of civilized femininity, and deferential behavior toward women, constituted a central marker of evolutionary progress. The term "women" itself tended to reference privileged Anglo-European groups; those lower on the vector of development were more likely to be called "females." But even the most prosperous civilized women were considered less evolved than the men of their nation, ethnicity, and class and could not fully embody the mental, cultural, and productive achievements of civilization. Though Anglo-European women of the privileged classes gained access to education and many of the professions during the nineteenth century, their access was far from equal. So while the pages of sexology texts like Krafft-Ebing's were increasingly filled with extensive case histories and even first-person narratives of male perverts, inverts, Urnings, and "aunties" who were identified as clergymen, doctors, and gentlemen of "high social position" as well as artists and writers, there were few cases of women, and none in the first person before the publication of the first edition of Havelock Ellis's *Sexual Inversion* in 1897.[8]

When women appeared in sexology texts under case listings for antipathic or contrary sexual instinct or inversion, their positioning in the story of evolutionary or racial progress was especially contradictory. For a woman's physiology, psyche, or behavior to be described as in any way "like" a man's raised a perplexing conundrum: Was she like a man of her class and therefore a "higher" type than if she were "normal"? Was she "like" a man of a lower position and therefore a degraded or degenerate female? Or was she a freak of nature or, more benignly, a quirk or anomaly to be placed on a horizontal scale between male and female, like the Urning?

The sexologists, from the most conservative to the homophile reformers, equivocated and at times flatly contradicted themselves. But they also proliferated classification schemes and explanatory frameworks that were expansive and flexible enough to contain contradictions, and to stretch to accommodate observations of an increasingly visible social world of multiplying gendered embodiments, sexual styles, and relational practices. Krafft-Ebing, for example, divided cases of antipathic sexual instinct into acquired and congenital forms and divided each of these into grades extending from psychic hermaphroditism, to inversion, and on to androgyny or gynandry. The boundaries among the forms and grades were blurred; cases might be narrated to fit any number of slots. And as Judith Halberstam has argued, the details of the cases always exceeded the taxonomic imaginations of sexologists.[9]

The texts of Anglo-European sexology were therefore expansive, contradictory, multivocal, and politically ambivalent. They contained pathologizing attacks on populations of perverts, imagined and real, but they also contained a naturalizing if not normalizing homophile discourse right from the start. This defensive discourse emphasized that Urnings or inverts were represented among civilization's most respected citizens and displayed crucial qualities of civilized interiority—feeling, morality, creativity, self-restraint, and the capacity for self-articulation. These Urnings were to be distinguished from those whose unreflective lives of vice and immorality justifiably excluded them from civilization's highest benefits. This discourse therefore applied most completely to privileged men, more partially and ambivalently to privileged women, and not at all to races and classes mired in primitive inarticulate unselfconsciousness.[10]

The Alice Mitchell–Freda Ward murder case entered the literature of sexology through the U.S. mass circulation press and Frank Sim's extensive recounting of the story and the courtroom scene in his *Memphis Medical Monthly* article (which was the source for Krafft-Ebing's addition of the case to later editions of *Psychopathia Sexualis*).[11] It was taken up within a relatively small and derivative U.S. medical literature on the subject of sexuality, which began to appear with a trickle of articles during the 1880s.[12] Many of these early articles were summaries or reprints of European publications. Among the first to include a U.S. case history was P. M. Wise's account of Lucy Ann Slater, alias Rev. Joseph Lobdell.[13] Lobdell had entered the Willard Asylum for the Insane, where Wise was an assistant physician, in 1880—a year after the *National Police Gazette* story appeared (see chapter 5)—in an apparently deteriorated physical and mental condition. Wise's report described excited and confused behavior that he diagnosed as "erotomania" and "dementia," and it also supplied a brief life history, mentioning Slater/Lobdell's book about her adventures and her reputation as "The Female Hunter of Long Eddy." But she was not described as simply an eccentric Female Husband, as she had been in the press. Wise presented her as "a case of sexual perversion" and described her marriage as an instance of "Lesbian love." He quoted Krafft-Ebing but argued against his opinion that "these sufferers should be excepted from legal enactments for the punishment of unnatural lewdness." Wise then continued on to argue that "true sexual perversion is always a pathological condition and a peculiar manifestation of insanity," though "[t]he subject possesses little forensic interest, especially in this country, and the case herewith reported is offered as a clinical curiosity in psychiatric medicine."

Within a decade, such cases were no longer regarded as curiosities. The number of cases reported and the volume of the U.S. literature on the subject of sexual perversion had increased dramatically, though the American branch of the field remained much less developed than the European until well after 1900. No major book on the subject was produced by an American, though a small number of American writers, largely European-influenced neurologists, did publish original material such as P. M. Wise's case. Their contributions were scattered among the medical journals—including older journals like *The American Journal of Insanity*, general medicine publications such as *The Medical Record* or *The New York Medical Review*, and the newer neurological publications like *The Journal of Nervous and Mental Disease*. Most of these journals published only a handful of articles on sexual perversion and inversion or homosexuality from 1880 to 1900, with only a handful of writers appearing in many different journals.

One journal took a rather dramatic lead. The *Alienist and Neurologist* published more than twenty articles during this period, by far the highest concentration of material on the subject in any U.S. medical journal. The *Alienist and Neurologist* featured the work of those Americans whose writing on sexual perversion and inversion was most ubiquitous and influential—especially the journal's own editor, Charles Hughes, and the uniquely prolific James G. Kiernan.

Charles H. Hughes, M.D., of St. Louis, was president and Professor of Neurology and Psychiatry of the Barnes Medical College, as well as editor of the *Alienist and Neurologist*.[14] He spoke and published widely on the subject of the sexual perversions and was among the primary conduits in the United States for the ideas of Krafft-Ebing, Westphal, and other Europeans. He first addressed the Alice Mitchell murder case in an editorial published as the trial was in progress during July 1892 and framed as a direct response to continuing press reports:

Alice Mitchell, the "Sexual Pervert," and Her Crime, are now being psychically and medico-legally considered before a Memphis, Tennessee, court and jury. Her trial began on the eighteenth instant, and her counsel have interposed the plea of insanity, to avert the legal penalty for murder of her fated female fiancé Freda Ward.

The newspapers are discussing, and have discussed this case as if it were a foregone conclusion that a woman who, possessed of the reversed sexual instinct, or the erotism of a man in a woman's organism, the *contrare sexualempfindung* of Westphal, the man's brain in a woman's body of Kiernan, and dominated by that feeling toward one of her sex as a man be toward the woman he loves, and making no resistance to its imperious sway and inspired by jealousy, destroys for strong motive the object who having once returned her love suddenly ceases to requite it, by transferring it to another, is necessarily insane. . . .

. . . Novices in psychiatry who never had any considerable experience in the treatment of insanity, will not be wanting, doubtless, who on the trial may boldly say, the act establishes Alice Mitchell's mental status, but this will not be the testimony of authority, nor will it be a reasonable deduction from the history of the thus far recorded cases.

It is not the dictum of psychiatry that a flagrant crime like that of murder, perpetrated for revenge or jealousy, or both, by a sexual pervert is of necessity an insane act. . . .

Alice Mitchell may or may not be insane, but the facts concerning her which have thus far been made public, or rather which have come to us through the public press, have not been sufficient to fix her mental status as an impossible lunatic, though they do seem to establish sexual perversity, but so are sodomy, pederasty or what the law calls the unnatural *crime* of buggery. Their perpetrators are moral perverts not lunatics. . . .

. . . Gentlemen, neurologists, brother alienists, let us pause and consider before we conclude that irresponsibility is a necessary sequel to reversed sexual feeling unrequited and revenged in murder. If this is always insanity, then is extreme normal love, vented in violence upon the object of the opposite sex who responds not reciprocally? And if Alice Mitchell was insane, then what was the mental condition of her dead associate, for the testimony says, "they loved each other alike?"

The court and jury may find Alice Mitchell to have been insane, but will her insanity be that popular insanity which shields the wayward, passionate scions of the wealthy and influential or that undoubted mental disease of which the murder of her companion was but one expression— . . . In the light of all facts thus far made public it would seem that the insanity of Alice Mitchell is still a mooted and mootable question. Yet this girl may be insane, but if she should be insane it will be because of other facts than that of contrary sexual feeling.[15]

Besides misstating the legal facts of the case (Mitchell's attorneys did not plead "not guilty" by reason of insanity but asked that she be declared unfit to stand trial), Hughes blurred the conditions of sexual perversion described by Krafft-Ebing and Westphal with categories of illegal vice or moral perversity, including sodomy and buggery. His mixing and matching of warring terminologies broke down the very distinctions that defined and ordered the emerging field of sexology, but such confusions were characteristic of much of the literature—especially in the United States.

In a theoretical article, "Erotopathia.—Morbid Erotism," Hughes considered the Mitchell case more extensively, within a broader context. He laid out the evolutionary framework and noted the difficulty of distinguishing between perversity and perversion:

> We make no plea here in extenuation of genesic perversity, lust, rapine, pederasty, homo-prostitution, etc. Disease does not ordinarily originate them. It only sometimes exceptionally excuses them. Salacity and sexual perversity may be solely immoral with no excuse in disease or pre-natal organic perversion. Sexual orgies the most revolting may co-exist with erotic disease on the part of some and without disease on the part of others who participate in them, as the London orgies of 1885, the Manhaters' dance in Berlin and the floral festivals honoring the prostitute Flora of Ancient Rome. . . .[16]

In taking up the demanding task of making such distinctions, a task clearly requiring scientific expertise, Hughes sometimes echoed the vocabulary and concepts of the Europeans, but he often also turned to biblical references or to terms and assumptions derived from earlier medical frameworks or from popular or literary sources. He described Zola's novel *Nana* as featuring a "tribadist" and argued that such practices were often introduced in insane hospitals by nymphomaniacs, sexual perverts, pubescent lunatics, hysterics, and imbeciles.

Newspapers were among Hughes's most important nonmedical sources. He quoted extensively from the Mitchell trial coverage and recounted another similar case from the Indianapolis press:

> Two girls are arrested in the streets of a western city (Indianapolis, June 27th) whose erotopathia simulates that of Alice Mitchell and Freda Ward, without, thus far, the tragic ending of the latter. Their names are given as Delia Perkins and Ida Preston. They had run away from home together because of their love for each other. Delia had cut off her hair and offered it for sale in order that she might obtain money on which to help defray the joint expenses of herself and the loved Ida. When Delia's step-father was summoned by the Chief of Police to come for his run-away daughter, she threatened to kill him, and when he came treated him coldly. To her step-father's importunities to go back home with him she only finally agreed on promise of being permitted to see Ida whenever she should desire to, imprinting burning kisses upon the cheeks and lips of the paramour of her own sex on parting. These

two devoted girls had been together almost constantly since their departure from home and they had not been in the company of gentlemen. The intense and active passion seemed to be on the part of Delia, Ida being reported as regarding the matter "as a huge joke." When Delia was returned home the following colloquy took place with her mother (now Mrs. Mendenhall):

MOTHER: "You will not run away again, will you?"

DELIA: "Not if you let me go with Ida."

MOTHER: "That I will not do."

DELIA: "Then I will kill myself and you will be responsible."

MOTHER: "Don't say that. We will try to make you happy and you must try to forget all about Ida. I can't understand why you do not forget this foolish fancy and fall in love with a man and marry him."

DELIA: "I do not care for the best man that ever walked, and never will. Ida is the only one I ever loved and I will continue to love her until I die, and if we are not allowed to go together, *I will kill myself and her too.*"

Miss Perkins told the reporter that she had not left home because she had been mistreated, but because of her love for Ida Preston. "My parents refused to let me go with Ida," said she, "and I decided to be with Ida, let the consequences be what they might."

Miss Preston stated that she had been met in the street by Miss Perkins; that the latter said she was tired of staying at home and said she was going to leave.

"I didn't want to leave home," said Miss Preston, "but Delia told me she loved me so dearly that if I did not consent to go with her she would kill herself and me, too. I like the girl, but don't believe I care as much for her as she does for me." [17]

Through such cases, the lesbian love murder narrative entered the pages of the medical press, where physicians searched for similar stories and end-lessly recirculated those they discovered. Hughes referenced an article by his associate James Kiernan:

In Kiernan's contribution to our subject, to which we have already referred, another homicide resulting from this perverted passion is cited in the person of Miss D., a young lady of Pocomoke City, Maryland. An attempt was made to break off the relationship, and an engagement was entered into with a young man, where-upon Miss D. shot her "lover" dead. She was tried and found guilty of "manslaughter in heat of passion."

This account of the Lily Duer/Ella Hearn case, reported in the *National Police Gazette* in 1879 (see chapter 5), was followed by references to an instance of "another violent Lesbian lover whose passion passed into the insane delusion of being with child by the woman she loved" and to "several instances of actual marriage as man and wife between women." [18]

Such reports in the medical literature, taken either directly from the newspapers or secondhand from other medical articles based on news stories, varyingly included some or all four elements of the lesbian love murder narrative: the masculine/feminine contrast, the triangle, the marriage plan, and the violence. But medical articles, addressed to an elite and insular profession engaged in classifying sexual types, generally stressed the case histories of individuals rather than the plots of stories elaborated in the press. The medical writers also added sexual specifics that the newspapers only obliquely referenced. For cases drawn from the newspapers such inclusion required speculation. In the case of Alice Mitchell and Freda Ward, Charles Hughes queried:

How much may not mutual masturbation have had to do with the development of a morbid and perverse erotism in both? Libidinousness, impurity and lascivious sensuality are developed in this way, and by early and bad companionship and salacious literature.[19]

An article on the Mitchell-Ward case in the *Medical Fortnightly* elaborated this hypothesis with more detail:

This masturbation probably began alone, was taught to her school-girl friend, mutual masturbation followed, then the well-developed perverted sexual love with all its disgusting details, was the almost inevitable result. From this came the desire to consummate the unnatural love by marriage, the enforced separation, the breaking up of a habit which had made sexual monsters of the two maidens—then the climax—murder.[20]

Of course such speculations characteristically blurred the distinction between environmental and hereditary causes of perversity versus perversion. In the overall context of the medical literature, the distinction was nonetheless hazily made between populations prone to vice and perversity, who occupied the lower rungs on the vector of development, and populations who might be said to suffer from an involuntary condition—the difference was romance. Though Hughes speculated about Mitchell's sexual activities and fantasies with or without Freda Ward, he did not doubt that the tale was one of love gone awry:

Alice Mitchell and Freda Ward, two young women, loved each other, "not wisely, but too well." Their love culminated in a matrimonial engagement as between man and woman. . . .[21]

Romance was not attributed to "primitive" populations, or to degenerate, if elite, denizens of vice-ridden demimondes. As the lesbian love murder narrative worked its way into the medical literature, it contributed to the emergence of a new type—a woman whose sexual deviance was marked primarily by *feelings* that distinguished her from the prostitute, criminal, primitive, or degraded female. Her difference was not sited in her sexual actions, interpreted as signs or symptoms of deviance, but in her being, located in both body and psyche from which the telltale feelings arose. Though these distinctions were fluid, and at moments vice, disease, and anomaly were indistingishably conflated, the romance of the lesbian love murder story generally marked its characters as respectable "girls" in trouble.

The lesbian love murder narrative appeared within the medical literature in relation to other types and stories that shaped its meanings. First-person narratives and naturalizing defenses appeared primarily via citations of the European sexologists; a rare American treatise by Edward I. Prime Stevenson, author under the pseudonym Xavier Mayne of *The Intersexes: A History of Similisexualism as a Problem in Social Life,* was printed privately in Italy in 1908 and circulated very narrowly.[22] Such defenses, which coexisted with pathologizing theories and moral condemnations, applied almost exclusively to privileged Anglo-European men. At the other end of the vector of development, the U.S. medical literature repeated the Anglo-European evolutionary framework but also added special American preoccupations with indigenous populations and black people. In his 1893 article, Charles Hughes quoted eminent New York neurologist William Hammond on the subject of the "mujerado":

The Pueblo Indians are in the habit of selecting some one male from among those living in a village and rendering him sexually impotent, reserving him at the same time for pederastic purposes. This person is called a mujerado. . . . A mujerado is an essential person in the saturnalia or orgies in which these Indians, like the Ancient Greeks, Egyptians and other nations indulge. He is the chief passive agent in the pederastic ceremonies, which form so important a part in the performance. . . . For the making of the mujerado one of the most virile men is selected, and the act of masturbation is performed upon him many times every day; at the same time he is made to ride almost continuously on horseback. From over-excitement comes abolition of the orgasm, the organs atrophy, the temperature changes, and he becomes assimilated with the female sex, perhaps at first with reluctuance, but finally with entire complaisance and assent.

Hughes then remarked that "[s]anity in a savage may be lunacy in a civilized being," and he quoted James Kiernan to argue that "[t]he Zuni 'mujerado' is hence not the evidence of either immorality or insanity it would be in an Anglo-Saxon race."[23]

Discussions of black sexuality in the same articles were more consistently hostile and pathologizing than the patronizing, voyeuristic imaginings of Native American practices. In a note appended to "Erotopathia.—Morbid Erotism," Hughes described "an annual convocation of negro men called the drag dance, which is an orgie of lascivious debauchery beyond pen power of description" in Washington, D.C.:

> In this sable performance of sexual perversion all of these men are lasciviously dressed in womanly attire. . . . Standing or seated on a pedestal, but accessible to all the rest, is the naked queen (a male), whose phallic member, decorated with a ribbon, is subject to the gaze and osculations in turn, of all the members of this lecherous gang of sexual perverts and phallic fornicators.
>
> Among those who annually assemble in this strange libidinous display are cooks, barbers, waiters and other employees of Washington families, some even higher in the social scale—some being employed as subordinates in the Government departments.[24]

In 1907 he followed up this report with a "Note on a Feature of Sexual Psychopathy" in the *Alienist and Neurologist*:

> Male negroes masquerading in woman's garb and carousing and dancing with white men is the latest St. Louis record of neurotic and psychopathic sexual perversion. Some of them drove to the levee dive and dance hall at which they were arrested in their masters' auto cars. All were gowned as women at the miscegenation dance and the negroes called each other feminine names. They were all arrested, taken before Judge Tracy and gave bond to appear for trial, at three hundred dollars each signed by a white man.
>
> . . . The names of these negro perverts, their feminine aliases and addresses appear in the press notices of their arrest, but the names of the white degenerates consorting with them are not given.
>
> Social reverse complexion homosexual affinities are rarer than non reverse color affinities, yet even white women sometimes prefer colored men to white men and

vice versa. Homosexuality may be found among blacks, though this phase of sexual perversion is not so common or at least has not been so recorded, as between white males or white females. . . .[25]

Needless to say, romantic feeling was not a feature of Hughes's fantasies of these proceedings.

Such racializing reports were ubiquitous in the psychiatric journals. Few articles there repeated or responded to the lynching narrative directly, however, as was more common in medical articles under the broad rubric of turn-of-the-century eugenics. F. E. Daniel, M.D., editor of the *Texas Medical Journal* in Austin, argued in 1893 for castration as the appropriate eugenic puninshment for rape, sodomy, bestiality, pederasty, and habitual masturbation. He suggested that punishment "to lessen the evil of transmission of vice, disease, and the propensity to crime" and offered it as an alternative to capital punishment, including by lynching:

It may be answered that capital punishment does fulfill two of the ends; it prevents a repetition of the offense, and stops hereditary transmission; but that it lessens crime cannot be admitted. After the abolition of the death penalty for rape in England the crime greatly increased; but in Texas, although the offense is visited with swift retribution, and often a cruel death is inflicted by a mob; yet rape, and that too, in its most horrible, cruel and revolting form, that of tender young girls, is greatly on the increase. Not a newspaper can be picked up that does not contain the announcement of something of the kind, and it is by no means confined to Texas. Even the horrible execution by fire of the wretch at Paris, Texas, seems to have been forgotten, if it has not, indeed, *acted as a suggestion or excitant*, to that incomprehensible race, the negro, so different from his immediate progenitors of only one or two generations ago.[26]

Though Daniel's position was extreme and unusual, even for eugenicists in the South,[27] his views were not outside the mainstream of medical discussion. The *Texas Medical Monthly* article included a summary of other physicians' views, including those of G. Frank Lydston, a prominent U.S. specialist in genitourinary and venereal diseases, a professor at the Chicago College of Physicians and Surgeons, and the author of a widely cited classification scheme for the sexual perversions:[28]

. . . Dr. Frank Lydston (*Va. Medical Monthly*) in reply to a question from Dr. Hunter McGuire as to the cause of so much rape by negroes in the South, advises castration as a remedy for the evil; and there is much wisdom in the advice. He would castrate the rapist, thus rendering him incapable of a repetition of the offense, and of propagating his kind, and *turn him loose*—on the principle of the singed rat—to be a warning to others. Dr. Lydston says, and very truly, that a hanging or even a burning is soon forgotten; but a negro buck at large amongst the ewes of his flock, minus the elements of manhood, would be a standing terror to those of similar propensities.[29]

Daniel wrote at the intersection of eugenic and sexological discourses in 1893. He remained primarily within the frame of reference of hard-line eugenics, but he also referenced Krafft-Ebing and other European sexologists in arguing for the "powerful influence of the sexual sense," which in the healthy person "dominates life, and is the great incentive to action, to the acquisition of property, the struggle for social eminence, and the foundation of a home." His objective—to locate the threats to property and the white home—led him to focus on an especially wide range of sexual perversions. He noted that "in light of the Alice Mitchell case it might be well enough to . . . asexualize all criminals of whatever class."[30]

In Daniel's article, the Mitchell case was only briefly referenced and lumped into the undifferentiated mass of crimes and perversions. More commonly, the Mitchell-Ward story appeared in more elaborated form along with "similar cases." The lesbian love murder narrative, thus assembled, stood uneasily at the boundary between vice and perversity on one side and the natural romantic intensities of normal elite white women on the other. The figure of the lesbian killer, allied with masculinity, expressed the danger of romance out of its gendered place; the figure of the "passive" or "feminine" partner expressed the fear that any white woman might be susceptible. Though the element of violence marked the lesbian love murder's characters as pathological and dangerous, and set them off from the honorable Urnings of Ulrichs, the element of romance distinguished them from females of the "lower" races and classes.

The most prolific and influential U.S. sexologist, James G. Kiernan, circulated this typical framework throughout the international medical press, helping to integrate American cases with Anglo-European theories. His career followed the common trajectory for sexologists from asylum work and forensic experience to neurological practice and university-based research. After receiving his medical degree from New York University in 1874, Kiernan worked as assistant physican at Ward's Island Asylum in New York until 1878. He then moved to Chicago as Superintendent of the Cook County Insane Asylum. During the next decade he held a series of chairs in nervous and mental disease at Chicago medical schools, taught forensic psychiatry at the Union Law School, and contributed to a long list of general medical and neurological publications. He appeared as a witness in the notorious Guiteau trial in 1881 and wrote extensively on issues of the criminal responsibility of the insane.[31]

In his earliest articles on sexual perversion, Kiernan reported on the writings of Ulrichs, Westphal, and Krafft-Ebing, and he began summarizing and numbering their cases, adding to them the handful of cases reported by Americans during the 1880s. From the beginning he exhibited a particular interest in female sexual inverts, devoting more space proportionately to such cases than to cases of male inverts or any other perversions. In an 1884 article in the *Detroit Lancet* he summarized a case of Westphal's as well as P. M. Wise's 1883 article on Lucy Ann Lobdell, and he also contributed a case history from his own practice.[32] Alice Mitchell first appeared in one of his most ambitious articles, "Responsibility in Sexual Perversion."

This 1892 article provided a typical rhetorical mixture — an extended discussion of the evolution of the sexual instinct, from the primitive protoplasmic hunger of the amoeba through savage human lusts, to the romances of the civilized races; charts detailing G. Frank Lydston's and Krafft-Ebing's classification systems for the sexual perversions; and a series of numbered case histories. The cases included Lucy Ann Lobdell, Alice Mitchell, and Miss H. D. (who must have been the *National Police Gazette*'s Lily Duer), "a young lady of masculine tastes" who " 'loved' another young lady also of Pocomoke City, Md." Kiernan concluded with reference to the source of many of his case reports:

> It should be remembered that sexual pervert crimes of all types are likely to increase, because of newspaper agitation of the subject, among hysterical females, from a desire to secure the notoriety dear to the hysteric heart.[33]

More than twenty years later, Kiernan was still invoking the same notorious lesbian love murders in his column for *The Urologic and Cutaneous Review,* headlined "Sexology." In 1916 he wrote:

> . . . Since the dramatic sex-invert homicide of Hattie Deuel at Pocomoke City, Md., in 1878, followed by that equally sensational one by Alice Mitchell of Memphis in 1892, female sex invert manifestations of all kinds have been much exploited by the press. Attention has been attracted to it. As a result sex invert friendships not hitherto viewed with alarm have been suspected by mothers. In an Illinois town

the mothers dreaded girl friendships with a local poetess more than intimacies with young men. The androphobia, so to speak, of the deeply ingrained sex invert has led to her leadership in social purity movements and a failure to recognize inversion. Such inverts see no harm in seduction of young girls while dilating on the impurity of even marital coitus.[34]

But by 1916 he was also responding to the claims of Havelock Ellis (1859–1939), the most influential sexologist since Krafft-Ebing, that sexual inversion was increasing among Americans. Though Kiernan labored to refute the English sexologist's claim, his own reports of U.S. cases based on newspaper stories had in fact shaped Ellis's conclusions. In the 1915 edition of *Sexual Inversion* Ellis recounted a series of U.S. cases:

. . . Inverted women, who may retain their feminine emotionality combined with some degree of infantile impulsiveness and masculine energy, present a favorable soil for the seeds of passional crime, under those conditions of jealousy and allied emotions which must so often enter into the invert's life.

The first conspicuous example of this tendency in recent times is the Memphis case (1892) in the United States. . . . In this case a congenital sexual invert, Alice Mitchell, planned a marriage with Freda Ward, taking a male name and costume. This scheme was frustrated by Freda's sister, and Alice Mitchell then cut Freda's throat. There is no reason to suppose that she was insane at the time of the murder. She was a typical invert of a very pronounced kind. Her mother had been insane and had homicidal impulses. She herself was considered unbalanced, and was masculine in her habits from her earliest years. Her face was obviously unsymmetrical and she had an appearance of youthfulness below her age. She was not vicious, and had little knowledge of sexual matters, but when she kissed Freda she was ashamed of being seen, while Freda could see no reason for being ashamed. She was adjudged insane.

There have been numerous cases in America more recently. One case (for some details concerning which I am indebted to Dr. J. G. Kiernan, of Chicago) is that of the "Tiller Sisters," two quintroons, who for many years had acted together under that name in cheap theaters. One, who was an invert, with a horror of men dating from early girlhood, was sexually attached to the other, who was without inborn inversion, and was eventually induced by a man to leave the invert. The latter, overcome by jealousy, broke into the apartment of the couple and shot the man dead. She was tried, and sent to prison for life. A defense of insanity was made, but for this there was no evidence. In another case, also occurring in Chicago . . . , a trained nurse lived for fourteen years with a young woman who left her on four different occasions, but was each time induced to return; finally, however, she left and married, whereupon the nurse shot the husband, who was not, however, fatally wounded. The culprit in this case had been twice married, but had not lived with either of her husbands; it was stated that her mother had died in an asylum, and that her brother had committed suicide. She was charged with disorderly conduct, and subjected to a fine.

In another later case in Chicago a Russian girl of 22, named Anna Rubinowitch, shot from motives of jealousy another Russian girl to whom she had been devoted since childhood, and then fatally shot herself. The relations between the two girls had been very intimate. "Our love affair is one purely of the soul," Anna Rubinowitch was accustomed to say; "we love each other on a higher plane than that of earth." (I am informed that there were in fact physical relationships; the sexual organs were normal.) This continued, with great devotion on each side, until Anna's "sweetheart" began to show herself susceptible to the advances of a male wooer. This aroused uncontrollable jealousy in Anna, whose father, it may be noted, had committed suicide by shooting some years previously. . . .

The infatuation of young girls for actresses and other prominent women may occasionally lead to suicide. Thus in Philadelphia, a few years ago, a girl of 19, belonging to a very wealthy family, beautiful and highly educated, acquired an absorbing infatuation for Miss Mary Garden, the *prima donna*, with whom she had no personal acquaintance. The young girl would kneel in worship before the singer's portrait, and studied hairdressing and manicuring in the hope of becoming Miss Garden's maid. When she realized that her dream was hopeless she shot herself with a revolver. . . .[35]

These cases sat like an undigested lump within what Siobhan Somerville has called Ellis's hybrid text.[36] Though educated as a physician, Ellis never practiced. He did not come to sexology with the asylum or courtroom experience of many of his predecessors, though his first book, *The Criminal* (1890), drew on the criminal anthropology of Lombroso.[37] He made his career as a writer, beginning his lifelong study of sexuality with the first edition of *Sexual Inversion* (1897).[38] He uneasily combined a naturalist's emphasis on nonjudgmental observation of benign variation with the framework of an evolutionist and the concerns of a eugenicist. Influenced strongly by his coauthor of *Sexual Inversion*, John Addington Symonds, as well as by Ulrichs, Hirschfeld, and his personal friend Edward Carpenter, Ellis penned strong arguments for legal and cultural tolerance for the invert.[39] But he combined such pleas with the vocabulary of abnormality and degeneration derived from Krafft-Ebing.

Though *Sexual Inversion* included far fewer female than male cases of inversion, it contained the first women's first-person narratives to appear in the published cases of the sexological literature. Ellis's wife, Edith Lees, helped collect the women's cases for him. An invert herself, her own case history was also recounted in her husband's text. Altogether, Ellis's six numbered cases of female inversion did not feature the violence of the American newspaper reports that also appeared in the book. They shifted the portrayal of women inverts more in the direction of the naturalized Urning, but the histories and analysis were nonetheless still more negative, reductively generalizing, and ambivalently pathologizing than those in the men's cases.

Ellis disputed the congenital versus acquired distinction that marked most sexologists' discussions of inversion, stressing that such conditions (as opposed to vices) were generally congenital. In describing female inverts, Ellis insisted that they were characterized by some degree of masculinity, in body and psyche. This theoretical strategy worked to fix the female invert as an identifiable type, decidedly differentiable from normal femininity. But in his case histories, Ellis recounted numerous contradictory instances of ardent "womanly" partners of more markedly masculine or even only boyish inverts. He labored to resolve this contradiction:

A class in which homosexuality, while fairly distinct, is only slightly marked, is formed by the women to whom the actively inverted woman is most attracted. These women differ, in the first place, from the normal, or average, woman in that they are not repelled or disgusted by lover-like advances from persons of their own sex. They are not usually attractive to the average man, though to this rule there are many exceptions. Their faces may be plain or ill-made, but not seldom they possess good figures: a point which is apt to carry more weight with the inverted woman than beauty of face. Their sexual impulses are seldom well marked, but they are of strongly affectionate nature. On the whole, they are women who are not very robust and well developed, physically or nervously, and who are not well adapted for child-bearing, but who still possess many excellent qualities, and they are always womanly. One may, perhaps, say that they are the pick of the women whom the average man would pass by. No doubt, this is often the reason why they are open to homosexual advances, but I do not think it is the sole reason. So far as they may constitute a class, they seem to possess a genuine, though not precisely sexual, preference for women over men, and it is this coldness, rather than lack of charm, which often renders men rather indifferent to them.[40]

This residual category, required to shore up the portrait of inversion without implicating "normal" women, addressed the competitive anxiety of the "normal" man rather obliquely by arguing that the partners of inverts were women likely to be passed over by men. Ellis's textual anxiety may or may not be related to the fact that as he began his work on *Sexual Inversion*, his wife was simultaneously embarking on her first serious affair with a woman since their marriage.[41]

Ellis thus included the versions of the lesbian love murder narrative derived from U.S. press reports, but he reworked the competitive triangle of invert–normal man–normal woman in his case histories and analysis. Ellis's cases of female inversion were not violent; they posed less of an immediately dangerous threat to the Anglo-Saxon home. The threat they still posed was contained in Ellis's text with notions of congenital abnormality, mixed with defensive condescension.

Ellis's text repeated the evolutionary framework in a less starkly judgmental but still hierarchizing mode. His cases of inversion were nearly all from the privileged classes. His discussion of female inversion thus marked a shift over time in the preponderance of cases from the asylum-based populations and forensic interests of the earliest reports, such as P. M. Wise's article on Lucy Ann Lobdell, to the love murder stories involving respectable women like Alice Mitchell, to the speaking inverts who appear in *Sexual Inversion*. This shift in preponderance did not involve a fundamental change in the overall framework for analyzing the sexual perversions, however. The latter kinds of cases did not supersede the earlier kinds, nor did they emerge over time as parallel discourses. The privileged invert of homophile reform emerged more distinctly over time, but she always appeared in relation to vice-ridden or criminal, primitive others. The discourse of sexuality that defined the speaking invert in the texts of sexology was from its inception interarticulated with hierarchies of race, class, and gender. The homophile discourse embedded within the contradictions of sexology depended for its coherence on the discourses of morality, crime, and disease, in relation to which, and in terms of which, its pleas were constructed.[42]

The sexologists served up a strong brew of materials gathered from fiction, fantasy, clinical experience, newspapers, and autobiographical reports. The resulting vocabularies, concepts, and frameworks were influential beyond the scope of professional scientific, medical, and legal interests. But their categories and theories never dominated the social or cultural landscapes.

They were constructed in relation to the social world and reflected the stories and "types" of social life. The figure of the unusually masculine, elite woman in pursuit of more ordinarily feminine women was not an invention of the sexologists. Anne Lister's diaries, for instance, record strikingly similar representations from the early nineteenth century.[43] By mid-century when sexologists' texts proliferated, many modes of embodiment, experiences of desire, and forms of relationship organized social worlds in Anglo-European cities, and by the end of the century in U.S. cities as well.[44] The sexologists condensed these multiple forms into the types charted by their byzantine classification schemes, and interpreted them from the point of view of those authorized to speak as professionals. Readers, writers, and patients participated, contributing ethnographic detail and appropriating ideas.[45] The narratives of social life thus interacted constantly with those of many varieties of texts, including sexological tomes, though not in an open-ended or egalitarian give-and-take. The most subordinated and deprived populations appeared entirely as objects, never as subjects of sexological discourse.

The literature of sexology thus operated as an interactive public sphere, though in a more constrained arena than the mass circulation press or the courtroom. In referencing other public spheres in their discussions of women's sexuality, the sexologists tended to repeat the press's emphasis on the dangers of the brothel, the theater, and the school, though the European literature also referenced convents and U.S. writers worried over women's social reform organizations. When lesbianism was linked to prostitution, the language emphasized vice and immorality as well as physical or mental abnormality. The theater appeared in discussions of the dangers of cross-dressing or as a site of heterosocial leisure offering abundant opportunities for female immorality. But sexologists centrally featured the school as the primary location of elite female homosociality, lending itself not only to the predations of inverts but also to "epidemics" of sexual desire among students.[46] Sexologists' focus on these public spheres highlighted the contradiction between their description of a fixed type of female invert and their observations of rampant sapphic desire in nondomestic, collective settings.

When Sigmund Freud (1856–1939) published his article "The Psychogenesis of a Case of Homosexuality in a Woman," in 1920, the prosperous young woman featured desired a prostitute, an actress, and a teacher.[47] For all its departures from the theories of sexologists, and its particularly crucial abandonment of the vocabulary of degeneration, Freud's psychoanalysis nonetheless repeated many features of the earlier literature, such as this emphasis on homosocial public spheres as magnets for or generators of alternative desires and domesticities. Though psychoanalysis more fully psychologized sexuality, and more fully naturalized and normalized the sexual perversions than any of the sexologists' frameworks during this time period,[48] Freud's theories still invoked an evolutionary model (especially in *Totem and Taboo*) and a vector of psychosexual development.[49] The biological theories of sexology inflected Freud's discussion of universal human *drives*, and the sexological stress on the central diagnostic importance of feelings over acts influenced the psychoanalytic concept of *libido*.

Like psychoanalysis, some of the social sciences and U.S. social studies of the early twentieth century emphasized the role of environment, focused on prosperous white populations, and pointed to a plurality of sexual experiences rather than a sharp divide between the normal and abnormal. Most notably, beween the pioneering sexual surveys of Magnus Hirschfeld and the groundbreaking researches of Alfred Kinsey published during the 1950s, Katherine Bement Davis's *Factors in the Sex Life of Twenty-Two Hundred Women* established that homosexual experience, defined as feelings only or as also including actions, was widespread among "normal" educated white women.[50]

But the discourses of vice and disease, and the contradictory presumptions of biology as the primary ground for behavior, did not recede, to be replaced by more enlightened theories. They remained powerfully present in religious and moral arenas, in the mix of social and biological studies of insane, feebleminded, imprisoned or impoverished populations, and in popular conceptions of the aberrations found among "other" races, nations, and classes. During the first half of the twentieth century, reformers and professionals located lesbian vice or pathology in women's prisons, where such relations were often represented as characteristically and alarmingly interracial.[51] Biological theories of sexuality, both pathologizing and naturalizing, were also rejuvenated by the eugenics movement and by the new sciences of genetics and endocrinology during the early twentieth century.[52]

The sexually defined subcultures that proliferated during the twentieth century produced new vocabularies, types, and explanatory frameworks, many of them complexly intertwined with the evolutionary frameworks of sexology, as well as some quite independent of them. Elements of the lesbian love murder story reappeared in cultural productions expressive of such subcultures, less prominently in popular forms like the blues,[53] and more clearly in the forms produced and circulated by readers of mainstream newspapers and sexology—forms such as literary fiction.

A THOUSAND STORIES

In the newspaper accounts of Memphis' strange
love-murder there is a vivid background upon
which mystery-story writers might base a thousand
stories, but the scientist-writer sees nothing
thrilling in the bizarre killing . . . .

D. O. Cauldwell, *Sexology* (1950)[1]

The "continuum of publication" surrounding the Mitchell-Ward trial included newspaper stories, medical articles, and legal summaries, all of
which were inextricably intertwined with fiction.[2] In addition to the imaginative and fantastic elements constitutively embedded in the genres of sensationalism, legal storytelling, and scientific sexual classification, writing
about the Mitchell-Ward murder referenced French novels from the very
start and eventually included English-language novels, stories, plays, and
even a ballad.[3] And during the late 1920s and after, the lesbian love murder
narrative was decisively transformed by the impact of a novel—Radclyffe
Hall's *The Well of Loneliness*.

The intersections and interactions among mass circulation newspapers,
scientific reports, and differing formats and genres of fiction circulated versions of the lesbian love murder tale through the overlapping territories of
"high" and "low" culture. Newspapers marketed to urban workers drew references from elite European fiction, narrowly circulated professional medical articles collected data from sensationalized news reports, and writers of
fiction absorbed plots and concepts from courtroom testimony. The lesbian
love narrative, chameleonlike, changed its language, forms of address, and
generic features as it traveled through these interacting circuits of culture

and communication. But it also developed and transported its central elements across multiple cultural locations.[4]

Beginning with the first reports of the murder in 1892, both the newspapers and the medical journals noted that this case seemed to echo the plots of novels by Honoré de Balzac, Théophile Gautier, Gustave Flaubert, Adolphe Belot, and Émile Zola, which were beginning to appear in widely available U.S. editions during the 1890s.[5] Those plots became resources for the elaboration of the elements of the lesbian love murder story, headlined as "A Tragedy Equal to the Most Morbid Imaginings of Modern French Fiction,"[6] and for accompanying moralizing pronouncements or "lessons." As physician G. Frank Lydston humbly noted in an editorial on the Mitchell-Ward case:

... a layman has done more to bring the subject of sexual perversion, as illustrated in the Mitchell-Ward case, before the public than has any scientific physician.[7]

The layman was Adolphe Belot, the writer most often mentioned in connection with the Memphis murder case. Belot's novel *Mademoiselle Giraud, Ma Femme* began as a serial in *Le Figaro* in 1870 and was published in several editions in book form by 1880. Possibly drawing on Karl Westphal's 1869 publication of a case of "contrary sexual feeling" in a woman,[8] Belot's novel featured a relationship begun in a girls' boarding school. The central character, Paule, marries but continues her sapphic liaison until she dies from brain fever (ostensibly brought on by the affair); her husband then murders the more aggressive "reptile," Mme. Blangy, with the approval of M. Blangy. Though Belot's plot did not include the masculine/feminine contrast or the elopement plan of the lesbian love murder, the setting of the girls' boarding school, and the erotic triangle resulting in murder, resonated with the Mitchell-Ward case in the minds of newspaper and medical writers—though the normal man, and not his female rival, committed the violence in Belot's story.

Théophile Gautier's much earlier novel, *Mlle. De Maupin* (1835), was cited nearly as often as Belot's. Gautier's story of a cross-dressing orphaned heiress, who has affairs with both men and women, was supposedly based on the life of seventeenth-century actress Madeleine Maupin d'Aubigny, but it bears a closer resemblance to Gautier's acquaintance in Paris, George Sand. The central character describes herself as a "third sex" with many "masculine" qualities—she is tall, wide shouldered and slim hipped, skilled in riding and fencing—that attract more feminine women as well as some men. But Maupin's masculinity is not positioned within a consistent masculine/feminine contrast, nor is she portrayed as embroiled in violence-producing love triangles. The novel was associated with the lesbian love murder through the setting of the theater and the elements of cross-dressing and erotic fluidity.[9]

Other French novels mentioned in connection with the Mitchell-Ward murder and "similar" cases during the 1890s included Honoré de Balzac's *The Girl with the Golden Eyes* (1835) and Émile Zola's *Nana* (1880). Balzac's plot featured a triangle resulting in the murder of the beautiful girl of the novel's title. The girl is held prisoner by a wealthy marquise, until she is discovered and seduced by the Marquise's half brother, then murdered in a jealous rage by her captor. Zola's fictionalized life history of a courtesan included sapphic relations and premature death from the excesses of vice but no violent triangles. Neither novel organized its sapphic relations around a masculine/feminine contrast, though Balzac presented a starkly active/passive pairing, and Zola depicted the Paris demimonde as having a coarsening and masculinizing effect on its female denizens.[10]

The mass circulation press in the United States, and the Anglo-American medical journals, turned to French novels for reference in assembling the lesbian love murder story, noting repeatedly that no American authors produced any similar literature. The cited French works were available in English translations for the U.S. market by 1900. After the turn of the century, a larger international literature of sapphism, inversion, or lesbianism grew along with public controversy, including significant contributions written in English (though these were largely by British authors, published after 1915).[11]

The French novels mentioned as the lesbian love murder narrative was assembled focused primarily on vice, degeneration, and violence, with the notable exception of Gautier's adventuring heroine. None of these novels centered on respectable romance with the obsessive interest of nineteenth-century English domestic novels, which featured representations of intense friendship between women as well as the ubiquitous marriage plot. This element of elaborated romantic feeling characterized an extensive female-authored literature of romantic friendship in English, from Mary Wollstonecraft's *Mary, A Fiction* (1788) to Florence Converse's *Diana Victrix* (1897) and Gertrude Stein's *Q.E.D., or Things as They Are* (1903). Such novels generally defended, and sometimes celebrated, intense emotional attachments between proper bourgeois Anglo-American women; they also often depicted the failures and frustrations of women's relationships with men.[12] They avoided representing overt sexuality between women, though many were laced with intensely erotic language and sexual implications. And though they portrayed jealousy and competition between women's friendships and their marriage ties, they did not explicitly sexualize these rivalries.[13]

The Mitchell-Ward story, and the lesbian love murder narrative elaborated through it, drew both from representations of intense, ambiguously sensual, though spiritual and noble attachments between girls, and from more explicitly sexualized language and images — like those of the French novels or the medical articles on sexual perversion. Soon after 1892, the Memphis news reports and medical analyses of them began, in turn, to produce fiction more directly based on the particular plot, characters, and details of the Mitchell-Ward murder.

In 1895, an obscure novel published in Austin, Texas, and clearly based on the Alice Mitchell case, became one of the earliest American defenses of "satisfaction of the erotic desire" between two women. Dr. John Wesley Carhart's *Norma Trist; or Pure Carbon: A Story of the Inversion of the Sexes* drew from both the newspaper accounts and the recent medical reports.[14] The lead character, Norma Trist, is the daughter of a wealthy Texas widow. She becomes infatuated with her music teacher, Mrs. Marie LaMoreaux, a widow who is beautiful, young, and cultured. When Norma is sent to Maplewood Young Ladies Seminary in Massachusetts, her passionate letters to Mrs. LaMoreaux are intercepted by the faculty, who find them mystifying. Carhart explains that they have never heard of a "pathological psychical vita sexualis," because American literature in philosophy, science, and fiction is "entirely barren" of enlightenment on the subject. Norma graduates as valedictorian and returns to find Mrs. LaMoreaux engaged to be married to a Spanish captain. She stabs her former teacher. Every daily newspaper in the country covers the crime with headlines such as:

A GIRL MURDERS HER FEMALE LOVER
SEXUAL PERVERSION
A GIRL IN LOVE WITH A WOMAN
KILLS HER IN THE PUBLIC STREET[15]

Mrs. LaMoreaux recovers, marries, and leaves for Mexico, while Norma is declared insane in court and committed to the Austin, Texas, asylum. The publicity surrounding the attempted murder leads a few "investigators and original thinkers" to turn their attention to reports of other such cases in courts and the casebooks of physicians.

When the superintendent of the asylum determines that Norma is not insane, she is returned for trial on the charges against her. Her defense is that her love for Mrs. LaMoreaux is natural to her (though abnormal to the majority), and that the "jealous frenzy" behind the stabbing was no different than the "transports" of jealousy for the opposite sex that so often motivate transient acts of desperation. This defense is expressed by several characters at the trial. Her attorney argues:

. . . a state of psychopathia sexualis might exist, and frequently does exist between one man and another, and between one woman and another woman. It might be congenital or it might be induced or acquired.[16]

Norma herself takes the stand to argue that her love is "as pure as the deepest, purest, most God-given passion between two of the opposite sexes can possibly be, and I may modestly say, as intelligent," and that it is "according to the profoundest and most irresistible instincts of my nature. . . ." When the prosecutor asks if her relations with Marie brought her "perfect satisfaction," Norma replies with what Jonathan Ned Katz has called the most explicit defense of genital-orgasmic relations between women published in English during the nineteenth century:[17]

Norma, apprehending the exact purport of the question, and wishing to relieve him from all embarrassment, said:
"I understand you to mean satisfaction of the erotic desire?"
"That is what I mean."
"I have no hesitancy in answering frankly and freely, that my love for and relations with Marie afforded the highest and profoundest satisfaction of which the entire human being is capable in the realm of human love."[18]

This unusual, early, ringing defense is followed, however, by the "cure" of Norma by a Dr. Jasper, who has determined that she is a noncongenital case who can be treated with hypnosis. She marries, has children, and leads a life of "bliss."

This novel assembled a defense of the "invert" that clearly called on the homophile discourses of Ulrichs, Hirschfeld, and others whose concepts and ideas were embedded within nineteenth-century sexology. Carhart's characters mobilize the argument that "inverted" feelings and acts are "natural" to a minority of the population, and use it to attack the link between female inversion and violence seemingly established in Norma's case (and Alice Mitchell's). They argue, along with some of the newspaper editorialists and medical writers who commented on the Mitchell case, that jealous violence is no more caused by an invert's sexual nature than is an ordinary passionate attack on a sweetheart caused by the love of the "opposite" sex.[19] Of course, the impact of this defense is limited by the last-minute conversion of Norma—though Dr. Jasper also asserts that "congenital" cases cannot be cured and are deserving of sympathy rather than censure.

Carhart's sapphic-slasher story closely echoed the details of the Mitchell-Ward case but replaced the "chumming" friends with a romance between a girl and an older teacher bearing a suspiciously French name. Carhart also imagined a new ending to the Mitchell story, allowing the stabbing victim to recover and Norma to be found sane and ultimately curable. This rewriting of the lesbian love murder story thus repeated its four central elements but downplayed, displaced, or deferred their impact. The masculine congenital invert does not appear in the story but is invoked by a physician; the triangle exists but is not thematized through development of the male rival in the plot (who is exoticized as Spanish and exiled to Mexico); and the violence is committed but does not result in murder. The novel appeared, like the Mitchell case itself, as a kind of hybrid form between the French novels' narratives and English-language tales of respectable, intense female love.

According to Lillian Faderman's study of romantic friendship, *Surpassing the Love of Men*, there were two other fictional publications probably written with the Mitchell-Ward murder in mind—one novel and one short story, both published by women in 1895.[20] Mary Hatch's *The Strange Disappearance of Eugene Comstock* featured a cross-dressing heroine/villain portrayed with marked authorial ambivalence: she spends time in Paris, participates in robberies, breaks male and female hearts, and ultimately commits suicide. This portrayal seems influenced primarily by the French novels, however, rather than by the U.S. newspaper stories. Hatch's heroine is alternately attractive and repulsive, presented in a manner much more reminiscent of Gautier's Mlle. de Maupin than of the Alice Mitchell of American news reports. The path from cross-dressing to crime to suicide may very well have been influenced by those reports, however.

Hatch was a relatively obscure novelist, but Mary E. Wilkins Freeman was well known and highly regarded as a "local colorist" at the turn of the century.[21] Her 1895 story, "The Long Arm," is a mystery surrounding the murder of the father of the narrator, Sarah Fairbanks. The details of the story seem to owe at least as much to the widely reported case of Lizzie Borden (which also occurred in 1892) as to the Mitchell-Ward murder. Like Borden, Sarah Fairbanks is charged with her father's murder but is released for lack of evidence (Borden was acquitted for this reason).[22] Unlike Borden, Sarah succeeds in removing the town's continuing suspicion of her by solving the case, with the help of a detective disguised as a book agent. The guilty party is Phoebe Dole, whose housemate and partner for forty years, Maria Woods, was planning to marry Sarah Fairbanks's father.

Though the murder story and its connection to the women's relationship may have been influenced by the Mitchell-Ward case, or by the publicity given to many "similar" cases in the early 1890s, it did not repeat all elements of the lesbian love murder story as closely as Carhart's novel. There is no elaboration of romantic intensity between the women housemates—the story is of the detective genre rather than the domestic romance. Phoebe Dole is presented as a "proper" lady; she and Maria have separate bedrooms, and their relationship bears no trace of sensuality. Dole's evil, and her violence, is linked to her determination to dominate Maria—a determination shown as being parallel to the determination of Sarah's father to dominate *her* and prevent a marriage she greatly desired.

It is the motive Freeman assigned to Phoebe Dole that most resonates with the Mitchell case. Phoebe declares as she confesses her crime to Sarah Fairbanks:

> She was going to marry your father—I found out. I stopped it once before. This time I knew I couldn't unless I killed him. She's lived with me in that house for over forty years. There are other ties as strong as the marriage one, that are just as sacred. What right had he to take her away from me and break up my home?[23]

Phoebe is also described as more athletic and masculine than the weaker Maria. But Freeman doesn't link Dole's crime with her sexual nature or her appearance; she links it to her frustration at her failure to control Maria. Dole is presented as an evil individual, whose domineering ways and determination to maintain her "home" lead to the murder; she is not portrayed as a recognizably pathological "type."[24]

Neither Carhart's novel nor Freeman's story are domestic romances; both focus more centrally on the crime story. But both contain marriage plots, ultimately successful for both female characters in *Norma Trist* and aborted by the murder in "The Long Arm." The marriage plot, the central feature of the English-language domestic novel throughout the nineteenth century, produced notions of psychic interiority and privacy linked to the domestic gender relations and to the racial and national interests of emergent imperial classes. As Nancy Armstrong has argued, following Foucault, these domestic novels did not merely reflect the marriage practices of the privileged, or offer trivial distraction for idle bourgeois women, but actively worked (in company with other material and cultural institutions) to refigure relations of economic and political power through innovation in representations of self-regulated subjects—subjects whose personal virtues might dependably support newly dominant institutions for love, work, and global domination.[25] Marriage, ostensibly private and personal, lay at the core of this complex of institutions, as well as at the center of the domestic novel.

In the United States as well as Britain, marriage laws and practices operated as linchpins at the intersection of economic and political institutions regulating race and reproduction, and defining the American nation. At the end of the nineteenth century, the limited democratization of marriage laws —expanded to apply to black citizens after the end of slavery and to accommodate women's increasing independence—led to a perceived "marriage crisis," as limits, frustrations, and conflicts surfaced in literary and popular culture.[26] The simultaneous spread of education and literacy expanded the markets for fiction as well as the pool of novel writers. These novel writers and readers addressed the marriage crisis and simultaneously struggled over the racial definitions and hierarchies of modern American nationalism, and over the gender relations and domestic arrangements that shaped economic and political institutions, through reworkings of the marriage plot.

For example, as Hazel Carby, Claudia Tate, and Ann duCille have argued, African American women's novels at the turn of the century articulated political claims to desire and democracy, equality and freedom, through innovative versions of what duCille has called "the coupling convention."[27] At the same time, such claims were limited through their containment within discourses of morality and class-based propriety. Calls for greater gender equality in marriage or access to a multiracial middle class, however radically innovative within the genre of domestic fiction, could not exceed the novel form's gendered terms of upward class aspiration during this time period.

The possibilities for more fundamental challenges expanded during the early twentieth century, as forms of the novel proliferated along with multiplying manifestations of political feminism and cultural modernism. During these decades the challenge posed to the gendered domestic arrangements of the white business and professional classes by increasingly visible lesbian populations energized a wave of "high" culture Anglo-American novels. From Henry James's *The Bostonians* and Gertrude Stein's *Fernhurst*, written early in the century (though Stein's novella wasn't published until 1971), to D. H.

Lawrence's *The Fox*, published during the 1920s, these novels featured elements of the lesbian love murder narrative—often the masculine/feminine
contrast and sometimes a version of the elopement plan, rarely the violence,
but nearly always the erotic triangle.   •

One novel published during the 1920s transformed the cultural landscape
in Britain and the United States more profoundly than any other published
discussion of female inversion or homosexuality before the 1950s.[28] Radclyffe Hall's *The Well of Loneliness*, published in 1928, became an immediate best-
seller in the United States, circulating substantially beyond any of the other
popular, obscure, or elite literary novels with sapphic themes. Many critics
have noted the novel's reliance on sexology's portrait of the invert for the
character of Stephen Gordon—*The Well* included a preface by Havelock Ellis
and mentioned Richard von Krafft-Ebing. Much has also been written about
the censorship battles *The Well* encountered in England and New York and
about the press coverage of those battles.[29] The novel has thus been clearly
situated within the discursive fields of sexology, sensationalism, and the law.
But the appeal of *The Well* to many readers may have extended beyond its
popularization of sexology and its sensational trials. Radclyffe Hall's plot for
this novel mixed "high" and "low" elements and qualities, and appropriated
and reworked the terms of the lesbian love murder in a manner that substantially altered it as the dominant interpretive frame for white elite women's
same-sexual attachments.

The reception of Hall's novel was shaped by the Anglo-European experience of World War I, which had profoundly altered conceptions of family
life, women's citizenship, and representations of gendered aesthetics.[30] In
the United States, particularly in New York, *The Well's* reception was no doubt
also influenced by the immense popularity of the 1926 Broadway production of Edouard Bourdet's play *The Captive*, which was raided and closed for
obscenity in a furor of publicity during 1927.[31] *The Captive* features the erotic
triangle of a normal married couple, menaced by a predatory older woman
of sapphic inclinations. The sapphist succeeds in her pursuit of the young
normal woman at the end of the play, to the man's horror. Echoing Adolphe
Belot's *Mlle. Giraud, Ma Femme*, *The Captive* repeats the warnings and lessons of
the lesbian love murder story, though it ends with conquest, not violence.
The play was ultimately closed because of objections to any public airing of
the topic—no one claimed that the play defended the women's relationship.

In the wake of *The Captive*, especially, Radclyffe Hall's novel appeared as the story retold from the invert's perspective.

The reception of *The Well* in the United States also always involved a complex cultural translation from its British aristocratic and French bohemian contexts. The *Well's* lead character, Stephen Gordon, grows up among Britain's landed gentry at Morton, an idealized estate in England's midlands. From her childhood at Morton through her adult life as a writer in Paris, Stephen grows in self-knowledge as she passes through three versions of the erotic triangle. In childhood she pines after the housemaid, Collins, but is enraged to find herself defeated by the footman. As a young adult, she courts a married American actress, Angela Crossby, who uses and betrays her. The ending of each of these affairs is set as a kind of primal scene, at which Stephen witnesses the erotic embraces of her unworthy beloved and her male rival. But the final triangle of the novel rewrites this scene of misdirected love and hopeless defeat. Exiled to Paris by her intolerant and unkind mother, and active in the women's ambulance corps during the war, Stephen meets and sets up housekeeping with a normal woman who fully returns her passion. But Stephen stages an elaborate ruse to drive her lover, Mary Llewellan, into the arms of her idealized best friend, the normal Martin Hallam. Stephen sacrifices Mary because she perceives her as a normal woman who might have a conventional life and social respect if she married Martin. But Mary will not leave Stephen, will not choose Martin over her. Stephen, out of martyred honor, must sacrifice her own desire and relinquish Mary, against the latter's wishes but for her own good.

Radclyffe Hall's novel thus repeats elements of the lesbian love murder story: the masculine/feminine contrast, the triangle, and the wish to set up a household (Stephen at one point wishes for marriage for the invert). But the defeat of and/or violence by the masculine woman is rewritten as her noble sacrifice of the normal woman's love. This rewriting ingeniously formulates a plea for social tolerance for inverts, defined as a fixed minority who pose no serious threat to the contours of normal elite domestic life. The gesture of Stephen's sacrifice of Mary to an assumed marriage to Martin (the novel ends before any marriage actually occurs) can be read as a gesture of deference to ancestral conventions and the normal home on the part of one who seeks a place in the institutions of economic and political life (Stephen is a fine writer and participates heroically in the World War I ambulance corps) but only a peripheral, nondisruptive place.

As Esther Newton has argued, *The Well of Loneliness* marked out and publicized a crucial line of defense for overt sexuality between women, as well as for female masculinity more generally.[32] This defense was staged as a forceful counter to the lesbian love murder narrative, but a counter framed substantially within that narrative's terms. The masculine woman competes with the normal man for the normal woman, with the goal of establishing access to the home and through it, to the institutions of national modernity. Stephen Gordon is exiled from the home/nation of Morton, but that estate remains the ideal of perfection that she yearns to occupy. Her claim to Morton is framed as a right of inheritance, a right manifested throughout *The Well* in Stephen's nobility of character, her moral virtue, her intellectual and physical gifts and achievements. Ultimately, she lays claim to her inheritance by sacrificing the normal woman's love and loyalty.[33]

In the U.S. context, the English setting of *The Well of Loneliness* may have translated as a marker of the American nation's racial heritage; Morton may have appeared as an ancestral white home. The terms of the novel's plea for tolerance—on the basis of virtue and achievement, and of sacrifice—certainly translated easily into a claim for race and class-based American cultural, economic, and political citizenship. Such a translation is peripherally suggested in the novel's treatment of Lincoln and Henry Jones, two "very nice Negroes" invited to sing the spirituals of the southern U.S. plantations at a party in Paris. The Jones brothers mark an ambivalent site for both identification, as fellow outcasts, and differentiation, as less civilized racial others. Lincoln is described as bearing the "patient, questioning expression common to the eyes of most animals and to those of all slowly evolving races," while Henry is presented as exuding a "primitive force rendered dangerous by drink" yet redeemed by his singing, which left him "pure, unashamed, triumphant."[34]

Hall's ambivalent and often contradictory address for social tolerance, at once expansive and limited, emerged partly in relation to the lesbian love murder story. (Hall may have read about the Mitchell case directly in either Ellis's or Krafft-Ebing's books, or absorbed its elements more indirectly.) *The Well of Loneliness*'s pleas poured forth from the perspective of the masculine woman in the triangle, a perspective that limited its scope in class and racial terms, as well as in its sexual-identity parameters.

The Well's representations of lesbian relationships and sapphic practices greatly exceeded the scope of its identity politics, however. The novel's characters include normal women who toy with inverts, normal women who fall in love with them, and an array of other characters who don't fit the masculine woman/normal woman pairing at all. As in Radclyffe Hall's social worlds in London and Paris, the pages of her novel include feminine couples, masculine couples, and many in-between and uncategorized types, from a wide range of economic/class backgrounds, with variable character and achievements.[35] Though the normal women are clearly not included as subjects of Hall's polemical address—they are objects of desire described with great ambivalence, both idealized and rendered as inferior—the non-invert women (the male characters are all either normal or clearly inverted) in lesbian relationships are more ambiguously positioned in the text. They are at times embraced in Stephen Gordon's appeals for tolerance but at other times clearly not included among the noble inverts for whom she speaks.

The Well of Loneliness's narrative pushed aside the lesbian love murder story as a dominant interpretive frame for modern female homosexuality, offering a portrait of noble suffering in the place of dangerous violence. But the violent masculine figure was not replaced altogether; she continued to appear in popular and mass cultural forms, from the predatory vampire to the lesbian serial killer.[36] Meanwhile Radclyffe Hall's novel contributed substantially to the transmission of the lesbian love murder story's legacy, however powerfully and effectively transformed, to the post–World War II homophile movement and beyond. As The Well addressed, and worked to create, expanded lesbian publics in the second half of the twentieth century—cultural work that the earlier, more hostile lesbian love murder narratives could not have performed—it circulated ambivalent, contradictory, limited, and exclusionary calls for inclusion and tolerance. It circulated rhetorical strategies and modes of political resistance framed as claims to morality and normality—claims therefore trapped within the terms of privileged whiteness.[37]

MORE THAN LOVE: AN EPILOGUE

I am an anomaly to myself as well as to others. I
do not wish to be married but I do wish for the
society of gentlemen.

Ida B. Wells [1]

Given the pressure for respectability placed on black women, it is not surprising that Ida Wells did eventually marry, despite her earlier wish to avoid
the altar; Wells and her fellow black female activists could not call on a tradition of "single blessedness" available to respectable white reformers like
Frances Willard or Susan B. Anthony. Aspersions on Wells's virtue shadowed
her during her years of antilynching work before her marriage; after marriage, the assumption of marital duties and motherhood curtailed her visibility and impact in the world of national civil rights agitation. She remained
a respected local activist for many decades, however; local political organizing was then (as now) more open to women's equal participation than
national leadership. During those decades, the impact of lynching, disfrans-
chisement, and segregation imposed special contraints on the freedoms of
black women hemmed in by the gendered burden of embodying proper
ladyhood and symbolizing the virtuous black home as a project of "uplift"
within middle-class communities. Such constraints restricted Wells's access
to the world stage but never succeeded in driving her off. [2]

Alice Mitchell, having committed a horrendous crime, disappeared from
public view after her lunacy inquisition. She was committed to the Western
State Insane Asylum at Bolivar, Tennessee, on August 1, 1892; after that date,
she was interviewed occasionally by reporters for brief articles in the local
press but was never asked to comment on her crime, her mental state, or the
legal proceedings that committed her.

The few press accounts of her life in the asylum were not particularly revealing; they were largely conventional, highly sentimental portraits of a "bright, happy, laughing girl," as Edward H. Taylor described her in 1893 in the *Brownsville States-Democrat*. Taylor wrote that Mitchell spent her time reading, conversing, playing the guitar, performing needlework and embroidery, and keeping her "pretty little room" a "gem of neatness." He concluded:

> It is said that she is never sad. The dances and concerts in the amusement hall are, we are told, dull and spiritless without Alice Mitchell's presence. She dances well and never misses a set.[3]

According to an article in the *Bolivar Bulletin*, though she often attended dances (as Taylor had reported), she refused to dance with any of the men other than the male asylum attendants, saying, "No, I don't care to dance or have anything to do with the Bolivar boys, for I know they want to meet me merely from curiosity."[4] The *Memphis Commercial Appeal* reporter noted simply that in 1895 she committed no violence, was obedient, and "showed no outward sign of insanity."[5]

Alice Mitchell's condition and treatment in the asylum can't be discerned in much greater detail or accuracy from the hospitals records, either. Founded as the third state insane asylum in Tennessee (after Central State in Nashville and Eastern State in Knoxville), the Western State Insane Asylum opened its doors in 1889, built to accommodate three hundred patients.[6] By 1892, it was already overcrowded with patients sent (like Alice Mitchell) for insanity believed caused primarily by hereditary predisposition. The treatment provided was primarily the "moral treatment" common during the nineteenth century: exercise, healthy diet, and work and amusements considered appropriate and strictly divided according to race and gender. No other treatments are recorded.[7]

The patient rolls for the Western State Insane Asylum show Alice Mitchell on the first — or healthiest — roster from her commitment in 1892 until 1897, when her condition apparently began to decline rapidly. By July 1897, she was listed on the last roster, no. 6; in January 1898, she was back up to roster no. 3. She died on March 31, 1898.[8]

The patient rolls don't list the cause of Mitchell's death, but the local press reported that she died of "consumption" and that she had been "wasting away" for some time before her death.[9] The use of the vague diagnosis of "consumption" (used sometimes to designate a general wasting and deterioration rather than the specific disease of tuberculosis) seemed to confirm what the Bolivar Bulletin printed in 1892:

> In the opinion of the experts . . . her insanity is progressive, and it is only a question of time when this victim of erratic [sic] mania will be a drivelling idiot through the decay of brain tissue.[10]

The Memphis Commercial Appeal reporter understood "consumption" in this way when he concluded:

> . . . for some months she has not been in good health, and gradually failed until the end came as it usually does to the insane—a collapse of the whole system.[11]

The reports of Mitchell's death from consumption (if interpreted as death from tuberculosis) accord with the decline in her condition recorded in the patient rolls; they also seem to be supported by the large increase in deaths due to tuberculosis reported by the asylum during 1896–1898.[12] But this view of Alice Mitchell's demise was eventually disputed. At least one newspaper reported that Mitchell had been much improved and in a good state of health, appearing at two dances just days before her death,[13] a discrepancy later (perhaps) explained by Paul Coppock's 1930 interview with Malcolm Patterson in the Memphis Commercial Appeal. According to Patterson:

> Those closest to the case knew . . . that she had taken her own life by jumping into a water tank on top of the building. But that story was never printed.[14]

Whether Mitchell died of tuberculosis or perhaps starved herself and then committed suicide, we can't now know.[15] Though repeatedly "examined" during her lifetime and extensively dissected in print for over a hundred years, she rarely spoke for the "public" record when alive and was yet more rarely listened to.[16] We therefore know very little about her life or death; we know a great deal more about the fears, fantasies, and strivings of those who wrote about her.

The genres of sensationalism and sexology continued to mention Alice Mitchell at the end of the nineteenth century and well into the twentieth. Medical journals cited the murder among their cases of female sexual perversion, often in company with other "similar" crimes (increasingly referred to in the later articles as "female homosexuality" or "lesbianism" rather than perversion or inversion). An 1899 report in Medicine, reprinted in the Alienist *and Neurologist*, analyzed the attempted murder of Charles Seibert by Nettie Miller in Chicago, "seemingly consequent on sexual inversion jealousy." Seibert had married Hattie Leonard, who claimed that for fourteen years prior to her marriage she had been under Nettie Miller's "hypnotic influence." *Medicine* commented on two other "striking homicides of this character," including the one committed by Alice Mitchell.[17]

In the arena of newspaper sensationalism, an extensive rehash of the orginal press coverage was published in the *Memphis Commercial Appeal* in 1930. The article, by well-known Memphis journalist Paul Coppock, "Memphis' Strangest Love Murder Had All-Girl Cast," gave the Mitchell-Ward story new life. Coppock trumpeted the case as "the most interesting and widely discussed in the city's annals of killings," the facts of which "still live in the history of famous cases taught young lawyers and in the world's anthologies of sex psychology and sex pathology."[18]

Most of this article simply recycled the earlier news reports, adding an interview with former governor Malcolm Patterson (Lillie Johnson's attorney in 1892, who told Coppock, "I remember the scene when court opened as though it were yesterday. . . ."). But Coppock placed the murder in a framework somewhat altered from that of the 1892 news and editorial commentary. He maintained the distinction made at the trial—between the "unnatural love" attributed to Alice and Freda and the "sexual depravity" that was carefully ruled out as a factor in the case. But he stated this distinction in slightly (but significantly) changed language, saying that "there had been an extremely developed Platonic or brain love" between the two (words he quoted from trial testimony), but that there was not the least evidence of "homosexuality" (a word that was never used at trial or in the 1890s press coverage). In commenting on the causes of the murder, he didn't question the diagnosis of insanity offered by experts at the trial, but he also emphasized the social context of the murder, from the vantage point of the "modern" critique of Victorian "separate spheres":

> Out of their close companionship in a social order that very closely restricted the association of girls of their ages with men, there developed a love that duplicated the love of a young man for a girl.[19]

This article became the source of references to the Mitchell-Ward case in other sensational reports of lesbian love murders. One Sunday newspaper used the notoriety of a 1931 double murder, allegedly involving three women in a love triangle, to reprint most of Coppock's account under the heading "Trunk Murder Recalls '91 [sic] Tragedy":

Weird as they are calling the Judd-Samuelson-LeRoi trunk murder case, it is not exactly unique. Some forty years ago, in Memphis, Tenn., there was another celebrated case with an all-girl cast.[20]

As late as 1950, the journal *Sexology* recyled the 1930 Coppock article from the *Memphis Commercial Appeal* in an article by Dr. D. O. Cauldwell, "Lesbian Love Murder." Dr. Cauldwell took the opportunity to congratulate his profession for the progress made in understanding such cases in the years since the Mitchell-Ward murder:

This article is a study of a Lesbian love-murder which, in 1892, shook the nation. . . .

The strangeness of the case depended largely on the fact that its circumstances were so little understood in those days. Strangely enough a court-at-law found no evidence of homosexuality in a case which today would correctly be termed homosexual by any qualified student of sexology and sex psychology. . . .

The year 1892 was a part of the so-called age of chivalry—and this had special application in the southern city of Memphis, Tennessee. The association of the sexes was much restricted. . . . Alice Mitchell and Freda Ward evidently had early Lesbian careers which resulted from the stilted environment in which they lived and the pseudo-chivalrous atmosphere of the day. . . .

Freda Ward must have been of the submissive type. Alice was of the aggressive type with a strong *mortido* principle. . . . Alice Mitchell probably had no distinct heterosexual leanings . . . and hence aspired to the male role in Lesbian love. Freda Ward apparently was potentially heterosexual. . . .

. . . [T]he physicians who testified in Alice Mitchell's trial were guided by pseudo-chivalry rather than by science. . . . *We* are moving slowly toward a better civilization through education and the advancement of science. Looking back on Memphis' strange case of female homosexual infatuation, we can take pride in the progress made during the 58 years just passed—yet we still have a long road ahead of us. (Emphasis added)[21]

This article (along with its source, the 1930 *Memphis Commercial Appeal* article) then became the basis for the use of the Mitchell-Ward murder as an illustration of "sadistic" lesbianism in the influential, widely cited 1954 text by Dr. Frank Caprio, *Female Homosexuality: A Psychodynamic Study of Lesbianism*.[22]

Few accounts of the Mitchell-Ward murder appeared outside the realms of sensational news and sexology. There were the few fictional reworkings (discussed above) and one ballad passed down through oral tradition in the mid-South. The date of origin of this ballad is unknown, but it was discovered and recorded in 1961 by folklorist John Quincy Wolf. The ballad, sung to him in Memphis by Mrs. Grace Hastings, probably had nonelite origins at the time of the crime itself. Mrs. Hastings knew nothing of the actual case behind the ballad, which she called "Alice Mitchell and Freda Ward" and recreated as follows:

You have heard of Freda Ward
Who lived many miles from town.
As she went down the stone-paved walk,
Alice Mitchell cut her down.

They won't do anything to her,
She has two of the best lawyers in town.

She says she killed her because she loved her,
But love was not the thing,
For Alice and Freda both loved the same man . . .

There goes that Alice Mitchell
With arms strong tightly bound down.
For the crime she did in Memphis,
She's bound for Bolivar now.[23]

It's clear exactly how little persuasive power the physicians' testimony had with this unknown balladist. (It's also clear that the story of Alice's love for Freda was received as in some sense "unbelievable.")[24]

As these examples suggest, the press, sexologists, and others continued to pluck the story of Alice Mitchell from its context in 1892 Memphis, and set it down as part of the empirical basis of changing theories, from the somatic hereditarianism of 1890s neurology to the vulgar Freudian psychodynamic formulations of the 1950s.[25]

Beginning in the 1970s, following on the successes of the civil rights movement, the rebirth of feminism, and the inauguration of a gay liberation movement at the Stonewall Rebellion in 1969, new defenses for lesbian women were forged. Alice Mitchell's story was taken up again and retold as the tale of a lesbian who was misunderstood and persecuted by an ignorant society. Fred Harris's 1975 "Lesbian Slaying Shocked 'Gay Nineties' Memphians" was included in his series on Memphis gay history in *Gaiety . . . Reflecting Gay Life in the South* and was drawn from the original Memphis newspaper reports—as was Sherre Dryden's "That Strange Girl: The Alice Mitchell Murder Case," published in the Nashville, Tennessee, lesbian and gay newspaper *DARE* in 1988.[26] Jonathan Ned Katz's account of the Mitchell case, included in his pioneering *Gay American History* (1976), was drawn from the medical reports of the case, especially Frank Sim's *Memphis Medical Monthly* article.[27] The 1985 play by Dan Ellentuck, "Alice and Fred" (presented at New York City's Cherry Lane Theater) was probably adapted from Katz's book.[28]

These accounts of Mitchell's crime and trial were placed within the context of a search for the history of "lesbians" in all times and places—a search based on modern sexual-identity categories that the Mitchell-Ward case helped to forge. *Sapphic Slashers'* intervention in these contemporary retellings of the Mitchell-Ward story is to demonstrate, in company with the writings of many other historians and queer theorists, that the boundaries of these identities have been too reactive and restrictive to contain the complex history and politics of dissenting female embodiments and enactments of gender and desire. For instance, the figure of the "normal" woman in the lesbian love murder story cannot be regarded as "lesbian" or "gay" in the contemporary sense; it would also be anachronistic to call her "bisexual." To name her in any of these ways would be to obscure her particular place in pre–World War II narratives—the place marking the instability and nontransparency of the "normal" position itself. She might be understood within a genealogy of the contemporary "femme"—a contested position in stories of lesbian life and love, marked sometimes as a straight woman available for lesbian experience or, from the 1950s on, sometimes as lesbian, though often unreliably so.[29] The history of these femmes can not be written within the parameters of histories of lesbianism. A history of femmes would necessarily be a history of normative femininities and their subversive mobility—a queer history certainly, though not a gay or lesbian one.

Sapphic Slashers is also written with the hope of illuminating the limits and dangers of political strategies grounded, like Radclyffe Hall's novel, in melodramatic, normalizing scenarios of martyrdom and sacrifice. After the horrifying murder of Wyoming college student Matthew Shepard in October 1998, expressions of national outrage and mourning were mobilized around the image of Shepard's violated body. These mobilizations, and the claims

to national citizenship for gay people surrounding them, generated a vigorous counter-response to antigay rhetoric and legislative initiatives. But they
also relied unselfconsciously on the normative figure of the white college
boy, unintentionally highlighting the failures of LGBT/Q constituencies to
mobilize in response to the far more common persecution and murder of
transgender sex workers of color, for instance.[30] Thus, for all their oppositional energy, the calls for expanded citizenship raised over the corpse of
Matthew Shepard, like earlier claims such as Hall's, excluded as much as they
claimed.

In responding to pathologizing representations of sexual minorities as
violent or dangerous, it is important to resist the countermove of representing exclusion as innocence violated or nobility scorned. The moral terms
of such melodramas limited the scope of political resistances in the United
States throughout the twentieth century. At the start of the twenty-first, we
need new narratives to claim greater equality without qualification or exclusion.

APPENDIX A

HYPOTHETICAL CASE.

Facts and Questions Presented by Counsel
To Expert Physicians.

Alice J. Mitchell is the youngest child of George Mitchell and Isabella Mitchell, and was born in the year 1873.

During the mother's pregnancy with Alice she was the subject of perceptible mental alienation; and these mental disturbances continued until some time after Alice's birth. Among the evidences of disturbed mentality was a groundless and absurd antipathy to a devoted sister, that she fondly loved, and a like groundless aversion against a highly cherished female friend. About the same time she was possessed with the unfounded belief that a step-daughter, 12 years of age, who was much attached to her children, intended to kill them, and would not allow her to sleep in the same room with them. She formed the purpose of putting this step-child to death, without any cause whatever. She could not be reasoned out of her belief that the step-child intended to kill her children, or her purpose to take the life of her step-child. Efforts to do so only inflamed and excited her, and her husband was compelled to send the step-child to live with his relatives. The malady passed off after a few months, and Mrs. Mitchell has ever since been apparently of sound mind, but has a sad and melancholy expression. She never laughs, and rarely is seen to smile.

Mrs. Mitchell was afflicted in the same way, but in a more violent form, with her first child.

She was the subject of a marked case of puerperal insanity, which manifested itself a few days after the birth of this child. She became wild, and

Reprinted from "Sane or Insane?" *Memphis Commercial*, July 19, 1892, 1. Also published in F. L. Sim, "Forensic Psychiatry: Alice Mitchell Adjudged Insane," *Memphis Medical Monthly*, Aug., 1892, 379–90.

wholly ungovernable. Her condition was such that Dr. Comstock, the family physician, advised that she be sent to an asylum for the insane, which was done. After being treated for two or three months, she was discharged as restored. She was, however, in feeble health, and so continued for two or three years.

A sister of Mrs. Mitchell took this child upon the committal of Mrs. Mitchell to the asylum, to keep and care for, and it was with her at her home, upon the discharge of Mrs. Mitchell from the asylum. She and her husband were on the eve of going for it when she heard of its sudden and unexpected death. The shock upon her weak condition, mentally and physically, was very great. Always thereafter she was profoundly gloomy, seeming to rest under some great sorrow.

Between the birth of the first and second child a period of four years elapsed.

She gave birth to six children between the first and Alice.

With each child her mental trouble appeared in a more or less marked degree.

She would be seized with imaginings, for which there were no grounds whatever. These delusive ideas would pass off generally in a few weeks after childbirth.

Four years intervened between the birth of Alice and that of the next youngest child.

The parents of Mrs. Mitchell died when she was an infant. One of her brothers was insane for a considerable period, one of her uncles was insane and several of her first cousins were insane.

Alice was a nervous, excitable child, somewhat undersize. As she grew she did not manifest interest in those childish amusements and toys that girls are fond of.

When only 4 or 5 years old she spent much time at a swing in the yard of the family, in performing such feats upon it as skinning the cat and hanging by an arm or leg. She was fond of climbing, and expert at it.

She delighted in marbles and tops, in base ball and foot ball, and was a member of the children's base ball nine. She spent much time with her brother Frank, who was next youngest, playing marbles and spinning tops. She preferred him and his sports to her sisters. He practiced with her at target shooting with a small rifle, to her great delight. She excelled this brother at tops, marbles and feats of activity.

She was fond of horses, and from early childhood, would go among the mules of her father and be around them when being fed. About six or seven years ago her father purchased a horse. She found great satisfaction in feeding and currying him. She often rode him about the lot bareback, as a boy would. She was expert in harnessing him to the buggy, in looking after the harness and mending it when anything was amiss. To the family she seemed a regular tomboy.

She was willful and whimsical. She disliked sewing and needle work. Her mother could not get her to do such work. She undertook to teach her crocheting, but could not. She was unequal in the manifestation of her affections. To most persons, even her relatives, she seemed distant and indifferent. She was wholly without that fondness for boys that girls usually manifest.

She had no intimates or child sweethearts among the boys, and when approaching womanhood, after she was grown, she had no beaux and took no pleasure in the society of young men. She was sometimes rude, and always indifferent to young men. She was regarded as mentally wrong by young men toward whom she had thus acted.

About the time her womanhood was established she was subject to very serious and protracted headaches. She had far more than the usual sickness at that period. She was subject to nervous spells, in which she would visibly tremble or shake. She is still, at times, subject to these attacks of extreme nervous excitement; but does not now, and never did, wholly lose consciousness in them but upon one occasion.

For Fred Ward, a girl about her own age, she had an extraordinary fondness. Whenever she could do so she was with her. They lived as neighbors and spent as much of their time together as possible. The attachment seemed to be mutual, but was far stronger in Alice Mitchell than in Fred.

They were very different in disposition. Fred was girl-like and took no pleasure in the boyish sports that Alice delighted in. Her instincts and amusements were feminine. She was tender and affectionate. Time strengthened the intimacy between them. They became lovers in the sense of that relation between persons of different sexes. May, a year ago, the Ward family moved from Memphis to Golddust, a small town on the Tennessee side of the Mississippi river, about eighty miles north of Memphis. The separation greatly distressed Alice, but an active correspondence by mail was at once opened, and in this way they modified the regret caused by the separation. The summer after the removal of the Wards Alice visited her beloved Fred and remained with her two or three weeks. They were continually together and often seen embracing and clasped in each other's arms.

Alice got a promise that Fred should visit her in the fall or winter, and this promise was kept, Fred spending about two weeks with Alice in December, 1890.

During this visit Alice entertained the idea of taking her own life or that of Fred. She bought laudanum with that view. She considered the plan of giving it to Fred whilst sleeping, but in some way Fred was aroused and suspected that Alice had some design, either on her own life or that of Fred, and remained awake the greater part of the night. Alice showed her the bottle marked poison. The next day she went with Fred to the boat on her way home at Golddust, carrying the bottle of laudanum with her. She locked herself and Fred in a state room on the boat and took the contents of the bottle with suicidal intent. She suffered greatly for many days for this rash act. The reason assigned by Alice was that Fred loved Harry Bilger and Ashley Roselle and she meant to end her existence and troubles and leave Fred free to become the wife of her choice of the young men named. She cautioned Fred if she wrote to her again as to what she might write, as she had no doubt she would be dead before it came to hand.

During this visit Alice manifested the most ardent attachment for Fred, and some days after Fred reached home she wrote Fred of her recovery, and then began again a regular correspondence, showing all the warmth of lover for lover.

In February, 1891, Alice proposed marriage. She repeated the offer in three separate letters. To each Fred replied, agreeing to become her wife. Alice wrote her upon the third promise that she would hold her to the engagement, and that she would kill her if she broke the promise.

Alice again visited Fred in June, 1891. She had saved from time to time small sums of money, amounting in the aggregate to about $15. With this sum she purchased a ring, and on her June visit formally tendered it to Fred as their engagement ring, and Fred accepted it as such.

They were often seen in each other's embraces, and the married sister of Fred, Mrs. Volkmar, remarked that they were disgusting in their demonstrations of love for each other.

Alice felt a sense of shame in allowing others to see her hug and kiss Fred. She did not think it proper for lovers to be openly hugging and kissing. Fred did not take that view, and rather reproached Alice for being ashamed of showing her love for her in that way.

On leaving Alice got a pledge that Fred would pay her a visit in the coming November. Their engagement was a secret then only known to themselves.

It was agreed that Alice should be known as Alvin J. Ward, so that Fred could still call her by the pet name, Allie, and Fred was to be known as Mrs. A.J. Ward. The particulars of formal marriage and elopement were agreed upon. Alice was to put on man's apparel, and have her hair trimmed by a barber like a man; was to get the license to marry, and Fred was to procure the Rev. Dr. Patterson of Memphis, and of whose church she was a member, to perform the marriage ceremony, and if he declined, they intended to get a justice of the peace to marry them. The ceremony performed, they intended to leave for St. Louis. Alice was to continue to wear man's apparel, and meant to try and have a mustache, if it would please Fred.

She was going out to work for Fred in men's clothes.

In the latter part of June, 1891, Ashley Roselle, before mentioned, began to pay court to Fred, who gave him one of her photographs. The watchful vigilance of Alice got track of this affair, and she remonstrated warmly with Fred, and charged her with deception and infidelity. Fred acknowledged she had done wrong, vowed unshaken fidelity to Alice, and promised never more to offend.

The scheme of marrying and eloping seemed almost ready for execution in the latter part of July. Fred was to take a St. Louis packet at Golddust and come to Memphis and notify Alice of her arrival, and they were then to marry and go at once by boat to St. Louis, as they had agreed to do. The boat Fred was to take was to reach Golddust at night between 10 and 2 o'clock.

By chance, Mrs. Volkmar, the married sister before referred to, with whom Fred was living, saw part of the correspondence of the girls, which disclosed the relations between them, and the plans to elope and marry. She was surprised and indignant. She communicated the fact to her husband, and he determined to watch Fred and prevent her from taking the boat for Memphis. He suspected a man was at the bottom of the affair and watched with his Winchester rifle. No man appeared. When the boat whistled announcing her arrival, he went to the room of Fred. He found a light burning in her room, and she was dressed, had her valise packed, and was ready to take the boat. An exciting scene ensued. Mrs. Volkmar wrote to Mrs. Mitchell, the mother of Alice, and at the same time wrote Alice, returning the engagement ring, and other love tokens, and declaring that all intercourse between the girls must at once cease. Mrs. Mitchell knew that Mrs. Volkmar was in feeble health, and thought that she had grossly exaggerated and misunderstood the matter. She told Alice of the letter received from Mrs. Volkmar. Alice listened in silence. Mrs. Mitchell destroyed the letter. She then knew nothing of Alice's secret.

The effect on Alice of the return of the engagement ring and the inhibition of all communication with Fred was almost crushing. She wept, passed sleepless nights, lost her appetite, frequently declined even to come to the table.

She hid the returned tokens of love in the kitchen, in a cigar box, to which there was a lock and key. She would often go alone to this hiding place and gaze in an abstracted way upon these tokens of affection.

She spent hours in the kitchen, alternately crying and laughing.

She told the cook that she was engaged to marry; said her father and mother were good to her, but her sisters were not kind. The cook supposed she was engaged to marry some man, and the sisters of Alice opposed the match. She had no notion that it was a woman she was engaged to marry. She thought they were not treating Alice right in the house, in some way, but did not know how. She thought Alice was not right in her mind. Alice showed her the engagement ring—would gaze upon it and pass from tears to laughter whilst doing so. The cook had a child about six years old, and Alice talked a great deal to this child—seemed to take a fancy to the child, in her distress. She said they would not lift her troubles off her.

In August and September, the winter supply of coal for the family was being delivered, and she receipted five of the coal bills in the name of Fred Ward, and on being asked why she did so, replied that she was not conscious of doing so; that she was thinking of Fred, and used her name without knowing it. For weeks before the killing her eyes shone with a strange lustre.

Alice was plump and round before the passion for Fred possessed her. After that she grew thin, and her face wore an anxious expression. She seemed absent, and absorbed, and quite strange to her acquaintances.

That singularity of behavior which always characterized her, increased, until those who had long known her concluded that she was mentally wrong.

November was the time when Fred was again to visit Memphis, according to her promise to Alice. On the first of November, Alice, clandestinely, possessed herself of her father's razor. When she took it she was thinking of Fred. She feared they would take Fred from her. She could not bear the thought of losing her. Sooner than lose her, she would kill her. As she says she had no use for the razor but to kill Fred. If she used it for that purpose, it would be because she loved her, and feared they would take her away.

Her father missed his razor, and inquired about it in Alice's hearing, but she left the room, lest she should be questioned about it. She secreted it, and generally carried it with her on going out after November 1st, thinking that she might meet Fred. She thought of Fred and the razor together, and had no use for it unless it became necessary to kill Fred with it.

In the hope of hearing something of Fred and ascertaining also if Ashley Roselle was likely again to make love to Fred, Alice wrote him in December, 1891, and in January, 1892.

To sound this matter in this correspondence with Roselle, who was almost a stranger to her, she gave expression to sentiments of regard which she did not feel for him, and never felt for any man. This correspondence continued, to a date near the homicide. Her love for Fred, and her fear that Roselle, in some way, might be made the means of taking Fred from her, inspired this correspondence. She got her friend, Miss Johnson, to write to him, expressing her admiration for him, the real object being to try and see if he was again a lover of Fred. But not satisfied with Miss Johnson's efforts, she took the correspondence in her own hand. She also met him on the Rosa Lee several times, pretending to do so out of her regard for him, but only to discover, if she could, how he felt toward Fred. This was in December, 1891, and January, 1892.

In January, 1892, Fred came to Memphis, but went to stay with Mrs. Kimbrough, instead of Alice. She did not see or write to Alice, who had a burning desire to be with her, or receive some message from her. She tried to communicate with her by letter—wrote her two letters, and managed to get one of them into her hands during her stay at Mrs. Kimbrough's. These letters told of her love in the most passionate terms. One was returned with the word "returned" written upon it in Fred's handwriting.

Alice sought opportunities to see Fred—to look upon her, to speak to her, but in vain. Fred's sister, or some one else, was on the lookout, and her desire was thus thwarted.

One day while upon the watch she saw Fred go, unattended, into a photograph gallery. In a short time she came out, but did not observe or speak to Alice. She went from the photograph gallery to Mrs. Carroll's.

Alice thought of using the razor, which she had with her on the occasion, but found some difficulty in getting it out, and the feeling then to take the life of Fred with the razor passed off, and she returned to her home. At the time she thus thought of killing Fred she loved her as much, or more, than ever. On January 18 Alice got the last letter she ever received from Fred. This letter told of Fred's continued love for Alice; but said she was not allowed to see her, or speak to her, and prayed the forgiveness of Alice.

Alice and Miss Lillian Johnson, an estimable neighbor girl, about the same age, were intimate, and loved each other, but as one girl loves another. She was aware of the ardent attachment of Alice for Fred, but did not at first suspect that it was different from the love of one girl for another.

Alice often took Miss Johnson in her buggy, and made her the companion of her drives. In her sorrow she confided in Miss Johnson, who understood her on every subject, except her relations to Fred. This was incomprehensible. The inclement weather in the greater part of the month of January permitted no buggy-riding, and for many days prior to the killing of Fred these girls had not been out driving. Miss Johnson had never heard a word from Alice that did not breathe devotion to Fred. Her love and her grief at the separation filled her mind.

On the morning of the homicide Alice had the buggy horse shod and engaged Miss Johnson to drive with her that evening. Alice, Miss Johnson and the nephew of the latter, about 6 years old, occupied the buggy in the evening drive. Alice knew that Fred would probably take the boat that evening for home. On the Friday before she had gone with Miss Johnson on foot to the boat under the impression that Fred would leave on that day. Miss Johnson accompanied Alice to the boat at the request of the latter, who expressed a desire to see Fred again before she left. Fred was not on board and the next trip of the boat would be on the following Monday evening, and Alice thought Fred would then leave for home. Without disclosing her purpose she drove so as to meet Fred on her way to the boat. Josie Ward and Miss Purnell were with Fred. Alice turned her buggy on meeting Fred and her companions and drove in the direction that Fred was going. She drove slowly so as to keep nearly abreast of Fred and her companions. Miss Johnson's father was walking in the same direction and came to the buggy and gave his little grandson his gloves. Miss Johnson talked with her father as they drove along until they reached Union street, where he stopped. At one point the clothes of Fred became entangled or disarranged, and one of the girls with her relieved her from this embarrassment. They stopped a very short time in order to do so. Alice then drove still more slowly so as not to pass them. At one time as they thus drove along Alice slipped off her rubbers, and Miss Johnson suspected that she was going to leave the buggy and run to Fred and kiss her. But she remained in the buggy. When Madison street was reached Alice still drove slowly, but passed Fred and her companions. She drove directly to

the custom house, and all three got out of the buggy. In a few seconds, Fred
and her companions came up and turned north, in order to reach the way
that led to the steamboat upon which Fred and her sister proposed to leave.
Fred passed within less than two feet of Alice, who turned to Miss Johnson
and said: "Oh, Lil; Fred winked at me." In a few seconds Alice said she must
see Fred once more, and walked after Fred. She soon overtook her, and without a word cut her with a razor. Fred's sister undertook to interfere, but was
slightly cut by Alice and forced to retire. Alice then turned upon Fred and
again cut her, one of the wounds being mortal, cutting her throat almost
from ear to ear. Fred fell to the earth and Alice ascended the steep walk to the
buggy, in which she found Miss Johnson and her nephew. Alice had cut her
own hand in the struggle. Miss Johnson heard some one cry out, "She has
cut that woman's throat," and supposing by Alice's appearance, her hat being
off and the blood flowing from the wound in her hand, that some one had
cut Alice, she asked her what they had done to her. Alice paid no attention
to her question, but putting her foot on the hub of one of the buggy wheels
sprang into the buggy. She seized the reins, took the whip and drove off at
a rapid rate, lashing the horse to his full speed. She drove north until Court
street was reached, then east until she got to Main street and south on Main,
the most public street in the city, until she reached Monroe, a distance of
several hundred yards, and thence by the way of Monroe and Union streets
until she reached home.

Persons who saw the prisoner as she ascended the hill from the scene of
the homicide describe her as almost in a run, looking wildly, with her hat off
and her hair disheveled and streaming down behind her and her face bloody.
She moved with a quick determined step to the buggy in which Lillian Johnson and her little nephew were seated, and seemed to take possession of it
by violence—seizing the reins and grabbing the whip, she lashed the horse
and moved off at a dangerous speed. One of these persons followed her fearing that she would overturn the buggy and injure the occupants. This person
supposed from her appearance and manners that she was insane, and had
violently taken possession of the buggy of some other person and was driving it in her mad fury in the most reckless manner. He followed her until
she reached Main street. Her manner and the speed at which she was driving impressed those who witnessed her actions with the belief that she was
crazy.

As they dashed along she asked Miss Johnson if there was not blood on
her face, and being told there was she requested Miss Johnson to take her

handkerchief and wipe it off, but instantly checked her by saying, "No, let it remain; it is Fred's blood, and I love her so." Miss Johnson asked her what she had done. She replied, "Cut Fred." On reaching home Alice drove in the back way, and on entering the house asked for her mother, who was not in, and turning to her sister said, "Do not excite my mother," but declined to say what had occurred. Presently her mother came, and she told her that she had cut Fred's throat. She appeared to be quite nervous. The blood was washed from her face, her cut fingers were tied up, and by that time the chief of police arrived and told Mrs. Mitchell that he had come to arrest one of her daughters. She asked him not to take her away until her father could see her. He soon came, and Alice then went with the chief of police to the county jail. She appeared to be cool, and said that she cut Fred because she loved her and because Fred did not speak to her. That night and the next morning she did not seem to realize that she had committed a criminal act. Nor does she yet realize it.

Alice intended to follow Fred on the boat and there kill her. Why she did so before she got on the boat she cannot tell. In her language she more than loved Fred. She took her life because she had told her she would, and because it was her duty to do it. The best thing would have been the marriage, the next best thing was to kill Fred. That would make it sure that no one else could get her, and would keep her word to Fred. She saw no wrong in keeping her word and doing her duty, and now sees none.

On being asked when in the act of taking the life of Fred what she was doing, according to her own version she replied: "What I intended to do, and I don't care if I am hung for it," and according to another: "What I intended; I want to die anyhow."

A significant incident occurred on the morning of the homicide. In giving an account of it the manner and actions of the prisoner are striking. She details the circumstances in the most artless and unreserved manner. She drops her voice to a low tone, and her face assumes a sharp and alert expression. She discovered her sister, so she says, looking for something in a drawer, in which she had the razor concealed, it being enclosed in an old spectacle case. She watched closely. Her sister in her search put her hand on the spectacle case containing the razor. Instantly she seized it, taking it from her, hurried out of the room, took it out of the spectacle case, wrapped it in a rag and concealed it at another point. The occurrence gave her the greatest concern, and she exclaims in describing it: "What would I have done if she had got the razor?" Being asked why she wanted the razor, she replied: "To do what

I did with it." Being further asked if she could not have used something else her reply was: "I don't know; I never thought of it."

For many nights before the killing she was all the time dreaming of Fred. She says she now sees Fred, when awake and asleep, and can't understand that Fred is dead.

She shows no remorse or regret for the bloody deed, but weeps when her love for Fred is referred to.

On the night of the homicide, on being asked if she and Fred had ran [sic] off and married in St. Louis, what they would have done, she looked puzzled—said she never had thought of that, and in turn, inquired, what would they have done?

On the next morning she asked where Fred was. She showed no feeling or emotion when making this inquiry. Being told that her body was at Stanley & Hinton's, she turned to her mother, and with great feeling and with tears pouring from her eyes, begged her mother to take her to Fred and let her lie down with her.

She kisses passionately all the pictures and cuts of Fred she can lay hands on, and hunts the newspapers for them.

She is anxious that the attorney-general shall ask her more questions than he asked Miss Johnson on the application for bail, and that more persons shall attend her trial than did Miss Johnson's.

Alice J. Mitchell has been tenderly and carefully brought up by christian parents. Her family is one of the best in Memphis, and Fred Ward's family is above exception.

Nothing coarse or immoral is known of Alice or Fred.

Alice was a slow pupil at school. Efforts to teach her music and drawing were a failure. She would ask to have instructions repeated in a confused and absent way. She could not get her mind on the subject or remember what was said to her. The teachers were the of opinion that she was badly balanced and not of sound mind. Since quitting school she has shown no taste for books or newspapers, and reads neither the one nor the other.

END

APPENDIX B: LETTERS

I. LETTERS BETWEEN ALICE MITCHELL AND FREDA WARD

LETTER I
From Alice Mitchell to Freda Ward

Memphis, Tenn., Sunday, May 11, 1891

"LOVE"—As I have nothing to do and nobody to talk to I will write to my Pitty Sing. Mattie has gone to church with Mr. Farl and Addie is talking to Frank and Ida. Will did not come today. I thought you might come this evening. I watched for you.

Hun, please tell me why you thought that ivy would not grow; will you? I tell you almost anything you ask me.

May 12

I started this last night, but will finish it now. I don't think I will stay all night with you Friday. I suppose you know why. You were two weeks after me before, and it will be two weeks Friday since you stayed all night with me. As it is Joe's time to stay with me, I don't think I will get to sleep with you.

Sing, I have a rose for you; if it is not withered by the next time I see you, I will give it to you. I have been trying to get one for a long time. It beats all other roses. Good-bye.

ALLIE

Small changes have been made for consistency of spelling and/or to correct glaring grammatical errors. Letters 3, 5, and 6 appeared in "Still in Doubt," *Memphis Commercial*, July 20, 1892, 1. Letters 2, 4, 9, and 20 were published in "Silly Letters," *Memphis Commercial*, July 21, 1892, 1. Letters 10, 18, and 19 were included in "None but Freda," *Memphis Commercial*, July 22, 1892, 1. Letters 1 and 7 appeared in "Myra Is a Myth," *Memphis Commercial*, July 23, 1892, 1. Letter 8 was published in "Fair Lillie" *Memphis Commercial*, February 25, 1892, 1. Letters 11 through 17 were included in "Letters in Demand," *Memphis Appeal Avalanche*, Feb.16, 1892, 4–5.

LETTER 2
From Freda Ward to Alice Mitchell

GOLDDUST, TENN., July 11, 1891

Sunday Afternoon

My True Sweetheart, YBIR [cypher for LOVE]:

I will start your letter this afternoon so I can write you a long one. I have still got the blues. Sweet love, you know that I love you better than anyone in the wide world. I am trying not to love others, and when I stop loving "A" [Ashley Roselle] and "H" [Harry Bilger], . . . I will tell you. I know that you are awfully jealous, sweet, but try not to be. Allie, do you mean that if I make you worse jealous you will hate me? For God's sake, Allie, don't ever hate me, for I believe it would kill me if you did. You don't know how much I worship you, sweetheart. Alvin, please be perfectly happy when you marry me, for I am true to you, and always will be forever. Maybe other women are not happy when they love others beside their husbands, but I will be perfectly happy when I become Mrs. Alvin J. Ward. I know you would do anything for me, loved one, for you love me. Sweetheart, I am not half as crazy to go on the stage as I was. When I marry you I will be happy and satisfied without going on the stage. I want to be with you all the time, for I more than love you. Good-bye until tomorrow.

SING

LETTER 3
From Freda Ward to Alice Mitchell

GOLDDUST, Tenn., July 26, 18[91]

YBIR—Your letter was received and I enjoyed it, oh, so much, even if you did fuss at me all the way through it. Yes, loved one; I loved Freda [Alice's alter ego] dearly, and I would give anything in this world (but A.J.W.) [Alvin J. Ward—Alice's "husband" identity] if she had only lived. I wanted to see her so bad. We all [g]ot to talking about her this afternoon at Mrs. Matthews', and I couldn't help but cry. Mrs. M made them stop talking about [her]. She said she don't want to make me feel bad. I tried . . . not to cry, but I couldn't help it. I know you love me best. Love, I knew it long before Freda (YBIR) died. I know you are so sweet, but I love you better than any one in the world. Monday afternoon, Alvin, forgive me. I have done what you heard me tell Lil I was going to do. No, love, I am not keeping my promise, but I will be true to you this time and tell you all about it. Sweetheart, I didn't think what I was doing when I did it. I did not think I was deceiving you when I did it. But I more than worship you, sweetheart, and I only love A.R. [Ashley Roselle]. I swear I don't even love him now as much as I did when you were here. Believe me, Alvin, I am trying not to love him.

I didn't even think of doing such a thing until Lil told me to do it, and a week after you left this is what I wrote to him. Sweetheart, BELIEVE me, I will tell you the honest truth.

[*Following is a copy of Freda's letter to Ashley*]

GOLDDUST, TENN., July, 18[91]

Mr. Ashley Rosell[e], Featherstone, Ark.:

Friend Ashley — I suppose you will be somewhat surprised when you receive this missive, but I write to ask you to forgive me for the way I have treated you. My friend, Alvin Ward, knew you had my picture. He was jealous and asked me to let him write for it and I did so. I knew I did you wrong and I don't blame you for tearing the picture up, but I do blame you for telling Dr. Vance and all the men on the boat about it. If you are my friend at all, please don't tell any one else. If you forgive me, write and say so; if not send my letter back. Remember, Ashley, I don't BEG you to forgive me. I merely ASK you to address

Your friend, SERG. JUEQ.
334 Vance st.
Memphis, Tenn.

I SWEAR, Alvin, that is ALL I wrote to him, but I have received no answer yet. When it comes I will send it to YOU.

Can you, will you forgive me, Alvin? I swear before God from this on I will be true to you as the stars above. Sweetheart, you know I want to marry you; I don't only want to, but I am going to marry you.

I will prove my love . . . by marrying you soon, and being true to you as long as I live. If you chew tobacco, love, I won't let you kiss me. I know I did wrong in writing that letter, and I can't blame you for being ji-—, sweet love, but BELIEVE me once, hun. I am so sorry I did it, Alvin. I beg you with all my heart to forgive me. Will you, sweet? I didn't deceive Ashley. I merely stopped writing to him because you told me to, and I never did tell him right out that I loved him. Whenever he asked me I would tell him that I didn't love him, but I liked him. You said you did not suppose I would keep it up now, since you knew all about it. What do you mean by that? I have only written the one letter to him since I stopped writing that time you told me to.

I will always be careful, love, about getting my feet wet for your sake, but I have been careless all the time about it, and I know that is why I always suffer so much.

I would have written you a short letter so you could have gotten it this morning, but I was sick in bed almost all day Friday. My throat was so sore I couldn't talk at all. I am not near over my cold yet.

We are going to a picnic next Thursday with Mr. and Mrs. Matthews. Maybe Ashley will be there, but I swear, Alvin, I will not speak to him. Trust me, I won't even notice him. Of course when I come home from the picnic I will be all dressed, so that night, Thursday, I will try to get off on the City of Monroe, that is, if she comes after 10 o'clock at night. If I don't get to come, then I can't come before way next Monday, for Saturday night there would be no boat down, for the Cairo is laid up. If you can't get ready by next Friday, why, let me know Thursday. You can take the letter down to the boat, but if you can get ready by that time I will try to come Thursday. We will have to get married on Friday, but I don't care. I will be thankful if we get married at all, let alone what day.

If I come I will telephone to you early Friday morning. You can tell your mamma it was Lil that telephoned, and make up some lie about going over there right away, and you can meet me in front of the "custom-house" or any place, it doesn't make any difference. Be sure to get up early that morning so no one else will come to the telephone. If you do not hear from me by half-past 8 o'clock anyway, you may know I didn't come.

I received the ring all O.K. I know you are true to me Love and I more than idolize you. I will be so happy when we are married. I will stop. I will always be true to you hereafter. Yours Forever,

PETTY SING.

Don't write by Saturday's boat for I might come Friday. I more than love you.

MRS. A.J. WARD.

LETTER 4
From Alice Mitchell to Freda Ward

MEMPHIS, TENN., Aug. 1, 1891

YBIR:—Dearest Love—If you only knew it, you are getting me in trouble. I have stood it long enough. I am too jealous. I love you, Fred, and would kill Ashley before I would see him take you from me. You think I am only saying that for fun, but I really mean it. I know you love him, but if you would tell me the truth about it and wouldn't be so mean I would not be so jealous.

I have done something and I know you will get mad at me for it, but I can't help it. As long as you do me this way I will keep it up. Please be true to me, Sing, and I won't do anything wrong as long as you are true to me. I don't mean to do Ashley any harm, but if you still make me j-— and deceive me I will. I hate to do it, but you will be the cause of it. He has done nothing to me, but I am mad with jealousy.

I am writing tonight, for I may go over to Lill's tomorrow evening. I can't write much for it is late. After this I will write only when I get a letter from my Sing.

Sweet one, you have done me mean, but I love you still with all your faults. I wish we were married, but it will be best for us to wait until next winter, unless you say no. We can get off all right, then, and take all the clothes or anything else we want. I won't write any more tonight, but will try to write more some time tomorrow.

I love you. I love you.

Sunday Evening.—I wish I could see "Lovey." If I could squeeze you just once it would do me good. I wish you knew how I love you. I would give anything for you. I more than love you. Be sure and tell me when Miss Ada will let you come. If it is too long, run off, for I am afraid some boy will take you from me if we wait too long. You are so changeable. Fred, do you love me one-half as much as you did the first winter? I believe you loved me truer then than you ever did. You didn't fall in love with every boy that talked sweet to you then.

We went to see Miss Ward at 319 Georgia street yesterday. She wasn't there, but we sprinkled her woodhouse, and Lill drank some of her water out of her new hydrant. I took a piece of ivy and some slips of rose bushes. The pink one is gone. Water was standing in the yard. I wish my little sweetheart was living there now. Then I would have some one to kiss. I thought of how you loved me when you lived there. Sing, I don't do a thing but have the blues all the time. I am always thinking of you, and crying. You don't know how I hated to leave you on that day. I knew you would write that as soon as I left, and I was thinking about it the whole time you was on the boat. When we were in the pilot-house I put my arm around you and you told me to take it away. I suppose you were thinking of some one else and wanted his arm around you. I know you were disappointed because he was not on the boat. I knew as soon as I heard what you told Lill that you didn't care for me, and you were deceiving me. If you don't love me you needn't but I will love you forever. I worship you love. I hope you will be true to me after this, but it is no use, as long as you think of Ashley and Harry so much. If you loved me as you say you do you would deceive them instead of me. I will try not to fuss at you any more, love, unless you say something about that until I see you. [?] Do you remember what I said I would do if you would deceive me? That's what I was coming for, sweet one, honest; but Lill begged me. I love you, Fred, and hate to do it. Be true to me, will you, love? I had the nerve to price the pistols. They only had one size, and that was too big. That was all that kept me from getting it. They were $12. Then I went for Lill and if it hadn't been for her I would have tried every place in Memphis until I got the right one. I didn't know what I was doing, Fred, if you only knew how I love you! Please try to stop loving them before you marry me, love. Nothing could make me happier than to have you love no one but me. If you loved me one-third as much as I do you I would feel better. I am so j-—, I will ask you once more, for my last time, to desert all for my sake: even Ashley and Harry, and be true to me from this on forever. It is the last time I will ask it of you. If you love me you will do it. You can't love all at once, and love them truly. You will have to give up some. Will you have me? I have always been your friend. I am not merely your friend, but your true lover. I have done nothing to you, as I know of, to make you do me this way. I have always been true to you. You might think enough of me to tell me the truth once. Yours forever.

SWEETHEART

LETTER 5
From Mrs. W. H. Volkmar to Alice Mitchell

GOLDDUST, TENN., Aug. 1, 1891

Miss Allie Mitchell:

Ere now you must fully realize that your supposed well laid plans to take Fred away have all gone awry. You should have taken into consideration that Fred had a sister watching over her who had good eyes and plenty of common sense, and was fully competent to take care of her sister. I return your "engagement ring" as you called it, and all else that I know of your having [sent] Fred, as you won't marry her yet awhile. Don't try in any way, shape, form or manner to have any intercourse with Fred again. I thought you were a lady. I have found out to the contrary. Stay at home and attend to your own business, and Fred will do likewise. I hope you will live to see the day that you will realize how very foolish such proceedings were.

MRS. W. H. VOLKMAR.

P.S. — I enclose $2.40 all I can find out that Fred owes you. $1.75 for the dress and 50 cents for the harp and 15 cents that you sent to pay the porter for the ring. If she owes you any more, please let me know and I will send it to you.

MRS. W. H. V.

LETTER 6
From Alice Mitchell to Freda Ward
(The original was destroyed by Mrs.Volkmar before reaching Freda. The following is based on Alice's copy of the letter.)

MEMPHIS, TENN., Aug. 7, 1891

Dear Fred — As Miss Ada sent my things back I will return yours all except the picture. I won't part with that. I told mama and she said I could keep that. If there is anything else I have let me know and I will send it.

Remember, Fred, there is no hard feeling toward you on my side. They have turned you against me, although I know you did not think as much of me as you said you did. You did it only to save your life. When I first asked you to marry me I gave you a chance to think and say no. You wrote and said yes in three letters before I said for certain you had promised. I told you then to think what we were risking, but you still said you would be mine. After that I wouldn't let you break the engagement. I not merely begged you to marry me, but I forced you. I am sorry I have gotten you in trouble, "Sing," but I beg you to forgive me. Mr. and Mrs. Volkmar opened our letters unknown to us and have turned you against me. Of course, I don't ask you to marry me after this, for if they would miss us it would be worse than ever. I have told everything to mama. You told and I did too. I even told her about you running off and going on the stage with Harry, and about Ashley asking you to marry him and you had Ashley's ring and all. You said if it wasn't for me you would have been Mrs. R[oselle]. I suppose it would have been better in the end. If they give you this letter it will be the last I will write. If I could see you just once it would be all I would want. I have one thing to ask you. After that you needn't even speak to me.

I will forgive you for writing that letter to A[shley]. I forgive you for everything you have done.

Please do me a favor, and that is *destroy every* letter I have ever written to you. Don't let this cause hard feelings between you and Lil, for she had nothing to do with it. I LOVE YOU STILL and will forever. Will you forgive me? Please answer and I won't write any more or have anything else to do with you, for your sake.

Yours forever, ALLIE

LETTER 7
From Alice Mitchell, writing as her alter ego, "Freda Myra Ward," to Freda Ward
(The letter was apparently sent from Memphis to Chicago, where it was then mailed to Freda in Golddust.)

Chicago, Ill., Aug. 30, 1891

Dear Freddie:

I know you will be surprised when you get this, for it was reported that I was dead, but I am still alive. I am all right now. Better than I have ever felt. Rob Ritchie was in New York at the same time I was, and when he heard I was not expected to live he said I was dead.

They thought I was dying and gave me up in July, and that is when he said I was dead. I don't thank him one bit for it. I was only supposed to be dead. I hope you will soon go to Memphis and meet the dead girl. I will go next week. It is too changeable here for me. How long did Alice and Lillie stay at the wonderful city of Golddust?

I know you enjoyed their visit. I passed there on the boat while they were there, but I did not see any of you. I suppose you were out viewing the wonderful city or calling on the great people. Hoping you are not angry with me for not writing before, I remain your friend,

FREDA M. WARD

Address general delivery C.S., Memphis, Tenn.
P.S.—I will be there before your letter will.

LETTER 8
From Freda Ward to Alice Mitchell
(This letter was in Alice's possession during the murder and was found in a bloodstained envelope.)

MEMPHIS, Tenn., Jan. 18, 1892

DEAR ALLIE:

I love you now and always will, but I have been forbidden . . . to speak to you and I have to obey. You say I am as much to blame as you are. If I have done you any harm or caused you any trouble, I humbly beg your forgiveness. Please don't let any one know I wrote this. No one knows about that last summer's business except our family, that is unless you have told some one. We go back to Golddust this evening.

FREDA

LETTER 9
Alice Mitchell's last letter to Freda Ward

MEMPHIS, Tenn., Jan. 21, 1892

Fred—Send me my photo, which you have that was taken with Estelle. Also send me the silver ring that I gave you. Maybe you think I believe you left Memphis Monday. You knew as well as I did that the steamer Rosa Lee was not running regular. I suppose you will go home on the Ora Lee tomorrow, or wait for the Rosa Lee Monday.

Don't let any one know you wrote to me! If you trouble me any more I will not only let any one know, but will send the letter to Mrs. W. H. Volkmar, and something else, too. Do you remember who you met on Union street, near Hernando street, this afternoon? I heard more scandal about Mr. ———— and Mrs. ———— that kept the saloon on Poplar street, near Front Row today.

7 Madison street.   ALLIE

II. LETTERS TO MEN FROM ALICE MITCHELL AND LILLIE JOHNSON

LETTER 10

From Alice Mitchell (using a hybrid pseudonym, "Freda Mitchell") and Lillie Johnson to an actor they met on the electric car line.

Memphis, Tenn., Aug. 22, 1890

Mr. R. F. Chartrand:

KIND FRIEND—As you have been so kind to us, and you are going away, we thought we would return it by sending you a few flowers. Hoping this will not be the last time we will see you, we remain yours truly,

FREDA MITCHELL and
LILLIE JOHNSON

The above note was accompanied by a card with "Compliments of Lillie and Freddie" written upon it.

LETTER 11

From Alice Mitchell (writing as her alter ego, Freda Myra Ward) to Jim, an unknown correspondent in Wellsville, Mo.

Memphis, Tenn., Sept. 15, 1890

Unknown Friend—I am an actress. I have pearl-white teeth, blue eyes and light hair. I am 17 years of age, I have been in Memphis this summer with the Fisher Opera Co. After I left Memphis I went to Greenville for three nights and then to St. Louis. I will not go on the stage this winter, and thought I would write to you for pastime, or what may follow. Next summer, I will join the Fisher Opera Co. again, and next winter will travel with the "Said Pasha" Opera Company. I will not write to many, as I will be studying. I was going to join the Baker Opera Co. this winter, but I will rest and write to you. If I like you I will write to you while I am traveling, and tell you all that goes on. My home is in Memphis, but as I belong to a St. Louis troupe I am in St. Louis more than any other place.

Please send me your photo, and I will do the same. Well, I will stop now and write you a long letter next time. Hoping you will do the same, I am very truly yours.

Freda Ward

Please address Miss Freda Ward, care general delivery, Memphis, Tenn.

LETTER 12
From *Alice Mitchell (as Freda Ward) to Jim in Wellsville, Mo.*

Memphis, Tenn., Sept. 17, 1890

My Own Dear Jim—Your appreciated letter was received yesterday with much pleasure. I knew very well Freda's Jim would not go back on her. He is too cute to do anything like that.

You may think I was joking, but, really, I admire you very much. I have written to two others, and I think you are the nicest of the three. I prefer you and think I will drop the others entirely. I received a letter from one yesterday. I do not like him very much, and don't think I will answer it.

My dear Jim beats them all. He is my favorite.

I will wait once more for your photo, but this is the last time I will trust you. As you have kept your promises thus far, I suppose you will send it. It is to be hoped you will.

You are just the right age for me; you hit it exactly. I will always have you for my Jim, even if you do go back on me. I don't think I will ever forget you, dear Jim.

Yes, Freda Ward is my name. My true name is Freda Myra Ward, but my stage name is Myra Ward. I didn't change it much as most of them in the first troupe I joined didn't change their names at all.

I am glad you and your girl "don't speak as you pass by" or some other girl would be jealous. The fair commenced here yesterday. I expect I will go Wednesday.

I wish you were here to go with me. I would enjoy it so much more if you were only with me. You asked me where my company plays when in St. Louis. Once when I was there, I played three nights at the Standard Theater, but the other times I played at the Grand Opera House. I have played everything from soubrette parts to tragedy roles. I do not care much for tragedy.

A comic opera suits me best. I dearly love the stage, and in fact, I enjoy my part. Litty Lind has left the London Gaiety Company.

Ben Lodge, one of our troupe, wrote me week before last and said he was looking for a job. I heard from him Friday, and he is engaged as leading comedian of the Bancroft Opera Company. He is a great favorite in Boston, where the company appears.

As a professional, Miss Ruth Carpenter made her first appearance with Roland Reed in "The Woman Hater," as Alice Lane.

Will you please tell me the name of your chum that traveled with the company to which Edith Kingdon belonged?

I will not send you a lock of my hair this time, but as I admire you so much will be sure to send it next time, and it will be my own hair. Have you a photo of yourself that I could put in my watch? That is the latest here.

The little actress you were badly "gone on" last winter was Kate Castleton (or Mrs. Mary Phillips). I don't much blame you. She is cute. I am her height; not quite so flashy: my eyes are a darker blue, and my hair is the same color (although she wore a wig). I think she sings the "Spider and the Fly" and "I Dreamt I Dwelt in Marble Halls" in that play. It was "A Paper Doll."

I am almost certain it was the same one you were speaking of.

They have new words for the "Spider and the Fly" now.

I can truly say I have loved some boys, but I think if I would meet you I "wouldn't fall in love, but I would rise in love" with you.

I loved one of the actors last summer, and I think he thought a great deal of me, too, but he has joined the Said Pasha Opera company now. He will come back again this spring.

You come, too, and see if you can't get ahead of him. He is handsome, but I don't care for that.

There is one in St. Louis now that I love. He is not good-looking, but I am almost certain he thinks more of me than I do of him. Don't get jealous, now, Jim. I don't intend to marry an actor: in fact, I think I am too young yet to.

Well, I think this letter is long enough; longer than I expected.

Don't fall in love with another married actress before I come along.

Kate Castleton owns property in California. I suppose that is what you were after. Please write soon to your

Freda (Yes, I.L.Y.)

LETTER 13

From *Alice Mitchell (as Freda Ward) to Jim in Wellsville, Mo.*

YBIR

Memphis, Tenn., Sept. 29, 1890

Dear Jim—I received your more than welcome letter yesterday.

I wrote to two others at the same time, but yours was the only one I received an answer to. I have a Memphis beau named Jim, but I don't think he is as nice as Wellsville Jim. Is he? I think Jim is a cute name.

I am almost certain you are giving a false name. Please tell me your proper name.

If you come to St. Louis next spring as you said, perhaps I may see you there. I think I will go there next spring and join the Fischer Company. I tried to get some one to take my place until they come to Memphis. The Fischer Opera Company will be here for the summer operas again next summer.

I asked Jessie Hatcher, as she was in it last summer, but she is so taken with Baker Opera Company that she will not leave it. If I cannot get some one to take my place I will have to go. I don't mind that if I thought my dear Jim would be there.

Please send your photos as soon as possible, as I want to know who and what I am writing to. Don't keep it back because you think you are bad looking; I can love an ugly boy just as much as a pretty boy. I don't care for that at all. I will acknowledge I am pretty. But don't think I am vain. I have had so many to tell me so that I think it is time I was knowing it. If one of us are pretty, I think that will answer for both. I am very much taken with you and think I will like you more after I am better acquainted with you. You asked me what kind of a letter I liked best. I am full of fun; all my stage friends call me "Funny." But, of course, we must have some love. "This world is but a fleeting shore of love."

I will take them mixed. I am writing for fun and a nice beau, and I want it. You won't be so cruel as to disappoint me, will you, Jim?

Last Monday I commenced taking elocution again. I only take it for practice while I am not on the stage. That takes more of my time, but don't you fool yourself, I have time to write to Jim (my Jim), Is he? Please tell me in your next letter the color of your eyes. I hope our correspondence will continue, and some time we will meet. I do not have much time to see my friends when I am traveling, but I expect I can be with you some summer. It is fun to be an actress, but it is hard work. I have gone on the stage and sung and danced when I was so sick I could hardly hold my head up. I ran off with a friend of mine when I was young and went to New York. When I first started I was a chorus girl, and received $10 to $20 a week. I was a chorus girl for two months, when I took a principal part and have been taking principal parts since. Now, I receive from $50 to $60 a week and sometimes $70.

My friend I ran off with is in Memphis now. He will stay here until the Primrose & West Minstrels come, and then he will go with them. Be sure and answer this, Your

Freda

. . . P.S. — Don't forget to send your photo,

"Love"

LETTER 14

From Alice Mitchell (as Freda Ward) to Jim in Wellsville, Mo.

Memphis, Tenn., Oct. 27, 1890

Dear Jim — Your welcome letter was handed to me during performance the night before I left Cincinnati.

I didn't have time to read them, as it was nearly 12 o'clock when the play was over.

Please excuse me for not writing sooner, but they sent for me and said no one could take that part, so I had to go. I had a Memphis boy with me. He has been with the company over a year.

I met them in Chicago on the 7th. We were in Louisville, Ky. on the 10, Monday, 13, Frankfort, Ky; Tuesday, 14, Lexington, Ky.; Thursday, 16, Ironton, O.; Friday, 17, Portsmouth, O.; Cincinnati, O., October 21, one week.

I left for "Home, Sweet, Home" on the 26th. I was with the "Mr. Barnes, of New York," company. I had a delightful time while I was gone. I am very sorry you didn't send your photo. I will have some taken soon and send you one of the latest. That is if you send yours.

You said you were an usher at an opera house. I suppose you saw some pretty girls there, but you can't always tell when they are on the stage. I wish I would pass through Wellsville while you were there.

You needn't be afraid of me getting stuck on some one else and giving you the grand bounce, dear Jim. I have struck the right one now, and that is my Jim.

You asked me how I pronounced my name. It is pronounced Freda (Friedar), but the home folks call me Fred, or Freddie, sometimes. I met a young man whose name was Ellis. I think J. H. Ellis, but I don't suppose he was your chum. He was with the Baker Opera Co. when I met him.

As you waited for a lock of my hair, and I admire you and think so much of you, I will send it this time.

Now don't forget your photo.

I can't say for certain when I will go to St. Louis. I have been offered from $95 to $100 a week by "Mr. Barnes, of New York," company, and I think I may join that.

I prefer an opera troupe, as I have a splendid voice, but don't know for certain yet which I will join.

I have a chance to join the Emma Juch English Opera Company, but I am not allowed to use my voice any this autumn. That is the reason I went with this last company. It was a drama.

When I wrote to your chums B and C I had forgotten it was your advertisement, and was going to write to A (which was you) the next day, and found it was my Jim.

I had mailed the two letters, and it was too late.

By no means, I am not tired of your letters, and am glad to hear from you any time.

Accept my thanks for those cards you sent me. I appreciate them very much, and am ever so much obliged to you for your kindness. Now I know you think something of me.

You said you could not read the initials on the envelope. I have forgotten what I wrote, but it was either

Sealed With A Kiss

Look Under the Stamp, or

Read Inside of Envelope.

I read every initial you had in your letter and my answer is "Yes."

Please answer this letter immediately, as I may be called for unexpected at any time.

Your Freda

P.S. — If I go off in a hurry again I will let you know and give you some addresses ahead.

LETTER 15
From *Alice Mitchell (as Freda Ward) to Jim in Wellsville, Mo.*

Memphis, Tenn., October 29, 1890

My Dear Jim — I answered your letter as soon as I could. I was not in Memphis, and it was not sent to me until the night before I left Cincinnati.

I did not have time to answer it then, so I answered it as soon as I returned home. I didn't write to you while I was gone, because I had not heard from you.

Thought you had forsaken me, but I see you think as much of me as ever.

I will not write any more now until I get a letter from you.

Hoping everything is all right, I remain, sincerely,

Freda

LETTER 16

From Alice Mitchell (writing as her alter ego, Freda Ward's sister, Wander) to Jim in Wellsville, Mo.

Memphis, Tenn., November 23, 1890

Dear Jim—I have heard Freda speak of you so much that I have come to the conclusion that I can love you also.

I am her sister and am the same size, same age, just like her and everything, except she is about an inch taller than I am, and she has dark blue eyes and I have dark brown.

She says your eyes are blue. I love blue eyes, although I prefer dark blue, but of course you cannot get everything you wish for.

Next Wednesday is my birthday. I will be 18.

You are just the right age for me, dear Jimmie. Have me for your sweetheart, will you, Jim dear?

I neither would want for my beau a silly little boy nor an old man. I think you will suit me exactly.

Darling Jim, please don't drop me as you did Freddie.

I had my photo taken last week, and every time the photographer looked at me I laughed.

In the end he took it while I was laughing.

Send me one of yours, and I will send you one of mine in return.

If you think Freddie is pretty you will think I am pretty, because you can hardly tell us apart, unless you look at our eyes.

I will not write any more this time, so write me a sweet letter Jim dear. Yours truly,

Wander

Please address Miss Wander Ward, care Edmonson's drug store, corner Lauderdale street and Mississippi avenue, Memphis, Tenn.

LETTER 17

Alice Mitchell's last letter (writing as Freda Ward) to Jim in Wellsville, Mo.

Memphis, Tenn. Nov. 30, 1890

Jim — If I have done or said anything to hurt your feelings please let me know. If not, please return my hair which I sent you, and oblige

Freda Ward

LETTER 18

From Lillie Johnson (writing as her alter ego, "Jessie James") to an unknown correspondent, "Mr. Robins."

MEMPHIS, Tenn., Nov. 30, 1890

Mr. Robins:

UNKNOWN FRIEND — As I have heard Freda [Alice Mitchell's alter ego] speak of you so much, I thought I would write to you. Freda told me you were going to a candy pulling, and I hope you will enjoy yourself. I wish I was there to go with you. I know you will have a fine time. When you are pulling the candy just think of me.

I suppose you would like to have a description of myself as you have never heard of or seen me. I have light hair and blue eyes. I live in St. Louis, near Freda, on West Eighth street near Charles avenue. So you said you would exchange photos with Freda. I would like to do the same. Excuse this short letter as this is the first. I will write you a long one next time. Hoping to hear from you soon, I remain,

Yours truly,
JESSIE R. JAMES.

P.S. — Please address Miss Jessie James, care general delivery, Memphis, Tenn.

Write soon.   JESSIE.

LETTER 19

Lillie Johnson writing to the same unknown correspondent as above (letter 18), using her own name this time.

Memphis, Tenn., Friday, Jan. 2, 1891

Mr. Robins:

DEAR FRIEND — As I have heard my friend Freda [Alice Mitchell's alter ego] speak of you so much, I thought I would write you. You told Freda you would like to correspond with me. Mr. Robins, don't think I am a flirt for writing to you, for I am not. It was your wish that I should correspond with you. I hope if you ever come to Memphis, I will meet you. My friend Allie Mitchell went to Mrs. Volkmar's to see her sisters Fred and Joe, and she said she saw you in Golddust, and she said you were just handsome. If she says anybody is pretty she means it, for Allie is a good judge of beauty. I am going up to Mrs. V's to see Fred and Joe next summer, and I hope I will get to meet you, that is, if you would like to meet me.

Well, I suppose you would like to know the color of my hair and eyes. My hair is light and I have blue eyes. Freddie and Joe Ward, at "G'd," spent two weeks with me, and I tell you we had a nice time. I am going to the theater tonight with my best friend. I wish you were here to go along with us. If you ever come to Memphis and I get acquainted with you, I tell you, I will make you have a good time. My friend Jessie [her own alter ego] is coming down from St. Louis to spend three weeks with me, and I tell you we will have great times.

I will take my friend Jessie's name, and I will tell you now to add it.

Well I must close, hoping you will answer this letter real soon. I remain yours truly,

LILLIE JOHNSON

P.S.—Please address Miss Jessie James, care general delivery, Memphis, Tenn.

LETTER 20
From Alice Mitchell (writing as Freda Ward) to "Virg" in Carbon, Texas

MEMPHIS, TENN., Jan. 11, 1892

Dearest Virg—Your highly appreciated letter was enjoyed and read with much pleasure. I thought you had forgotten me. I waited until December 30 and you didn't come, so I then went to St. Louis with Jess [Lillie Johnson's alter ego]. Had just an elegant time. Returned home night before last. Made a complete mash there. He just begged me to elope with him, but I loved some one better. A young man come to see Jess and me last evening and fell in love with my singing. I was real glad to be home with my friends again. Saw a great many pretty boys, but then their charms and sweet smiles are to me as naught when I think of one sweet boy in Texas. I would love to see you just splendid. I am quite fascinated with your letters, and also what is more precious your darling self. I am very sorry to hear of your illness and sincerely hope you will be able to come and see your Freda real soon. Certainly I will forgive you for not writing, as you were so ill. Give your brother my congratulations for me. I hope he has a sweet pretty girl. I hope you won't get married, dear, until you see me. I love you. I didn't realize what real love was until you stopped writing, and I looked for you all in vain. Dearest, I love you devotedly. I have one question to ask you, and you must be sure and answer. Would you associate with an actress? I won't worry you with a long letter, as you are not well. Please write me a long letter real soon.

Yours, forever, FREDA

NOTES

Introduction

1   I borrow the term "calendrical coincidence" from Benedict Anderson, *Imagined Communities: Reflections on the Origin and Spread of Nationalism* (London: Verso, 1983), 33–36.

2   By "containment" I do not mean the repression of knowledge but the shaping and channeling of both objects of investigation and methods of communication; this containment is productive as well as disciplinary.

3   Phillip Brian Harper, *Private Affairs: Critical Ventures in the Culture of Social Relations* (New York: New York University Press, 1999), 29.

4   These authors provide methods for analyzing cultural narratives that usefully modify historical approaches that stress the *adoption* of elite formulations (like medical conceptions of sexuality) by passive populations, or the simple or direct *reflection* of "real" relations in scientific or literary texts. Instead, these scholars combine aspects of social and cultural history methodologies with discourse analysis; they show how texts, practices, and identities are formulated interactively and circulate through concrete institutions and material practices. See Judith R. Walkowitz, *City of Dreadful Delight: Narratives of Sexual Danger in Late Victorian London* (Chicago: University of Chicago Press, 1992); Jacquelyn Dowd Hall, "'The Mind That Burns in Each Body': Women, Rape, and Racial Violence," in *Powers of Desire: The Politics of Sexuality*, ed. Ann Snitow, Christine Stansell, and Sharon Thompson (New York: Monthly Review Press, 1983), 328–49; Hazel Carby, *Reconstructing Womanhood: The Emergence of the Afro-American Woman Novelist* (New York: Oxford University Press, 1987); Judith Halberstam, *Female Masculinity* (Durham: Duke University Press, 1998); Lisa Lowe, *Immigrant Acts: On Asian American Cultural Politics* (Durham: Duke University Press, 1996).

5   Mary P. Ryan, *Civic Wars: Democracy and Public Life in the American City during the Nineteenth Century* (Berkeley: University of California Press, 1997); Evelyn Brooks Higginbotham, *Righteous Discontent: The Women's Movement in the Black Baptist Church, 1880–1920* (Cambridge: Harvard University Press, 1993); Elsa Barkley Brown, "Negotiating and Transforming the Public Sphere: African American Political Life in the Transition from Slavery to Freedom," in *The Black Public Sphere: A Public Culture Book*, ed. The Black Public Sphere Collective (Chicago: University of Chicago Press, 1995), 111–50; Nancy Fraser, "Rethinking the Public Sphere: A Contribution to the Critique

of Actually Existing Democracy," in *The Phantom Public Sphere*, ed. Bruce Robbins (Minneapolis: University of Minnesota Press, 1993), 1–32; Miriam Hansen, *Babel and Babylon: Spectatorship in American Silent Film* (Cambridge: Harvard University Press, 1991); Lauren Berlant, *The Queen of America Goes to Washington City: Essays on Sex and Citizenship* (Durham: Duke University Press, 1997); and Michael Warner, *The Letters of the Republic: Publication and the Public Sphere in Eighteenth-Century America* (Cambridge: Harvard University Press, 1990).

6 Michel Foucault, *The History of Sexuality*, vol. 1: *An Introduction*, trans. Robert Hurley (New York: Pantheon, 1978).

7 Throughout this book, I use "United States" or "U.S." to designate the historical, legal institutions of the state and "American" to refer to the ideological nation.

8 For a critique of the treatment of sexuality as disconnected from issues of material distribution, see Judith Butler, "Merely Cultural," *Social Text* 52–53 (fall/winter 1997): 265–77.

Chapter 1   Girl Slays Girl

1 Henry P. Lundsgaarde, *Murder in Space City: A Cultural Analysis of Houston Homicide Patterns* (New York: Oxford University Press, 1977), 3.

2 This narrative of events is constructed from numerous newspaper accounts of testimony at the legal proceedings following the murder. Specific citations are noted throughout this and the following chapters. Only those events reported in a local newspaper as corroborated in court by more than a single witness are included.

3 "Girl Slays Girl," *Memphis Appeal Avalanche*, Jan. 26, 1892, 5.

4 "I Loved Her So!" *Memphis Public Ledger*, Jan. 26, 1892, 1.

5 There are numerous accounts of these events. See especially Ida B. Wells, "Lynching at the Curve," chapter 6 of her *Crusade for Justice: The Autobiography of Ida B. Wells*, ed. Alfreda M. Duster (Chicago: University of Chicago Press, 1970), 47–52. See also Linda O. McMurry, *To Keep the Waters Troubled: The Life of Ida B. Wells* (New York: Oxford University Press, 1998), chapter 7; Paula Giddings, *When and Where I Enter: The Impact of Black Women on Race and Sex in America* (New York: William Morrow, 1984), 17–31; Mildred I. Thompson, *Ida B. Wells-Barnett: An Exploratory Study of an American Black Woman, 1893–1930* (Brooklyn, N.Y.: Carlson Publishing, 1990), 27–34; Fred L. Hutchins, *What Happened in Memphis* (Kingsport, Tenn.: Kingsport Press, 1965), 36–41; "LYNCHED! Memphis Jail Broken Open. Three of the Curve Rioters Taken Out by Masked Men," *Memphis Appeal Avalanche*, Mar. 9, 1892, 1; "The Lynching," *Memphis Appeal Avalanche*, Mar. 10, 1892, 4.

6 Quoted in Wells, *Crusade for Justice*, 65–66.

7 Quoted in Ida B. Wells-Barnett, *Southern Horrors: Lynch Law in All Its Phases* (New York: The New York Age, 1892), 5. The events are described in Wells, *Crusade for Justice*, 53–67.

8 For an assessment of the historical importance of Wells's analysis, see Hazel Carby, *Reconstructing Womanhood: The Emergence of the Afro-American Woman Novelist* (New York: Oxford University Press, 1987), 108.

9 Recent historians who provide discussions of Wells's activism and writing placed in broad context include Gail Bederman, *Manhood and Civilization: A Cultural History of Gender and Race in the United States, 1880–1917* (Chicago: University of Chicago Press, 1995); Kevin Gaines, *Uplifting the Race: Black Leadership, Politics and Culture in the Twentieth Century* (Chapel Hill: University of North Carolina Press, 1996); Sandra Gunning, *Race, Rape and Lynching: The Red Record of American Literature, 1890–1912* (New York: Oxford University Press, 1996).

10 The Mitchell case was brought to the attention of contemporary historians by Jonathan Ned Katz, *Gay American History* (New York: Thomas Crowell, 1976), 53–58. Some discussion also appeared in Lillian Faderman, *Surpassing the Love of Men: Romantic Friendship and Love between Women from the Renaissance to the Present* (New York: William Morrow, 1981), 291–94. The only scholarly article on the case is by Lisa J. Lindquist, "Images of Alice: Gender, Deviancy, and a Love Murder in Memphis," *Journal of the History of Sexuality* 6, no. 1 (winter 1995): 30–61. There are many other contemporary recreations of the Mitchell-Ward murder and its aftermath in newspapers, fiction, and drama; these are discussed in later chapters.

11 Significant histories of these developments in the late-nineteenth-century South are provided by Joseph H. Cartwright, *The Triumph of Jim Crow: Tennessee Race Relations in the 1880s* (Knoxville: University of Tennessee Press, 1976); Joel Williamson, *The Crucible of Race: Black-White Relations in the American South* (New York: Oxford University Press, 1984); Edward Ayers, *The Promise of the New South: Life after Reconstruction* (New York: Oxford University Press, 1992).

12 For a discussion of the economic, political, and cultural dimensions of corportate liberalism, as it defined Americanness in the twentieth century, see Martin J. Sklar, *The Corporate Reconstruction of American Capitalism, 1890–1916: The Market, the Law, and Politics* (Cambridge: Cambridge University Press, 1988). For a summary of the arguments about three globally dominant modernities—seventeenth-century Dutch mercantile, nineteenth-century British industrial, and twentieth-century American consumerist—see Peter Taylor, *Modernities: A Geohistorical Interpretation* (Minneapolis: University of Minnesota Press, 1999). Taylor also synthesizes debates about how these dominant modernities emerged in a world of different modern times, different modern spaces, and multiple modernities (12). For detailed elaborations of such arguments, see Paul Gilroy, *The Black Atlantic: Modernity and Double Consciousness* (Cambridge: Harvard University Press, 1993), and Arjun Appadurai, *Modernity at Large: Cultural Dimensions of Globalization* (Minneapolis: University of Minnesota Press, 1997).

13 Here I am borrowing and extending the concept of race as a "metalanguage," introduced by Evelyn Brooks Higginbotham, "African-American Women's History and the Metalanguage of Race," *Signs* 17 (winter 1992): 251–74. For an analysis

of the production of masculine sameness, through whiteness, as national citizenship in the early republic, see Dana Nelson, *National Manhood: Capitalist Citizenship and the Imagined Fraternity of White Men* (Durham: Duke University Press, 1998). For this period see also Alexander Saxton, *The Rise and Fall of the White Republic: Class Politics and Mass Culture in Nineteenth-Century America* (London: Verso, 1990), though I disagree with Saxton's argument that the central significance of whiteness for American nationalism declined after World War I. For a discussion of the fracturing of "whiteness" during the period of mass European immigration to the United States, and the reconsolidation of that category in the early twentieth century, see Matthew Frye Jacobson, *Whiteness of a Different Color: European Immigrants and the Alchemy of Race* (Cambridge: Harvard University Press, 1998). For a discussion of Mexican, black, and Anglo/white relations and overlapping conflicts of class and gender in central Texas, see Neil Foley, *The White Scourge: Mexicans, Blacks, and Poor Whites in Texas Cotton Culture* (Berkeley: University of California Press, 1997). For an account of the production of "whiteness" through law, see Ian F. Haney Lopez, *White by Law: The Legal Construction of Race* (New York: New York University Press, 1996).

14   For a riveting picture of the crises of late-nineteenth-century politics, see Nell Irvin Painter, *Standing at Armageddon: The United States, 1877–1919* (New York: W. W. Norton, 1987).

15   For a discussion of the central place of whiteness at the heart of modern American institutions, see Grace Elizabeth Hale, *Making Whiteness: The Culture of Segregation* (New York: Pantheon Books, 1998). Hale stresses the significant place of the New South in nationalizing race relations during the twentieth century.

16   I am *not* arguing that class was a fundamental organizing principle of social and economic life, while race, gender, or sexuality were epiphenomenal distractions. Rather, I am arguing that these modes of producing identity and difference were inextricable and mutually constituting. Different categories were thematized in mass culture at specific historical moments and sometimes worked to obscure the operations of other inequalities and conflicts. At the turn of the century in the United States, the master discourse of whiteness worked explicitly *with* narratives of gender and sexuality and often *against* narratives of class antagonism.

17   I draw the phrase "the best white people" from Frances Willard, the national Women's Christian Temperance Union leader who argued, following an 1890 organizing tour of the South, that lynching was justified. She had been assured by "the best white people" that the "safety of woman, of childhood, the home is menaced in a thousand localities at the moment." Willard was rebuked by Wells for such remarks. Willard responded by condemning Wells in an 1894 WCTU address for her implication that white women ever encouraged sexual liaisons with black men. Quoted in Carby, *Reconstructing Womanhood*, 113–14.

18   Biographical details of Ida B. Wells's life are contained in her autobiography, *Crusade for Justice*, in Alfreda Duster's introduction to that volume, in Miriam DeCosta-

Willis, ed., *The Memphis Diary of Ida B. Wells* (Boston: Beacon Press, 1995), in DeCosta-Willis's introduction to the diary, and in the afterword by Dorothy Sterling. For recent research into Wells's life, see also McMurry, *To Keep the Waters Troubled*.

19 Hale, *Making Whiteness*, chapter 4. Hale points out the central significance of the train and general store in the history of battles over segregation during the late nineteenth century. Both locations play crucial roles in Ida B. Wells's life in Memphis and in motivating her later activism. She sued a railroad and responded to a lynching that resulted from racial competition over ownership of a general store.

20 Bederman, *Manhood and Civilization*, 53–57; Evelyn Brooks Higginbotham, *Righteous Discontent: The Women's Movement in the Black Baptist Church, 1880–1920* (Cambridge: Harvard University Press, 1993), 234.

21 For an extended discussion of splits within African American leadership between "uplift" advocates and agitators such as Wells and Fortune with a more militant agenda, see Gaines, *Uplifting the Races*, especially pp. 24–30. See also Gunning, *Race, Rape and Lynching*, 81.

22 These statistics are the best available estimates. Christopher Waldrep has argued persuasively, however, that it is impossible to accurately count the number of lynchings in the United States during this period. See his "Word and Deed: The Language of Lynching, 1820–1953," in *Lethal Imagination: Violence and Brutality in American History*, ed. Michael A. Bellesiles (New York: New York University Press, 1999), 229–58. For details and interpretations of the practice of lynching, see Howard N. Rabinowitz, *The First New South 1865–1920* (Arlington, Ill.: Harlan Davidson, 1992), 141; Mary Frances Berry, "Repression of Blacks in the South 1890–1945," in *The Age of Segregation: Race Relations in the South, 1870–1945*, ed. Robert Haws (Jackson: University Press of Mississippi, 1978), 41; Williamson, *The Crucible of Race*, 180–223; Elsa Barkley Brown, "Negotiating and Transforming the Public Sphere: African American Political Life in the Transition from Slavery to Freedom," in *The Black Public Sphere: A Public Culture Book*, ed. The Black Public Sphere Collective (Chicago: University of Chicago Press, 1995), 116; Higginbotham, *Righteous Discontent*, 1993, 4; Gaines, *Uplifting the Race*, 25; Bederman, *Manhood and Civilization*, 47; W. Fitzhugh Brundage, ed., *Under Sentence of Death: Lynching in the South* (Chapel Hill: University of North Carolina Press, 1997), introduction; Stewart Emory Tolnay, *A Festival of Violence: An Analysis of Southern Lynchings, 1882–1930* (Urbana: University of Illinois Press, 1995). For analyses of lynching in specific southern states, see George C. Wright, *Racial Violence in Kentucky 1865–1940* (Baton Rouge: Louisiana State University Press, 1990), and W. Fitzhugh Brundage, *Lynching in the New South: Georgia and Virginia 1880–1930* (Urbana: University of Illinois Press, 1993).

23 For accounts of the meanings attached to voting, see Eric Foner, "From Slavery to Citizenship: Blacks and the Right to Vote," in *Voting and the Spirit of American Democracy*, ed. Donald Rogers (Chicago: University of Illinois Press, 1992), 55–65. For a discussion of white fear of the economic independence of the growing black middle class, see Hale, *Making Whiteness*. For an analysis of the meanings of bodily

and domestic privacy, see Phillip Brian Harper, "Private Affairs: Race, Sex, Property and Persons," *GLQ: A Journal of Lesbian and Gay Studies* 1, no. 2 (1994), 111–33. For an extended argument about the foundational importance of household relations for politics and citizenship, see Laura F. Edwards, *Gendered Strife and Confusion: The Political Culture of Reconstruction* (Chicago: University of Illinois Press, 1997).

24 Gunning, *Race, Rape and Lynching*, 7.

25 One of the most influential analyses of the lynching narrative is Jacquelyn Dowd Hall, " 'The Mind That Burns in Each Body': Women, Rape, and Racial Violence," in *Powers of Desire: The Politics of Sexuality*, ed. Ann Snitow, Christine Stansell, and Sharon Thompson (New York: Monthly Review Press, 1983), 328–49. The historical operations of cultural narratives of sexual danger have been meticulously theorized in Judith R. Walkowitz's *City of Dreadful Delight: Narratives of Sexual Danger in Late Victorian London* (Chicago: University of Chicago Press, 1992). See also Peter Stallybrass and Allon White, *The Politics and Poetics of Transgression* (Ithaca, N.Y.: Cornell University Press, 1986), 25, 202.

26 See Amy Kaplan, "Manifest Domesticity," *American Literature* 70, no.3 (Sept. 1998), 581–606, and also her "Romancing the Empire: The Embodiment of American Masculinity in the Popular Historical Novel of the 1890s," *Amercian Literary History* 2, no. 4 (winter 1990): 659–90.

27 See Lora Romero's discussion of "manhood" rights in Maria Stewart's early-nineteenth-century black nationalism in *Home Fronts: Domesticity and Its Critics in the Antebellum United States* (Durham: Duke University Press, 1997), chapter 3. See also Edwards, *Gendered Strife and Confusion*, 21–23, for a description of the limits imposed on class and racial politics by "manhood" rhetoric.

28 For analyses of masculinity and the racialized politics of citizenship, see Robyn Wiegman, *American Anatomies: Theorizing Race and Gender* (Durham: Duke University Press, 1995), and Bederman, *Manhood and Civilization*.

29 Gunning offers a way of reading the lynching narrative and its resistances that puts black women back into the triangle that overtly excludes them. See *Race, Rape and Lynching*, especially p. 77.

30 Eve Kosofsky Sedgwick's historical analysis of the nineteenth-century erotic triangle of British literature in *Between Men: English Literature and Male Homosocial Desire* (New York: Columbia University Press, 1985) has influenced my own thinking substantially.

31 Martha Hodes makes clear the links between sexuality and the politics of citizenship in her "The Sexualization of Reconstruction Politics: White Women and Black Men in the South after the Civil War," *Journal of the History of Sexuality* 3, no. 3 (1993): 402–17.

32 Wells drew from collective political and intellectual resources in formulating her critique of lynching. See Martha Hodes, *White Women, Black Men: Illicit Sex in the Nineteenth-Century South* (New Haven: Yale University Press, 1997), chapter 8.

33 Bederman, *Manhood and Civilization*, 59.

34 See Patricia A. Schechter's articles, "Unsettled Business: Ida B. Wells against

Lynching, or, How Antilynching Got Its Gender," in *Under Sentence of Death: Lynching in the South*, ed. W. Fitzhugh Brundage (Chapel Hill: University of North Carolina Press, 1997), 292–317, and " 'All the Intensity of My Nature': Ida B. Wells, Anger, and Politics," *Radical History Review* 70 (winter 1998): 48–77. See also Gunning, *Race, Rape and Lynching*, 82, 88.

35 I am borrowing the concept of the politics of narrative from Gunning, *Race, Rape and Lynching*; see especially p. 8.

36 See John D'Emilio and Estelle Freedman, *Intimate Matters: A History of Sexuality in America* (New York: Harper and Row, 1988), 171–235.

37 See Elizabeth Pleck, *Domestic Tyranny: The Making of Social Policy against Family Violence from Colonial Times to the Present* (New York: Oxford University Press, 1987), 217–25; Roger Lane, *Violent Death in the City: Suicide, Accident and Murder in Nineteenth Century Philadelphia* (Cambridge: Harvard University Press, 1979), 100–109.

38 For succinct discussions of women's political activities in the United States at the close of the nineteenth century, see Giddings, *When and Where I Enter*; Louise Michele Newman, *White Women's Rights: The Racial Origins of Feminism in the United States* (New York: Oxford University Press, 1999); Mary Ryan, "Gender and Public Access: Women's Politics in Nineteenth Century America," in *Habermas and the Public Sphere*, ed. Craig Calhoun (Cambridge: MIT Press, 1996), 258–88; Suzanne Lebsock, "Women and American Politics 1880–1920," in *Women, Politics and Change*, ed. Louise Tilly and Patricia Gurin (New York: Russell Sage Foundation, 1990), 35–62. For descriptions of women's reform work in the South see Valeria Gennaro Lerda, " 'We Were No Class at All': Southern Women as Social Reformers," in *Race and Class in the South Since 1890*, ed. Melvyn Stokes and Rick Halpern (Oxford: Berg Publishers, 1994), 121–37; Jacqueline Jones, "The Political Implications of Black and White Women's Work in the South, 1890–1965," in Tilly and Guerin, eds., *Women, Politics and Change*, 108–29. For accounts of women's political interventions in Memphis specifically, see Marsha Wedell, *Elite Women and the Reform Impulse in Memphis, 1875–1915* (Knoxville: University of Tennessee Press, 1991); Grace Elizabeth Prescot, "The Woman Suffrage Movement in Memphis: Its Place in the State, Sectional and National Movements," *The West Tennessee Historical Society Papers*, no. 18 (1976): 87–106.

39 For the story of Lizzie Borden's trial, see Catharine Ross Nickerson, " 'The Deftness of Her Sex': Innocence, Guilt, and Gender in the Trial of Lizzie Borden," in Bellesiles, ed., *Lethal Imagination*, 260–81; Ann Jones, *Women Who Kill* (New York: Holt, Rinehart & Winston, 1980), 222–35; and Victoria Lincoln, *A Private Disgrace: Lizzie Borden by Daylight* (New York: International Polygonics, 1986).

40 "Alice Mitchell's Crime," *New York World*, Jan. 31, 1892, 6.

41 There were a number of precursors to the Mitchell-Ward murder's press coverage. See, for example, "A Female Romeo . . . A Queer Psychological Study," *The National Police Gazette*, June 7, 1879, 6. These will be discussed at length in later chapters.

42 Jeannette Foster's *Sex Variant Women in Literature* (New York: Vantage Press, 1956)

provided a pioneering study of lesbian themes in Anglo-European and U.S. literature. For synopses of the French novels alluded to here, see her part 4. See also Faderman, *Surpassing the Love of Men*, 254–94.

43 The importance of the boundaries of circulation defined by print capitalism for developing nationalism is stressed in Benedict Anderson, *Imagined Communities: Reflections on the Origin and Spread of Nationalism* (London: Verso, 1983). These issues will be developed further in chapter 2.

44 Jonathan Ned Katz, *Gay/Lesbian Almanac: A New Documentary* (New York: Harper & Row, 1983), 231–32.

45 Surveys and analyses of the range of variation in gender and sexual meanings and practices in Anglo-Europe are provided by Lisa L. Moore, " 'Something More Tender Still Than Friendship': Romantic Friendship in Early Nineteenth Century England," *Feminist Studies* 18, no. 3 (fall 1992), 499–520; Judith Halberstam, *Female Masculinity* (Durham: Duke University Press, 1998); Emma Donoghue, *Passions between Women: British Lesbian Culture 1668–1801* (New York: Harper Collins, 1993); Martha Vicinus, "Lesbian History: All Theory and No Facts, or All Facts and No Theory?" *Radical History Review* 60 (fall 1994): 57–75; Louise O. Fradenburg and Carla Freccero, "The Pleasures of History," *GLQ: A Journal of Gay and Lesbian Studies* 1, no. 4 (1995): 371–84.

46 Havelock Ellis, *Sexual Inversion* (Philadelphia: F. A. Davis, 1901); Richard von Krafft-Ebing, *Psychopathia Sexualis, with Special Reference to Antipathic Sexual Instinct: A Medico-Forensic Study*, 10th ed. (London: Rebman, 1899), 550. For a detailed account of the side-by-side emergence of dissimilar popular and elite vocabularies and categories of sexual identity in the early twentieth century, see George Chauncey Jr., *Gay New York: Gender, Urban Culture and the Making of the Gay Male World, 1890–1940* (New York: Basic Books, 1994).

47 Forms of female partnership and same-sex desire had existed for centuries—see Martha Vicinus, " 'They Wonder to Which Sex I Belong': The Historical Roots of Modern Lesbian Identity," *Feminist Studies* 18, no. 3 (fall 1992): 467–97. But the social identity "lesbian" did not appear until the nineteenth century and was not widely publicized until well into the twentieth century.

48 Ann-Louise Shapiro has argued that the *witch* and the *hysteric* were generic constructions, covering over diverse experiences and phenomena. See her "Disordered Bodies/Disorderly Acts: Medical Discourse and the Female Criminal in Nineteenth-Century Paris," *Genders* 4 (1989): 68–86.

49 Hale, *Making Whiteness*, provides an extended analysis of the cultural work of the "white home" in her chapter 3.

50 A benchmark debate on the meanings of the "mannish lesbian" is elaborated in Carroll Smith-Rosenberg, "Discourses of Sexuality and Subjectivity: The New Woman, 1870–1936," and Esther Newton, "The Mythic Mannish Lesbian: Radclyffe Hall and the New Woman," both in *Hidden from History: Reclaiming the Gay and Lesbian Past*, ed. Martin Duberman, Martha Vicinus, and George Chauncey Jr. (New York: New American Library, 1989), 264–93.

51 For an analysis of the material embeddedness of cultural productions that has greatly influenced my own thinking, see Lisa Lowe, *Immigrant Acts: On Asian American Cultural Politics* (Durham: Duke University Press, 1996).

Chapter 2   *A Feast of Sensation*

1 Quoted in John D. Stevens, *Sensationalism and the New York Press* (New York: Columbia University Press, 1991), 7.

2 See Martin J. Sklar, *The Corporate Reconstruction of American Capitalism, 1890–1916: The Market, the Law, and Politics* (Cambridge: Cambridge University Press, 1988); Richard Ohmann, *Selling Culture: Magazines, Markets, and Class at the Turn of the Century* (London: Verso, 1996); Matthew Schneirov, *The Dream of a New Social Order: Popular Magazines in America, 1893–1914* (New York: Columbia University Press, 1994).

3 Michael Schudson, *Discovering the News: A Social History of American Newspapers* (New York: Basic Books, 1978).

4 The now classic account of the role of print capitalism in the development of nationalism is Benedict Anderson, *Imagined Communities: Reflections on the Origin and Spread of Nationalism* (London: Verso, 1983). For an analysis of the specific U.S. context, see Michael Warner, *The Letters of the Republic: Publication and the Public Sphere in Eighteenth-Century America* (Cambridge: Harvard University Press, 1990). For an argument about the emergence of "mass" readerships in the British context, see Raymond Williams, *The Long Revolution* (New York: Harper and Row, 1965), 173–213.

5 An analysis of the ideological work of disconnection and fragmentation accomplished through newspaper page layouts is provided by Richard Terdiman, *Discourse/Counter-discourse: The Theory and Practice of Symbolic Resistance in Nineteenth-Century France* (Ithaca, N.Y.: Cornell University Press, 1985), 120–42. Terdiman draws significantly on the work of Walter Benjamin. See also the discussion of "calendrical coincidence" as an organizing principle of the newspaper in Anderson, *Imagined Communities*, 33–36.

6 For an account of the development of multiple "publics" in nineteenth-century U.S. cities, see Mary P. Ryan, *Civic Wars: Democracy and Public Life in the American City during the Nineteenth Century* (Berkeley: University of California Press, 1997). For an analysis of the contested public sphere of the early-twentieth-century cinema that has significantly influenced my discussion of the newspaper as public sphere here, see Miriam Hansen, *Babel and Babylon: Spectatorship in American Silent Film* (Cambridge: Harvard University Press, 1991). See also Hansen's foreword to Oskar Negt and Alexander Kluge, *Public Sphere and Experience: Toward an Analysis of the Bourgeois and Proletarian Public Sphere*, trans. Peter Labanyi, Jamie Owen Daniel, and Assenka Oksiloff (Minneapolis: University of Minnesota Press, 1993). For one of the most influential recent theoretical formulations of the work of publics, counterpublics, and alternative public spheres see Nancy Fraser, "Rethinking the Public Sphere: A Contribution to the Critique of Actually Existing Democracy," in *The Phantom Pub-*

lic Sphere, ed. Bruce Robbins (Minneapolis: University of Minnesota Press, 1993), 1–32. All of these writers are drawing upon and modifying Jürgen Habermas, The Structural Transformation of the Public Sphere: An Inquiry into a Category of Bourgeois Society, trans. Thomas Burger and Frederick Lawrence (Cambridge: Polity Press, 1989). Other reworkings of Habermas's framework are included in The Black Public Sphere Collective, editors, The Black Public Sphere: A Public Culture Book (Chicago: University of Chicago Press, 1995), and Craig Calhoun, ed., Habermas and the Public Sphere (Cambridge: MIT Press, 1996).

7   My analysis of the work of cultural narratives is heavily indebted to Judith R. Walkowitz, City of Dreadful Delight: Narratives of Sexual Danger in Late Victorian London (Chicago: University of Chicago Press, 1992). For a discussion of the intersections of news and fiction in nineteenth-century popular culture, see Michael Denning, Mechanic Accents: Dime Novels and Working-class Culture in America (London: Verso, 1987). See also Stevens, Sensationalism and the New York Press.

8   For an analysis of the work of sensationalism in British fiction that informs my discussion here, see Ann Cvetkovich, Mixed Feelings: Feminism, Mass Culture, and Victorian Sensationalism (New Brunswick, N.J.: Rutgers University Press, 1992). For discussion of the politics of sensationalism in the U.S. context, see David Ray Papke, Framing the Criminal: Crime, Cultural Work and the Loss of Critical Perspective, 1830–1900 (Hamden, Conn.: Archon Books, 1987); Amy Gilman Srebnick, The Mysterious Death of Mary Rogers: Sex and Culture in Nineteenth-Century New York (New York: Oxford University Press, 1995); Patricia Cohen, The Murder of Helen Jewett: The Life and Death of a Prostitute in Nineteenth-Century New York (New York: Knopf, 1998); and Karen Halttunen, Murder Most Foul: The Killer and the American Gothic Imagination (Cambridge: Harvard University Press, 1998).

9   My analysis here has been deeply influenced by Lauren Berlant's notion of the privatization of citizenship and the workings of the "intimate public sphere." See Lauren Berlant, The Queen of America Goes to Washington City: Essays on Sex and Citizenship (Durham: Duke University Press, 1997), and her "Introduction to 'Intimacy: A Special Issue,'" Critical Inquiry 24 (winter 1998): 281–88. For a concise theorization of the displacement of political and economic questions to "mere" affective interest, see Phillip Brian Harper, "Private Affairs: Race, Sex, Property, and Persons," GLQ: A Journal of Lesbian and Gay Studies 1, no. 2 (1994): 111–33.

10 For a brief history of newspaper publishing in Memphis, see Paul Coppock, Memphis Sketches (Memphis: Friends of Memphis and Shelby County Libraries, 1976), 130–32. The panic of 1893 and intense competition left its mark on the Memphis newspaper business—by 1894 there were only two major dailies, the Memphis Commercial Appeal (a merger of the two morning papers publishing in 1892) and the Evening Scimitar. Circulation figures for the Appeal Avalanche were advertised on February 5, 1892, 4. Population figures are from R. L. Polk & Co.'s Memphis Directory (1892) and Dow's Memphis Directory, vol. 30 (1892). In addition to the dailies, several major weeklies and a few limited circulation papers were also published in Memphis; Polk's 1892 city directory lists twelve, including the African Ameri-

can *Memphis Free Speech* and a handful of trade journals, religious publications, and profesional journals.

11 See Lynette Boney Wrenn, *Crisis and Commission Government in Memphis: Elite Rule in a Gilded Age* City (Knoxville: University of Tennessee Press, 1998), and Kathleen C. Berkeley, *"Like a Plague of Locusts": From an Antebellum Town to a New South City, Memphis, Tennessee, 1850–1880* (New York: Garland Publishing, 1991). Raymond Williams, in *The Long Revolution*, points to the transition from individual proprietorship to corporate conglomerate ownership of the British press by the early twentieth century (173–213), a change that was beginning to occur in the largest U.S. urban centers during the 1890s. In Memphis, however, individual proprietorship and partnerships persisted as the dominant form of newspaper ownership well into the twentieth century.

12 For a discussion of the relation of marketing strategies and racial segmentation, see Grace Elizabeth Hale, *Making Whiteness: The Culture of Segregation* (New York: Pantheon Books, 1998), chapter 4, 121–97. See also Ohmann, *Selling Culture*, 255–65.

13 See Joshua Brown, "Reconstructing Representation: Social Types, Readers, and the Pictorial Press, 1865–1877," *Radical History Review* 66 (fall 1996): 5–38, especially p. 27.

14 My categorization of "types" in the late-nineteenth-century newspapers is a modification of the "fiend" and "rogue" types decribed for earlier in the century by Papke, *Framing the Criminal* see especially pp. 20–29.

15 "Crushed Their Skulls," *Memphis Appeal Avalanche*, Jan. 19, 1892, 1; "Fiends Assault a Bride," *Memphis Commercial*, July 30, 1892, 1; "Murdered by a Maniac," *Memphis Commercial*, July 28, 1892, 3; "Work of a Madman," *Memphis Commercial*, Jan. 14, 1892, 1; "Now It's Jack the Sculptor," *Memphis Appeal Avalanche*, Feb. 7, 1892, 1; "Eight Mangled Forms," *Memphis Appeal Avalanche*, Jan. 20, 1892, 1; "Killed By a Swelling Tongue," *Memphis Appeal Avalanche*, Feb. 27, 1892, 2.

16 "Rapist May Cause War of Races, A Negro Brute Assaults a Little White Girl, Negroes Rescue the Scoundrel and Are Guarding Him," *Memphis Appeal Avalanche*, July 26, 1892, 2; "Blow Rich Men to Bits," *Memphis Appeal Avalanche*, Jan. 10, 1892, 1. This story was about English anarchists, but closer to home the same paper reported that in Knoxville, the "Miners Are Murderous," Jan. 7, 1892, 1.

17 "Her Babes Saw Her Murdered," *Memphis Appeal Avalanche*, March 10, 1892, 7; "Shot His Mistress to Death," *Memphis Appeal Avalanche*, Feb. 7, 1892, 1; "Torture for Children," *Memphis Appeal Avalanche*, Feb. 26, 1892, 1; "Vitriol as Revenge," *Memphis Public Ledger*, Jan. 30, 1892, 3; "The Old, Old Story," *Memphis Commercial*, Feb. 17, 1892, 8; "Dashed Vitriol in Her Face," *Memphis Commercial*, July 30, 1892, 1.

18 "She Stooped to Folly," *Memphis Appeal Avalanche*, July 31, 1892, 1; "An Irate Father's Success," *Memphis Commercial*, July 31, 1892, 1.

19 For a discussion of the workings of scandal and publicity in the British context, see William A. Cohen, *Sex Scandal: The Private Parts of Victorian Fiction* (Durham: Duke University Press, 1996). For the U.S. context, see P. Cohen, *The Murder of Helen Jewett*, and Srebnick, *The Mysterious Death of Mary Rogers*.

20 See Sandra Gunning, *Race, Rape and Lynching: The Red Record of American Literature, 1890–1912* (New York: Oxford University Press, 1996).

21 An original and detailed account of the emergence of lynching as a modern spectacle, involving publicity, mass spectatorship, and the development of a definable narrative is provided by Hale, *Making Whiteness*, 199–239.

22 See Henry Lewis Suggs, ed., *The Black Press in the South, 1865–1979* (Westport, Conn.: Greenwood Press, 1983).

23 For a detailed rendition of these events, see Linda O. McMurry, *To Keep the Waters Troubled: The Life of Ida B. Wells* (New York: Oxford University Press, 1998), 128–29.

24 The school board debates were actually quite complicated, involving disputes between more privileged, established African Americans and relatively more impoverished freedpeople, as well as complex alliances with different factions of the white elite in Memphis. See Berkeley, "Like a Plaque of Locusts," 178–87.

25 See Suggs, *The Black Press in the South*, 326–27.

26 See P. Cohen, *The Murder of Helen Jewett*; Halttunen, *Murder Most Foul*; and Srebnick, *The Mysterious Death of Mary Rogers*.

27 See Mary Ryan, "Gender and Public Access: Women's Politics in Nineteenth-Century America," in Calhoun, ed., *Habermas and the Public Sphere*, 258–88; Sharon R. Ullman, *Sex Seen: The Emergence of Modern Sexuality* (Berkeley: University of California Press, 1997); Dina M. Copelman, "The Gendered Metropolis: Fin-de-siècle London," *Radical History Review*, no. 60 (Fall 1994): 38–56; Suzanne Lebsock, "Women and American Politics 1880–1920," in *Women, Politics and Change*, ed. Louise Tilly and Patricia Gurin (New York: Russell Sage Foundation, 1990), 35–62.

28 Marsha Wedell, *Elite Women and the Reform Impulse in Memphis, 1875–1915* (Knoxville: University of Tennessee Press, 1991); Ann Firor Scott, *Making the Invisible Woman Visible* (Chicago: University of Illinois Press, 1984); Ann Firor Scott, *The Southern Lady: From Pedestal to Politics* (Chicago: University of Chicago Press, 1970); Grace Elizabeth Prescot, "The Woman Suffrage Movement in Memphis: Its Place in the State, Sectional and National Movements," *The West Tennessee Historical Society Papers*, no. 18 (1964): 87–106; Mattie Duncan Beard, *The WCTU in the Volunteer State* (Kingsport, Tenn.: Kingsport Press, 1962); Elizabeth Avery Meriwether, *Recollections of Ninety-Two Years, 1824–1916* (Nashville: Tennessee Historical Commission, 1958); Lide Meriwether, "State Report—Tennessee," *The Woman's Journal*, Feb. 6 1892, 44; Paul Coppock, "A Fighting Daughter of the South—Elizabeth Avery Meriwether," *Memphis Commercial Appeal*, June 7, 1981.

29 E. Meriwether, *Recollections*, v.

30 Sterling Tracy, "Clara Conway, Jenny Higbee and Others Made This City Notable for Cultural Study," *Memphis Commercial Appeal*, April 30, 1950; Buford C. Utley, "The Early Academies of West Tennessee," *The West Tennessee Historical Society Papers*, no. 8 (1954): 5–38; Walter J. Fraser Jr., "Three Views of Old Higbee School," *West Tennessee Historical Society Papers*, no. 20 (1996): 46–60; Coppock, *Memphis Sketches*, 149–52.

31 See Wedell, *Elite Women*; Cynthia Neverdon-Morton, *Afro-American Women of the South*

and the *Advancement of the Race, 1895–1925* (Knoxville: University of Tennessee Press, 1989); Stephanie J. Shaw, *What a Woman Ought to Be and to Do: Black Professional Women Workers during the Jim Crow Era* (Chicago: University of Chicago Press, 1996); Barbara Solomon, *In the Company of Educated Women: A History of Women and Higher Education in America* (New Haven: Yale University Press, 1985).

32 Robert A. Sigafoos, *Cotton Row to Beale Street: A Business History of Memphis* (Memphis: Memphis State University Press, 1979), 78.

33 R. L. Polk & Co., *Memphis Directory* (1892); Dow, *Dow's Memphis Directory* (1892); John M. Keating, *History of the City of Memphis and Shelby County, Tennessee,* vol. 2 (Syracuse, N.Y.: D. Mason, 1888), 94–121; "Souvenir Edition," *Memphis Evening Scimitar,* Oct. 1891.

34 See Mary Louise Roberts, "Gender, Consumption, and Commodity Culture," *American Historical Review* 103, no. 3 (June 1998): 817–44.

35 " 'I Loved Her So! And That Is Why I Cut Her Throat.' A Very Unnatural Crime," *Memphis Public Ledger,* Jan. 26, 1892, 1.

36 "Alice Mitchell's Crime," *New York World,* Jan. 31, 1892, 6, and "A Most Shocking Crime, A Memphis Society Girls Cuts a Former Friend's Throat," *New York Times,* Jan. 26, 1892, 1. The Mitchells were prosperous but were not among the cotton families who controlled the Memphis economy. Freda Ward's family was considered "respectable" but was not well off at the time of her death. She had to be buried in an unmarked, church-owned charity plot in a Memphis cemetery. (See the Elmwood Cemetery records, available in the cemetery's business office in Memphis, Tennessee.)

37 "Freda Ward's Murder, Investigating the Story of Strange Passion and Death," *San Francisco Examiner,* Jan. 30, 1892, 1; "Love Runs Mad and Deadly, Unnatural Passion . . . Steeled the Arm of Alice Mitchell," *San Francisco Examiner,* Jan. 31, 1892, 3.

38 *Memphis Public Ledger,* Jan. 26, 1892, 1. Since eyewitnesses reported that Freda arose and walked a short distance after the final slashing, it seems unlikely that she was in fact "almost beheaded."

39 These were the subheads under the lead headline, "Girl Slays Girl," *Memphis Appeal Avalanche,* Jan. 26, 1892, 5. The quick action taken by "Uncle George" in warding off the press and procuring attorneys is detailed in "Girl Slays Girl," *Memphis Appeal Avalanche,* Jan. 26, 1892, 5.

40 The statement was published in "Who Is This 'Jessie James?' *Memphis Appeal Avalanche,* Jan. 29, 1892, 5. The claims of her attorneys appeared in that article and in two others in the same paper: "The Grand Jury Has the Case," Jan. 30, 1892, 5, and "Present Insanity," Feb. 2, 1892, 5.

41 "Both Are Indicted," *Memphis Commercial,* Jan. 31, 1892, 5. The unnamed physician was later identified as E. P. Sale (in "Evidence!" *Memphis Commercial,* Feb. 23, 1892, 1), who later testified at the lunacy inquisition. At this early stage, it isn't clear how much control the defense attorneys exerted over quoted physicians. It seems likely that they were recruited by the defense, however, as they are the same ones who eventually testified on that side.

42 D. Hack Tuck, ed., *A Dictionary of Psychological Medicine* . . . , 2 vols. (Philadelphia: P. Blakiston, Son, 1892), vol. 1, 460. Quoted in Stanley W. Jackson, M.D., *Melancholia and Depression* (New Haven: Yale University Press, 1986), chapter 15, "Love Melancholy," 370. This chapter provides a historical overview of the meanings of the diagnosis "erotomania." (For more detailed discussion, see later chapters.)

43 "Both Are Indicted," *Memphis Commercial*, Jan. 31, 1892, 5; "Sent for the Doctor . . . , This Disease Which Doctors Call Erotomania," *Memphis Commercial*, Feb. 5, 1892, 5. The second article went on, in contradictory fashion, to state that medical evidence didn't actually show that murderous intent was formed.

44 Memphis physician B. F. Turner told the *New York World* (quoted in "Alice Mitchell's Crime," Jan. 31, 1892, 6) that Alice suffered from "abnormal erotic instinct," the only other medical diagnosis to appear in the press before courtroom testimony began. Turner later testified for the defense, at which time several new diagnoses were offered (see chap. 4).

45 "Miss Alice Mitchell's Lunacy, Counsel Have Confidence That Erotomania Can Be Established, The Perverted Affection of One Girl for Another," *Memphis Appeal Avalanche*, Feb. 4, 1892, 4.

46 For an analysis of how the avoidance of sexual specificity in the language of scandal reporting helped produce the sexual deviant as an embodied "type," see Ed Cohen's analysis of the Oscar Wilde trial in *Talk on the Wilde Side* (New York: Routledge, 1993), especially pp. 144–46.

47 "Marrying a Maiden! Can a Woman Legally Marry a Woman?" *Vanity Fair*, Feb. 13, 1892, 1. This publication carried news of the popular theater and was much more explicit and sensational in its coverage of sexuality than the mainstream dailies.

48 "Cold, Cruel Law, Holds Two Girls for Murder," *Memphis Appeal Avalanche*, Jan. 31, 1892, 5. (For a detailed discussion of the importance of heredity in late-nineteenth-century diagnoses of mental disease, see chaps. 4 and 6.)

49 "Miss Alice Mitchell's Lunacy," *Memphis Appeal Avalanche*, Feb. 4, 1892, 4.

50 "Two Girls in Jail," *Memphis Appeal Avalanche*, Jan. 27, 1892, 5.

51 The first mention that the police were searching for a man behind the tragedy was in "Her Affectionate Letters," *Memphis Appeal Avalanche*, Feb. 12, 1892, 4. A summary of theories about Alice's motives—including the suggestion that Alice attacked Freda after being ignored and that there was probably a man behind it all—appeared in "Evidence! Facts Will Be Revealed in the Celebrated Case," *Memphis Commercial*, Feb. 23, 1892, 1. This same article also pointed to the existence of correspondence between Alice and young men (discussed below) as evidence that she was not indifferent to the other sex, as the defense claimed she was. It also suggested that Alice had intended to disfigure Freda with the razor, out of jealousy, rather than murder her. The first reports in the *New York Times* ("A Most Shocking Crime," Jan. 26, 1892, 1) and the *San Francisco Morning Call* ("Deliberate Murder, Sensational Tragedy on a Street in Memphis," Jan. 26, 1892, 7) reported the rumor that Alice had attacked because Freda had made "remarks of a decidedly uncomplimentary nature" regarding her. Christina Purnell first suggested

that Freda Ward's relatives considered Alice "fast" in an interview quoted in "Girl Slays Girl," *Memphis Appeal Avalanche*, Jan. 26, 1892, 5.

52 Mr. Volkmar's opinion was printed in "The Case in Court," *Memphis Public Ledger*, Jan. 29, 1892, 2. The letters between Alice and Freda, which Mrs. Volkmar turned over to Peters, were withheld from the press until the lunacy inquisition in July 1892. The defense went to court to argue for access to them and failed. Reporters became so frustrated with this secrecy that they printed jokes about Peters's mangled form being found in the dungeons of the Press Club. For discussion of the letters, see "Murder's Aftermath . . . , Tell-Tale Letters," *Memphis Public Ledger*, Jan. 28, 1892, 2; "Both Are Indicted," *Memphis Commercial*, Jan. 31, 1892, 5; "Cold, Cruel Law," *Memphis Appeal Avalanche*, Jan. 31, 1892, 5; "They Want to See the Letters," *Memphis Appeal Avalanche*, Feb. 14, 1892, 4; and "Begs to See Her Freda, . . . Passionate Love Letters Such as a Man Might Write," *New York World*, Jan. 29, 1892, 1.

53 "Evidence!" *Memphis Commercial*, Feb. 23, 1892, 1. The *Appeal Avalanche* was never so skeptical, but one of its reporters did question a defense attorney about whether erotomania could be a defense to murder. The reporter queried by analogy: "In other words, while proof of kleptomania might be sufficient to procure a discharge of the crime of theft, would it be considered in law a sufficient degree of insanity to warrant a discharge of any other crime?" The attorney replied, "It would show a diseased condition of the mind." See "Miss Alice Mitchell's Lunacy," *Memphis Appeal Avalanche*, Feb. 4, 1892, 4.

54 These designations appeared repeatedly in all the news reports.

55 Single articles often included competing characterizations. "Girl Slays Girl," *Memphis Appeal Avalanche*, Jan. 26, 1892, 5, included the phrase "bloodthirsty Amazon" as well as descriptions of Alice as sullenly resigned and "simple." "Alice Mitchell's Crime," *New York World*, Jan. 31, 1892, 6, referred to her as a "hardened criminal" who was "sullenly cool" and "self-possessed" but also mentioned the fear that she would erupt in a "sudden frenzy." The mention of the "craving desire of her mad mind" appeared in "Cold, Cruel Law," *Memphis Appeal Avalanche*, 31, 1892, 5, which also described her dramatic mood swings from tears to gaiety.

56 "Both Are Arraigned," *Memphis Commercial*, Feb. 2, 1892, 4.

57 "Letters in Demand," *Memphis Appeal Avalanche*, Feb. 16, 1892, 4–5. The report that she was plump appeared in "The Recent Horror," *Memphis Appeal Avalanche*, Jan. 28, 1892, 5. The *Public Ledger's* description was published in "Pulling for Proof, The Motion by the Defense in the Mitchell Case," Feb. 15, 1892, 1. Both of these papers and the *Memphis Commercial* (see note 56). paid especially close attention to the length of Alice's dress, and to her feet and shoes.

58 The *New York World* stated specifically that Freda was Alice's "opposite." In "Alice Mitchell's Crime," Jan. 31, 1892, 6, Alice and Freda were described as students at the Higbee School. Alice was vivacious, devoted to a few friends, fond of rifles and prone to expressions of temper, while Freda was gentle, loved music, and stood higher in her classes than Alice. The Lincoln, Nebraska, issue of *Vanity Fair*, in its long, highly sensationalized report of the case, described Alice as "mas-

culine" and Freda as "gentle" and "refined." See "Marrying a Maiden!" Feb. 13, 1892, 1.

59 These statements all appeared Feb. 2, 1892, in "Present Insanity," *Memphis Appeal Avalanche*, 5; "Both Are Arraigned," *Memphis Commercial*, 4; and "Insanity the Defense, The Murderers of Freda Ward Asked to Plead at Memphis," *New York Times*, 1. For an extended discussion of the characterization of Lillie Johnson, see chapter 3.

60 The "three sorrowing fathers" first appeared in "Two Girls in Jail," *Memphis Appeal Avalanche*, Jan. 27, 1892, 5. Complete portraits of all of them (with the reference to Mitchell as a "poor old man") were published in "Alice Mitchell's Crime," *New York World*, Jan. 31, 1892, 6. Mr. Johnson's sleepless vigilance was noted in many articles, including "The Recent Horror," *Memphis Appeal Avalanche*, Jan. 28, 1892, 5. The description of Mr. Ward as almost "unmanned" appeared in "I Loved Her So!" *Memphis Public Ledger*, Jan. 26, 1892, 1.

61 Descriptions of the mothers and mother figures were included in "Their First Sunday in Jail," *Memphis Appeal Avalanche*, Feb. 1, 1892, 5; "Begs to See Her Freda," *New York World*, Jan. 29, 1892, 1; "Alice Mitchell's Crime," *New York World*, Jan. 31, 1892, 6.

62 See "Two Girls in Jail," *Memphis Appeal Avalanche*, Jan. 27, 1892, 5, and "The Case in Court," *Memphis Public Ledger*, Jan. 29, 1892, 2.

63 Articles featuring the judge provided comic relief for readers and vented reporters' disapproval and occasional frustration. See "More Room for Judge DuBose," *Memphis Appeal Avalanche*, Feb. 11, 1892, 4.

64 "Will Be Disappointed, An Expectant Throng Will Gather at the Court House To-Day," *Memphis Commercial*, Feb. 17, 1892, 2.

65 "I Loved Her So!" *Memphis Public Ledger*, Jan. 26, 1892, 1.

66 "Freda Ward's Murder," *San Francisco Examiner*, Jan. 30, 1892, 1.

67 "Both Are Indicted," *Memphis Commercial*, Jan. 31, 1892, 5.

68 "Made Love Like a Man, Alice Mitchell's Unseemly Conduct with a Girl in Cincinnati," *Memphis Appeal Avalanche*, Feb. 22, 1892, 4.

69 "Did Alice Mitchell Write It?" *Memphis Appeal Avalanche*, Feb. 6, 1892, 5. The attorney general was said to have received many anonymous as well as credited letters concerning the Mitchell case; one suspected of being written by Alice herself was, according to Peters, probably "the ebullition of a crank."

70 "Memphis Murder Case," *New York Times*, Jan. 31, 1892, 1.

71 The young women's claim that they had overheard someone named Alice speaking to a man and threatening to cut Freda's throat was repeated and dismissed in all the papers. See, for instance, "Murder's Aftermath," *Memphis Public Ledger*, Jan. 28, 1892, 2.

72 "After the Tragedy . . . Did Allie Intend to Mar Miss Ward's Beauty?" *Memphis Commercial*, Jan. 27, 1892, 1.

73 "The Recent Horror," *Memphis Appeal Avalanche*, Jan. 28, 1892, 5; "Murder's Aftermath," *Memphis Public Ledger*, Jan. 28, 1892, 2.

74 "Who Is This Jessie James?" *Memphis Appeal Avalanche*, Jan. 29, 1892, 5.

75 "Bernhardt Jailed," *Memphis Public Ledger*, Feb. 17, 1892, 2.

76 "The Case in Court," *Memphis Public Ledger*, Jan. 29, 1892, 2.

77 "The Grand Jury Has the Case," *Memphis Appeal Avalanche*, Jan. 30, 1892, 5.

78 "Letters in Demand," *Memphis Appeal Avalanche*, Feb. 16, 1892, 4; "The Case in Court," *Memphis Public Ledger*, Jan. 29, 1892, 2.

79 "Will Be Disappointed, An Expectant Throng Will Gather at the Court House Today," *Memphis Commercial*, Feb. 17, 1892, 2; "Sent for the Doctor," *Memphis Commerical*, Feb. 5, 1892, 5.

80 "The Mitchell Case," *Memphis Appeal Avalanche*, Jan. 28, 1892, 4.

81 *Memphis Appeal Avalanche*, Feb. 24, 1892, 4.

82 Quoted in "Ward-Mitchell Case," *Memphis Commercial*, Feb. 9, 1892, 4.

83 Lillie's version of events appeared in "I Loved Her So!" *Memphis Public Ledger*, Jan. 26, 1892, 1, in a section subheaded "Miss Lillie Johnson Interviewed"; in "Girl Slays Girl," *Memphis Appeal Avalanche*, Jan. 26, 1892, 5; and in "Alice Mitchell's Crime . . . , History of the Girl Who Killed Her Boarding School Friend Because She Wouldn't Marry Her," *New York World*, Jan. 31, 1892, 6.

84 "Letters in Demand . . . A Batch of Letters That She Wrote to a Missouri Man," *Memphis Appeal Avalanche*, Feb. 16, 1892, 4–5. Transcripts of several of these letters appear in appendix B.

85 In "The Recent Horror," Jan. 28, 1892, 5, the *Memphis Appeal Avalanche* reported that Freda had exhibited a "decided turn for amateur theatricals" and was known for her sweet singing voice in her church's choir. Another set of letters from Alice to a young man in Pittsburgh, also signed Freda Ward and telling of life as an actress, had been turned over to Memphis police before the Missouri letters appeared. They were withheld from the press before trial. See "Her Affectionate Letters, Alice Mitchell Corresponded with a Young Man," *Memphis Appeal Avalanche*, Feb. 12, 1892, 4. Reports that Alice had signed Freda's name to coal receipts appeared in "Present Insanity," *Memphis Appeal Avalanche*, Feb. 2, 1892, 5.

Chapter 3   Habeas Corpus

1 Alexis de Tocqueville, *Democracy in America* (New York: Vintage Books, 1945), 290, quoted in Robert Hariman, *Popular Trials: Rhetoric, Mass Media and the Law* (Tuscaloosa: University of Alabama Press, 1990), 7.

2 See Martin J. Sklar, *The Corporate Reconstruction of American Capitalism, 1890–1916: The Market, the Law, and Politics* (Cambridge: Cambridge University Press, 1988); Mary P. Ryan, *Civic Wars: Democracy and Public Life in the American City during the Nineteenth Century* (Berkeley: University of California Press, 1997); and Joseph H. Cartwright, *The Triumph of Jim Crow: Tennessee Race Relations in the 1880s* (Knoxville: University of Tennessee Press, 1976).

3 For this argument about nationalism and publication I am deeply indebted to Michael Warner, *The Letters of the Republic: Publication and the Public Sphere in Eighteenth-Century America* (Cambridge: Harvard University Press, 1990), and to Lauren Ber-

lant, *The Queen of America Goes to Washington City: Essays on Sex and Citizenship* (Durham: Duke University Press, 1997). Neither author may agree with my formulation here, but both significantly influenced my thinking.

4   For an especially pointed account of the connection between violence, politics, and state action, see Kenneth C. Barnes, *Who Killed John Clayton? Political Violence and the Emergence of the New South* (Durham: Duke University Press, 1998). For an analysis of the formation of the state through race in the post-Reconstruction period, see Ian F. Haney Lopez, *White by Law: The Legal Construction of Race* (New York: New York University Press, 1996).

5   Memphis Board of Commissioners, "Report of the Chief of Police," (1892), 202–5. For the reputation of Memphis as the "Murder Capital" after 1900, when its vice districts gained a national reputation, see Fred L. Hutchins, *What Happened in Memphis* (Kingsport, Tenn.: Kingsport Press, 1965), chapter 4, "Crime in Memphis," 34–51. The low representation of women in the arrest statistics was of course not unique to Memphis. According to Roger Lane, women were accused of only 9.8 percent of murders in Philadelphia in the period 1839–1901. See Roger Lane, *Violent Death in the City: Suicide, Accident and Murder in Nineteenth-Century Philadelphia* (Cambridge: Harvard University Press, 1979), 100–101.

6   In covering the Mitchell case, the *Appeal Avalanche* noted in passing that on some days only the "regular business of the court" was proceeded with—"cases of assault and battery, carrying concealed weapons" and such. See "Lillie Is at Home," Feb. 28, 1892, 5. The *Public Ledger* summarized crimes in its police columns but rarely went into any detail. Sexual crimes merited some mention but never any explicit description. On January 1, 1892, 1, the paper reported that "Melville Peoples, a negro man, was charged with a beastly and revolting crime against nature. The evidence adduced was clear as day, and he was fined $15 for the city and sent before the Criminal Court." On January 19, 1892, 1, a melee at a "house of ill-fame" on Short Third Street was described for comic effect, a charge of sodomy was reported, and three "darkies" charged with hog larceny were said to be entertaining the audience in police court with "some very racy testimony." Oddly, though the "crime against nature" and "sodomy" appear in the crime columns of the newspapers, they don't appear in the arrest statistics.

7   An outline of this case is included in "Murder in Good Society," *New York World*, July 17, 1892, 28. King occupied the Shelby County jail at the same time as Alice Mitchell and Lillie Johnson—the only other prisoner to have a private cell and special privileges. See "Miss Alice Mitchell's Lunacy," *Memphis Appeal Avalanche*, Feb. 4, 1892, 4. A complete description of the jail and its differential treatment of prisoners by sex, race, and class is contained in "Behind Barred Doors," *Memphis Commercial*, July 24, 1892, 11.

8   My discussion of the law here is influenced by the writings of the critical legal studies, critical race theory, and law and narrative movements. See Mark Kelman, *A Guide to Critical Legal Studies* (Cambridge: Harvard University Press, 1987); Kimberle Crenshaw et al., eds., *Critical Race Theory: The Key Writings That Formed the Movement*

(New York: The New Press, 1995), and Peter Brooks and Paul Gewirtz, eds., *Law's Stories: Narrative and Rhetoric in the Law* (New Haven: Yale University Press, 1996).

9 For accounts of the role of female defendants in producing persuasive narratives in trial settings, see Ruth Harris, *Murders and Madness: Medicine, Law and Society in the Fin de Siècle* (Oxford: Oxford University Press, 1989); Edward Berenson, *The Trial of Madame Caillaux* (Berkeley: University of California Press, 1992); and Catharine Ross Nickerson, " 'The Deftness of Her Sex': Innocence, Guilt, and Gender in the Trial of Lizzie Borden," in *Lethal Imagination: Violence and Brutality in American History*, ed. Michael A. Bellesiles (New York: New York University Press, 1999), 261–81.

10 For analyses of notorious trials framed explicitly as political, see Michael R. Belknap, ed., *American Political Trials* (Westport, Conn.: Greenwood Press, 1994), and J. Anthony Lukas, *Big Trouble: A Murder in a Small Western Town Sets Off a Struggle for the Soul of America* (New York: Simon and Schuster, 1997).

11 See Patricia Cohen, *The Murder of Helen Jewett: The Life and Death of a Prostitute in Nineteenth-Century New York* (New York: Knopf, 1998), and Altina Waller, *Reverend Beecher and Mrs. Tilton: Sex and Class in Victorian America* (Amherst: University of Massachusetts Press, 1982).

12 There are no existing records of the grand jury's proceedings; only its findings (not its makeup or its deliberations) were reported in the newspapers. Lillie and Alice were indicted jointly for murder under the state's theory that Lillie knew Alice's purpose when she followed Freda but did nothing to prevent the crime. Anyone who thus aided and abetted a murder was considered as guilty as the principal under the law. See "Cold, Cruel Law," *Memphis Appeal Avalanche*, Jan. 31, 1892, 5.

The Tennessee state constitution stipulated that a defendant charged with a capital crime was not bailable if the proof was "evident" or the "presumption great" that the defendant was guilty as charged. The indictment against Lillie Johnson on the charge of murder created a presumption against her, so the burden of proof fell on her to show that the evidence against her was not "evident." Her attorneys were obliged to interrogate the state's witnesses as well as present their own. The case would thus be laid out before the public. For a full explanation of the legal process, see "Lillie Is at Home," *Memphis Appeal Avalanche*, Feb. 28, 1892, 5.

13 Testimony had been taken at the coroner's inquest and before the grand jury that produced the indictments for murder against Alice Mitchell and Lillie Johnson. These were closed proceedings, however; neither press nor public had been welcome. The habeas corpus hearing was the first occasion for the public to hear and see the principals and witnesses.

14 "More Room for Judge DuBose," *Memphis Appeal Avalanche*, Feb. 11, 1892, 1; "No Decision Today," *Memphis Public Ledger*, Feb. 16, 1892, 2; "The Web of Fate," Feb. 24, 1892, 1.

15 These were subheads on the articles "The Web of Fate" and "Fair Lillie" in the *Memphis Appeal Avalanche*, Feb. 24, 25, 1892, both on p. 1.

16   "In the Balance," *Memphis Public Ledger*, Feb. 23, 1892, 1. As an evening paper, the *Ledger* had an advantage in presenting each installment in the "drama"; its version got to readers the night before the morning *Appeal Avalanche* and *Commercial* reports.

  For an extended discussion of the importance of the theaters and opera houses in Memphis, especially for Alice Mitchell and Freda Ward, see chapter 5.

17   For a reporter's description of the coming trials as entertainment, see "More Room for Judge DuBose," *Memphis Appeal Avalanche*, Feb. 11, 1892, 1. On the first day of the habeas corpus hearing, Judge DuBose referred to the court as "entertainment"; see "The Web of Fate," *Memphis Appeal Avalanche*, Feb. 24, 1892, 1. The newspapers occasionally used other metaphors—those of battle or of literature (such as the "first chapter")—to describe the courtroom action, but the theatrical metaphors predominated.

18   In *Communication and Litigation: Case Studies of Famous Trials* (Carbondale: Southern Illinois University Press, 1988), Janice Schuetz and Kathryn Holmes Snedaker argue that courtroom drama is a complex theatrical spectacle that presents a play within a play. The "external play" persuades by mimesis as advocates re-present facts with second-order interpretations. The "internal play" persuades through "phantasia" as people tell the story directly and persuade by appeal to imagination, experience, and understanding. See their chapter 7, "Courtroom Drama—The Trial of the Chicago Eight," especially pp. 220–24.

  The charactertistics of late-nineteenth-century trials, as examined in this chapter, are of course shared by public trials in many times and places.

19   For a discussion of the ideological underpinnings of "classic realism," see Catherine Belsey, *Critical Practice* (London: Methuen, 1980), chapters 4–6.

20   Ann-Louise Shapiro, "Disordered Bodies/Disorderly Acts: Medical Discourse and the Female Criminal in Nineteenth-Century Paris," *Genders*, no. 4 (spring 1989), 68.

21   "Fair Lillie," *Memphis Appeal Avalanche*, Feb. 25, 1892, 1.

22   "Second Day!" *Memphis Public Ledger*, Feb. 24, 1892, 1.

23   Angus McLaren describes the sensational trial of a serial killer in London, also during 1892, at which the large number of women in attendance was commented on in very similar terms. See his *A Prescription for Murder: The Victorian Serial Killings of Dr. Thomas Neill* (Chicago: University of Chicago Press, 1993), 53. William A. Cohen argues that the public for scandal was routinely represented as female—a feminized, endangered social body. See his *Sex Scandal: The Private Parts of Victorian Fiction* (Durham: Duke University Press, 1996), 15, 107–8.

24   The nursery rhyme paraphrase appeared in "Second Day!" *Memphis Public Ledger*, Feb. 24, 1892, 1, under the heading "Personal and General." In addition to the two professional reporters, the *Ledger* reported the presence of six "amateur" lady reporters—a designation laced with some sarcasm. The *Appeal Avalanche*'s admonition was contained in "The Web of Fate," Feb. 24, 1892, 5; this article reported the presence of seven women pretending to be reporters. The reference to a "tidal wave" was in "Unfolded," *Memphis Commercial*, Feb. 24, 1892, 1.

For further discussion of the contested status of women's spectatorship at the turn of the century, see Ann Jones, *Women Who Kill* (New York: Holt, Rinehart and Winston, 1980), especially p. 147, and Mary S. Hartman, *Victorian Murderesses* (London: Robson Books, 1977), 51–84.

25   "The Pity of It," *Memphis Appeal Avalanche*, Feb. 26, 1892, 4; "The Criminal Court Goes On," *Memphis Appeal Avalanche*, Feb. 27, 1892, 5. In the second article, she was identified as "the female who undertook to argue with Judge DuBose last Thursday in the course of the Lillie Johnson proceedings."

26   The reference to Alice and Lillie on "exhibition" is in "The Web of Fate," *Memphis Appeal Avalanche*, Feb. 24, 1892, 1. The description of Lillie "devoured" by the eyes of spectators is in "Fair Lillie," *Memphis Appeal Avalanche*, Feb. 25, 1892, 1. An account of Judge DuBose's order that the defendants unveil is in "Unfolded," *Memphis Commercial*, Feb. 24, 1892, 1. "Fair Lillie" reports that Lillie pulled her veil back over her face while leaving the stand after testifying.

27   Drawings of the female principals were published often in Memphis's two illustrated papers—the *Appeal Avalanche* and the *Commercial*. They also appeared in the *New York World* coverage. The razor appeared in the pre-hearing article in the *Memphis Commercial*, "Evidence!" Feb. 23, 1892, 1. Freda Ward's bleeding corpse on the coroner's slab appeared in "Girl Slays Girl," *Memphis Appeal Avalanche* 26, 1892, 5.

28   The first drawing appeared in "Unfolded," *Memphis Commercial*, Feb. 24, 1892, 1. The second was included in "Fair Lillie," *Memphis Commercial*, Feb. 25, 1892, 1.

29   My discussion of the trial as public sphere is informed by Miriam Hansen's analysis of early cinema audiences in her *Babel and Babylon: Spectatorship in American Silent Film* (Cambridge: Harvard University Press, 1991), and by her foreword to Oskar Negt and Alexander Kluge, *Public Sphere and Experience: Toward an Analysis of the Bourgeois and Proletarian Public Sphere*, trans. Peter Labanyi, Jamie Owen Daniel, and Assenka Oksiloff (Minneapolis: University of Minnesota Press, 1993).

30   In "Present Insanity," *Memphis Appeal Avalanche*, Feb. 2, 1892, 5, Lillie's tendency to nervous prostration and hysteria was stressed, but the reporter also commented that many thought it strange that Lillie willingly shared Alice's jail cell. The case against Lillie was summarized in "Miss Johnson's Case," *Memphis Public Ledger*, Feb. 8, 1892, 2. In "Who Is This Jessie James?" *Memphis Appeal Avalanche*, Jan. 29, 1892, 5, Lillie's improper behavior in corresponding with young men using the pseudonym "Jessie Rita James" was recounted, and the possibility that she knew Alice's "secrets" was suggested. But the reporter assured readers that the weight of the evidence was in Miss Johnson's favor. Rumors that Lillie and Alice flirted with conductors on the electric streetcar were reported in "Evidence!" *Memphis Commercial*, Feb. 23, 1892, 1.

31   Cartwright, *The Triumph of Jim Crow*, pp. 239, 246.

32   An outline of Malcolm Patterson's career is contained within the Malcolm Rice Patterson Papers, Tennessee State Library and Archives. A brief biographical sketch also appears in Margaret I. Phillips, *The Governors of Tennessee* (Gretna, La.:

Pelican, 1978), 122–26. The "promising" reference is in "Evidence!" *Memphis Commercial*, Feb. 23, 1892, 1, and the assertion that he was never "outclassed" appears in "Second Day!" *Memphis Public Ledger*, Feb. 23, 1892, 1.

33 Judge J. P. Young's *The Standard History of Memphis, Tennessee* (Knoxville, Tenn.: H. W. Crew, 1912), includes accounts of the local leadership of both Gantt and Patterson during the postepidemic years. Hon. William S. Speer's *Sketches of Prominent Tennesseans* (Nashville: Albert B. Tavel, 1888) refers to Gantt as "decidedly the best advocate (i.e. before a jury)" in Memphis—see p. 521. Both Young's and Speer's compilations are of the hagiographical variety, however.

A biographical sketch of Luke Wright is contained in Paul Coppock, *Memphis Memoirs* (Memphis: Memphis State University Press, 1980), "Persuasive General," 152–56. Coppock mentions that Wright's appointment as secretary of war was an extraordinary combination of a Republican president and a Confederate veteran. But Wright was a "Gold Democrat" who left the party when William Jennings Bryan and the silverites took over, and had been "Good Old Luke" to Roosevelt for years.

The "tear starter" reference to Gantt is in "She Bides in Bonds," *Memphis Public Ledger*, Feb. 26, 1892, 2. The reference to Gantt and Wright as among the strongest lawyers in the South is in "Evidence!" *Memphis Commercial*, Feb. 23, 1892, 1.

34 Winters was always present during the hearing, but he never spoke—he advised the lead attorneys. The quoted reference to him is from "Evidence!" *Memphis Commercial*, Feb. 23, 1892, 1.

35 A biographical sketch of Peters is contained in his obituary in the *Memphis Commercial Appeal*, Dec. 9, 1906. For an account of the scandal surrounding the murder of Van Dorn, see Hugh Walker, "A Crime of Passion? The Day the Doctor Shot the General," *The Nashville Tennesseann Magazine*, July 14, 1963, 8–9. This article suggests that the motive for the murder may have been an effort by Dr. Peters to please the Federals by eliminating Van Dorn, thus ensuring the return of his land in Mississippi. For a report of Thomas Peters's suicide, see "Distressing Case of Suicide," *Memphis Avalanche*, Apr. 10, 1866.

36 "Evidence!" *Memphis Commercial*, Feb. 23, 1892, 1.

37 For an account of the political conflicts surrounding Judge DuBose's career, see Lynette Boney Wrenn, *Crisis and Commission Government in Memphis: Elite Rule in a Gilded Age City* (Knoxville: University of Tennessee Press, 1998), 138–39.

38 "Judge DuBose Dies," *Memphis Commercial Appeal*, Mar. 22, 1912. This obituary details his career and reputation. Luke Wright prosecuted DuBose before the state senate on thirty-four counts; he was convicted and impeached on two (failing to recognize a writ of habeas corpus and overstepping his authority). The following legislature restored his rights, however.

39 "Unfolded," *Memphis Commercial*, Feb. 24, 1892, 1.

40 Ibid.

41 "The Web of Fate," *Memphis Appeal Avalanche*, Feb. 24, 1892, 1.

42 This account of the first day of the hearing is based on "The Web of Fate," *Memphis*

Appeal Avalanche, Feb. 24, 1892, 1, 2 and 5; "Unfolded," *Memphis Commercial*, Feb. 24, 1892, 1–3; and "In the Balance," *Memphis Public Ledger*, Feb. 23, 1892, 1.

43 "Unfolded," *Memphis Commercial*, Feb. 24, 1892, 1.

44 The *Appeal Avalanche* and the *Commercial* printed the letter with the errors, and the latter commented on them. Only the *Public Ledger* corrected the note for publication.

45 These were subheads for "Unfolded," *Memphis Commercial*, Feb. 24, 1892, 1. The reference to the "sensation of the morning" is on the same page of this article.

46 "Unfolded," *Memphis Commercial*, Feb. 24, 1892, 2.

47 Ibid.

48 Ibid., 1.

49 "The Web of Fate," *Memphis Appeal Avalanche*, Feb. 24, 1892, 1.

50 "Fair Lillie," *Memphis Appeal Avalanche*, Feb. 25, 1892, 3.

51 Ibid., 2.

52 "Fair Lillie," *Memphis Commercial*, Feb. 25, 1892, 2. Note that both the major Memphis morning papers gave their front page coverage the same headline on this date.

53 "Fair Lillie," *Memphis Appeal Avalanche*, Feb. 25, 1892, 3.

54 "Second Day!" *Memphis Public Ledger*, Feb. 24, 1892, 1.

55 "Fair Lillie," *Memphis Commercial*, Feb. 25, 1892, 1.

56 "Fair Lillie," *Memphis Appeal Avalanche*, Feb. 25, 1892, 1.

57 "The Pity of It," *Memphis Appeal Avalanche*, Feb. 26, 1892, 4.

58 "Still in Doubt," *Memphis Public Ledger*, Feb. 25, 1892, 1.

59 "Argument!" *Memphis Commercial*, Feb. 26, 1892, 1.

60 "The Pity of It," *Memphis Appeal Avalanche*, Feb. 26, 1892, 5.

61 Ibid., 1.

62 "Argument!" *Memphis Commercial*, Feb. 26, 1892, 1.

63 "The Pity of It," *Memphis Appeal Avalanche*, Feb. 26, 1892, 5.

64 "Lillie Is at Home," *Memphis Appeal Avalanche*, Feb. 28, 1892, 5.

65 "She Is Out on Bail," *Memphis Commercial*, Feb. 28, 1892, 8.

66 See especially "Fair Lillie," *Memphis Appeal Avalanche*, Feb. 25, 1892, 1–3.

67 For a discussion of late-nineteenth-century melodrama and its multiple connections to the trials of Lillie Johnson and Alice Mitchell, see chapter 5.

Chapter 4   Inquisition of Lunacy

1 From a lecture at the College de France, Aug. 1, 1975. Quoted in Hillary Allen, *Justice Unbalanced: Gender, Psychiatry and Judicial Decisions* (Philadelphia: Open University Press, 1987), 111.

2 For a very detailed account of the aftermath of the Memphis lynching, including the commentary of the white and black press, see Linda O. McMurry, *To Keep the Waters Troubled: The Life of Ida B. Wells* (New York: Oxford University Press, 1998), chapters 7 and 8.

3 The lunacy inquisition was designed to investigate the defendant's *present* mental state, not her condition at the time of the crime. But the circumstances of the crime were considered relevant in establishing the existence of "prior insane conduct," one of the categories of evidence normally admissible in court in cases of possible insanity. Evidence of physical malformation and physical diseases likely to affect the mental nervous systems, and evidence concerning the insanity of near relatives, was also admissible, both at a murder trial and a lunacy inquisition. For an account of the state of turn-of-the-century forensic psychiatry, see Charles Rosenberg, *The Trial of the Assassin Guiteau: Psychiatry and Law in the Gilded Age* (Chicago: University of Chicago Press, 1968). See also Janet Ann Tighe, "A Question of Responsibility: The Development of American Forensic Psychiatry, 1838–1930" (Ph.D. diss., University of Pennsylvania, 1983), and Janet Colaizzi, *Homicidal Insanity, 1800–1985* (Tuscaloosa: University of Alabama Press, 1989).

4 Defendants charged with homicide and found insane, at any point in the legal process, were seldom discharged once committed. Alienists and legal experts agreed that homicidal lunatics should be incarcerated indefinitely, and asylum superintendents were usually reluctant to pronounce such an inmate cured. See Colaizzi, *Homicidal Insanity*, 42, and Thomas Maeder, *Crime and Madness: The Origins and Evolution of the Insanity Defense* (New York: Harper and Row, 1985), 114.

In Alice Mitchell's case, the medical experts testifying for the *defense* pronounced her essentially incurable.

5 For a discussion of the controversy among alienists over whether so-called "partial insanity" (or "moral insanity" earlier in the century) could lead to criminal irresponsibility, see Tighe, *A Question of Responsibility*. See also Colaizzi, *Homocidal Insanity*, especially chapter 3, "The Development of a Medical Jurisprudence of Insanity."

6 For the role of the M'Naghten rule in a late-nineteenth-century murder trial, see Rosenberg, *The Trial of the Assasin Guiteau*, chapter 3, "The Prisoner, Psychiatry and the Law."

7 The state's legal code was quoted by the judge in his charge to the jury and reprinted in "Not a Murder," *Memphis Commercial*, July 31, 1892, 4.

8 This strategy was criticized by some observers. A local attorney's comments were quoted as follows in the *Memphis Public Ledger* ("Present Insanity," Feb. 5, 1892, 2):

> The gentlemen who represent Miss Mitchell know their case better than anybody else does, and, of course, no one will dispute their ability to make the best of it, but the way they have started out is a puzzle to me. Should they fail to prove to the satisfaction of the jury of lunacy that their client is now insane, the verdict would naturally be used by the State on the trial for murder that would follow, and it couldn't fail to influence the jury against the presumption that Miss Mitchell was crazy when she did the killing. And you must remember that in the inquisition the burden of proof is on the defense. Some decisions go so far as to say that the defense must prove insanity beyond a reasonable doubt.

On the other hand, if they go to trial first on the indictment, they can plead not guilty and insanity too. The burden of proof will be on the State, and the jury must acquit unless it be shown beyond a reasonable doubt that the defendant was sane in the estimation of the law when she killed Freda Ward. If they can show that Alice Mitchell is crazy now they certainly should be able to establish the fact of her irresponsibility on the 25th of January.

This attorney apparently saw no important difference in the standards for determining the sanity of a defendant in the two types of legal proceedings.

9 Nineteenth-century American newspaper readers were likely to have encountered any of a number of trials in which overly enthusiastic defenders of the nuptial couch had been acquitted as temporarily insane. For a discussion of the successful use of a temporary insanity plea to defend a woman accused of passion murder in Washington, D.C., in 1865, see Lee Chambers-Schiller, "Seduced, Betrayed and Revenged: The Murder Trial of Mary Harris," in Michael A. Bellesiles, ed., *Lethal Imagination: Violence and Brutality in American History* (New York: New York University Press, 1999), 185–209. By the end of the century, the "mania transitoria" diagnosis was in ill repute and less likely to be used as a legal defense. But temporary insanity defenses did not disappear entirely, especially in cases involving "crimes of passion," as in the notorious 1906 murder trial of millionaire Harry K. Thaw.

10 For discussion of the kinds of stories most effective in nineteenth-century Frenchwomen's defenses to violent crime, see Ruth Harris, "Melodrama, Hysteria and Feminine Crimes of Passion in the Fin-de-Siecle," *History Workshop 25* (spring 1988): 31–63, or her *Murders and Madness: Medicine, Law and Society in the Fin de Siecle* (Oxford: Clarendon Press, 1989), chapter 6, "Female Crimes of Passion." For both French and English women, see Mary S. Hartman, *Victorian Murderesses* (London: Robson Books, 1977). For American cases, see Ann Jones, *Women Who Kill* (New York: Holt, Rinehart and Winston, 1980).

11 The differential availability of different defenses to different categories of defendants is clearly indicated by the anecdotal, unsystematic evidence of nineteenth-century newspapers. There are no national crime statistics available for periods prior to 1930. But only prosperous defendants could afford a serious defense to a serious charge, and only prosperous white men could be certain of controlling the kind of defense that was mounted for them.

12 For discussion of the "hypothetical question" in insanity trials, see Tighe, "A Question of Responsibility," 113–17.

13 A provocative analysis of the medical case report and its history can be found in Kathryn Montgomery Hunter's *Doctor's Stories: The Narrative Structure of Medical Knowledge* (Princeton: Princeton University Press, 1991), especially pp. 56, 93. Hunter makes an extended analogy between the case report and the mystery story, both of which developed during the 1830s.

14 For a discussion of the ways psychiatric diagnosis stripped social suffering of

its meanings, rendered active subjects passive, and offered a biological "sense" for what seemed culturally senseless, see Roger Smith, *Trial by Medicine: Insanity and Responsibility in Victorian Trials* (Edinburgh: Edinburgh University Press, 1981), especially pp. 127, 141, 149.

15 The trial was an event in which all these discourses entered into "dialogic" relation, in Mikhail Bakhtin's sense. See "Discourse in the Novel," in his *The Dialogic Imagination*, ed. and trans. Michael Holquist and Caryl Emerson (Austin: University of Texas Press, 1981), 259–422.

16 See Barbara Sicherman, *The Quest for Mental Health in America, 1880–1917* (New York: Arno Press, 1980), and Charles Rosenberg "Bitter Fruit—Heredity, Disease and Social Thought," in his *No Other Gods: On Science and American Social Thought* (Baltimore: Johns Hopkins University Press, 1976).

17 Isabella Mitchell's life history is drawn here from her husband's testimony, reported in "Sane or Insane?" *Memphis Commercial*, July 19, 1892, 1, and from the hypothetical case reprinted in appendix A. I am not assuming that these are the "true facts" but wish to analyze them as the representations constructed for use at the lunacy inquisition. Mrs. Mitchell's commitment to the asylum was verified at trial by a certificate of confinement and the deposition of her physician.

18 For a discussion of puerperal insanity and its symptoms, especially as a defense to infanticide in British trials, see Smith, *Trial by Medicine*, 150–54. For an analysis of the representation of women's social stresses as physical maladies, see Carroll Smith-Rosenberg, "Puberty to Menopause: The Cycle of Femininity in Nineteenth-Century America," in her *Disorderly Conduct: Visions of Gender in Victorian America* (New York: Knopf, 1985).

19 "Still in Doubt," *Memphis Commercial*, July 20, 1892, 1.

20 The hypothetical case (appendix A) reports the seven childbirths. At the time of trial, only four adult children were resident in Memphis, no others were mentioned, and there is no record (either with the family plot at the cemetery or in connection with the trial or commitment) of any others. The only child's death specifically mentioned is the first one, however.

21 According to the *New York World*, Dr. Comstock's deposition said that Mrs. Mitchell believed herself dead when she was committed to the asylum. See "Alice Mitchell Laughs while Counsel Are Trying to Build Up Her Plea of Insanity," July 20, 1892, 1. References to the stepdaughter are repeated in the hypothetical case, George Mitchell's testimony, and the stepdaughter's deposition to the court. See "Sane or Insane?" and "Still in Doubt," *Memphis Commercial*, July 19, 20, 1892, 1.

22 At present, the causes of postpartum depression are vigorously debated. Some medical experts argue that it is primarily a psychological disorder, some believe its causes are somatic, and others adhere to mixed explanations. See Katharina Dalton, *Depression after Childbirth* (New York: Oxford University Press, 1980).

23 These depositions are summarized in "Still in Doubt," *Memphis Commercial*, July 20, 1892, 1.

24 Mattie's testimony was reported in "None but Freda," July 22, while Addie's was contained in "Myra Is a Myth," July 23, both in the *Memphis Commercial*, 1892, 1.

25 The testimony cited below was reported in the 1892 *Memphis Commercial* in "Sane or Insane?" July 19, 1; "Still in Doubt," July 20, 1; "Silly Letters," July 21, 1; "None but Freda," July 22, 1; "Myra Is a Myth," July 23, 1; and "Not Love at All," July 24, 4.

26 "An Analysis of Love," *Memphis Appeal Avalanche*, July 24, 1892, 6.

27 Frank reported a suicide attempt aboard the riverboat the Friday before the murder (see "None but Freda," *Memphis Commercial*, July 22, 1892, 1). No other witness reported such an event at that time, though the hypothetical case tells of a suicide attempt with laudanum that took place *before* the planned elopement (see appendix A).

28 This comment was reported in "Alice Mitchell Laughs," *New York World*, July 20, 1892, 1.

29 "Is This Girl Murderer Insane?" *New York World*, July 19, 1892, 5.

30 Ruth Harris describes the importance of feminine "love sickness" in the turn-of-the-century crime of passion, and its role in eliciting compassion and rendering a portrait of feminine irresponsibility in a legal context. See "Melodrama, Hysteria and Feminine Crimes of Passion," especially p. 41.

31 "None but Freda," *Memphis Commercial*, July 22, 1892, 1.

32 For a discussion of the deployment of legal voluntarist and medical determinist discourses in nineteenth-century insanity trials, see Smith, *Trial by Medicine*, chapter 8, "Knowledge and Responsibility."

33 According to Frank Sim, the prosecution claimed "that the insanity of the ancestry of the mother was purely accidental and due to recognized causes, other than the insane [inheritable] temperament," but the newspapers did not report any testimony specifically to that effect. See Sim, "Forensic Psychiatry. Alice Mitchell Adjudged Insane," *Memphis Medical Monthly* 12 (Aug. 1892): 378.

34 The *Memphis Commercial* summarized the efforts of the prosecution through the first four days of testimony: "The chief object was to refute the testimony of . . . witnesses in reference to what was testified to about Alice Mitchell's fondness for outdoor sports, and to disprove that such was unusual or indicative of an unsound mind." "None but Freda," July 22, 1892, 1.

35 The testimony of the medical experts was reported during the summer of 1892 in (1) three articles in the *Memphis Commercial*: "Not Love at All," July 24, 4; "More Evidence," July 26, 4; and "They All Agree," July 27, 4; (2) three articles in the *Memphis Appeal Avalanche*: "An Analysis of Love," July 24, 6; "Diagnosis of Insanity," July 26, 5; and "The Deed of a Maniac," July 27, 4–5; and (3) the article by F. L. Sim, "Alice Mitchell Adjudged Insane," *Memphis Medical Monthly* (Aug. 1892), 377–429.

36 A complete account of Callender's career can be found in his obituary in the *Nashville Journal of Medicine and Surgery* 80, no. 3 (Sept. 1896): 135–46. There is a brief biographical listing for him in Howard A. Kelly and Walter L. Burrage, *Dictionary of American Medical Biography* (New York: D. Appleton, 1928), 195.

37 Summaries of Sim's career can be found in obituaries published in the *Journal of the American Medical Association* 23, pt. 2 (Dec. 1, 1894): 840; the *Medical Record* 46, no. 25 (Dec. 22, 1894): 788; and the *Memphis Medical Monthly* 14, no. 12 (Dec. 1894): 565–71.

38 "The Deed of a Maniac," *Memphis Appeal Avalanche*, July 27, 1892, 4–5. A summary of Sale's career is included in his obituary in the *Memphis Medical Monthly* 21, no. 7 (July 1901): 387–88.

39 "More Evidence," *Memphis Commercial*, July 26, 1892, 4. A brief summary of his later career is included in Marcus J. Steward, M.D., William T. Black Jr., M.D., and Mildred Hicks, eds., *History of Medicine in Memphis* (Jackson, Tenn.: McCowat-Mercer Press, 1971), 282. The mention of his studies with Allan McLane Hamilton is included in "Alice Mitchell's Crime," *New York World*, Jan. 31, 1892, 6. In this article, he is quoted as saying that Alice's insanity took the form of "abnormal erotic instinct." He didn't reiterate this opinion at trial, however.

40 There is a biographical listing for Campbell in Samuel J. Platt and Mary Louise Ogden, *Medical Men and Institutions of Knox County, Tennessee (1789–1957)* (Knoxville, Tenn.: Knoxville Academy of Medicine, 1969), 236–37.

41 The article by F. L. Sim, "Alice Mitchell Adjudged Insane," included expert testimony—some of it reprinted from the newspapers, but some (particularly J. H. Callender's) clearly prepared in advance on the basis of the hypothetical case and prepared questions. In testimony at trial, defense attorneys used hypothetical questions drawn from their written case, and witnesses seemed completely familiar with its contents.

42 Sim, "Alice Mitchell Adjuged Insane," 409.

43 "Diagnosis of Insanity," *Memphis Appeal Avalanche*, July 26, 1892, 5, and Sim, "Alice Mitchell Adjuged Insane," 395.

44 For a discussion of the domestic focus of turn-of-the-century psychiatry, see Elizabeth Lunbeck, *The Psychiatric Persuasion: Knowledge, Gender and Power in Modern America* (Princeton: Princeton University Press, 1994), especially chapter 2. For an analysis of the crucial role of domestic privacy in negotiating race and gender relations, see Phillip Brian Harper, "Private Affairs: Race, Sex, Property and Persons," *GLQ: A Journal of Lesbian and Gay Studies* 1, no. 2: 111–33. Harper's essay is reprinted in his *Private Affairs: Critical Ventures in the Culture of Social Relations* (New York: New York University Press, 1999), 1–32. See also his introduction, ix–xvii.

45 Kathryn Montgomery Hunter argues that the crisis of the medical plot is the quest for an uncertain diagnosis. See her *Doctors' Stories*. Lunbeck concentrates on this problematic quest, located in the "psychiatrists' atom," the case, in chapter 5 of *The Psychiatric Persuasion*, especially pp. 130–31, 143.

46 For an extended discussion of the growing importance of "loss of control" in nineteenth-century psychiatry, see Tighe, "A Question of Responsibility." Alienists succeeded in having a "loss of control" test added for legal insanity in some states, as a supplement to the M'Naghten rule.

47 Sim suggested that the colonial governor of New York, Lord Cornbury, had this sort of partial insanity. Cornbury occasionally paraded in public dressed as a

woman but fulfilled his governing duties without difficulty. He was later seated in the British House of Lords. See Sim, "Alice Mitchell Adjuged Insane," 393.

48 July 27, 1892, 4.

49 The depositions are reprinted in Sim, 425–28. Frank Ingram also wrote an occasional column on medical issues for the New York World, and he contributed one on the Alice Mitchell case, which was appended to "Alice Mitchell's Crime," Jan. 31, 1892, 6. A summary of William Fletcher's career is included in his obituary in Transactions of the Indiana State Medical Association, 58th Annual Session (May 22–24, 1907): 496–99.

50 Colaizzi, Homicidal Insanity, especially pp. 8, 75, 110–16.

51 Sim, "Alice Mitchell Adjudged Insane," 427–28. For an exhaustive survey of Hammond's career, see Bonnie Ellen Blustein, Preserve Your Love for Science: Life of William A. Hammond, American Neurologist (Cambridge: Harvard University Press, 1991).

52 Sim, "Alice Mitchell Adjuged Insane," 428.

53 "Diagnosis of Insanity," Memphis Appeal Avalanche, July 26, 1892, 5.

54 "The Deed of a Maniac," Memphis Appeal Avalanche, July 27, 1892, 5; Sim, "Alice Mitchell Adjuged Insane," 405.

55 Earlier in the year the Memphis Public Ledger had printed an article on Annie Hindle, erroneously called Marie Hindle by the reporter, with the headline "The Case of Male Impersonator Marie Hindle, Who Beaued the Girls at Broome's Variety Theater. Almost a Parallel Case." This article was appended to the Mitchell-Ward-Johnson continuing coverage, "The Plea for Bail," Feb. 11, 1892, 2. For more on Hindle, see chapter 5.

56 "More Evidence," Memphis Commercial, July 26, 1892, 4.

57 "The Deed of a Maniac," Memphis Appeal Avalanche, July 27, 1892, 4.

58 The issue of hermaphroditism, or indeterminate genitals, did arise occasionally in the local press. On February 27, 1892, the Memphis Appeal Avalanche reported that "Gov. Bucanan pardoned a white convict today, because a dozen or more physicians were unable to determine the prisoner's sex, and the warden did not know to which ward the prisoner should be assigned" (see "Couldn't Tell the Prisoner's Sex," 2).

    For discussion of the connections between gender crossing, homosexuality, and assumed hermaphroditism in earlier centuries, see Valerie Traub, "The Psychomorphology of the Clitoris," GLQ: A Journal of Lesbian and Gay Studies 2, no. 1–2 (1995): 81–113, and Julia Epstein, "Either/Or—Neither/Both: Sexual Ambiguity and the Ideology of Gender," Genders 7 (Mar. 1990): 99–142. For an account of the "scientific" inspection of lesbians' genitals for signs of difference in the twentieth century, see Jennifer Terry, "Lesbians under the Medical Gaze: Scientists Search for Remarkable Differences," The Journal of Sex Research 27, no. 3 (Aug. 1990): 317–39.

59 Sim, "Alice Mitchell Adjuged Insane," 393–94.

60 The debt to phrenology in this expert testimony is clear. For a discussion of the connections between phrenology and nineteenth-century psychiatry, see Colaizzi, Homicidal Insanity, 30–36.

61 Sim, "Alice Mitchell Adjuged Insane," 413.
62 "The Deed of a Maniac," *Memphis Appeal Avalanche*, July 27, 1892, 5.
63 Ibid.
64 Sim, "Alice Mitchell Adjuged Insane," 413. For a discussion of the nineteenth-century psychiatrists' struggle with definitions of insanity, especially in a courtroom context, see Tighe, "A Question of Responsibility."
65 See Thomas Maeder, *Crime and Madness*, 53–54. Maeder describes popular fiction that portrayed psychiatrists as readily duped by families with ulterior motives and quick to conclude that any criminal behavior was pathological. He quotes an 1870 story by Mark Twain, "A New Crime," about a wealthy man who claimed temporary insanity. Twain wrote, "Insanity certainly is on the increase in the world and crime is dying out."
66 "The Deed of a Maniac," *Memphis Appeal Avalanche*, July 27, 1892, 4.
67 The prosecution's case was reported in "Her Own Best Witness," *Memphis Appeal Avalanche*, July 28, 1892, 4, 5, 8, and "Her Own Story," *Memphis Commercial*, July 28, 1892, 4. Alice's testimony was also summarized in Sim, "Alice Mitchell Adjuged Insane," 414–24, but this account is drawn entirely from the newspapers.
68 "Her Own Best Witness," *Memphis Appeal Avalanche*, July 28, 1892, 5.
69 Freda and Ashley had conducted their correspondence through Alice Mitchell, ostensibly to keep Mr. Volkmar, the postmaster for Golddust, Tennessee, from intercepting their letters. When Alice withdrew from this arrangement, angry and jealous, Freda apparently told Ashley that Alice and Lillie had gone to Chicago and could no longer pass their letters. The Ashley-Freda correspondence stopped at this point, according to Ashley.
70 Nearly all the newspaper articles on the lunacy inquisition, cited above, include descriptions of Alice in court. For accounts of her behavior and activities in jail, see "Ready for Her Trial," July 18, 5; "Behind Barred Doors," July 24, 11; and "Sunday at the Jail," July 25, 5, all in the *Memphis Commercial*, 1892.
71 "Alice Mitchell Insane," *San Francisco Examiner*, July 19, 1892, 1.
72 "More Evidence," *Memphis Commercial*, July 26, 1892, 4.
73 "Her Own Best Witness," *Memphis Appeal Avalanche*, July 28, 1892, 4.
74 Ibid.
75 "Her Own Story," *Memphis Commercial*, July 28, 1892, 4.
76 "Her Own Best Witness," *Memphis Appeal Avalanche*, July 28, 1892, 4.
77 "Her Own Story," *Memphis Commercial*, July 28, 1892, 4.
78 Sim, "Alice Mitchell Adjuged Insane," 424, summarized the impact of Alice Mitchell's testimony for his readers in the medical community: "The statement of the prisoner, her appearance, her emotional and non-emotional psychic changes, etc., together with the developments that preceded, wholly disarmed the prosecution, and the case was given to the jury without argument."
79 "The Last of Alice Mitchell," *Memphis Appeal Avalanche*, July 31, 1892, 5. Other accounts of the verdict are included in "Not a Murder," *Memphis Commercial*, July 31, 1892, 4, and the *New York World*, July 31, 1892, 3.

80 "Alice Mitchell Is Crazy," *New York World*, July 31, 1892, 3.

81 "She Visits Freda's Grave," *Memphis Commercial*, August 2, 1892, 5.

82 "The Mitchell Case," *Memphis Appeal Avalanche*, July 31, 1892, 4.

83 "Not A Murder," *Memphis Commercial*, July 31, 1892, 4.

84 Memphis juries were composed entirely of white men in this period but could be mixed as to class position. The Mitchell jury, from all reports, was composed primarily of "the best men of Memphis"—the prosperous white business and professional class.

85 Karen Halttunen argues that late-nineteenth-century notions of insanity preserved the innocence of the primary personality by imputing criminal agency to an alien invasive disease. See her *Murder Most Foul: The Killer and the American Gothic Imagination* (Cambridge: Harvard University Press, 1998), chapter 7, "The Murderer as Mental Alien," 208–40.

86 "Diagnosis of Insanity," *Memphis Appeal Avalanche*, July 26, 1892, 5.

87 F. L. Sim's comments are reported in "An Analysis of Love," *Memphis Appeal Avalanche*, July 24, 1892, 6. Callender's remarks are quoted in "The Deed of a Maniac," *Memphis Appeal Avalanche*, July 27, 1892, 5.

88 Ed Cohen demonstrates the central importance of journalistic decorum in reporting of the Wilde trial to producing a notion of sexual difference as deviant embodiment rather than acts. See his *Talk on the Wilde Side* (New York: Routledge, 1993), especially p. 131.

89 "Myra Is a Myth," *Memphis Commercial*, July 23, 1892, 1, and "Still In Doubt," *Memphis Commercial*, July 20, 1892, 1.

90 Quoted from appendix B, section 1, letter 2.

91 Quoted from appendix B, section 1, letter 4.

92 "Still in Doubt," *Memphis Commercial*, July 20, 1892, 1.

93 Ibid.

94 Her relatives all reported her weight loss in the fall preceding the murder, but not one seemed to grasp its import.

95 For discussions of the importance of the regulation of marriage, see Harper, "Private Affairs"; Norma Basch, *Framing American Divorce: From the Revolutionary Generation to the Victorians* (Berkeley: University of California Press, 1999); Candice Lewis Bredbenner, *A Nationality of Her Own: Women, Marriage and the Law of Citizenship* (Berkeley: University of California Press, 1998); Peggy Pascoe, "Miscegenation Law, Court Cases, and Ideologies of 'Race' in Twentieth-Century America," in Martha Hodes, ed., *Sex, Love, Race: Crossing Boundaries in North American History* (New York: New York University Press, 1999), 464–90; John D'Emilio and Estelle Freedman, *Intimate Matters: A History of Sexuality in America* (New York: Harper and Row, 1988); Elaine Tyler May, *Great Expectations: Marriage and Divorce in Post-Victorian America* (Chicago: University of Chicago Press, 1980); Ian F. Haney Lopez, *White by Law: The Legal Construction of Race* (New York: New York University Press, 1996); Lisa Lowe, *Immigrant Acts: On Asian American Cultural Politics* (Durham: Duke University Press, 1996); Ann duCille, *The Coupling Convention: Sex, Text and Tradition in Black Women's Fiction* (New York:

Oxford University Press, 1993); and Katherine M. Franke, "Becoming a Citizen: Reconstruction Era Regulation of African American Marriages," *Yale Journal of Law and the Humanities* 11, no. 2 (summer 1999): 251–309.

96 For an argument about marriage law as *constitutive* of gender relations, see Nan D. Hunter, "Marriage, Law, and Gender: A Feminist Legal Inquiry," *Law and Sexuality* 1 (1991): 9–30.

97 The work of this novel in rewriting the lesbian love murder is analyzed in chapter 7.

Chapter 5   *Violent Passions*

1 Catherine Clement, *Opera, or the Undoing of Women*, trans. Betsy Wing (Minneapolis: University of Minnesota Press, 1988), 43.

2 For an in-depth analysis of the Borden trial, see Catherine Ross Nickerson, " 'The Deftness of Her Sex': Innocence, Guilt and Gender in the Trial of Lizzie Borden," in *Lethal Imagination: Violence and Brutality in American History*, ed. Michael A. Bellesiles (New York: New York University Press, 1999), 261–81.

3 For a discussion of state interventions in the sexual lives of working-class daughters, see Mary Odem, *Delinquent Daughters: Protecting and Policing Adolescent Female Sexuality in the United States, 1885–1920* (Chapel Hill: University of North Carolina Press, 1995). For a discussion of the ridicule of single women as "old maids" in early cinema at the turn of the century, see Sharon R. Ullman, *Sex Seen: The Emergence of Modern Sexuality* (Berkeley: University of California Press, 1997), 19–31.

4 For discussions of "female husbands" and "passing women," see Judith Halberstam, *Female Masculinity* (Durham: Duke University Press, 1998), 45–73; Jonathan Ned Katz, *Gay American History: Lesbians and Gay Men in the U.S.A.* (New York: Thomas Y. Crowell, 1976), "Passing Women: 1782–1920," 209–79; and San Francisco Lesbian and Gay History Project, " 'She Even Chewed Tobacco': A Pictorial Narrative of Passing Women in America," in Martin Duberman, Martha Vicinus, and George Chauncey Jr., eds., *Hidden from History: Reclaiming the Lesbian and Gay Past* (New York: New American Library, 1989), 183–94. For a study of romantic friendship, see Lillian Faderman, *Surpassing the Love of Men: Romantic Friendship and Love between Women from the Renaissance to the Present* (New York: William Morrow, 1981).

5 For a more extended discussion of the development of newspaper sensationalism and mass circulation imagined as national, see chapter 2.

6 "A Curious Career," *National Police Gazette*, Oct. 25, 1879, 7. This article is from the research of James Foshee, shared with me from the files of Jonathan Ned Katz. Katz publishes extensive excerpts from documents relating to Lobdell's life in his *Gay American History* but does not include this story. There is further discussion of Lobdell's "case" in chapter 6.

7 Lisa Moore persuasively argues that romantic friendship was not viewed quite as benignly as many historians have portrayed it but always contained the possibility of dangerous excess. See her " 'Something More Tender Still Than Friend-

ship': Romantic Friendship in Early Nineteenth Century England," *Feminist Studies* 18, no. 3 (fall 1992): 499–520.

8 "A Female Romeo," *National Police Gazette*, June 7, 1879, 6. This article is also from the research of James Foshee, shared with me from the files of Jonathan Ned Katz.

9 "Similar Cases Recalled," *Memphis Commercial*, Feb. 24, 1892, 3.

10 The "Ladies of Llangollen" were the subject of much commentary and represented an aristocratic British tradition at the intersection of "female husbands" and "romantic friends." See Elizabeth Mavor, *The Ladies Llangollen: A Study in Romantic Friendship* (London: Joseph, 1971). Anne Lister is another British aristocratic woman, described as a "female husband" in Halberstam, *Female Masculinity*, 65–73. But Lister did not "pass" or marry, as in the tradition I reference here. She comes to our attention through the recent publication of her extraordinary diaries, which, as Halberstam notes, show the ways a masculine woman and her feminine lovers achieved satisfactions within an aristocratic marriage culture. See Helena Whitbread, ed., *No Priest but Love* and *I Know My Own Heart: The Diaries of Anne Lister, 1819–1926* (New York: New York University Press, 1992).

11 "United in Death," *Memphis Public Ledger*, Jan. 27, 1892, 1.

12 "Instances Multiply," *Memphis Commercial*, Feb. 24, 1892, 3.

13 "A Strange Affection," *Memphis Weekly Commercial*, March 23, 1892, 12.

14 For discussion of the cultural narratives of sexual danger surrounding the prostitute in the mid-nineteenth-century United States, see Amy Gilman Srebnick, *The Mysterious Death of Mary Rogers: Sex and Culture in Nineteenth-Century New York* (New York: Oxford University Press, 1995), and Patricia Cohen, *The Murder of Helen Jewett: The Life and Death of a Prostitute in Nineteenth-Century New York* (New York: Knopf, 1998). For a description of the uses of the term "fast," see Laurence Senelick, "Boys and Girls Together: Subcultural Origins of Glamour Drag and Male Impersonation on the Nineteenth-century Stage," in *Crossing the Stage: Controversies on Cross-dressing*, ed. Lesley Ferris (London: Routledge, 1993), 89–90.

15 This story was contained within the larger article "The Plea for Bail," *Memphis Public Ledger*, Feb. 11, 1892, 2.

16 "Marrying a Maiden!" *Vanity Fair*, Feb. 13, 1892, 1. This article appears to be adapted from "Stranger Than Fiction: The True Story of Annie Hindle's Two Marriages," *New York Sun*, Dec. 27, 1891. Its inclusion along with the Mitchell-Ward murder report gives it its force of rebuttal. For an account of Hindle's career, see Senelick, "Boys and Girls Together," 80–95, and Senelick, "The Evolution of the Male Impersonator on the Nineteenth-Century Popular Stage," *Essays in Theatre* 1, no. 1 (1982): 31–46.

17 See Faye Dudden, *Women in the American Theatre: Actresses and Audiences, 1790–1870* (New Haven: Yale University Press, 1994); Benjamin McArthur, *Actors and American Culture, 1880–1920* (Philadelphia: Temple University Press, 1984); and for Britain, Tracy Davis, *Actresses as Working Women: Their Social Identity in Victorian Culture* (London: Routledge, 1991).

18 The phenomenon of "matinee girls" and "stage struck girls" and the social "prob-

lem" they presented is discussed in Albert Auster, *Actresses and Suffragists: Women in the American Theater, 1890–1920* (New York: Praeger, 1984). Auster notes that in 1893 the *New York Dramatic Mirror* began a weekly column titled "The Matinee Girl," who was assumed to be a product of education, economic self-sufficiency, leisure, and the relaxing moral constraints on young bourgeois women (39). In 1903, the surge of young women pursuing stage careers was estimated to outpace that of young men by twenty-five to one (49).

19   The *Memphis Commercial*, in an article on "Early Memphis Theaters," commented that "the Memphis public has ever been noted for its fondness and liberal patronage of the theater" (July 31, 1892, 9). Cross-dressing was a regular feature of this theater experience. On Feb. 12, 1892, the *Memphis Appeal Avalanche* noted the appearance at the Lyceum Theatre of the Kimball Opera Comique and Burlesque Company: "The role of Michaela was sustained by Charles Fostelle, a very clever female impersonator, while Miss Maud Dixon, a handsome and symmetrical young woman, appeared as Don Jose" (4). The *Memphis Commercial*, *Memphis Appeal Avalanche*, and *Memphis Public Ledger* all reviewed Bernhardt's appearances at the Lyceum Theatre on February 15, 16, and 17, 1892. The *Memphis Public Ledger*, in "Strife of the Stars. The Pitou Company and Sarah Bernhardt in Rivalry," pointed to the theme of "maddening jealousy" and described the act of murder: "A knife lies upon the table in easy reach. Twice she essays to grasp it before her woman's horror of taking life can be overcome. Then, reaching forth, she conceals it only to bury it in Scarpia's heart . . ." (Feb. 16, 1892, 4). The "bloodcurdling" quote appears in "Thespis in the Swim . . . Sarah Bernhardt in 'La Tosca' at the Lyceum," *Memphis Commercial*, Feb. 16, 1892, 2.

20   See "Bernhardt Jailed . . . She Tries to See Alice Mitchell and Lillie Johnson but Failed," *Memphis Public Ledger*, Feb. 17, 1892, 2, and "Bernhardt at the Jail . . . The Great Actress Wanted to See Miss Allie Mitchell," *Memphis Appeal Avalanche*, Feb. 17, 1892, 4. The editorial "The Drama of 'Alice Mitchell,'" *Memphis Appeal Avalanche*, Feb. 28, 1892, 4, noted that Bernhardt was putting together a scrapbook for Victorien Sardou so that he might write a play for her. The editorial writer wagered that the play "will not be wanting in thrilling situations and sensational development" but would be "a necessarily lurid drama." The editorialist then speculated about which role would be suitable for the star.

21   For an analysis of the role of theatricality in late Victorian British life, see Nina Auerbach, *Private Theatricals: The Lives of the Victorians* (Cambridge: Harvard University Press, 1990). Auerbach argues that dying well was an art that Sarah Bernhardt, whose onstage life was "a pageant of vibrant deaths," perfected (94). Eric Salmon, in the introduction to *Bernhardt and the Theatre of Her Time* (Westport, Conn.: Greenwood Press, 1984), argues that the later work of Bernhardt was given to the emotionalism, vulgarity, empty spectacle, and overemphasis on sensational narrative that was characteristic of theatrical romanticism in decay.

22   Diana Fuss makes a compelling case for the importance of the girls' school, and

the importance of the emergence of adolescence as a stage of life occurring at the same historical moment as the emergence of homosexuality. See her *Identification Papers* (New York: Routledge, 1995), 107–40. The classic article about girls' school crushes and the emergence of lesbianism is Nancy Sahli, "Smashing: Women's Relationships before the Fall," *Chrysalis* 8 (summer 1979): 17–27. For the importance of the school in the British context, see Martha Vicinus, "Distance and Desire: English Boarding School Friendships," *Signs* 9, no. 4 (summer 1984): 600–622, and also Vicinus, *Independent Women: Work and Community for Single Women, 1850–1920* (Chicago: University of Chicago Press, 1985).

23 "Like Miss Mitchell . . . An Infatuation Which Existed between Two School Girls," *Memphis Commercial*, Feb. 14, 1892, 13.

24 My argument converges here with Ed Cohen's discussion of the role of the newspaper and its descriptive taboos in producing Oscar Wilde as a "type." See his *Talk on the Wilde Side* (New York: Routledge, 1993).

25 Halberstam, *Female Masculinity*, argues persuasively for the historical existence of a wide variety of practices, modes of embodiment, and forms of relationship that have been collapsed into concepts of "lesbian" identity. See her chapter 2.

26 For discussion of blues lyrics, and blues performance venues, as contexts for the communication of ideas about female sexuality quite at odds with the white bourgeois standards and categories, see Angela Y. Davis, *Blues Legacies and Black Feminism: Gertrude "Ma" Rainey, Bessie Smith, and Billie Holiday* (New York: Pantheon Books, 1998), and Hazel Carby, "It Jus Be's Dat Way Sometime: The Sexual Politics of Women's Blues," in *Unequal Sisters: A Multicultural Reader in U.S. Women's History*, ed. Ellen Carol DuBois and Vicki Ruiz (New York: Routledge, 1990), 238–49. For a description of the early-twentieth-century prison context, see Estelle B. Freedman, "The Prison Lesbian: Race, Class and the Construction of the Aggressive Female Homosexual, 1915–1965," *Feminist Studies* 22, no. 2 (summer 1996): 397–423. These and other contexts will be discussed more extensively in chapters 6, 7, and 8.

27 For a groundbreaking discussion of the politics of practices of identification and disidentification, see José Esteban Muñoz, *Disidentifications: Queers of Color and the Performance of Politics* (Minneapolis: University of Minnesota Press, 1999). See also Fuss, *Identification Papers*.

28 Analysis of the modes of reception for the late-nineteenth-century mass circulation press is beyond the scope of this project. It may be largely impossible to research this question directly, given the sources available for this period. But the newspapers themselves, as interactive public spheres, reveal modes of reception within the terms of their production. In trial coverage, for instance, responses to the newspaper stories were contained in each day's continuing account of events; such responses affected the trials themselves, as all good lawyers knew.

29 For an analysis of the limits of the politics of "uplift," see Kevin Gaines, *Uplifting the Race: Black Leadership, Politics and Culture in the Twentieth Century* (Chapel Hill: Uni-

versity of North Carolina Press, 1996). But even within the terms of the moral language of domestic desire that inflected uplift politics, resistant meanings circulated. See Ann duCille, *The Coupling Convention: Sex, Text and Tradition in Black Women's Fiction* (New York: Oxford University Press, 1993).

Chapter 6   Doctors of Desire

1 Edward C. Mann, "Medico-Legal and Psychological Aspects of the Trial of Josephine Mallison Smith," *Alienist and Neurologist* 14, no. 3 (July 1893), 473.

2 The discussion of sexology in this chapter is influenced especially by Jennifer Terry's essays (see note 52 below), integrated and revised in her book, *An American Obsession: Science, Medicine, and Homosexuality in Modern Society* (Chicago: University of Chicago Press, 1999), and also by the essays in Vernon Rosario, ed., *Science and Homosexualities* (New York: Routledge, 1997). On Anglo-European sexology, see also Lucy Bland and Laura Doan, eds., *Sexology in Culture: Labelling Bodies and Desires* (Chicago: University of Chicago Press, 1998); Daniel Pick, *Faces of Degeneration: A European Disorder, c.1848–1918* (Cambridge: Cambridge University Press, 1989); Sander L. Gilman, *Difference and Pathology: Stereotypes of Sexuality, Race and Madness* (Ithaca, N.Y.: Cornell University Press, 1985); and Jennifer Terry and Jacqueline Urla, eds., *Deviant Bodies: Critical Perspectives on Difference in Science and Popular Culture* (Bloomington: Indiana University Press, 1995). For discussions of evolutionary theory, the science of heredity, and the eugenics movement, see Marouf Arif Hasian Jr., *The Rhetoric of Eugenics in Anglo-American Thought* (Athens: University of Georgia Press, 1996); Nancy Stepan, *The Idea of Race in Science: Great Britain, 1800–1960* (Hamden, Conn.: Archon Books, 1982); Nancy Stepan, *"The Hour of Eugenics": Race, Gender and Nation in Latin America* (Ithaca, N.Y.: Cornell University Press, 1991); George Stocking Jr., *Race, Culture and Evolution: Essays in the History of Anthropology* (London: Collier-Macmillan, 1968); John Haller, *Outcasts from Evolution: Scientific Attitudes of Racial Inferiority, 1859–1900* (Urbana: University of Illinois Press, 1971); and Stephen Gould, *Ontogeny and Phylogeny* (Cambridge: Harvard University Press, 1977). For discussions of ideas about heredity and eugenic proposals in the United States, see Edward J. Larson, *Sex, Race, and Science: Eugenics in the Deep South* (Baltimore: Johns Hopkins University Press, 1995); Daniel J. Kevles, *In the Name of Eugenics: Genetics and the Uses of Human Heredity* (New York: Knopf, 1985); Nichole Hahn Rafter, ed., *White Trash: The Eugenic Family Studies, 1877–1913* (Boston: Northeastern University Press, 1988); and Mark H. Haller, *Eugenics: Hereditary Attitudes in American Thought* (New Brunswick, N.J.: Rutgers University Press, 1963). For analysis of the complex appropriations of evolutionary science and eugenic ideas within the U.S. women's rights and birth control movements, see Louise Michele Newman, *White Women's Rights: The Racial Origins of Feminism in the United States* (New York: Oxford University Press, 1999); and Linda Gordon, *Woman's Body, Woman's Right: Birth Control in America*, rev. ed. (New York: Penguin, 1990).

3 Julian Carter's article, "Normality, Whiteness, Authorship: Evolutionary Sexology

and the Primitive Pervert," in Rosario, ed., *Science and Homosexualities*, 155–76, especially influenced my argument here.

4   For an especially lucid discussion of the flexible political valences of European degeneration theory in particular, see Pick, *Faces of Degeneration*.

5   For a succinct account of Krafft-Ebing's career, see Brian King's introduction to Richard von Krafft-Ebing, *Psychopathia Sexualis, with Especial Reference to Contrary Sexual Instinct: A Clinical-Forensic Study*, 12th English ed., 1906, ed. Brian King (Burbank, Calif.: Bloat, 1999). See also Harry Oosterhuis, "Richard von Krafft-Ebing's 'Step-Children of Nature': Psychiatry and the Making of Homosexual Identity," in Rosario, ed., *Science and Homosexualities*, 67–88, and Merl Storr, "Transformations: Subjects, Categories and Cures in Krafft-Ebing's Sexology," in Bland and Doan, eds., *Sexology in Culture*, 11–26.

6   See Hubert Kennedy, "Karl Heinrich Ulrichs: First Theorist of Homosexuality," 26–45, and James Steakley, "*Per scientiam ad justitiam*: Magnus Hirschfeld and the Sexual Politics of Innate Homosexuality," 133–54, both in Rosario, ed., *Science and Homosexualities*. See also Hubert Kennedy, *Ulrichs: The Life and Work of Karl Heinrich Ulrichs, Pioneer of the Modern Gay Movement* (Boston: Alyson Publications, 1988); James D. Steakley, *The Homosexual Emancipation Movement in Germany* (New York: Arno, 1975); and Charlotte Wolff, *Magnus Hirschfeld: A Portrait of a Pioneer in Sexology* (London: Quartet Books, 1986).

7   For discussions of Carpenter, and of Symonds as Havelock Ellis's collaborator, see Sheila Rowbotham and Jeffrey Weeks, *Socialism and the New Life: The Personal and Sexual Politics of Edward Carpenter and Havelock Ellis* (London: Pluto Press, 1977). See also Joseph Bristow, "Symonds's History, Ellis's Heredity: *Sexual Inversion*," in Bland and Doan, *Sexology in Culture*, 79–99.

8   For analyses of the the place of gender and women in sexological theory, see Margaret Gibson, "Clitoral Corruption: Body Metaphors and American Doctors' Constructions of Female Homosexuality, 1870–1900," in Rosario, ed., *Science and Homosexualities*, 108–32, and Carolyn Burdett, "The Hidden Romance of Sexual Science: Eugenics, the Nation and the Making of Modern Feminism," in Bland and Doan, *Sexology in Culture*, 44–59. For a strong argument about the centrality of gender in U.S. psychiatric practice in particular, see Elizabeth Lunbeck, *The Psychiatric Persuasion: Knowledge, Gender and Power in Modern America* (Princeton: Princeton University Press, 1994). See also Cynthia Eagle Russett, *Sexual Science* (Cambridge: Harvard University Press, 1989).

9   Judith Halberstam, *Female Masculinity* (Durham: Duke University Press, 1998), 75–83.

10   The force of my argument here is greatly influenced by Carter, "Normality, Whiteness, Authorship," in Rosario, ed., *Science and Homosexuality*.

11   Frank L. Sim, "Forensic Psychiatry: Alice Mitchell Adjudged Insane," *Memphis Medical Monthly* 12 (Aug. 1892): 377–428. The Alice Mitchell case was first added to the English translation of the tenth edition of *Psychopathia Sexualis* and appears in the 1999 reprint of the twelfth edition of 1906 (cited above) on pages 487–90.

12 For a comprehensive survey of the early U.S. cases of sexual inversion and homo-
    sexuality, see Bert Hansen, "American Physicians' 'Discovery' of Homosexuals,
    1880–1900: A New Diagnosis in a Changing Society," in *Framing Disease: Studies in
    Cultural History,* ed. Charles Rosenberg and Janet Golden (New Brunswick, N.J.: Rut-
    gers University Press, 1992), 104–33. Many of the early medical articles Hansen
    cites are excerpted in Jonathan Ned Katz, *Gay American History* (New York: Thomas
    Y. Crowell, 1976), and in Katz, *Gay/Lesbian Almanac: A New Documentary* (New York:
    Harper and Row, 1983).

13 P. M. Wise, "Case of Sexual Perversion," *Alienist and Neurologist* 4, no. 1 (Jan. 1883):
    87–91. Wise references Lucy Ann Lobdell, *Narrative of Lucy Ann Lobdell, the Female Hunter
    of Delaware and Sullivan Counties, N.Y.* (New York: Published for the authoress, 1855).
    Both are excerpted in Katz, *Gay American History*, 214–25.

14 For brief biographies of Charles Hughes, see his listings in R. French Stone, M.D.,
    Biography of Eminent American Physicians and Surgeons (Indianapolis: Carlon and Hollen-
    beck Publishers, 1894), 234–37, and in Howard A. Kelly and Walter L. Burrage,
    Dictionary of American Medical Biography (New York: D. Appleton, 1928), 615.

15 Charles H. Hughes, "Alice Mitchell, the 'Sexual Pervert' and Her Crime," *Alienist
    and Neurologist* 13, no. 3 (July 1892): 554–57.

16 Charles H. Hughes, "Erotopathia — Morbid Erotism," *Alienist and Neurologist* 14, no. 4
    (Oct. 1893): 531–78, quoted from p. 535.

17 Ibid., 558–59.

18 Ibid., 557.

19 Ibid., 545.

20 The editorial by "H." from the *Medical Fortnightly* was excerpted in the *Alienist and
    Neurologist* 13, no. 2 (Apr. 1892): 398–400.

21 Hughes, "Erotopathia — Morbid Erotism," 545.

22 Edward I. Prime Stevenson, *The Intersexes: A History of Similisexualism as a Problem in
    Social Life* (Naples: R. Rispoli, 1908), excerpted in Katz, *Gay American History*, 146–48.

23 Hughes, "Erotopathia — Morbid Erotism," 554.

24 Charles H. Hughes, "Postscript to Paper on 'Erotopathia' — An Organization of
    Colored Erotopaths," *Alienist and Neurologist* 14, no. 4 (Oct. 1893): 731–32. This note
    is reprinted in Katz, *Gay American History*, 42–43.

25 Charles H. Hughes, "Homo Sexual Complexion Perverts in St. Louis: Note on a
    Feature of Sexual Psychopathy," *Alienist and Neurologist* 28, no. 4 (Nov. 1907): 487–88.
    Excerpted in Katz, *Gay American History*, 48–49.

26 F. E. Daniel, "Castration of Sexual Perverts," *Texas Medical Journal* 9, no. 6 (Dec. 1893):
    255–71, quoted from p. 263.

27 For a discussion of the eugenics movement in the U.S. South, see Larson, *Sex, Race,
    and Science.*

28 For a summary of Lydston's career, see his listing in Stone, *Eminent American Physi-
    cians,* 294–95.

29 Daniel, "Castration of Sexual Perverts," 264.

30 Ibid., 256, 263.

31 For accounts of Kiernan's career, see H. B., "Editor, Doctor, Teacher: A Brief Review of the Contributions Made to Science and Society by James George Kiernan. . . . ," *New York University Alumnus* 9 (Feb. 20, 1929): 7–8, and "Noted Alienist Dies, Dr. James G. Kiernan Was Expert for the Defense in Guiteau Trial," *New York Times,* July 3, 1923, 13. See also his listing in Stone, *Eminent American Physicians,* 266–67. For an account of his role in the Guiteau trial, see Charles Rosenberg, *The Trial of the Assassin Guiteau: Psychiatry and Law in the Gilded Age* (Chicago: University of Chicago Press, 1968).

32 James G. Kiernan, "Insanity: Sexual Perversion," *Detroit Lancet* 7, no. 11 (May 1884): 481–84.

33 James G. Kiernan, "Responsibility in Sexual Perversion," *Chicago Medical Recorder* 3, no. 3 (May 1892): 185–210, quoted from p. 210.

34 James G. Kiernan, "Sexology: Increase of American Inversion," *Urologic and Cutaneous Review* 20, no. 1 (Jan. 1916): 44–49, quoted from p. 46.

35 The 1915 edition of *Sexual Inversion* is included as volume 1, part 4, of Havelock Ellis, *Studies in the Psychology of Sex* (New York: Random House, 1942). Quoted from pp 201–2.

36 Siobhan B. Somerville, *Queering the Color Line: Race and the Invention of Homosexuality in American Culture* (Durham: Duke University Press, 2000), 19. Somerville's argument in chapter 1, "Scientific Racism and the Invention of the Homosexual Body," 15–38, has greatly influenced my argument in this chapter.

37 Jane Caplan notes the poor reception of Ellis's *The Criminal* and describes the contested reception of Lombroso's ideas in England. See her "'Educating the Eye': The Tattooed Prostitute," in Bland and Doan, *Sexology in Culture,* 100–115. See also David G. Horn, "This Norm Which Is Not One: Reading the Female Body in Lombroso's Anthropology," in Terry and Urla, eds., *Deviant Bodies,* 109–28.

38 See Jeffrey Weeks, "Havelock Ellis and the Politics of Sex Reform," in part 2 of Rowbotham and Weeks, *Edward Carpenter and Havelock Ellis,* 141–85.

39 There was significant conflict as well as mutual influence in the Symonds/Ellis collaboration. See Bristow, "Symonds's History, Ellis's Heredity," in Bland and Doan, *Sexology in Culture,* and Wayne Koestenbaum, *Double Talk: The Erotics of Male Literary Collaboration* (New York: Routledge, 1989).

40 Ellis, *Psychology of Sex,* 222.

41 For discussions of the Ellis-Lees marriage, see Phyllis Grosskurth, *Havelock Ellis: A Biography* (New York: New York University Press, 1985), and Havelock Ellis, *My Life: Autobiography of Havelock Ellis* (Boston: Houghton Mifflin, 1939).

42 Some specific interarticulations of race and sexuality in the sexological literature are outlined in Somerville, *Queering the Color Line,* 15–38.

43 There are no doubt other examples, and from earlier periods, but Lister's diaries are exceptionally explicit in a way that is quite rare in published, first-person sources prior to the mid-nineteenth century. See Anne Lister, *No Priest but Love and I*

Know My Own Heart: The Diaries of Anne Lister, ed. Helena Whitbread (New York: New York University Press, 1992). An especially illuminating analysis of these diaries can be found in Halberstam, *Female Masculinity*, 66–73.

44 A selection of documents describing "The Homosexual Underworld in American Cities" is included in Katz, *Gay American History*, 39–53.

45 Vernon Rosario argues that homosexuals played an active part in the "fictioning" of their experience in his provocative article "Inversion's Histories, History's Inversions: Noveling Fin-de-Siecle Homosexuality," in Rosario, ed., *Science and Homosexualities*, 89–107.

46 Krafft-Ebing lists sources from which homosexual love in woman may spring, including "female teachers in seminaries," "prostitutes disgusted with intercourse with men," and "opera singers and actresses who appear on the stage in male attire by preference." See Krafft-Ebing, *Psychopathia Sexualis*, 328. Ellis notes that "actresses from the eighteenth century onward have frequently been more or less correctly identified with homosexuality" (197), and he asserts that the "frequency of homosexual practices among prostitutes is a fact of some interest" (210). He also includes an appendix to *Sexual Inversion* titled "The School-Friendships of Girls" (368–84). Krafft-Ebing and Ellis also cited "epidemics" of sexual desire or activity in female workplaces, such as among seamstresses or servants, but they rarely drew case histories from these locations or elaborated their dangers extensively.

47 Sigmund Freud, "The Psychogenesis of a Case of Homosexuality in a Woman (1920)," in *The Standard Edition of the Complete Psychological Works of Sigmund Freud*, ed. James Strachey (London: Hogarth Press, 1955), 145–72. Diana Fuss notes that Freud's patient selects these three objects in *Identification Papers* (New York: Routledge, 1995), 74. See also Ronnie C. Lesser and Erica Schoenberg, eds., *That Obscure Subject of Desire: Freud's Female Homosexual Revisited* (New York: Routledge, 1999).

48 For a strong argument about Freud's depathologizing interventions, see Henry Abelove, "Freud, Male Homosexuality, and the Americans," in *The Lesbian and Gay Studies Reader*, ed. Henry Abelove, Michele Aina Barale, and David M. Halperin (New York: Routledge, 1993), 381–93.

49 Fuss, *Identification Papers*, 32–36.

50 Katharine B. Davis, *Factors in the Sex Life of Twenty-Two Hundred Women* (New York: Harper and Row, 1929). For a discussion of Davis's findings about homosexual experience, see John D'Emilio and Estelle Freedman, *Intimate Matters: A History of Sexuality in America* (New York: Harper and Row, 1988), 193. See also Erin G. Carlston, " 'A Finer Differentiation': Female Homosexuality and the American Medical Community," in Rosario, ed., *Science and Homosexualities*, 177–96.

51 See Estelle B. Freedman, "The Prison Lesbian: Race, Class and the Construction of the Aggressive Female Homosexual, 1915–1965," *Feminist Studies* 22, no. 2 (summer 1996): 397–423. See also Carter, "Normality, Whiteness, Authorship," in Rosario, ed., *Science and Homosexualities*, 168–73.

52 Jennifer Terry's discussions of George Henry's late 1930s New York study under the auspices of the Committee for the Study of Sex Variants are especially illuminating about the emerging mid-century mixtures of biological and anatomical investigations and sociological surveys and interviews. See her "Lesbians under the Medical Gaze: Scientists Search for Remarkable Differences," *The Journal of Sex Research* 27, no. 3 (Aug. 1990): 317–39; "Anxious Slippages between 'Us' and 'Them': A Brief History of the Scientific Search for Homosexual Bodies," in Terry and Urla, eds., *Deviant Bodies*, 129–69; and "The Seductive Power of Science in the Making of Deviant Subjectivity," in Rosario, ed., *Science and Homosexualities*, 271–95.

53 Angela Y. Davis's study of early-twentieth-century women's blues reveals a sexual world largely independent of sexology and mass circulation newspaper sensationalism. See her *Blues Legacies and Black Feminism: Gertrude "Ma" Rainey, Bessie Smith, and Billie Holiday* (New York: Pantheon Books, 1998).

Chapter 7   A Thousand Stories

1 D. O. Cauldwell, M.D., "Lesbian Love Murder," *Sexology* 16 (July 1950): 776–77.

2 I borrow the phrase "continuum of publication" from Robert Ferguson, "Untold Stories in Law," in Peter Brooks and Paul Gewirtz, eds., *Law's Stories: Narrative and Rhetoric in the Law* (New Haven: Yale University Press, 1996), 84.

3 I refer here to late-twentieth-century productions discussed in the epilogue to follow, as well as the earlier publications described in this chapter.

4 I am grateful to Ann Cvetkovich for suggestions about the work of "high" and "low" cultural forms in this case.

5 For discussions of these novels, see Jeannette Foster, *Sex Variant Women in Literature* (New York: Vantage Press, 1956), chaps. 3 and 4, and Lillian Faderman, *Surpassing the Love of Men: Romantic Friendship and Love between Women from the Renaissance to the Present* (New York: William Morrow, 1981), 254–94.

6 "I Loved Her So! And That Is Why I Cut Her Throat. A Very Unnatural . . . Crime A Tragedy Equal to the Most Morbid Imaginings of Modern French Romances," *Memphis Public Ledger*, Jan. 26, 1892, 1.

7 G. Frank Lydston, "A Phase of Sexual Perversion as Illustrated by the Recent Tragedies," *St. Louis Medical Mirror* 3 (Mar. 1 1892): 118.

8 For a discussion of the cross-fertilization between sexology and the nineteenth-century French novel, see Vernon Rosario, "Inversion's Histories/History's Inversions: Novelizing Fin-de-Siecle Homosexuality," in Rosario, ed., *Science and Homosexualities* (New York: Routledge, 1997), 89–107.

9 See Foster, *Sex Variant Women in Literature*, 64–66.

10 Ibid., 63, 83–85.

11 There is a huge literature on early-twentieth-century "lesbian" literature—both literary-critical and biographical. See, for example, Blanche Wiesen Cook, "Women Alone Stir My Imagination: Lesbianism and the Cultural Tradition," *Signs*

4 (1979): 718–39; Shari Benstock, *Women of the Left Bank: Paris 1900–1940* (Austin: University of Texas Press, 1986); and Julie Abraham, *Are Girls Necessary? Lesbian Writing and Modern Histories* (New York: Routledge, 1996).

12 Foster, *Sex Variant Women in Literature*, 60 and *passim*, argues that there are two traditions dealing with "variant" women in fiction—one extending from Diderot's *The Nun*, which links explicit sexuality and pathology, and the other extending from Mary Wollstonecraft's *Mary, A Fiction*, celebrating the romantic friendships of women.

13 For an extended analysis of the treatment of romantic friendship and its sapphic dangers, interpreted in relation to domestic preoccupations of British imperialism, see Lisa L. Moore, *Dangerous Intimacies: Toward a Sapphic History of the British Novel* (Durham: Duke University Press, 1997).

14 Dr. John Wesley Carhart, *Norma Trist; or Pure Carbon: A Story of the Inversion of the Sexes* (Austin, Tex.: Eugene von Boeckmann, 1895). Eric Garber discovered this obscure novel, listed in an old science fiction bibliography. Jonathan Ned Katz supplied me with a photocopy and published excerpts of it in his *Gay/Lesbian Almanac: A New Documentary* (New York: Harper and Row, 1983), 277–84. Nothing is known about the author; Dr. John Wesley Carhart may be a pseudonym.

15 Carhart, *Norma Trist*, 182.

16 Ibid., 205–6.

17 Katz, *Gay/Lesbian Almanac*, 283.

18 Ibid., 207–11.

19 Specifically, the superintendent of the Austin asylum testifies that Norma is just as responsible for her act of violence as one would be who, in "a transport of jealousy for the opposite sex, should committ overt acts." See ibid., 215–17.

20 Mary R. P. Hatch, *The Strange Disappearance of Eugene Comstock* (New York: G. W. Dillingham, 1895), and Mary E. Wilkins Freeman, "The Long Arm," in *The Long Arm . . . and Other Detective Stories* (London: Chapman and Hall, 1895). "The Long Arm" is reprinted in Carolyn Wells, ed., *American Detective Stories* (New York: Oxford University Press, 1927), 134–78, and in Susan Koppelman, ed., *Two Friends and Other Nineteenth-Century Lesbian Stories by American Women Writers* (New York: Meridian, 1994), 140–73. See Faderman, *Surpassing the Love of Men*, 292–94.

21 There are several biographies and critical studies of Mary Eleanor Wilkins Freeman. See especially Mary E. Wilkins Freeman, *The Infant Sphinx: Collected Letters of Mary E. Wilkins Freeman*, edited with biographical/critical introductions and annotations by Brent L. Kendrick (Metuchen, N.J.: Scarecrow Press, 1985). Wilkins Freeman had several long, significant romantic friendships with other women, including Mary Wales and Evelyn Sawyer (who left her to marry), before her own marriage to Charles Freeman at the age of forty-nine. For a discussion of Freeman's story "The Long Arm" in the context of women's detective fiction, see Catherine Ross Nickerson, *The Web of Iniquity: Early Detective Fiction by American Women* (Durham: Duke University Press, 1998), chap. 7.

22 Many of the details of the Borden case appear in "The Long Arm," like a disap-

pearing bloody dress. See Victoria Lincoln, *A Private Disgrace: Lizzie Borden by Day-light* (1967; reprint, New York: International Polygonics, 1986)—one of the better "true crime" accounts of Borden's case. See also Catherine Ross Nickerson, "'The Deftness of Her Sex': Innocence, Guilt and Gender in the Trial of Lizzie Borden," in *Lethal Imagination: Violence and Brutality in American History*, ed. Michael A. Bellesiles (New York: New York University Press, 1999), 261–81.

23 Freeman, "The Long Arm," in Wells, ed., *American Detective Stories*, 174.

24 Sarah Fairbanks remarks following Phoebe Dole's confession, "I believe in de-moniacal possession after this." Ibid., 177.

25 Nancy Armstrong, *Desire and Domestic Fiction: A Political History of the Novel* (New York: Oxford University Press, 1987).

26 For discussions of the "marriage crisis," see Norma Basch, *Framing American Divorce: From the Revolutionary Generation to the Victorians* (Berkeley: University of California Press, 1999); Candice Lewis Bredbenner, *A Nationality of Her Own: Women, Marriage and the Law of Citizenship* (Berkeley: University of California Press, 1998); and Elaine Tyler May, *Great Expectations: Marriage and Divorce in Post-Victorian America* (Chicago: University of Chicago Press, 1980).

27 Hazel Carby, *Reconstructing Womanhood: The Emergence of the Afro-American Woman Nov-elist* (New York: Oxford University Press, 1987); Claudia Tate, *Domestic Allegories of Political Desire* (New York: Oxford University Press, 1992); Ann duCille, *The Coupling Convention: Sex, Text and Tradition in Black Women's Fiction* (New York: Oxford University Press, 1993). For a historical analysis of the role of marriage law in constraining the sexual and reproductive practices of African Americans after the Civil War, see Katherine M. Franke, "Becoming a Citizen: Reconstruction Era Regulation of African American Marriages," *Yale Journal of Law and the Humanities* 11, no. 2 (summer 1999): 251–309.

28 Abraham argues that the publication of Hall's novel concludes the first phase of the history of the lesbian novel in the United States, and inaugurates a second phase, lasting through the 1940s and dominated by responses to Radclyffe Hall, *The Well of Loneliness* (New York: Doubleday, 1928).

29 See Katz, *Gay/Lesbian Almanac*, 448–52, for excerpts from the extensive press cov-erage of the novel's publication and the legal controversy surrounding it.

30 See Laura Doan, "Passing Fashions: Reading Female Masculinities in the 1920s," *Signs* 24, no. 3 (fall 1998): 663–700.

31 See Kaier Curtin, *We Can Always Call Them Bulgarians: The Emergence of Lesbians and Gay Men on the American Stage* (Boston: Alyson Publications, 1987), 43–67, for a detailed discussion of the 1926 New York production of *The Captive* and its aftermath.

32 Esther Newton, "The Mythic Mannish Lesbian: Radclyffe Hall and the New Woman," in Martin Duberman, Martha Vicinus, and George Chauncey, Jr., eds., *Hidden from History: Reclaiming the Lesbian and Gay Past* (New York: New American Li-brary, 1989).

33 In a series of conversations about Hall's novel, Henry Abelove pointed out to me the Christian themes of sacrifice and suffering by a "people" who exhibit nobility

and thus earn redemption. He also noted the resonance of Hall's Christlike representation of Stephen Gordon with Oscar Wilde's self-imaging in his postimpris-
onment cri de coeur, *De Profundis* (1905; reprint, New York: Dover, 1997). I haven't
developed these themes here, but I hope that others will.

34   Hall, *Well of Loneliness*, 361–63.

35   For a discussion of Hall's social world, much more helpful than those contained
in the various biographies of Hall, see Judith Halberstam, *Female Masculinity* (Durham: Duke University Press, 1998), 75–110.

36   For popular and academic analyses of this figure as it recurs throughout the twen-
tieth century, see Lynda Hart, *Fatal Women: Lesbian Sexuality and the Mark of Aggression*
(Princeton: Princeton University Press, 1994), and Julie Glamuzina and Alison
Laurie, *Parker and Hulme: A Lesbian View* (Ithaca, N.Y.: Firebrand Books, 1995). B. Ruby
Rich's introduction to the Glamuzina and Laurie volume places the 1954 New
Zealand murder case that it analyzes (the case that provided the basis for the film
Heavenly Creatures) in historical context for the U.S. edition.

37   The reception of *The Well* might very well have overturned the limitations and
exclusions I describe here. A study of the novel's reception in the post–World
War II period would undoubtedly turn up many surprising appropriations and
uses for it by different populations and generations of readers.

More Than Love: An Epilogue

1   Quoted in Patricia A. Schechter, "'All the Intensity of My Nature': Ida B. Wells,
Anger, and Politics," *Radical History Review* 70 (winter 1998): 52.

2   For an extensive discussion of how the pressure for respectability and propriety
hobbled Wells's career, see ibid., 48–77. See also Linda O. McMurry, *To Keep the
Waters Troubled: The Life of Ida B. Wells* (New York: Oxford University Press, 1998).

3   Edward H. Taylor, writing in the *Brownsville States-Democrat*, excerpted as "Alice
Mitchell," in the *Bolivar Bulletin*, Mar. 10, 1893, 3. Taylor also said she mentioned
"the tragedy that ruined her life" only once or twice, and then in a light, careless
way.

4   This report from an issue of *The Bolivar Bulletin* is quoted by Sherre Dryden in "That
Strange Girl: The Alice Mitchell Murder Case," *DARE* 1 (June 29–July 5, 1988): 4.

5   "Alice Mitchell Dead," *Memphis Commercial Appeal*, Apr. 1, 1898, 4. In this article, the
reporter said he had visited Alice at the asylum in 1895, and he summarizes his
observations at that time.

6   See *Grains of Sand: A History of Western Mental Health Institute 1886–1986* (Bolivar, Tenn.:
Western Mental Health Institute History Committee, 1986). This official document includes a sketchy account of the period before 1900.

7   See the biennial *Report of the Board of Trustees of the Western Hospital for the Insane* for
the years 1890/92, 1892/94, and 1896/98. (The report for 1894/96 is missing.)
These reports include statistical tables describing the patient populations. In 1892,
there were 319 patients (151 males, 168 females)—37 percent (48 percent of the

women, 28 percent of the men) were admitted for insanity imputed to "hereditary predisposition." This was the largest single cause listed (next most important were alcoholism and epilepsy for men, uterine trouble, ill health, and the flu for women); by 1898, it had declined in importance, accounting for 20 percent of the admissions (23 percent of the women and 18 percent of the men).

The biennial reports described work as of central importance in treatment, with men at work on the farm and in the workshops, and women in the laundry and the sewing room. Exercise and amusements (dances, concerts, and magic lantern shows) were also described as helpful. The somatic diagnoses and medical treatments in use at more "advanced" public and private asylums at this time were not mentioned.

For the history of asylum organization and treatment during the nineteenth century, see Gerald Grob, *Mental Institutions in America* (New York: The Free Press, 1973); David Rothman, *The Discovery of the Asylum* (Boston: Little, Brown, 1971); and especially Ellen Dwyer, *Homes for the Mad: Life Inside Two Nineteenth-Century Asylums* (New Brunswick, N.J.: Rutgers University Press, 1987).

8 These patient rolls are available at the Tennessee State Library and Archives: Department of Mental Health Record Group no. 94, Series no. 7: Lists/Rolls of Employees, Inmates, Patients, Pupils and Veterans, box no. 35, folders 1–10.

9 See "Alice Mitchell Dead . . . Last Chapter of a Tragedy," *Memphis Commercial Appeal*, Apr. 1, 1898, 4, and "Alice Mitchell's Death," *Bolivar Bulletin*, Apr. 8, 1898, 3.

10 "Alice Mitchell Insane," *Bolivar Bulletin*, Aug. 5, 1892, 1.

11 "Alice Mitchell Dead," *Memphis Commercial Appeal*, Apr. 1, 1898, 4.

12 The 1890/92 biennial report of the Western State Insane Asylum listed six deaths due to "phthisis pulmonalis" or tuberculosis (19 percent of the thirty-one deaths reported). The 1892/94 report listed seven (17 percent of the forty-one deaths), while the 1896/98 report listed twenty-three (33 percent of the sixty-nine deaths reported).

13 Sherre Dryden, "That Strange Girl: The Alice Mitchell Murder Case," *DARE* vol. 1 (1988): 13 (June 15–21), 14 (June 22–28), 15 (June 29–July 5). Dryden says this report appeared in the *St. Louis Chronicle* and was reprinted in the *Bolivar Bulletin* on April 9, 1898, without comment.

14 Coppock, "Memphis' Strangest Love Murder," Sept. 7 (1930) section 4, 5.

15 For an account of the emergence of the modern disease of "anorexia nervosa" in the nineteenth century, see Joan Jacobs Brumberg, "Emergence of the Modern Disease," chapter 4 in *Fasting Girls: The History of Anorexia Nervosa* (Cambridge: Harvard University Press, 1988). Alice Mitchell's "wasting" may have been a related phenomenon.

16 Daphne de Marneffe argues that psychiatrists *looked at* but seldom really *listened to* their patients until the radical therapeutic innovations of Sigmund Freud. See her "Looking and Listening: The Construction of Clinical Knowledge in Charcot and Freud," *SIGNS* 17 (Autumn 1991): 71–111.

I'm arguing that Alice Mitchell's relatives and lawyers didn't really listen to her either; only Lillie Johnson seemed to know much about her life before the murder.

17 "Sexual Inversion, Jealousy and Homicide," *Alienist and Neurologist* 20 (Oct. 1899): 669–71. This unsigned account was included in the "Selection" section and was reprinted from *Medicine* (June 1899).

18 Paul Coppock, "Memphis' Strangest Love Murder Had All-Girl Cast," *Memphis Commercial Appeal*, Sept. 7, 1930, section 4, 5.

19 Ibid.

20 This clipping, dated October 25, 1931, from a newspaper identified only as the *Sunday News*, appears in a "Lesbian Scrapbook" in the Kinsey Institute archives in Bloomington, Indiana. It was given to me by Jonathan Ned Katz. Another clipping on this case from the same scrapbook appeared in the *Evening Graphic*, datelined Los Angeles, on October 21, 1931. The report begins:

> Jealousy, developed by the weird mutual attachment of three women, resulted in the gruesome murder of two figures in their unusual triangle, authorities believed today as they sought the third woman.
>
> So far their search for Mrs. Winnie Ruth Judd, minister's daughter, telephone operator and physician's wife, accused of killing Mrs. Agnes Ann Leroi and Miss Samuelson, has been futile. . . .
>
> Detective described Mrs. Judd as a beautiful woman, feverish from tuberculosis and passionate, as shown in letters to her husband. They said that Mrs. Leroi was a rather large woman of the mannish type. Miss Samuelson, also tubercular, was described as extremely feminine and of the "clinging vine" type.

21 D. O. Cauldwell, "Lesbian Love Murder," *Sexology* 16 (July 1950): 773–79.

22 Frank S. Caprio, *Female Homosexuality: A Psychodynamic Study of Lesbianism* (New York: Citadel Press, 1954), 175–76.

23 Edwin Howard, "Resurrected Ballad Recalls a Strange Memphis Killing," *Memphis Press Scimitar*, Nov. 13, 1961. Professor Wolf died before publishing a planned article on this ballad. I have not been able to locate his files or tapes.

24 Of course, it's impossible to say how many transformations this ballad underwent, and at whose hands, in the years from its original composition until Mrs. Hastings's version was recorded in 1961.

25 For an overview of the medical approaches to homosexuality from the nineteenth century to the present, see Ronald Bayer, *Homosexuality and American Psychiatry: The Politics of a Diagnosis* (New York: Basic Books, 1981). For a gripping personal account of the "treatment" authorized by the 1950s psychodynamic theories, see Martin Duberman, *Cures* (New York: Dutton, 1991).

26 Fred Harris, "Lesbian Slaying Shocked 'Gay Nineties' Memphians," *Gaiety . . . Reflecting Gay Life in the South* 1, no. 5 (Nov. 1975): 3, 12; Sherre Dryden, "That Strange Girl: The Alice Mitchell Murder Case," *DARE* vol. 1 (1988): 13 (June 15–21), 14 (June 22–28), and 15 (June 29–July 5).

27 Jonathan Ned Katz, *Gay American History: Lesbians and Gay Men in the U.S.A.* (New York:

Thomas Y. Crowell, 1976), 53–58. An account of the Mitchell-Ward case is also included in Daneel Buring, *Lesbian and Gay Memphis: Building Communities behind the Magnolia Curtain* (New York: Garland Publishing, 1997), 18–20.

28 See the highly critical review of this play by Alisa Solomon, "Butchery," *Village Voice*, Nov. 12, 1985, 34.

29 Elizabeth Lapovsky Kennedy and Madeline D. Davis have provided the most carefully researched, historically grounded discussion of the position of fem(me)s. In *Boots of Leather, Slippers of Gold: The History of a Lesbian Community* (New York: Routledge, 1993), 336–46, they argue that "femness" was dictated more by setting and circumstance than by identity or difference, and they note that a system that polarizes sexualities cannot properly conceptualize them; thus none of their fem informants considered herself bisexual. After the 1950s, Kennedy and Davis find some fems more likely to be considered gay, but not necessarily or consistently. For provocative discussions of femness in memoir, essay, poetic, or fictional form, see Joan Nestle, ed., *The Persistent Desire: A Femme-Butch Reader* (Boston: Alyson Publications, 1991), and Sally Munt, ed., *Butch/Femme: Inside Lesbian Gender* (London: Cassell, 1998).

30 For a discussion of violence against transgender sex workers of color in New York City, and the complicity of the police and of wealthy gay residents of the far West Village neighborhood, see Craig Horowitz, "Whose Village?" *New York Magazine*, (Nov. 8, 1998), 28–33, 88.

BIBLIOGRAPHY

Manuscript Sources

Federal Writers' Project Records. Includes 300 biographical sketches. Tennessee State Library and Archives, Nashville, Tenn.

Higbee School for Young Ladies. Annual catalogs. Memphis Room Collection, Tennessee Public Library.

Patterson, Malcolm Rice. Papers. Tennessee State Library and Archives, Nashville, Tenn.

Peters, George Boddie, Sr. Papers. Tennessee State Library and Archives, Nashville, Tenn.

Tennessee State Department of Mental Health. Archival records, including patient rolls. Tennessee State Library and Archives, Nashville, Tenn.

Newspapers, City Directories, Government Records and Reports

Bolivar Bulletin. Tennessee, 1892–98.

Dow's Memphis Directory. Tennessee, 1888, 1890, 1892.

Memphis Appeal Avalanche. Tennessee, 1892.

Memphis Board of Commissioners. Report of Chief of Police. Tennessee, 1892.

Memphis Commercial. Tennessee, 1892.

Memphis Commercial Appeal. Tennessee, 1898, 1930.

Memphis Evening Scimitar. Tennessee, 1891, 1898.

Memphis Public Ledger. Tennessee, 1892.

Memphis Weekly Commercial. Tennessee, 1892.

New York World. New York, 1892.

R. L. Polk and Co.'s Memphis Directory. Tennessee, 1892.

San Francisco Chronicle. California, 1892.

San Francisco Examiner. California, 1892.

San Francisco Morning Call. California, 1892.

Tennessee State Board of Charities. Report to the General Assembly, 1896.

Tennessee Western Hospital for the Insane. Biennial Reports, Bolivar, Tennessee, 1890–92, 1892–94, 1896–98.

Vanity Fair. Lincoln, Nebraska, 1892.

Primary Sources

Baner, J. L. "The Treatment of Some of the Effects of Sexual Excess." *Medical and Surgical Reporter* 1 (1884): 580, 614.

Beard, George M. *Sexual Neurasthenia*. New York: E. B. Treat, 1884.

Blumer, G. Adler. "A Case of Perverted Sexual Instinct (Contrare Sexualempfindung)." *American Journal of Insanity* 39 (1882): 22–35.

Caprio, Frank S. *Female Homosexuality: A Psychodynamic Study of Lesbianism*. New York: Citadel Press, 1954.

Carhart, Dr. John Wesley. *Norma Trist; or Pure Carbon: A Story of the Inversion of the Sexes*. Austin, Tex.: Eugene von Boeckmann, 1895.

Cauldwell, D. O. "Lesbian Love Murder." *Sexology* 16 (July 1950): 773–79.

Comstock, T. G. "Alice Mitchell of Memphis, A Case of Sexual Perversion or 'Urning' (A Paranoic)." *New York Medical Times* 20 (1892–93): 170–73.

Daniel, F. E. "Castration of Sexual Perverts." *Texas Medical Journal* 9 (1893): 255–71.

Duster, Alfreda, ed. *Crusade for Justice: The Autobiography of Ida B. Wells*. Chicago: University of Chicago Press, 1970.

Ellis, Havelock. "A Note on the Treatment of Sexual Inversion." *Alienist and Neurologist* 17 (1896): 257–64.

———. *Sexual Inversion*. 1st American printing. Philadelphia: F. A. Davis, 1901.

———. "Sexual Inversion in Men." *Alienist and Neurologist* 17 (1896): 115–50.

———. "Sexual Inversion in Women." *Alienist and Neurologist* 16 (1895): 144–58.

Freeman, Mary E. Wilkins. "The Long Arm." In *American Detective Stories*, edited by Carolyn Wells. New York: Oxford University Press, 1927. (Story orginally published 1895).

Garnier, Paul. "Sexual Pervert Impulses and Obsessions." *Alienist and Neurologist* 21 (1900): 634–41.

"A German Oscar Wilde." *Alienist and Neurologist* 17 (1896): 214.

"H." "Gynomania." *Medical Record* (Mar. 19, 1881): 336.

Hall, Radclyffe. *The Well of Loneliness*. New York: Doubleday, 1928.

Hamilton, A. MacLane. "The Civil Responsibility of Sexual Perverts." *American Journal of Insanity* 52 (1896): 505.

Hatch, Mary R. P. *The Strange Disappearance of Eugene Comstock*. New York: G. W. Dillingham, 1895.

Howard, William Lee. "Effeminate Men and Masculine Women." *New York Medical Journal* 71 (1900): 686.

———. "Psychical Hermaphroditism: A Few Notes on Sexual Perversion with Two Clinical Cases of Sexual Inversion." *Alienist and Neurologist* 18 (1897): 111–18.

———. "Sexual Perversion." *Alienist and Neurologist* 17 (1896): 1–6.

Hughes, Charles H. "Alice Mitchell, the 'Sexual Pervert' and Her Crime." *Alienist and Neurologist* 13 (1892): 554–57.

———. "Editorial: Perversions of the Sexual Feeling." *Alienist and Neurologist* 12 (1891): 423–25.

————. "Erotopathia—Morbid Erotism." *Alienist and Neurologist* 14 (1893): 531–78.

————. "Homo Sexual Complexion Perverts in St.Louis: Note on a Feature of Sexual Psychopathy." *Alienist and Neurologist* 28 (1907): 487–88.

————. "The Mitchell-Ward Tragedy." *Alienist and Neurologist* 13 (1892): 398–400.

"Impregnation of One Sexual Pervert Female by Another." *Alienist and Neurologist* 13 (1892): 545–46.

Kiernan, James G. "Aberrant Manifestations of the Sexual Appetite." *Neurological Review* (April 1886).

————. "Insanity: Sexual Perversion." *Detroit Lancet* 7 (1884): 481–84.

————. "Perverted Sexual Instinct." *Chicago Medical Journal and Examiner* 48 (1884): 263–65.

————. "Psychical Treatment of Congenital Sexual Inversion." *Review of Insanity and Nervous Disease* 4 (June 1884): 295.

————. "Psychological Aspects of the Sexual Appetite." *Alienist and Neurologist* 12 (1891): 188–219.

————. "Responsibility in Sexual Perversion." *Chicago Medical Recorder* 3 (1892): 185–210.

————. "Sexology: Increase of American Inversion." *Urologic and Cutaneous Review* 20 (1916): 44–49.

————. "Sexual Perversion and the Whitechapel Murders." *Medical Standard* 4 (1888): 170–72.

————. "Sexual Perversion in the Female." *Alienist and Neurologist* 15 (1894): 497–98.

Krafft-Ebing, Richard von. "Forensic Aspects of Sexual Pervert Impulses and Obsessions." *Alienist and Neurologist* 21 (1900): 680–82.

————. "Perversion of the Sexual Instinct: Report of Cases." *Alienist and Neurologist* 9 (1888): 565–81.

————. "Perverted Sexual Feeling." *Alienist and Neurologist* 3 (1882): 673–76.

————. *Psychopathia Sexualis with Especial Reference to Contrary Sexual Instinct*. Translated from the twelfth and final edition by Brian King. Burbank, Calif.: Bloat Publishing, 1999.

Leidy, P., and C. K. Mills. "Reports of Cases of Insanity from the Insane Department of the Philadelphia Hospital." *Journal of Nervous and Mental Disease* 13 (1886): 712.

"Lesbian Love and Murder." *New York Medical Record* 42 (July 23, 1892): 104.

Lydston, George Frank. *Addresses and Essays*. 2nd rev. ed. Louisville, Ky.: Renz & Henry, 1892.

————. *The Disease of Society (The Vice and Crime Problem)*. Philadelphia: J. B. Lippincott, 1904.

————. "Sexual Perversion: Satyriasis and Nymphomania." *Medical and Surgical Reporter* 61 (1889): 253.

"A Man in Petticoats." *Alienist and Neurologist* 16 (1895): 298–300.

Mann, Edward C. "Medico-Legal and Psychological Aspects of the Trial of Josephine Mallison Smith." *Alienist and Neurologist* 14 (1893): 467–77.

————. "Morbid Sexual Perversions As Related to Insanity." *Alienist and Neurologist* 14 (1893): 471–77.

Meriwether, Elizabeth Avery. *Recollections of Ninety-two Years, 1824–1916*. Nashville: Tennessee Historical Commission, 1958.

"Oscar Wilde As a Psychological and Psychiatric Study." *Alienist and Neurologist* 16 (1895): 320–21.

"Perversions of the Sexual Feeling." *Alienist and Neurologist* 15 (1894): 497–98.

Quackenbos, J. D. "Hypnotic Suggestion in the Treatment of Sexual Perversions and Moral Anaesthesia: A Personal Experience." *Transactions of New Hampshire Medical Society* (1899): 69–91.

Rosse, Irving C. "Increase in Sexual Depravity." *New Albany Medical Herald* 18 (1898): 699–700.

———. "Sexual Hypochondriasis and Perversion of the Genesic Instinct." *Journal of Nervous and Mental Disease* 17 (Nov. 1892): 795–811.

"Sexual Inversion, Jealousy and Homicide." *Alienist and Neurologist* 20 (1899): 669–671.

Shaw, J. C., and G. N. Ferris. "Perverted Sexual Instinct." *Journal of Nervous and Mental Disease* 10 (1883): 185–204.

Shrady, George. "Perverted Sexual Instinct." *Medical Record* 26 (1884): 70.

Sim, F. L. "Forensic Psychiatry. Alice Mitchell Adjudged Insane." *Memphis Medical Monthly* 12 (1892): 377–428.

Spitzka, E.C. "A Historical Case of Sexual Perversion." *Chicago Medical Review* (Aug. 20, 1881).

———. *Insanity: Its Classification, Diagnosis and Treatment*. New York: E. B. Treat, 1887.

Stefanowski, Dimitry. "Passivism—A Variety of Sexual Perversion." *Alienist and Neurologist* 13 (1892): 650–57.

———. "Uranism and Paederasty." *Alienist and Neurologist* 15 (1894): 455–58.

Stockham, Alice B. *Tokology: A Book for Every Woman*. Chicago: Alice B. Stockham, 1883.

Weir, J., Jr. "The Sexual Criminal." *Medical Record* 47 (1895): 581–83.

Wells-Barnett, Ida. B. *Southern Horrors: Lynch Law in All Its Phases*. New York: New York Age, 1892.

Whitbread, Helena, ed. *I Know My Own Heart: The Diaries of Ann Lister, (1791–1840)*. London: Virago, 1988.

———, ed. *No Priest But Love: Excerpts from the Diaries of Ann Lister (1824–1826)*. New York: New York University Press 1992.

Wise, P. M. "Case of Sexual Perversion." *Alienist and Neurologist* 4 (1883): 87–91.

Selected Secondary Sources

Abelove, Henry. "Freud, Male Homosexuality, and the Americans." In *The Lesbian and Gay Studies Reader*, edited by Henry Abelove, Michele Aina Barale and David M. Halperin, 381–93. New York: Routledge, 1993.

Abraham, Julie. *Are Girls Necessary? Lesbian Writing and Modern Histories*. New York: Routledge, 1996.

Alexander, Ruth. *The "Girl Problem": Female Sexual Delinquency in New York, 1900–1930*. Ithaca, N.Y.: Cornell University Press, 1995.

Allen, Hillary. *Justice Unbalanced: Gender, Psychiatry and Judicial Decisions.* Philadephia: Open University Press, 1987.

Anderson, Benedict. *Imagined Communities: Reflections on the Origin and Spread of Nationalism.* London: Verso, 1983.

Appadurai, Arjun. *Modernity at Large: Cultural Dimensions of Globalization.* Minneapolis: University of Minnesota Press, 1997.

Armstrong, Nancy. *Desire and Domestic Fiction: A Political History of the Novel.* New York: Oxford University Press, 1987.

Auerbach, Nina. *Private Theatricals: The Lives of the Victorians.* Cambridge: Harvard University Press, 1990.

Auster, Albert. *Actresses and Suffragists: Women in the American Theater, 1890–1920.* New York: Praeger, 1984.

Ayers, Edward. *The Promise of the New South: Life after Reconstruction.* New York: Oxford University Press, 1992.

Bakhtin, Mikhail. *The Dialogic Imagination.* Edited and translated by Michael Holquist and Caryl Emerson. Austin: University of Texas Press, 1981.

Barnes, Kenneth C. *Who Killed John Clayton? Political Violence and the Emergence of the New South.* Durham: Duke University Press, 1998.

Basch, Norma. *Framing American Divorce: From the Revolutionary Generation to the Victorians.* Berkeley: University of California Press, 1999.

Beard, Mattie Duncan. *The WCTU in the Volunteer State.* Kingsport, Tenn.: Kingsport Press, 1962.

Bederman, Gail. *Manhood and Civilization: A Cultural History of Gender and Race in the United States, 1880–1917.* Chicago: University of Chicago Press, 1995.

Belknap, Michael R., ed. *American Political Trials.* Westport, Conn.: Greenwood Press, 1994.

Bellesiles, Michael A., ed. *Lethal Imagination: Violence and Brutality in American History.* New York: New York University Press, 1999.

Benson, Susan Porter. *Counter Cultures: Saleswomen, Managers and Customers in American Department Stores, 1890–1940.* Chicago: University of Illinois Press, 1986.

Berenson, Edward. *The Trial of Madame Caillaux.* Berkeley: University of California Press, 1992.

Berkeley, Kathleen C. *"Like a Plague of Locusts": From an Antebellum Town to a New South City, Memphis, Tennessee, 1850–1880.* New York: Garland Publishing, 1991.

Berlant, Lauren. "Introduction to 'Intimacy: A Special Issue.' " *Critical Inquiry* 24 (winter 1998): 281–88.

———. *The Queen of America Goes to Washington City: Essays on Sex and Citizenship.* Durham: Duke University Press, 1997.

Berry, Mary Frances. "Repression of Blacks in the South 1890–1945." In *The Age of Segregation: Race Relations in the South, 1870–1945,* edited by Robert Haws. Jackson: University Press of Mississippi, 1978.

The Black Public Sphere Collective, eds. *The Black Public Sphere: A Public Culture Book.* Chicago: University of Chicago Press, 1995.

Bland, Lucy, and Laura Doan, eds. *Sexology in Culture: Labelling Bodies and Desires.* Chicago: University of Chicago Press, 1998.

Blustein, Bonnie Ellen. *Preserve Your Love for Science: Life of William A. Hammond, American Neurologist.* Cambridge: Harvard University Press, 1991.

Bredbenner, Candice Lewis. *A Nationality of Her Own: Women, Marriage and the Law of Citizenship.* Berkeley: University of California Press, 1998.

Brooks, Peter, and Paul Gewirtz, eds. *Law's Stories: Narrative and Rhetoric in the Law.* New Haven: Yale University Press, 1996.

Brown, Joshua. "Reconstructing Representation: Social Types, Readers, and the Pictorial Press, 1865–1877." *Radical History Review*, no. 66 (fall 1996): 5–38.

Brundage, W. Fitzhugh. *Lynching in the New South: Georgia and Virginia 1880–1930.* Urbana: University of Illinois Press, 1993.

———, ed. *Under Sentence of Death: Lynching in the South.* Chapel Hill: University of North Carolina Press, 1997.

Buhle, Mari Jo. *Women and American Socialism 1870–1920.* Urbana: University of Illinois Press, 1983.

Buring, Daneel. *Lesbian and Gay Memphis: Building Community behind the Magnolia Curtain.* New York: Garland Publishing, 1997.

Butler, Judith. *Gender Trouble: Feminism and the Subversion of Identity.* New York: Routledge, 1990.

Calhoun, Craig, ed. *Habermas and the Public Sphere.* Cambridge: MIT Press, 1996.

Capers, Gerald M., Jr. *The Biography of a River Town, Memphis: Its Heroic Age.* Chapel Hill: University of North Carolina Press, 1939.

Carby, Hazel. "It Jus Be's Dat Way Sometime: The Sexual Politics of Women's Blues." In *Unequal Sisters: A Multicultural Reader in U.S. Women's History*, edited by Ellen Carol DuBois and Vicki Ruiz, 238–49. New York: Routledge, 1990.

———. *Reconstructing Womanhood: The Emergence of the Afro-American Woman Novelist.* New York: Oxford University Press, 1987.

Cartwright, Joseph H. *The Triumph of Jim Crow: Tennessee Race Relations in the 1880s.* Knoxville: University of Tennessee Press, 1976.

Chauncey, George, Jr. "From Inversion to Homosexuality: Medicine and the Changing Conceptualization of Female Deviance." *Salmagundi* 58–59 (1982–83): 114–46.

———. *Gay New York: Gender, Urban Culture and the Making of the Gay Male World, 1890–1940.* New York: Basic Books, 1994.

Clarke, Anna. "Anne Lister's Construction of Lesbian Desire." *Journal of the History of Sexuality* 7, no. 11 (1996): 23–50.

Clement, Catherine. *Opera, or the Undoing of Women.* Translated by Betsy Wing. Minneapolis: University of Minnesota Press, 1988.

Cohen, Anne B. *Poor Pearl, Poor Girl! The Murdered-girl Stereotype in Ballad and Newspaper.* Austin: University of Texas Press/American Folklore Society, 1973.

Cohen, Ed. *Talk on the Wilde Side.* New York: Routledge, 1993.

Cohen, Patricia. *The Murder of Helen Jewett: The Life and Death of a Prostitute in Nineteenth-Century New York.* New York: Knopf, 1998.

Cohen, William A. *Sex Scandal: The Private Parts of Victorian Fiction.* Durham: Duke University Press, 1996.

Colaizzi, Janet. *Homicidal Insanity, 1800–1985.* Tuscaloosa: University of Alabama Press, 1989.

Copelman, Dina M. "The Gendered Metropolis: Fin-de-Siècle London." *Radical History Review,* no. 60 (Fall 1994): 38–56.

Coppock, Paul. "A Fighting Daughter of the South—Elizabeth Avery Meriwether." *Memphis Commercial Appeal,* June 7 1981.

———. *Memphis Memoirs.* Memphis: Memphis State University Press, 1980.

———. *Memphis Sketches.* Memphis: Friends of Memphis and Shelby County Libraries, 1976.

Crenshaw, Kimberle, Neil Gotanda, Gary Peller, and Kendall Thomas, eds. *Critical Race Theory: The Key Writings That Formed the Movement.* New York: The New Press, 1995.

Curtin, Kaier. *We Can Always Call Them Bulgarians: The Emergence of Lesbians and Gay Men on the American Stage.* Boston: Alyson Publications, 1987.

Cvetkovich, Ann. *Mixed Feelings: Feminism, Mass Culture, and Victorian Sensationalism.* New Brunswick, N.J.: Rutgers University Press, 1992.

D'Emilio, John, and Estelle Freedman. *Intimate Matters: A History of Sexuality in America.* New York: Harper and Row, 1988.

Dalton, Katharina. *Depression after Childbirth.* New York: Oxford University Press, 1980.

Davis, Angela Y. *Blues Legacies and Black Feminism: Gertrude "Ma" Rainey, Bessie Smith, and Billie Holiday.* New York: Pantheon Books, 1998.

Davis, Tracy. *Actresses as Working Women: Their Social Identity in Victorian Culture.* London: Routledge, 1991.

de Certeau, Michel. *The Practice of Everyday Life.* Berkeley: University of California Press, 1984.

Debord, Guy. *The Society of the Spectacle.* New York: Zone Books, 1995.

Denning, Michael. *Mechanic Accents: Dime Novels and Working-class Culture in America.* London: Verso, 1987.

Diggs, Marylynne. "'Romantic Friends' or a 'Different Race of Creatures'? The Representation of Lesbian Pathology in Nineteenth-Century America." *Feminist Studies* 21, no. 2 (summer 1995): 317–40.

Doan, Laura. "Passing Fashions: Reading Female Masculinities in the 1920s." *Signs* 24, no. 3 (fall 1998): 663–700.

Donoghue, Emma. *Passions between Women: British Lesbian Culture 1668–1801.* New York: Harper Collins, 1993.

Duberman, Martin, Martha Vicinus, and George Chauncey, Jr., eds, *Hidden from History: Reclaiming the Gay and Lesbian Past.* New York: New American Library, 1989.

duCille, Ann. *The Coupling Convention: Sex, Text and Tradition in Black Women's Fiction.* New York: Oxford University Press, 1993.

Dudden, Faye. *Women in the American Theatre: Actresses and Audiences, 1790–1870.* New Haven: Yale University Press, 1994.

Edwards, Laura F. *Gendered Strife and Confusion: The Political Culture of Reconstruction.* Chicago: University of Illinois Press, 1997.

Epstein, Julia. "Either/Or — Neither/Both: Sexual Ambiguity and the Ideology of Gender." *Genders* 7 (Mar. 1990): 99–142.

Evans, Sara. *Born for Liberty: A History of Women in America.* New York: The Free Press, 1989.

Faderman, Lillian. "Acting 'Woman' and Thinking 'Man': The Ploys of Famous Female Inverts." *GLQ: A Journal of Lesbian and Gay Studies* 5, no. 3 (1999): 315–29.

———. *Scotch Verdict.* New York: Columbia University Press, 1993.

———. *Surpassing the Love of Men: Romantic Friendship and Love between Women from the Renaissance to the Present.* New York: William Morrow, 1981.

Ferguson, Robert A. "Story and Transcription in the Trial of John Brown." *Yale Journal of Law and the Humanities* 6 (winter 1994): 37–73.

Fernando, Suman, David Ndegwa, and Melba Wilson. *Forensic Psychiatry, Race and Culture.* London: Routledge, 1998.

Foley, Neil. *The White Scourge: Mexicans, Blacks, and Poor Whites in Texas Cotton Culture.* Berkeley: University of California Press, 1997.

Foster, Jeannette. *Sex Variant Women in Literature.* New York: Vantage Press, 1956.

Foucault, Michel. *The History of Sexuality.* Vol. 1, *An Introduction.* Trans. Robert Hurley. New York: Pantheon, 1978.

Fradenburg, Louise O., and Carla Freccero. "The Pleasures of History." *GLQ: A Journal of Gay and Lesbian Studies* 1, no. 4 (1995): 371–84.

Franke, Katherine M. "Becoming a Citizen: Reconstruction Era Regulation of African American Marriages." *Yale Journal of Law and the Humanities* 11, no. 2 (summer 1999): 251–309.

Fraser, Walter J., Jr. "Three Views of Old Higbee School." *West Tennessee Historical Society Papers,* no. 20 (1966): 46–60.

Freedman, Estelle B. "The Prison Lesbian: Race, Class and the Construction of the Aggressive Female Homosexual, 1915–1965." *Feminist Studies* 22, no. 2 (summer 1996): 397–423.

———. *Their Sisters' Keepers: Women's Prison Reform in America, 1830–1930.* Ann Arbor: University of Michigan Press, 1981.

Fuss, Diana. *Identification Papers.* New York: Routledge, 1995.

Gaines, Kevin. *Uplifting the Race: Black Leadership, Politics and Culture in the Twentieth Century.* Chapel Hill: University of North Carolina Press, 1996.

Giddings, Paula. *When and Where I Enter: The Impact of Black Women on Race and Sex in America.* New York: William Morrow, 1984.

Gilman, Sander L. *Difference and Pathology: Stereotypes of Sexuality, Race and Madness.* Ithaca, N.Y.: Cornell University Press, 1985.

Gilmore, Glenda Elizabeth. *Gender and Jim Crow: Women and the Politics of White Supremacy in North Carolina, 1896–1920.* Chapel Hill: University of North Carolina Press, 1996.

Gilroy, Paul. *The Black Atlantic: Modernity and Double Consciousness.* Cambridge: Harvard University Press, 1993.

Glamuzina, Julie, and Alison Laurie. *Parker and Hulme: A Lesbian View*. Ithaca, N.Y.: Firebrand Books, 1995.

Goldberg, Jonathan. "The History That Will Be." *GLQ: A Journal of Lesbian and Gay Studies* 1, no. 4 (1995): 371–84.

Gordon, Linda. *Woman's Body, Woman's Right: Birth Control in America*. Rev. ed. New York: Penguin, 1990.

Gould, Stephen. *Ontogeny and Phylogeny*. Cambridge: Harvard University Press, 1977.

Grosskurth, Phyllis. *Havelock Ellis: A Biography*. New York: New York University Press, 1985.

Gunning, Sandra. *Race, Rape and Lynching: The Red Record of American Literature, 1890–1912*. New York: Oxford University Press, 1996.

Habermas, Jürgen. *The Structural Transformation of the Public Sphere: An Inquiry into a Category of Bourgeois Society*. Translated by Thomas Burger and Frederick Lawrence. Cambridge: Polity Press, 1989.

Halberstam, Judith. *Female Masculinity*. Durham: Duke University Press, 1998.

Hale, Grace Elizabeth. *Making Whiteness: The Culture of Segregation*. New York: Pantheon Books, 1998.

Hale, Nathan, Jr. *Freud and the Americans: The Beginnings of Psychoanalysis in the United States*. New York: Oxford University Press, 1971.

Hall, Jacquelyn Dowd. "'The Mind That Burns in Each Body': Women, Rape, and Racial Violence." In *Powers of Desire: The Politics of Sexuality*, edited by Ann Snitow, Christine Stansell, and Sharon Thompson, 328–49. New York: Monthly Review Press, 1983.

————. *Revolt against Chivalry: Jessie Daniel Ames and the Women's Campaign against Lynching*. New York: Columbia University Press, 1979.

Haller, John. *Outcasts from Evolution: Scientific Attitudes of Racial Inferiority, 1859–1900*. Urbana: University of Illinois Press, 1971.

Haller, Mark H. *Eugenics: Hereditary Attitudes in American Thought*. New Brunswick, N.J.: Rutgers University Press, 1963.

Halttunen, Karen. *Murder Most Foul: The Killer and the American Gothic Imagination*. Cambridge: Harvard University Press, 1998.

Hansen, Bert. "American Physicians' 'Discovery' of Homosexuals, 1880–1900: A New Diagnosis in a Changing Society." In *Framing Disease: Studies in Cultural History*, edited by Charles Rosenberg and Janet Golden, 104–33. New Brunswick, N.J.: Rutgers University Press, 1992.

Hansen, Miriam. *Babel and Babylon: Spectatorship in American Silent Film*. Cambridge: Harvard University Press, 1991.

Haraway, Donna. *Primate Visions*. New York: Routledge, 1990.

Hariman, Robert. *Popular Trials: Rhetoric, Mass Media and the Law*. Tuscaloosa: University of Alabama Press, 1990.

Harkins, John E. *Metropolis of the American Nile: An Illustrated History of Memphis and Shelby County*. Woodland Hills, Calif.: Windsor Publications, 1982.

Harper, Phillip Brian. *Private Affairs: Critical Ventures in the Culture of Social Relations*. New York: New York University Press, 1999.

Harris, Ruth. *Murders and Madness: Medicine, Law and Society in the Fin de Siecle*. Oxford: Oxford University Press, 1989.

Hart, Lynda. *Fatal Women: Lesbian Sexuality and the Mark of Aggression*. Princeton: Princeton University Press, 1994.

Hartman, Mary S. *Victorian Murderesses*. London: Robson Books, 1977.

Hasian, Marouf Arif, Jr. *The Rhetoric of Eugenics in Anglo-American Thought*. Athens: University of Georgia Press, 1996.

Higginbotham, Evelyn Brooks. "African-American Women's History and the Meta-language of Race." *Signs* 17 (winter 1992): 251–74.

————. *Righteous Discontent: The Women's Movement in the Black Baptist Church, 1880–1920*. Cambridge: Harvard University Press, 1993.

Hodes, Martha. "The Sexualization of Reconstruction Politics: White Women and Black Men in the South after the Civil War." *Journal of the History of Sexuality* 3, no. 3 (1993): 402–17.

————. *White Women, Black Men: Illicit Sex in the Nineteenth-Century South*. New Haven: Yale University Press, 1997.

Holquist, Michael. *Dialogism: Bakhtin and His World*. London: Routledge, 1990.

Hunter, Kathryn Montgomery. *Doctors' Stories: The Narrative Structure of Medical Knowledge*. Princeton: Princeton University Press, 1991.

Hunter, Nan D. "Marriage, Law, and Gender: A Feminist Legal Inquiry." *Law and Sexuality* 1 (1991): 9–30.

Hunter, Tera. *To 'Joy My Freedom: Southern Black Women's Lives and Labors after the Civil War*. Cambridge: Harvard University Press, 1997.

Hutchins, Fred L. *What Happened in Memphis*. Kingsport, Tenn.: Kingsport Press, 1965.

Jacobson, Matthew Frye. *Whiteness of a Different Color: European Immigrants and the Alchemy of Race*. Cambridge: Harvard University Press, 1998.

Jones, Ann. *Women Who Kill*. New York: Holt, Rinehart and Winston, 1980.

Jones, Jacqueline. "The Political Implications of Black and White Women's Work in the South, 1890–1965." In *Women, Politics and Change*, edited by Louise Tilly and Patricia Gurin, 108–29. New York: Russell Sage Foundation, 1990.

Kaplan, Amy. "Manifest Domesticity." *American Literature* 70, no. 3 (Sept. 1998): 581–606.

————. "Romancing the Empire: The Embodiment of American Masculinity in the Popular Historical Novel of the 1890s." *Amercian Literary History* 2, no. 4 (winter 1990): 659–90.

Kaplan, Amy, and Donald Pease, eds. *Cultures of United States Imperialism*. Durham: Duke University Press, 1993.

Katz, Jonathan Ned. *Gay American History: Lesbians and Gay Men in the U.S.A*. New York: Thomas Y. Crowell, 1976.

————. *Gay/Lesbian Almanac: A New Documentary*. New York: Harper and Row, 1983.

Kelman, Mark. *A Guide to Critical Legal Studies*. Cambridge: Harvard University Press, 1987.

Kennedy, Elizabeth Lapovsky, and Madeline D. Davis. *Boots of Leather, Slippers of Gold: The History of a Lesbian Community.* New York: Routledge, 1993.

Kennedy, Hubert. *Ulrichs: The Life and Work of Karl Heinrich Ulrichs, Pioneer of the Modern Gay Movement.* Boston: Alyson Publications, 1988.

Kevles, Daniel J. *In the Name of Eugenics: Genetics and the Uses of Human Heredity.* New York: Knopf, 1985.

Koestenbaum, Wayne. *Double Talk: The Erotics of Male Literary Collaboration.* New York: Routledge, 1989.

Kolko, Gabriel. *Main Currents in Modern American History.* New York: Harper and Row, 1976.

Kunzel, Regina G. *Fallen Women, Problem Girls: Unmarried Mothers and the Professionalization of Social Work, 1890–1945.* New Haven: Yale University Press, 1993.

Lane, Roger. *Murder in America: A History.* Columbus: Ohio State University Press, 1997.

———. *Violent Death in the City: Suicide, Accident and Murder in Nineteenth Century Philadelphia.* Cambridge: Harvard University Press, 1979.

Larson, Edward J. *Sex, Race, and Science: Eugenics in the Deep South.* Baltimore: Johns Hopkins University Press, 1995.

Lebsock, Suzanne. "Women and American Politics 1880–1920." In *Women, Politics and Change,* edited by Louise Tilly and Patricia Gurin, 35–62. New York: Russell Sage Foundation, 1990.

Lerda, Valeria Gennaro. "'We Were No Class at All': Southern Women as Social Reformers." In *Race and Class in the South since 1890,* edited by Melvyn Stokes and Rick Halpern, 121–37. Oxford: Berg Publishers, 1994.

Lesser, Ronnie C., and Erica Schoenberg, eds. *That Obscure Subject of Desire: Freud's Female Homosexual Revisited.* New York: Routledge, 1999.

Lincoln, Victoria. *A Private Disgrace: Lizzie Borden by Daylight.* 1976. Reprint, New York: International Polygonics, 1986.

Lindquist, Lisa J. "Images of Alice: Gender, Deviancy, and a Love Murder in Memphis." *Journal of the History of Sexuality* 6, no. 1 (winter 1995): 30–61.

Lopez, Ian F. Haney. *White by Law: The Legal Construction of Race.* New York: New York University Press, 1996.

Lowe, Lisa. *Immigrant Acts: On Asian American Cultural Politics.* Durham: Duke University Press, 1996.

Lukas, J. Anthony *Big Trouble: A Murder in a Small Western Town Sets Off a Struggle for the Soul of America.* New York: Simon and Schuster, 1997.

Lunbeck, Elizabeth. *The Psychiatric Persuasion: Knowledge, Gender and Power in Modern America.* Princeton: Princeton University Press, 1994.

Lundsgaarde, Henry P. *Murder in Space City: A Cultural Analysis of Houston Homicide Patterns.* New York: Oxford University Press, 1977.

Maeder, Thomas. *Crime and Madness: The Origins and Evolution of the Insanity Defense.* New York: Harper and Row, 1985.

Martin, Biddy. *Woman and Modernity: The (Life)Style of Lou Andreas-Salome.* Ithaca, N.Y.: Cornell University Press, 1991.

May, Elaine Tyler. *Great Expectations: Marriage and Divorce in Post-Victorian America.* Chicago: University of Chicago Press, 1980.

McArthur, Benjamin. *Actors and American Culture, 1880–1920.* Philadelphia: Temple University Press, 1984.

McHugh, Kathleen. *American Domesticity: From How-to Manual to Hollywood Melodrama.* New York: Oxford University Press, 1999.

McKee, Margaret. *Beale Black and Blue: Life and Music on Black America's Main Street.* Baton Rouge: Louisiana State University Press, 1981.

McLaren, Angus. *A Prescription for Murder: The Victorian Serial Killings of Dr. Thomas Neill.* Chicago: University of Chicago Press, 1993.

McMurry, Linda O. *To Keep the Waters Troubled: The Life of Ida B. Wells.* New York: Oxford University Press, 1998.

Meyerowitz, Joanne. *Women Adrift: Independent Wage Earners in Chicago, 1880–1930.* Chicago: University of Chicago Press, 1988.

Miller, D. A. *Narrative and Its Discontents: Problems of Closure in the Traditional Novel.* Princeton: Princeton University Press, 1981.

Miller, William D. "Rural Ideals in Memphis at the Turn of the Century." *West Tennessee Historical Society Papers,* no. 4 (1950): 41–49.

Moore, Lisa L. *Dangerous Intimacies: Toward a Sapphic History of the British Novel.* Durham: Duke University Press, 1997.

———. " 'Something More Tender Still Than Friendship': Romantic Friendship in Early Nineteenth Century England." *Feminist Studies* 18, no. 3 (fall 1992): 499–520.

Mosse, George L. *Nationalism and Sexuality: Middle-Class Morality and Sexual Norms in Modern Europe.* Madison: University of Wisconsin Press, 1985.

Muñoz, José Esteban. *Disidentifications: Queers of Color and the Performance of Politics.* Minneapolis: University of Minnesota Press, 1999.

Munt, Sally, ed. *Butch/Femme: Inside Lesbian Gender.* London: Cassell, 1998.

Negt, Oskar, and Alexander Kluge. *Public Sphere and Experience: Toward an Analysis of the Bourgeois and Proletarian Public Sphere.* Translated by Peter Labanyi, Jamie Owen Daniel, and Assenka Oksiloff. Minneapolis: University of Minnesota Press, 1993.

Nelson, Dana. *National Manhood: Capitalist Citizenship and the Imagined Fraternity of White Men.* Durham: Duke University Press, 1998.

Nestle, Joan, ed. *The Persistent Desire: A Femme-Butch Reader.* Boston: Alyson Publications, 1991.

Neverdon-Morton, Cynthia. *Afro-American Women of the South and the Advancement of the Race, 1895–1925.* Knoxville: University of Tennessee Press, 1989.

Newman, Louise Michele. *White Women's Rights: The Racial Origins of Feminism in the United States.* New York: Oxford University Press, 1999.

Newton, Esther. "The Mythic Mannish Lesbian: Radclyffe Hall and the New Woman." In *Hidden from History: Reclaiming the Gay and Lesbian Past,* edited by Martin Duberman, Martha Vicinus, and George Chauncey Jr. New York: New American Library, 1989.

Nickerson, Catherine Ross. "'The Deftness of Her Sex': Innocence, Guilt and Gender in the Trial of Lizzie Borden." In *Lethal Imagination: Violence and Brutality in American History*, edited by Michael A. Bellesiles, 261–81. New York: New York University Press, 1999.

———. *The Web of Iniquity: Early Detective Fiction by American Women*. Durham: Duke University Press, 1998.

Nye, Robert. *Crime, Madness and Politics in Modern France: The Medical Concept of National Decline*. Princeton: Princeton University Press, 1984.

Odem, Mary. *Delinquent Daughters: Protecting and Policing Adolescent Female Sexuality in the United States, 1885–1920*. Chapel Hill: University of North Carolina Press, 1995.

Ohmann, Richard. *Selling Culture: Magazines, Markets, and Class at the Turn of the Century*. London: Verso, 1996.

Painter, Nell Irvin. *Standing at Armageddon: The United States, 1877–1919*. New York: W. W. Norton, 1987.

Papke, David Ray. *Framing the Criminal: Crime, Cultural Work and the Loss of Critical Perspective, 1830–1900*. Hamden, Conn.: Archon Books, 1987.

Pascoe, Peggy. "Miscegenation Law, Court Cases, and Ideologies of 'Race' in Twentieth-Century America." In *Sex, Race, Love: Crossing Boundaries in North American History*, edited by Martha Hodes, 464–90. New York: New York University Press, 1999.

Peiss, Kathy. *Cheap Amusements: Working Women and Leisure in Turn-of-the-Century New York*. Philadelphia: Temple University Press, 1986.

Phillips, Margaret I. *The Governors of Tennessee*. Gretna, La.: Pelican, 1978.

Pick, Daniel. *Faces of Degeneration: A European Disorder, c. 1848–1918*. Cambridge: Cambridge University Press, 1989.

Pleck, Elizabeth. *Domestic Tyranny: The Making of Social Policy against Family Violence from Colonial Times to the Present*. New York: Oxford University Press, 1987.

Poovey, Mary. *Uneven Developments: The Ideological Work of Gender in Mid-Victorian England*. Chicago: University of Chicago Press, 1988.

Prescot, Grace Elizabeth. "The Woman Suffrage Movement in Memphis: Its Place in the State, Sectional and National Movements." *The West Tennessee Historical Society Papers*, no. 18 (1964): 87–106.

Rabinowitz, Howard N. *The First New South 1865–1920*. Arlington, Ill.: Harlan Davidson, 1992.

Rafter, Nichole Hahn, ed. *White Trash: The Eugenic Family Studies, 1877–1913*. Boston: Northeastern University Press, 1988.

Robbins, Bruce, ed. *The Phantom Public Sphere*. Minneapolis: University of Minnesota Press, 1993.

Roberts, Mary Louise. "Gender, Consumption, and Commodity Culture." *American Historical Review* 103, no. 3 (June 1998): 817–44.

Rogers, Donald, ed. *Voting and the Spirit of American Democracy*. Chicago: University of Illinois Press, 1992.

Romero, Lora. *Home Fronts: Domesticity and Its Critics in the Antebellum United States*. Durham: Duke University Press, 1997.

Rosario, Vernon, ed. *Science and Homosexualities*. New York: Routledge, 1997.

Rosenberg, Charles. *No Other Gods: On Science and American Social Thought*. Baltimore: Johns Hopkins University Press, 1976.

———. *The Trial of the Assassin Guiteau: Psychiatry and Law in the Gilded Age*. Chicago: University of Chicago Press, 1968.

Rowbotham, Sheila, and Jeffrey Weeks. *Socialism and the New Life: The Personal and Sexual Politics of Edward Carpenter and Havelock Ellis*. London: Pluto Press, 1977.

Russett, Cynthia Eagle. *Sexual Science*. Cambridge: Harvard University Press, 1989.

Ryan, Mary P. *Civic Wars: Democracy and Public Life in the American City during the Nineteenth Century*. Berkeley: University of California Press, 1997.

Sahli, Nancy. "Smashing: Women's Relationships before the Fall." *Chrysalis* 8 (summer 1979): 17–27.

Salmon, Eric. *Bernhardt and the Theatre of Her Time*. Westport, Conn.: Greenwood Press, 1984.

Saxton, Alexander. *The Rise and Fall of the White Republic: Class Politics and Mass Culture in Nineteenth-Century America*. London: Verso, 1990.

Schechter, Patricia A. "'All the Intensity of My Nature': Ida B. Wells, Anger, and Politics." *Radical History Review*, 70 (winter 1998): 48–77.

———. "Unsettled Business: Ida B. Wells against Lynching, or, How Antilynching Got Its Gender." In *Under Sentence of Death: Lynching in the South*, edited by W. Fitzhugh Brundage, 292–317. Chapel Hill: University of North Carolina Press, 1997.

Schneirov, Matthew. *The Dream of a New Social Order: Popular Magazines in America, 1893–1914*. New York: Columbia University Press, 1994.

Schudson, Michael. *Discovering the News: A Social History of American Newspapers*. New York: Basic Books, 1978.

Schuetz, Janice. *The Logic of Women on Trial*. Carbondale: Southern Illinois University Press, 1994.

Scheutz, Janice, and Kathryn Holmes Snedaker. *Communication and Litigation: Case Studies of Famous Trials*. Carbondale: Southern Illinois University Press, 1988.

Scott, Ann Firor. *Making the Invisible Woman Visible*. Chicago: University of Illinois Press, 1984.

———. *The Southern Lady: From Pedestal to Politics*. Chicago: University of Chicago Press, 1970.

Scott, James. *Domination and the Arts of Resistance: Hidden Transcripts*. New Haven: Yale University Press, 1990.

Sedgwick, Eve Kosofsky. *Between Men: English Literature and Male Homosocial Desire*. New York: Columbia University Press, 1985.

———. *Epistemology of the Closet*. Berkeley: University of California Press, 1990.

Senelick, Laurence. "Boys and Girls Together: Subcultural Origins of Glamour Drag and Male Impersonation on the Nineteenth-Century Stage." In *Crossing the Stage: Controversies on Cross-dressing*, edited by Lesley Ferris, 8–95. London: Routledge, 1993.

———. "The Evolution of the Male Impersonator on the Nineteenth-Century Popular Stage." *Essays in Theatre* 1, no. 1 (1982): 31–46.

Shapiro, Ann-Louise. "Disordered Bodies/Disorderly Acts: Medical Discourse and the Female Criminal in Nineteenth-Century Paris." *Genders* 4 (1989): 68–86.

Shaw, Stephanie J. *What a Woman Ought to Be and to Do: Black Professional Women Workers during the Jim Crow Era.* Chicago: University of Chicago Press, 1996.

Sicherman, Barbara. *The Quest for Mental Health in America, 1880–1917.* New York: Arno Press, 1980.

Sigafoos, Robert A. *Cotton Row to Beale Street: A Business History of Memphis.* Memphis: Memphis State University Press, 1979.

Sklar, Martin J. *The Corporate Reconstruction of American Capitalism, 1890–1916: The Market, the Law, and Politics.* Cambridge: Cambridge University Press, 1988.

Smith, Roger. *Trial by Medicine: Insanity and Responsibility in Victorian Trials.* Edinburgh: Edinburgh University Press, 1981.

Smith-Rosenberg, Carroll. "Discourses of Sexuality and Subjectivity: The New Woman, 1870–1936." In *Hidden from History: Reclaiming the Gay and Lesbian Past,* edited by Martin Duberman. New York: New American Library, 1989.

———. *Disorderly Conduct: Visions of Gender in Victorian America.* New York: Knopf, 1985.

Solomon, Barbara. *In the Company of Educated Women: A History of Women and Higher Education in America.* New Haven: Yale University Press, 1985.

Somerville, Siobhan B. *Queering the Color Line: Race and the Invention of Homosexuality in American Culture.* Durham: Duke University Press, 2000.

Spillers, Hortense. "Mama's Baby, Papa's Maybe: An American Grammar Book." *Diacritics* (summer 1987: 65–81.

Srebnick, Amy Gilman. *The Mysterious Death of Mary Rogers: Sex and Culture in Nineteenth-Century New York.* New York: Oxford University Press, 1995.

Stallybrass, Peter, and Allon White. *The Politics and Poetics of Transgression.* Ithaca, N.Y.: Cornell University Press, 1986.

Stam, Robert. *Subversive Pleasures: Bakhtin, Cultural Criticism and Film.* Baltimore: Johns Hopkins University Press, 1989.

Stansell, Christine. *City of Women: Sex and Class in New York, 1789–1860.* New York: Knopf, 1986.

Steakley, James D. *The Homosexual Emancipation Movement in Germany.* New York: Arno, 1975.

Stepan, Nancy. *"The Hour of Eugenics": Race, Gender and Nation in Latin America.* Ithaca, N.Y.: Cornell University Press, 1991.

———. *The Idea of Race in Science: Great Britain, 1800–1960.* Hamden, Conn.: Archon Books, 1982.

Stevens, John D. *Sensationalism and the New York Press.* New York: Columbia University Press, 1991.

Stocking, George, Jr. *Race, Culture and Evolution: Essays in the History of Anthropology.* London: Collier-Macmillan, 1968.

Suggs, Henry Lewis, ed. *The Black Press in the South, 1865–1979.* Westport, Conn.: Greenwood Press, 1983.

Tate, Claudia. *Domestic Allegories of Political Desire.* New York: Oxford University Press, 1992.

Taylor, Peter. *Modernities: A Geohistorical Interpretation*. Minneapolis: University of Minnesota Press, 1999.

Terdiman, Richard. *Discourse/Counter-discourse: The Theory and Practice of Symbolic Resistance in Nineteenth-Century France*. Ithaca, N.Y.: Cornell University Press, 1985.

Terry, Jennifer. *An American Obsession: Science, Medicine, and Homosexuality in Modern Society*. Chicago: University of Chicago Press, 1999.

Terry, Jennifer, and Jacqueline Urla, eds. *Deviant Bodies: Critical Perspectives on Difference in Science and Popular Culture*. Bloomington: Indiana University Press, 1995.

Thompson, Mildred I. *Ida B. Wells-Barnett: An Exploratory Study of an American Black Woman, 1893–1930*. Brooklyn, N.Y.: Carlson Publishing, 1990.

Tighe, Janet Ann. "A Question of Responsibility: The Development of American Forensic Psychiatry, 1838–1930." Ph.D. diss., University of Pennsylvania, 1983.

Tolnay, Stewart Emory. *A Festival of Violence: An Analysis of Southern Lynchings, 1882–1930*. Urbana: University of Illinois Press, 1995.

Tracy, Sterling. "Clara Conway, Jenny Higbee and Others Made This City Notable for Cultural Study." *Memphis Commercial Appeal*, April 30 1950.

Traub, Valerie. "The Psychomorphology of the Clitoris." *GLQ: A Journal of Lesbian and Gay Studies* 2, no. 1–2 (1995): 81–113.

Ullman, Sharon R. *Sex Seen: The Emergence of Modern Sexuality*. Berkeley: University of California Press, 1997.

Utley, Buford C. "The Early Academies of West Tennessee." *The West Tennessee Historical Society Papers*, no. 8 (1954): 5–38.

Vicinus, Martha. "Distance and Desire: English Boarding School Friendships." *Signs* 9, no. 4 (summer 1984): 600–622.

————. *Independent Women: Work and Community for Single Women, 1850–1920*. Chicago: University of Chicago Press, 1985.

————. "Lesbian History: All Theory and No Facts, or All Facts and No Theory?" *Radical History Review* 60 (fall 1994): 57–75.

————. " 'They Wonder to Which Sex I Belong': The Historical Roots of Modern Lesbian Identity." *Feminist Studies* 18, no. 3 (fall 1992): 467–97.

Walker, Hugh. "A Crime of Passion? The Day the Doctor Shot the General." *The Nashville Tennesseann Magazine*, July 14, 1963, 8–9.

Walkowitz, Judith R. *City of Dreadful Delight: Narratives of Sexual Danger in Late Victorian London*. Chicago: University of Chicago Press, 1992.

Waller, Altina. *Reverend Beecher and Mrs. Tilton: Sex and Class in Victorian America*. Amherst: University of Massachusetts Press, 1982.

Warner, Michael. *The Letters of the Republic: Publication and the Public Sphere in Eighteenth-Century America*. Cambridge: Harvard University Press, 1990.

Wedell, Marsha. *Elite Women and the Reform Impulse in Memphis, 1875–1915*. Knoxville: University of Tennessee Press, 1991.

Weeks, Jeffrey. *Sex, Politics and Society: The Regulation of Sexuality since 1800*. London: Longman, 1981.

Wiebe, Robert. *The Search for Order, 1877–1920*. New York: Hill and Wang, 1967.

Wiegman, Robyn. *American Anatomies: Theorizing Race and Gender.* Durham: Duke University Press, 1995.

Williams, Raymond. *The Long Revolution.* New York: Harper and Row, 1965.

Williamson, Joel. *The Crucible of Race: Black-White Relations in the American South.* New York: Oxford University Press, 1984.

Wolff, Charlotte. *Magnus Hirschfeld: A Portrait of a Pioneer in Sexology.* London: Quartet Books, 1986.

Woody, Thomas. *A History of Women's Education in the United States.* New York: Octagon Books, 1974.

Wrenn, Lynette Boney. *Crisis and Commission Government in Memphis: Elite Rule in a Gilded Age City.* Knoxville: University of Tennessee Press, 1998.

Wright, George C. *Racial Violence in Kentucky 1865–1940.* Baton Rouge: Louisiana State University Press, 1990.

Young, Judge J. P. *The Standard History of Memphis, Tennessee.* Knoxville, Tenn.: H. W. Crew, 1912.

INDEX

Abelove, Henry, 275 n.33
African Americans, 14, 26; arrests
    of, 63; as freedpeople, 37; guard
    comprised of, 11; lesbian love mur-
    der narratives featuring, 139–40,
    174–75; as lynching victims, 11–12,
    18–19; marriage laws extended to,
    187; newspapers' characterization of,
    55–56; newspapers written by, 12, 17,
    22, 41–42, 87–88, 243 n.10; novels
    written by women, 187; sexologists
    on, 170–71, 174–75; testimony of,
    about Alice Mitchell, 55, 96; in *Well
    of Loneliness*, 190. See also *Free Speech and
    Headlight*; Lynching narratives
Afro-American Council, 17
Agnes Scott College, 45
"Alice and Fred" (Ellentuck), 199
"Alice Mitchell and Freda Ward" (bal-
    lad), 198
Alienist and Neurologist, 164, 170, 195–96
American Journal of Insanity, The, 164
"Americanness": associations with, 25–
    27; newspapers' role in defining,
    33–34, 61–66. See also Modernity
Anglo-Europeans: Americans' iden-
    tification with, 15, 22, 25, 135; and
    sexology, 25–27, 156–79
Anthony, Susan B., 193
Antilynching narratives, 12, 20–22, 29,
    36, 42, 155, 193
Antimiscegenation laws, 118–19
Armstrong, Nancy, 186–87

Associated Press, 36
Association for the Advancement of
    Women, 43
Association of Medical Superinten-
    dents of American Institutions for
    the Insane, 98
Audiences. *See* Newspapers: readers of
Auerbach, Nina, 266 n.21
Auster, Albert, 266 n.18

Ballads, 198
Balzac, Honoré de, 24, 181, 182
Barrett, W. H., 11
Beale Street Baptist Church (Memphis),
    17, 41
Bederman, Gail, 21
Beecher, Henry Ward, 65
Belot, Adolphe, 24, 181, 188
Berlant, Lauren, 4
Bernhardt, Sarah, 149
Bilger, Harry, 112, 204, 214, 218, 220
Binaries: of gender, 19, 26–27, 62,
    86; of race, 14–16, 26; of sexuality,
    26–27, 190–91
Birth of a Nation, The (film), 40
Blues music, 179
Bolivar Bulletin, 194, 195
Borden, Lizzie, 23, 123, 185–86
Bostonians, The (James), 187
Bourdet, Edouard, 188
Brooks, E. H., 147
Broome's Variety Theater (Memphis),
    142–48

Brothels, 140–42, 178
Brown, Elsa Barkley, 4
Brown, John, 64
Burr, Aaron, 64
Brownsville States-Democrat, 194
Buffalo Courier, 135
Butler, Eleanor, 135

Callender, John Hill, 98, 100, 101, 103, 105–7, 115, 260 n.41
Campbell, Michael, 99, 103, 104, 106, 108
Capital punishment, 171
Caplan, Jane, 271 n.37
Caprio, Frank, 197
Captive, The (Bourdet), 188–89
Carby, Hazel, 4, 187
Carhart, John Wesley, 183–86
Carpenter, Edward, 161, 175
Castration, 171–72
Cauldwell, D. O., 197
Central State Hospital for the Insane (Nashville), 98, 194
Chartrand, R. F., 222
Chesapeake and Ohio Railroad, 17, 41
Chinese immigrants, 14, 15, 26
Chivalric rescue narratives, 19–20
"Chumming," 25, 27, 58, 100, 114, 150, 185
Citizenship. *See* Voting rights
Class: of Alice Mitchell and her friends, 11, 23, 46, 47, 84–85, 113–15, 211, 245 n.36; of Ashley Roselle, 109; conflicts of, over labor issues, 15, 35, 37, 39; cultural narratives' obscuring of inequalities in, 4, 16, 40, 65, 236 n.16; as difference between romance and perversity, 168–73, 177; of lawyers in Mitchell-Ward case, 75; legislation favoring one over another, 62; of newspaper owners, 34, 36–37; of people in newspaper scandals, 40; privileges associated with high,

43; in *Well of Loneliness*, 5, 189–90; of white people involved in lynching, 11, 13–14
Cohen, Ed, 263 n.88
Cohen, William A., 252 n.23
Committee for the Study of Sex Variants, 273 n.52
Comstock, Thomas Griswold, 94, 202
Convents, 178
Converse, Florence, 182
Conway, Clara, 44
Conway Institute, 44
Coppock, Paul, 195, 196–97
Cosgrove, Kate, 39
Courts: social domination in, 63–64. *See also* Criminal trials; Grand jury; Habeas corpus hearing; Jury; Lunacy inquisition; Lynching; Medical profession; Police; Violence
"Cranks." *See* "Maniacs"
Crimes of passion, 90, 97, 107, 114, 174, 257 n.9, 259 n.30. *See also* Jealousy; Lesbian love murder narratives
Criminal, The (Ellis), 175
Criminal trials: as nationalizing narratives, 62–66; theatrical metaphors used in, 67–68, 85, 252 n.18. *See also* Grand jury; Habeas corpus hearing; Jail; Jury; Lunacy inquisition; Lynching; Violence
Cross-dressing: by African Americans, 170; by Alice Mitchell, 55, 101, 111, 114, 174, 205; in fiction, 181–82, 185; as indicative of "partial insanity," 260 n.47; in theater, 149, 266 n.19. *See also* "Female husband" narratives
Culture (high and low), 180–81, 187–88
Curve, The (Memphis neighborhood), 11, 87

Daniel, F. E., 171–72
DARE (newspaper), 199
d'Aubigny, Madeleine Maupin, 181

Davis, Katherine Bement, 179

Davis, Madeline D., 279 n.29

Davis, Sarah, 70

Democracy: modernity's constraints on, 2, 3, 35–36, 61

Desplaines, Annette, 137–39

Detroit Lancet, 173

Diana Victrix (Converse), 182

Dictionary of Psychological Medicine (Tuke), 49

Diderot, Denis, 274 n.12

Domestic life. See Domestic scandals; Marriage; "White home"

Domestic scandals, 39–40, 46, 60, 75, 124

Douglass, Frederick, 22, 41–42

Drama. See Theater

Dryden, Sherre, 199

DuBose, Julius: background of, 37, 75; as judge in Johnson habeas corpus case, 66, 69–70, 76, 77, 84, 85; as judge in Mitchell lunacy inquisition, 13–14, 24, 90, 100, 110, 113; and lynchings, 11, 13–14; newspapers' characterization of, 54, 75

duCille, Ann, 187

Duer, Lily, 128–34, 167, 173

Eastern State Hospital for the Insane (Knoxville), 99, 194

Ellentuck, Dan, 199

Ellis, Havelock, 27, 162, 174–77, 188, 190, 269 n.7, 272 n.46

Elmwood Cemetery (Memphis), 113

England: same-sex relationships in novels from, 182–83, 188–91; Wells's speaking tour of, 22. See also Anglo-Europeans

English, Dick, 143

"Erotomania," 48–51, 103, 163

"Erotopathia.—Morbid Eroticism" (Hughes), 165, 170

Eugenics, 171–72, 175, 179

Evolutionary development, 157–63, 173, 175, 177, 179

Factors in the Sex Life of Twenty-Two Hundred Women (Davis), 179

Faderman, Lillian, 185, 235 n.10

"Fast" women, 24, 27, 30, 42–43; association of, with theater, 142; question of Alice Mitchell as, 47, 50, 55, 247 n.51

Female Homosexuality (Caprio), 197

"Female husband" narratives, 124–28, 134, 143–48, 163

"Femmes": definition of, 6, 279 n.29; in lesbian love murder narratives, 29–30, 86, 154, 172, 199

Fernhurst (Stein), 187

Fiction. See Novels

"Fiends," 38–39, 41, 46, 50–51

Fisk University (Nashville), 45

Fitzgerald, William, 106, 108

Flaubert, Gustave, 181

Fletcher, William Baldwin, 103

Fortune, T. Thomas, 17

Foshee, James, 264 n.6, 265 n.8

Foucault, Michel, 5, 186

Fox, The (Lawrence), 187–88

Franklin, Lucy, 96, 206

Fraser, Nancy, 4

Freeman, Mary E. Wilkins, 185–86, 274 n.21

Free Speech and Headlight (African American newspaper), 12, 17, 22, 87–88, 243 n.10

French novels, 24–26, 28, 180–83, 185

Freud, Sigmund, 178–79, 277 n.16

Fuller, Margaret, 44

Fuss, Diana, 154–55, 266 n.22, 272 n.47

Gaiety . . . Reflecting Gay Life in the South (Harris), 199

Galloway, M. C., 113

Gantt, George, 24, 47, 50, 74–76, 84–85

Garden, Mary, 175
Garfield, James, 98
Gautier, Théophile, 181–82, 185
Gay American History (Katz), 199
Gender: binaries of, 19, 26–27, 62, 86; in evolutionary theory, 158; as factor in citizenship, 62; newspaper sections divided by, 38; in whiteness discourse, 16; and women's crime, 23–25, 46, 93. See also White men; White women; Women
"Girl lovers." See Lesbians
Girls' schools. See Schools: for girls
Girl with the Golden Eyes, The (Balzac), 182
Golddust (Tennessee), 9, 53, 55, 112, 203–5, 220, 230, 262 n.69
Gomez, Pedro, 137–39
Grand jury (in Mitchell-Ward case), 66, 251 n.12
Grand Opera House (Memphis), 148
Grant, Macpherson, 135
Griffith, D. W., 40
Grocery store competition (in Memphis), 11, 42, 87
Guiteau, Charles, 98, 173
Gunning, Sandra, 19

Habeas corpus hearing (in Mitchell-Ward case), 4, 66–86, 135
Habermas, Jürgen, 4
Halberstam, Judith, 4, 162
Hall, Jacquelyn Dowd, 4, 238 n.25
Hall, Radclyffe, 2, 5, 119, 180, 188–91, 199, 200
Halttunen, Karen, 263 n.85
Hamilton, Allan McLane, 99
Hammond, William A., 104, 169
Hansen, Miriam, 4
Harper, Phillip Brian, 2–3
Harrell, Bob, 76
Harris, Fred, 199
Harris, Ruth, 259 n.30
Hastings, Grace, 198

Hatch, Mary, 185
Haymarket massacre, 65
Hearn, Ella, 128–34, 167
Hearst, William Randolph, 34
Henning, Z. B., 83
Henry, George, 273 n.52
Heredity: in evolution, 158, 160; in insanity, 49, 93–94, 100, 108, 174, 201–2
Hernando Street (Memphis), 9, 13
Higbee, Jenny, 44
Higbee School for Girls (Memphis), 9, 43–44, 58, 81, 95, 150
Higginbotham, Evelyn Brooks, 4
Hindle, Annie (or Marie), 105, 142–48, 155
Hirschfeld, Magnus, 160, 161, 175, 179, 184
Homosexuality: among women, 179, 240 n.47; concept of, 25–26, 196, 197. See also Lesbians
Hot Springs Graphic (Arkansas), 58
Household formation. See Marriage
Hubbard, C. G., 55
Hubbard, Minnie, 141
Hughes, Charles H., 164–71
Hunter, Kathryn Montgomery, 92

Illness (as feminine characteristic), 81–85. See also Insanity
Immigrants, 14, 15, 26, 37, 61
Imperialism, 15, 18–19, 157–58
Ingram, Frank, 103
Insanity: Alice Mitchell's plea of, 88–92, 113; alleged of Alice's mother, 49, 93–94, 100, 108, 109, 174, 201–2; in novels with lesbian love murder themes, 183–85; question of Alice Mitchell's, 24, 47, 48–50, 54–55, 58, 80, 84, 86–119, 164–65, 174, 194, 196, 206; question of lesbians', 104–5, 164–65, 183–85. See also "Erotomania"; Lunacy inquisition

Intersexes, The (Mayne), 169
Inverts. *See* Lesbians
Irish immigrants, 37

Jackson, Andrew, 136
Jackson (Tennessee) *Tribune-Sun*, 56, 58
Jail, 250 n.7; Alice Mitchell in, 47, 58,
    73, 109; Lillie Johnson in, 53, 73, 253
    n.30
James, Henry, 187
James, Jessie Rita (Lillie Johnson's
    pseudonym), 82, 229, 230, 253 n.30
Jealousy: as Alice Mitchell's motive, 50–
    51, 97, 107, 112, 119, 164–65, 214–18;
    as motive in domestic scandal, 39–
    40; as motive in same-sex murders,
    128–34, 137–40, 174–75, 184–85,
    196. *See also* Crimes of passion; Sexual
    triangle
Jewett, Helen, 65
Johnson, J. M. (Lillie's father), 53, 76,
    82, 84
Johnson, James, 95
Johnson, Lillie: as Alice Mitchell's
    friend, 9–10, 56, 58–59, 208–10,
    217, 218, 278 n.16; allegedly in men's
    clothing, 55; charges against, 66,
    71–74, 251 n.12; defense of, 68, 74–
    76, 84–85; descriptions of, 52–53,
    71, 72–74, 76, 79, 80–85, 253 n.30;
    flirtations of, with men, 72, 74, 79;
    habeas corpus plea of, 66–86, 135; in
    jail, 53, 73, 253 n.30; letters of, 78,
    82, 115–16, 222, 229–30, 253 n.30;
    prosecution of, 68, 75, 84; relation-
    ship of, with Alice Mitchell and Freda
    Ward, 79, 80–82, 96, 220; school of,
    44; testimony of, 80–82, 95, 96, 98,
    110; use of pseudonym by, 82, 229,
    230, 253 n.30
Johnson, Mrs. J. M. (Lillie's mother), 53,
    82, 84
Journal of Nervous and Mental Disease, The, 164

Jury (in Mitchell-Ward case), 54, 91,
    112, 113. *See also* Grand jury

Katz, Jonathan Ned, 184, 199, 235 n.10,
    264 n.6, 265 n.8
Kennedy, Elizabeth Lapovsky, 279 n.29
Kiernan, James G., 164, 167, 170, 172–74
Kimbrough, Mrs., 9, 53, 80, 207
King, H. Clay, 64
Kinsey, Alfred, 179
Krafft-Ebing, Richard von, 25, 159–60,
    162–65, 172–75, 188, 190, 272 n.46
Ku Klux Klan, 44, 75

"Ladies of Llangollen," 135
Lafitte, Jean, 136
LaGrange, Letitia, 150–53, 155
Lawrence, D. H., 187–88
Lees, Edith, 176–77
Leonard, Hattie, 196
Leroi, Agnes Ann, 278 n.20
"Lesbian Love Murder" (Cauldwell), 197
Lesbian love murder narratives: circu-
    lation of, 2, 32–60, 179–81; conse-
    quences of, 2, 3, 30; elements of, 5,
    27–29, 40, 46–60, 134–35, 153–54,
    168, 189; emergence of, 2, 4, 23–29,
    42–46, 154; in fiction, 24–26, 28,
    180–91; fictional challenges to, 2, 5,
    119, 180, 188–91, 199, 200; legacy of,
    5, 195–200; in medical case histo-
    ries, 163–69, 172; other cases of, 25,
    124–55, 239 n.41; purposes of, 30,
    35–36, 60, 119; sexology's influence
    on, 157. *See also* Lesbians; Mitchell,
    Alice; Ward, Freda
Lesbians: fictional challenges to hostile
    representations of, 2, 5, 119, 180, 188–
    91; as identity, 240 n.47; as men's
    competitors for "normal" white
    women, 4, 27–29, 43, 59, 86, 102,
    130–31, 154, 177, 190; persons identi-
    fied as, 163–64; question of sanity of,

Lesbians (*continued*)
104–5, 164–65, 183–85; sexologists'
interest in, 173–79. *See also* "Female
husband" narratives; "Femmes";
Homosexuality; Lesbian love murder
narratives; "Romantic friendship"
narratives; "Unnatural practices"
Lindquist, Lisa J., 235 n.10
Lister, Anne, 178, 265 n.10
Lobdell, Joseph Israel, 125–26, 163
Lobdell, Lucy Ann, 124–28, 163, 173, 177
Lombroso, Cesare, 160, 175
"Long Arm, The" (Freeman), 185–86
Lowe, Lisa, 4
Lunacy inquisition (in Mitchell-Ward
case), 4, 67, 86–119
Lyceum (Memphis), 148
Lydston, G. Frank, 171–73, 181
Lynching: as cause of Ida B. Wells's departure from Memphis, 3, 4, 12, 21,
42, 87; history of, 3, 4, 18–19, 236
n.17; lack of arrests for, 11, 18, 62–
63, 87–88; in Memphis, 3, 4, 11–12,
87; opposition to, 12, 18, 20–22, 88,
155. *See also* Antilynching narratives;
Lynching narratives
Lynching narratives: characteristics of,
27, 29, 40–42; consequences of, 4,
30, 42; role of, in modernity, 2–3,
19–20, 30, 32, 35–36, 60, 65, 118–
19, 155; sexual triangle in, 12, 20,
21, 29, 238 n.29. *See also* Antilynching
narratives

Mademoiselle de Maupin (Gautier), 181–82,
185
Mademoiselle Giraud, ma femme (Belot), 24,
181, 188
Male impersonators, 105, 142–48
"Maniacs" (or "Cranks"), 38–39, 46, 50.
See also Insanity
Marneffe, Daphne de, 277 n.16
Marriage: Alice Mitchell's desire to be

linked with Freda Ward in, 11, 23,
48, 78–79, 96, 97, 101–2, 107, 111–
12, 114, 116–18, 169, 174, 204–6, 210,
214–17, 219; "crisis" in, 187; death
as alternative to, 117; forbidding of,
across race, 118–19; of Ida B. Wells,
193; in novels, 186–87; other cases
of desire for, between women, 105,
125–26, 131–32, 134–35, 141, 143,
144–48, 150–52, 168; regulation of,
102, 115, 118–19; threats to, 154. *See also*
Domestic scandals; "White home"
Mary, A Fiction (Wollstonecraft), 182, 274
n.12
Mary Baldwin College, 45
"Masculine" inverts. *See* Lesbians
Mass circulation press. *See* Newpapers
Masturbation, 168, 169
"Matinee girls," 148
Mayne, Xavier, 169
McDowell, Calvin, 11, 63, 87
McGuire, Hunter, 171
McLaren, Angus, 252 n.23
Medical Fortnightly, 168
Medical profession: as expert witnesses
in Alice Mitchell's trial, 4, 48–49, 88,
89, 91–94, 98–110, 114–15; as expert
witnesses in Lillie Johnson's hearing,
5; on lesbian love, 4, 195–96; literature of, on same-sex love, 25–26,
156–79; on race, 5. *See also* Sexology
Medical Record, The, 164
Medicine, 195–96
Melodrama: in depictions of lesbians
and gays, 199–200; lynching narratives as, 20–22; trials and hearings as,
85, 149
Memphis (Tennessee): crime rates in,
63, 250 n.5; grocery store competition in, 11, 42, 87; lynching narratives
developed in, 36–42; as lynching
site, 3, 11–12; segregation in, 13, 17–
18, 42, 88; significance of, in 1892, 16;

as site of lesbian love murder, 2, 3–4, 9–11; Wells driven from, 3, 4, 12, 21, 42, 87; Wells's work in, 17, 41–42

Memphis Appeal Avalanche: on Alice Mitchell, 50, 52, 56, 59, 102, 110–11; attacks on black newspaper by, 41; circulation of, 36; on Jo Ward, 76–77; on Lillie Johnson's hearing, 80, 82–83; on Mitchell-Ward trial, 51, 69, 70, 105–6, 108–9, 113

Memphis Commercial, 36, 37; on Alice Mitchell, 48, 52, 56, 97, 110, 117, 194–97; on Ida Wells, 22; on Mitchell-Ward trial, 51, 54, 71, 75–76, 80–82, 97, 103, 113–14; other lesbian love murder narratives in, 135–40; other same-sex love stories in, 150–53

Memphis Commercial Appeal, 194–97

Memphis Evening Scimitar, 12, 36

Memphis Fertilizing Company, 53

Memphis Medical Monthly, 99, 101–3, 163, 199

Memphis Public Ledger, 36, 37, 75; on Alice Mitchell, 51, 54–55; attacks on black newspaper by, 41; on Mitchell-Ward murder case, 46–47, 67, 69, 70, 75, 82, 83, 85; on other lesbian love murder narratives, 136–39, 142–48

"Memphis' Strangest Love Murder Had All-Girl Cast," 196–97

Memphis Trades Council, 37

Meriwether, Elizabeth Avery, 43–44

Meriwether, Lide, 43–44

Mexican immigrants, 14, 15, 26

Miller, Nettie, 196

Mitchell, Addie, 94, 95

Mitchell, Alice, 16; as "Alvin Ward," 48, 79, 116, 117, 205, 214, 215; cross-dressing by, 55, 101, 111, 114, 174, 205; death of, 194–95; defense of, 47–50, 59, 88, 90–96, 98–105, 110, 113; descriptions of, 51–55, 71, 76, 83–84, 97, 109–10, 247 nn.55, 58;

desire of, to marry Freda Ward, 11, 23, 48, 78–79, 96, 97, 101–2, 107, 111–12, 114, 116–18, 169, 174, 204–6, 210, 214–17, 219; "hypothetical case" of, 91–94, 96, 97, 100, 103, 201–11; in jail, 47, 58, 73, 109; jealousy as motive of, 50–51, 97, 107, 112, 116, 119, 164–65, 214–18, 246 n.51; letters of, 51, 59, 76, 96, 98, 109, 115–19, 207, 213–31, 247 n.52; life of, after trial, 193–94; "masculine" characteristics of, 23, 54–55, 78–79, 95, 97, 102, 114, 202–3; motives of, as incomprehensible, 90–91, 97, 102–3, 119; as murderer, 2, 9–12, 208–11; possible physical abnormality of, 106; "present insanity" plea of, 88–92, 113; prosecution of, 47, 50–51, 59, 97–98, 104–10, 113; question of insanity of, 24, 47, 48–50, 54–55, 58, 80, 84, 86–119, 164–65, 174, 194, 196, 206; question of interest of, in men, 95, 97, 98, 109, 112, 194, 203, 207, 222–31, 246 n.51; relationship of, with Freda Ward, 11, 23, 48, 77–78, 96–97, 100–102, 105–7, 111–12, 114, 116–19, 169, 174, 204–6, 210–11, 214–17, 219; sexology's interest in, 163–68, 172–74, 177, 195–98; suicide threats by, 96, 97, 112, 116, 117, 195, 204, 218; testimony of, 109–13. *See also* Jealousy; Lesbian love murder narratives; Sexual triangle

Mitchell, Frank, 95, 96, 113, 202

Mitchell, George (Alice's father), 47, 53, 54, 76, 91, 113, 201, 210; testimony of, 93–96

Mitchell, Isabella Scott (Alice's mother), 11, 96, 106, 117–18, 205–6, 210, 211, 220; absence of, from trial, 53, 76, 93; in attendance on Alice in jail, 109; mental history of, 49, 93–94, 100, 108, 109, 174, 201–2

Mitchell, John, 42

Mitchell, Mattie, 94–95

Mitchell, Robert, 95, 96, 117

M'Naghten rule, 89–90

Modernity, 235 n.12; constraints on
democracy by, 2, 3, 35–36, 61, 236
n.16; discourse of whiteness in, 2,
14–16, 25, 135, 236 n.16; institutions
of, 1–3, 5, 32–34, 65, 102, 118, 190;
lynching narratives' role in, 2–3, 19–
20, 30, 32, 35–36, 60, 65, 118–19, 155;
narratives supporting, 14–16, 30–31,
60, 65. See also "Americanness"

"Monomania," 103–4

Montague, H. J., 146

Moore, Lisa, 264 n.7

Morel, Benedict Augustin, 160

Moss, Thomas, 11–12, 63, 87

"Mujerados," 169–70

Mundinger, Charles, 95–96

Mundinger, Mrs., 96

Muñoz, José, 154–55

Murders, 64, 65, 75, 128–34, 250 n.5. See
also Crimes of passion; Lesbian love
murder narratives; Violence

Mynott, Sallie, 40

Nana (Zola), 166, 182

Narratives. See Antilynching narratives; Chivalric rescue narratives;
"Female husband" narratives; Lesbian
love murder narratives; Lynching
narratives; "Romantic friendship"
narratives

Nashoba community, 44

Nationalism, 61–66

National Police Gazette: "female husband"
narratives in, 124–28, 163, 167, 173;
"romantic friendship" narratives in,
124, 128–34

Native Americans, 14, 15, 18, 26, 169–70

"New Crime, A" (Twain), 262 n.65

"New Negroes," 16

Newspapers: African American, 12, 17,
22, 41–42, 87–88, 243 n.10; decorum of, 115, 168; as institutions of
modernity, 1–3, 13, 32–34, 155; as
interactive public sphere, 4, 34; on
lynching, 87–88; in Memphis, 36–
42, 242 n.10; Mitchell-Ward murder
case in, 22–25, 32–60, 66–67, 97,
110, 163; readers of, 33–35, 38, 60,
62, 124, 128, 157; sensationalist strategies of, 4, 11, 34–36, 42–43, 46–60,
67–68, 85, 119, 252 n.18; treatment
of lesbian love murder narratives by,
155, 156–57

Newton, Esther, 190

"New Women," 16, 45–46

New York Advertiser, 150

New York Age, 42

New York Journal, 34

New York Medical Review, The, 164

New York Times, 46, 55

New York World, 24, 34, 36, 46, 97

Nightingale, Taylor, 17, 41

"Normal" women. See "Femmes"

Norma Trist; or Pure Carbon: A Story of the
Inversion of the Sexes (Carhart), 183–86

"Note on a Feature of Sexual Psychopathy" (Hughes), 170–71

Novels: with lesbian love murder
themes, 179–91; French, 24–26, 28,
180–83, 185

Nun, The (Diderot), 274 n.12

Olive, Julia, 40

Ora Lee, 73, 82

"Others": as depicted in newspapers,
38–39, 60, 62, 136–40; sexologists
on, 156–79. See also Class; Gender;
Race; Sexuality

"Paranoia," 103–4

Parsonby, Sarah, 135

Patterson, Josiah, 74

Patterson, Malcolm Rice ("Ham"), 73, 77–81, 83–85, 195, 196

People's Grocery Company, 11, 42, 87

People's Party, 15, 37

Perkins, Delia, 166–67

Peroda, Clara, 137–39

Perry, John, 54–55

Peters, George B., Jr., 50–51, 75–79, 81–84, 97–98, 104–7, 110

Peters, George B., Sr., 75

Peters, Thomas, 75

Phillips, Addie, 140–42

Phillips, Mrs. C. H., 45

Pocomoke City (Maryland). See Duer, Lily

Police, 63

Poor, 63. See also Class

Populism, 15, 37

Press. See Newspapers

Preston, Ida, 166–67

Prisons, 179

Prostitutes, 42–43, 65, 140–42, 178

"Psychogenesis of a Case of Homosexuality in a Woman, The" (Freud), 178–79

Psychopathia Sexualis (Krafft-Ebing), 25, 27, 159–60, 163

Pueblo Indians, 169–70

Pulitzer, Joseph, 34

Purnell, Christina, 9, 10, 54, 77, 80, 109, 208, 246 n.51

Q.E.D., or Things as They Are (Stein), 182

Race: as basis of exclusion, 62; binaries of, 14–16, 26; in coverage of Mitchell-Ward murder, 46, 47; hierarchy of, 15, 157–60, 163, 169–72; mixing of, 179; privileges associated with white, 43; in Well of Loneliness, 5. See also African Americans; Lynching narratives; "Racial uplift"; Segregation; White men; Whiteness; White women

"Racial uplift," 17, 193, 267 n.29

Railroads, 17, 41

Rape: of black women by white men, 20; castration proposed as punishment for, 171–72; enforcement of laws forbidding, 63; issues subsumed under claims of, 18–20; lynching as retaliation for claims of, 12; newspaper treatments of, 39

Reconstruction, 16, 18–20

"Responsibility in Sexual Perversion" (Kiernan), 173

Richardson, Eleanora, 139–40

Richmond Planet, 42

Ritchie, Rob, 220

Robinson, Richard P., 65

Romance, 168–73, 177

"Romantic friendship" narratives, 124, 128–34. See also "Chumming"

Roosevelt, Theodore, 75

Roselle, Ashley, 107, 109, 112, 116, 204, 205, 207, 214–18, 220

Rubinowitch, Anna, 175

Rudd, Winnie Ruth, 278 n.20

Rust College, 16

Ryan, Annie, 144–47

Ryan, Mary, 4

Sale, Eugene Paul, 99, 100, 102, 104, 107, 245 n.41

Salmon, Eric, 266 n.21

Samuelson, Miss, 278 n.20

Sand, George, 181

San Francisco Chronicle, 46

San Francisco Examiner, 46, 55, 110

Sardou, Victorien, 149

Saroney, Gilbert, 147

Saxton, Alexander, 236 n.13

School boards, 41, 244 n.24

Schools: dangers associated with, 58–59, 150–53, 178, 181; for girls, 150–

Schools (continued)
53; as institutions of modernity, 1–2;
women as teachers in, 43, 44–45. See
also Convents; School boards
Schuetz, Janice, 252 n.18
Scott, Vance, 94
Segregation, 61, 62, 118; in Memphis, 13,
88; opposition to, in Memphis, 17–18,
42
Seibert, Charles, 196
Sensationalism. See Newspapers: sensationalist strategies of
Seward, Anna, 135
Sexology, 26, 28, 115, 156–57; history
of, 157–63; influence of, on fiction,
184–85, 188; interest of, in lesbians,
173–79; literature of, 177–79; and the
Mitchell-Ward murder case, 163–68,
172, 173, 177, 195–98
Sexology, 197
Sexual Inversion (Ellis), 27, 162, 174–77
Sexuality: binaries of, 26–27, 190–91; in
evolutionary theory, 158; legitimate
vs. illegitimate, 65; production of
normative views of, 5, 25–26, 42–
46. See also Homosexuality; Lesbians;
Marriage; "Unnatural practices"
Sexual triangle: as element in lesbian
love murder narratives, 5, 27–28,
134–40, 168, 181, 182, 188, 189, 199;
in lynching narratives, 12, 20, 21, 29,
238 n.29; in same-sex love narratives,
144, 153, 154
Shapiro, Ann-Louise, 68
Shaw University, 16
Shepard, Matthew, 199–200
Sim, Frank L., 98–107, 115, 163, 199, 259
n.33
Sioux Indians, 15
Slater, George, 125, 127
Slater, Lucy Ann Lobdell. See Lobdell,
Lucy Ann
Snedaker, Kathryn Holmes, 252 n.18

Somerville, Siobhan, 175
Southern Horrors (Wells), 21, 22
Spanish-American War, 19
Spectators: at theater, 43, 45, 148–49,
265 n.18; at trials, 55–57, 68–71
Spelman College (Atlanta), 45
Stack, Mrs. Garrett, 140–42
Stanley & Hinton's (undertakers), 10
State. See Courts; Police
Stein, Gertrude, 182, 187
Stevenson, Edward I. Prime, 169
Stewart, Henry, 11, 63, 87
Strange Disappearance of Eugene Comstock, The
(Hatch), 185
Surpassing the Love of Men (Faderman), 185
Symonds, John Addington, 161, 175

Tate, Claudia, 187
Taylor, Edward H., 194
Taylor, Peter, 235 n.12
Temple, Miss, 135
Tennessee: insanity rules in, 89–90. See
also Memphis
Tennessee Rifles, 11
Tennessee Supreme Court, 13
Terry, Jennifer, 273 n.52
Texas Medical Journal, 171–72
"That Strange Girl: The Alice Mitchell
Murder Case" (Dryden), 199
Theater: Alice Mitchell and Freda
Ward's interest in, 59, 115–16, 148–
49, 220, 222–31; cross-dressing in,
149, 266 n.19; and female sexual re-
spectability, 142–48; metaphors of,
in describing Mitchell-Ward trial,
67–68, 85, 252 n.18; women's interest
in, 43, 45, 148–49, 178, 265 n.18. See
also Melodrama
"Tiller Sisters," 174
Tosca, La, 149
Totem and Taboo (Freud), 179
Trials. See Criminal trials
Tuke, D. Hack, 49

Turner, B. F., 99, 100, 103, 104–5, 107, 246 n.44
Twain, Mark, 262 n.65

Ulrichs, Karl, 160–61, 172, 173, 175, 184
Union Street (Memphis), 11
"Unnatural practices": denial of, between Mitchell and Ward, 49, 100, 113–15, 196; sexologists' description of, 168, 175
Urnings, 161–63, 172, 176
Urologic and Cutaneous Review, The, 173–74

Van Dorn, Earl, 75
Vanity Fair (Lincoln, Nebraska, theatrical newspaper), 49, 144–48
Veale, Father, 83
Violence, 36, 42, 63, 65, 250 n.5; and voting rights, 18, 40–41, 62; by whites, 18–21, 25, 29, 39. *See also* Crimes of passion; Lesbian love murder narratives; Lynching; Murders; Rape
Vivian, Charles, 146–47
Volkmar, Ada, 9, 50–51, 204; absence of, from trial, 53, 76; forbidding of contact among Alice Mitchell, Lillie Johnson, and Freda Ward by, 58–59, 78–79, 96, 98, 117–18, 205–6, 219–21; testimony of, 109
Volkmar, William, 97–98, 205, 220, 262 n.69
Voting rights: and lynching, 19–20; restrictions on, for blacks, 88; violence surrounding, 18, 40–41, 62; Wells's advocacy of, for African Americans, 17–18, 42; for women, 28, 43–44

Waldrep, Christopher, 237 n.22
Walkowitz, Judith, 4, 238 n.25
"Ward, Alvin J.", 48, 79, 116, 117, 205, 214, 215

Ward, Freda: Alice Mitchell's desire to marry, 11, 23, 48, 78–79, 96, 97, 101–2, 107, 111–12, 114, 116–18, 169, 174, 204–6, 210, 214–17, 219; boyfriends of, 107, 109, 116, 204, 205, 207, 214–18, 220; class background of, 46, 245 n.36; descriptions of, 52, 71, 203, 247 n.58; dramatic talents of, 59, 259 n.85; engagement ring of, 96; grave of, 113; letters of, 51, 76, 96, 109, 116, 207–8, 213–21, 247 n.52; murder of, 2, 9–11, 208–9; near-elopement of, 98, 205–6; relationship of, with Alice Mitchell, 58, 77, 80–82, 96–97, 100–102, 105–6, 111–12, 116–19; school of, 44, 58. *See also* Lesbian love murder narratives
Ward, Jo, 9, 10, 50, 112, 208; portrayals of, 54, 71, 76–77; testimony of, 76–79, 98, 110
Ward, Thomas (Freda's father), 53
Warner, Michael, 4
Well of Loneliness, The (Hall), 2, 5, 119, 180, 188–91, 199, 200
Wells, Ida B.: as anti-lynching campaigner, 12, 18, 20–22, 88, 155; background of, 16–18, 41–42, 45; driven from Memphis, 3, 4, 12, 21, 42, 87; and Frances Willard, 236 n.17; marriage of, 193
Wells, Jim, 16
Wesner, Ella, 146, 147
Western Hospital for the Insane (Bolivar), 104, 113, 193–94
Weston, Maggie, 146
Westphal, Karl, 160, 164, 165, 173, 181
"White home": challenges to, 18, 28, 30, 36, 42–43, 86, 91, 123–24, 140, 153, 154; in lynching and lesbian love murder narratives, 3, 6, 18, 28, 41; in *Well of Loneliness,* 190; women's aspirations to escape limitations of, 59, 153. *See also* Domestic scandals; Marriage

White men: attributes associated with, 102; authority of, in courtroom, 64, 68; female impersonation of, 105, 142–48; as jury in Mitchell-Ward case, 91; lesbians and black "rapists" seen as threat to, 3, 4, 18, 30; Lillie Johnson's flirtations with, 72, 74, 79; as Memphis newspaper owners, 36–38; as possible factor in Mitchell-Ward murder case, 50, 59, 107, 109, 116, 246 n.51; violence by, 20, 21, 29, 39. *See also* Lynching; "White home"

Whiteness: of characters in Mitchell-Ward trial, 71, 113–15; discourse of, and modernity, 2, 14–16, 25, 135, 236 n.16; as national identity, 40; violence associated with privileges of, 18–21, 25. *See also* "White home"

White women: as depicted in newspapers, 39–40; as instigators of sexual relations between black men and, 12, 21, 29; in lesbian love murder narratives, 4, 27–29, 43, 59, 86, 102, 130–31, 154, 177, 190; in lynching narratives, 20. *See also* "Femmes"; Lesbians

Wilde, Oscar, 263 n.88, 276 n.33

Willard, Frances, 193, 236 n.17

Willard Asylum for the Insane, 163

Williams, Emma, 139–40

Williams, Raymond, 243 n.11

Wilson, Marie Louise Perry, 126–27

Winters, Pat, 74–76

Wise, P. M., 163, 164, 173, 177

Wolf, John Quincy, 198

Wollstonecraft, Mary, 182, 274 n.12

Women: crimes of, 23–25, 46, 93, 250 n.5; economic opportunities for, 15, 23, 28, 43, 44–45, 124, 148–49; illness associated with, 81–85; lack of citizenship rights of, 28, 43–44, 54; lynching of, 18, 21; newspapers' characterization of, at trial, 55–56, 69–70, 83, 110; novels by African American, 187; sexologists on, 161–63. *See also* "Chumming"; "Fast" women; Lesbians; "New Women"; White women

Women's Christian Temperance Union (WCTU), 43, 45, 236 n.17

Women's clubs, 43

Women's suffrage. *See* Voting rights: for women

World War I, 188

Wounded Knee, 15

Wright, Fanny, 43–44

Wright, Luke E., 24, 37, 47, 74–76, 93, 98, 114

Zenger, John Peter, 64

Zola, Émile, 166, 181, 182

Lisa Duggan is Associate Professor of History and American Studies
at New York University, coauthor of *Sex Wars: Sexual Dissent and Political
Culture*, and coeditor of *Our Monica; Ourselves: The Clinton Affair and
National Interest*.

Library of Congress Cataloging-in-Publication Data
Duggan, Lisa
Sapphic slashers : sex, violence, and American modernity /
Lisa Duggan.
p.   cm.
Includes bibliographical references (p.) and index.
ISBN 0-8223-2609-4 (alk. paper) —
ISBN 0-8223-2617-5 (pbk : alk. paper)
1. Mitchell, Alice, 19th cent.   2. Ward, Freda, d. 1892.
3. Murder—Tennessee—Memphis—History—19th century.
4. Lesbian couples—Tennessee—Memphis—History—19th century.
5. Murder in mass media—Tennessee—Memphis—History—19th
century.   6. Trials (Murder)—Tennessee—Memphis—History—
19th century.   7. Lesbians in literature—History—19th century.
I. Title.
HV6534.M4 D84   2000
364.15′23′0976819—dc21   00-035426